EXCEL 2000

NO EXPERIENCE REQUIRED™

Gene Weisskopf

SYBEX®

San Francisco • Paris • Düsseldorf • Soest • London

Associate Publisher: Amy Romanoff
Contracts and Licensing Manager: Kristine O'Callaghan
Developmental Editor: Sherry Bonelli
Editor: Pat Coleman
Project Editors: Mike Anderson, Raquel Baker
Technical Editor: Maryann Brown
Book Designers: Patrick Dintino, Catalin Dulfu, Maureen Forys
Graphic Illustrator: Tony Jonick
Electronic Publishing Specialist: Adrian Woolhouse
Production Coordinators: Susan Berge and Lisa Reardon
Indexer: Rebecca Plunkett
Cover Designer: Design Site
Cover Photographer: Jack D. Meyers

Library of Congress Card Number: 99-60018
ISBN: 0-7821-2374-0

Manufactured in the United States of America

10 9 8 7 6 5 4 3 2

To Patricia, my favorite outlaw in-law,
whose first PC gave me a glimpse
of VisiCalc and things to come.

Acknowledgments

It may take just one person to write a few words, but it takes dozens of skilled people to bring those words to the public in a book. At Sybex, my thanks go to Kristine O'Callaghan, contracts and licensing manager; Sherry Bonelli, developmental editor; Raquel Baker and Mike Anderson, project editors; and the production team of Susan Berge, Lisa Reardon, and Adrian Woolhouse.

Special thanks go to Pat Coleman, editor and primary reviser of this edition. She wielded the red pencil with her usual skill and flare and also ensured that the updates to the book were comprehensive and accurate. She did it all on a very tight schedule, and her work is much appreciated.

Maryann Brown, the technical editor, was invaluable—not only in making sure that what I said was technically correct, but in making suggestions that always improved the book.

Many others contributed more indirectly to this book, but their presence is nonetheless felt in its pages. My thanks to all who have shared my enthusiasm for the personal computer, given me the support of friendship and good will, and tolerated my enthusiastic explanations.

Contents at a Glance

Table of Contents

Introduction

I first used Microsoft Excel for Windows soon after it came out in early 1988 (it was already a success on the Macintosh). It struck me as a real winner at the time, but on my 8Mhz 286 computer, the experience was more conceptual than productive.

Nonetheless, in the review I was writing, I described it as "a dazzling glimpse of life in the not too distant future." Of course, I was also prescient enough to predict that "considering that the Excel program takes a good 4MB of disk space, the 20MB hard disk may quickly give way to the 40MB drive." Ah yes, those were the days!

Since those golden times, Microsoft has expanded and improved Excel several times (and I have done the same to my computer hardware) to make it better in every way. No matter what your spreadsheet needs may be, Excel 2000 will undoubtedly be able to fill the bill.

Who Should Read This Book

I wrote *Excel 2000: No Experience Required* for three types of readers:

- Those who have no experience using Excel
- Those who've had brushes with Excel, maybe at the office, but who still think of themselves as having no experience
- Those who have experience with other spreadsheet programs but need to learn Excel

I do make a few assumptions about your experience, however. I assume that you know how to use a mouse, that you have some knowledge of Windows features, and that you know a few other basics such as how to open and close Windows programs. If you've worked with other Windows programs but come to Excel as a novice, you're ahead of the game. Many of the skills you use in Windows programs in general apply equally to Excel.

How to Use This Book

You can read this book as a tutorial, or you can use it as a reference. If you're very new to Excel, though, I recommend that you can work your way through each skill. In most cases, once you've familiarized yourself with Excel, you can read the sections that are pertinent to your work or your interests.

Each skill begins with a list of what you'll learn in it and ends with a list of what you've learned. You can use each of these lists to check your knowledge.

In some cases, I use real-world examples to explain how a feature works. You can either follow along by creating the simple worksheets I've included, or you can create your own. The steps will work with your data or mine. In most cases, however, I give you the general steps that will apply regardless of whether your data are budget figures, an employee directory, or an inventory price list.

What You'll Find in This Book

The skills in this book are arranged in order of their importance to the typical Excel user. If you're new to Excel, you should start with the first three skills. They lay the foundation for just about anything else you will do in Excel. The skills in the latter part of the book build to some extent on the material in the earlier skills.

Skill 1 is an all-around introduction to Excel and is a must for new users. Skill 2 discusses the many types of data you can work with in Excel, as well as some of the shortcuts Excel offers to help you work with your data. In Skill 3, you'll learn about the many commands and techniques that you can use to manipulate your data in the spreadsheet.

Skills 4 and 5 cover the important topic of spreadsheet calculations, perhaps the heart and soul of Excel.

Skill 6 shows you the many ways you can enhance the look of your work, such as by aligning entries in their cells and by applying fonts, numeric formats, and styles.

In Skill 7 you'll learn about working with files in Excel, and Skill 8 covers the everyday task of printing.

Skill 9 reveals the many tools you'll find in Excel for building, managing, and documenting your work.

Skill 10 shows you how to save Excel files as Web pages and how to publish them to a Web server, over the Internet or an intranet.

Skills 11 and 12 show you how to create eye-catching charts in Excel and how to include other graphic images in your work.

In Skill 13 you'll learn how to crunch your data with methods such as sorting data, filtering data based on criteria you specify, validating data as it is entered, and summarizing data with PivotTables.

Finally, Skill 14 discusses the many ways you can customize Excel to suit your working habits.

I've also provided an extensive index that will help you use this book as a reference. By looking up the topics that interest you in the index, you will find all the references to those topics in this book.

What You Won't Find in This Book

There is one topic that I simply could not broach in an introductory book of this size, and that is macros. A *macro* is an automated routine (essentially a computer program) that can perform repetitive or complex tasks in Excel. You can record a macro as you work in Excel and then play back that macro later to repeat exactly the same task. But that's just the very tip of the iceberg. There is a complete computer language for writing macros in Excel (and the other Microsoft Office programs) called Visual Basic for Applications (VBA). You'll need to become a bit of a VBA programmer if you're really interested in taking advantage of macros in Excel.

Another thing you won't find in this book is excess computer jargon. Explanations use everyday language with examples that are simple, uncluttered, and to the point. Boldface text indicates entries you type in. You'll find helpful notes, tips, and warnings throughout, which serve as adjuncts to the main body of text.

NOTE NOTE NOTE NOTE NOTE NOTE NOTE NOTE NOTE NOTE NOTE NOTE NOTE NOTE

The figures in this book were taken from a typical VGA computer screen while running Excel with its default settings. You might notice some small differences between the screen shots and your own screen if your computer is running at a higher resolution or if you have modified Excel's standard settings.

SKILL 1

Finding Your Way around in Excel

- Starting and closing Excel
- Looking at workbooks, worksheets, and cells
- Learning about cells and entering data
- Moving around in worksheets and workbooks
- Using toolbars and menus
- Finding help in all sorts of places

This skill introduces you to the essentials of Excel. If you're new to spreadsheets, this material will give you a quick boost up the learning curve. If you're already familiar with another spreadsheet program, the information in this skill will help you make the transition to Excel.

Once you've gone through this skill, you'll be ready to work through the skills that follow. But please don't feel as though you must study every golden word in Skill 1 before you can proceed to specific topics that interest you elsewhere in this book! You can always return to this skill later, either to continue your introduction to Excel or for a quick brush up.

Starting and Closing Excel

You can start Excel in several ways:

- Choose Start ➤ Programs ➤ Microsoft Excel, which opens Excel and a blank document.
- Select Excel from the Office shortcut bar, which opens Excel and a blank document.
- Double-click an Excel document icon, which opens Excel and that document.
- Choose Start ➤ Open Office Document to open the Open Office Document dialog box, and then select an existing workbook.
- Choose Start ➤ New Office Document to open the New Office Document dialog box, click the General tab, and then select Blank Workbook.

Once Excel is running, you'll find it as easy to use as any well-designed Windows program. For example, choosing File ➤ Save saves your current document, choosing Edit ➤ Copy and then Edit ➤ Paste copies data, and the Help menu contains online documentation and the answers to your questions. When you're ready to close Excel, you can:

- Choose File ➤ Exit.
- Click the Close button at the right side of Excel's title bar.
- Double-click the Control menu box, or choose Close from the Control menu.

If you have not saved an open document in which you've made changes, Excel prompts you to do so before it closes.

Looking at Excel's Workbooks, Worksheets, and Cells

An Excel document is called a *workbook*, which is the basic file in Excel, and each workbook can contain multiple pages, which are called *worksheets*. The active worksheet is displayed in the document window. Figure 1.1 shows the Excel application window with a worksheet open in the document window.

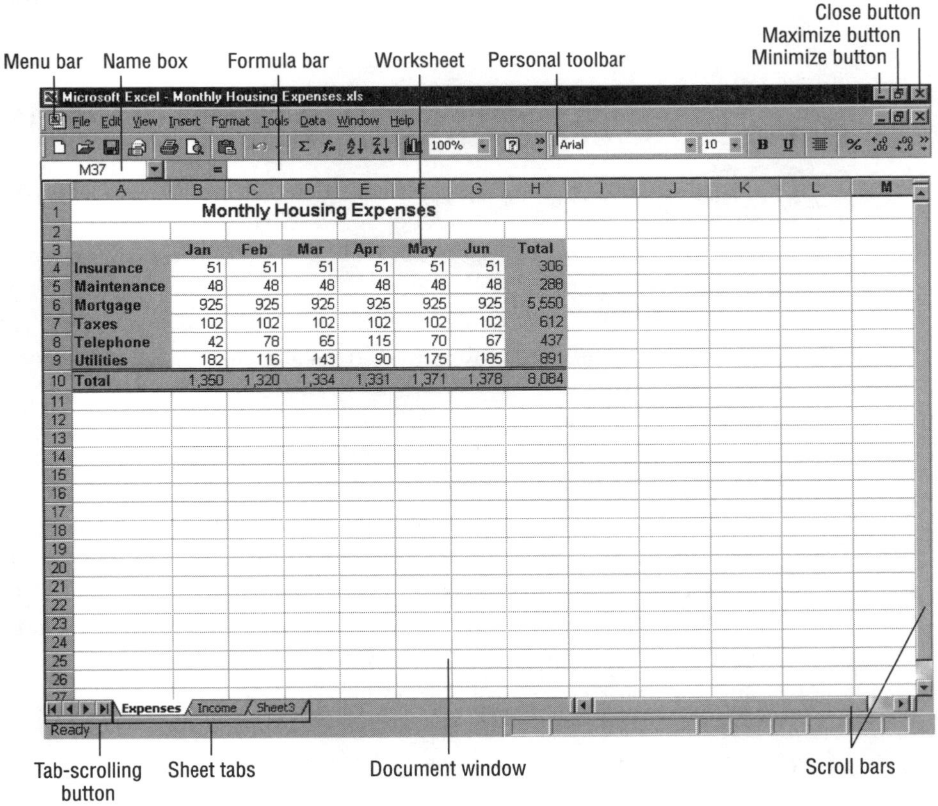

FIGURE 1.1: A worksheet open in Excel

You no doubt recognize many of the standard Windows controls and components. The title bar is at the top, with its Minimize, Maximize, and Close buttons on the right side. Beneath it is the menu bar with the commands File, Edit, View, and so on. Beneath the menu bar are two *toolbars*, which include a variety of buttons for performing common Excel tasks (you'll learn more about toolbars later in this skill).

In the main body of Excel's application window is the Monthly Housing Expenses worksheet. You use the horizontal and vertical scroll bars to navigate through the rows and columns of each worksheet in the workbook.

NOTE NOTE NOTE NOTE NOTE NOTE NOTE NOTE NOTE NOTE NOTE NOTE NOTE NOTE NOTE

You can hide or display many components. Use either the commands on the View menu or the settings in the View tab of the Options dialog box (choose Tools ➤ Options). See Skill 14 for more on changing the look of Excel.

Using Worksheets within a Workbook

The basic work area in an Excel workbook is a *worksheet*, which is sometimes called a spreadsheet. The electronic worksheet is based on the accountant's traditional green paper spreadsheet and consists of rows and columns in which you enter data and formulas.

A new Excel workbook contains three worksheets, and you can add as many more as you care to create—within the limits of your computer's memory resources, that is.

The default names of worksheets in a workbook are Sheet1, Sheet2, and so on. You can see the name of each sheet on its *sheet tab* at the bottom of the worksheet. The name of the sheet that is currently in use, the *active* sheet, is in bold.

To select a sheet, click its tab. The *tab scrolling* buttons to the left of the sheet tabs let you move through the tabs quickly (see "Moving around in Excel" later in this skill for more information).

To give a more meaningful name to a worksheet, double-click its tab and type a new name. In Figure 1.1, the names of the first and second sheets are Expenses and Income.

Understanding Cells in a Worksheet

Each worksheet in Excel is made up of rows and columns. The rows are identified by numbers, labeled down the left side of the worksheet in the heading area. In Figure 1.1, you can see only 26 rows of the 65,536 rows in each worksheet (yes, that really is a lot!).

The columns are identified by letters, labeled across the top of the sheet in the heading area. Each worksheet has a total of 256 columns; you can see columns A through M in Figure 1.1. Column Z is followed by columns AA, AB, AC, and column AZ is followed by BA, BB, BC, and so on, out through column IV.

At the junction of each row and column is a *cell*, and it is in the cells that you enter data, including text, numbers, and formulas. You refer to a cell by its *address* in formulas, commands, and so on. To refer to a cell:

On the current sheet Specify its column and row. For example, cell H4 is at the junction of column H and row 4.

On another sheet in the same workbook Include the sheet name before the cell address with an exclamation point as a separator. For example, the address Sheet3!A15 refers to cell A15 on Sheet3.

In another workbook Precede the cell address and sheet name with the workbook's filename, enclosed in square brackets. For example, the address [Sample.xls] Sheet2!B12 refers to cell B12 on Sheet2 in the workbook named Sample.xls.

Finally, hiding behind all the cells, worksheets, and workbooks is Excel's powerful calculating engine that can update thousands of your formulas in less time than it takes you to reach for a calculator. Without your even lifting a finger, Excel will keep track of all changes you make to the worksheet and update your formulas accordingly. All you have to do is sit back and be creative while Excel handles the number crunching.

Exploring the Excel Window

In Excel you can interact with the program by using menu commands and shortcuts, the Formula bar, and the status bar.

Accessing Commands in Excel

In Excel you can generally issue commands in two ways—through the menu bar and from shortcut menus.

Browsing through the menus is an easy way for you to take a quick tour of Excel's commands. Some menu commands also have shortcut keystrokes, such as Ctrl+S for File ➤ Save and Ctrl+C for Edit ➤ Copy. The shortcuts for all commands that have them are listed next to the command on the menu. But you may find that shortcuts really don't save all that much time or effort compared with the usual ways of accessing menus in Windows.

Excel also supports shortcut menus. Right-click a cell, a chart, a toolbar, or just about anything else to display a shortcut menu of commands you can select. You can also click a cell and press Shift+F10 to display a shortcut menu.

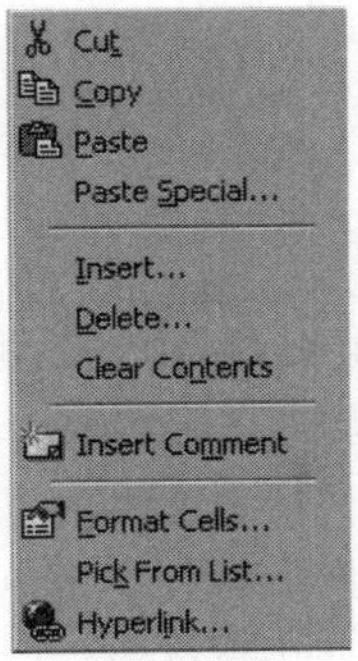

TIP TIP TIP TIP TIP TIP TIP TIP TIP TIP TIP TIP TIP TIP TIP TIP TIP TIP TIP TIP TIP TIP TIP TIP TIP

Shortcut menus list only commands that are relevant to the object you click (perhaps not every possible command, but the most commonly used ones). For example, the shortcut menu for a cell displays Cut and Copy, but not Save, Exit, or New Window.

Using the Formula Bar to See What's Inside

Beneath the toolbar and just above the worksheet is the Formula bar. It serves two important functions in Excel.

First, you can enter and revise data within the Formula bar for the current cell in the active worksheet. Second, the Formula bar displays whatever is *inside* the current cell. Here, you can see the formula =SUM(B5:G5) in the Formula bar. That formula is inside the selected cell, H5, and the selected cell displays only the *result* of that formula, 288. (Formulas are discussed in the section "Entering Data and Formulas into a Cell" later in this skill and in more detail in Skills 4 and 5.)

On the worksheet, and on paper when you print it, you really can't tell that there's a formula behind the value. To peek behind the scenes, keep your eye on the Formula bar as you're working in Excel.

At the left side of the Formula bar is the *Name Box*, which displays several types of names and addresses (you don't have to absorb all this right now; feel free to come back later on!):

- The address of the currently selected cell.
- The number of rows and columns you are selecting when you are selecting a range of cells, such as by dragging over them with the mouse.
- The name of the selected drawing or chart object.
- The named ranges in the workbook, which are accessed by clicking the Name Box's list arrow. When you can click a named range, Excel selects that range of cells (see Skill 3 for a discussion of names).

Watching the Status Bar to Keep Informed

Excel's *status bar* is at the very bottom of the application window. It displays various messages that keep you in touch with Excel.

NOTE NOTE NOTE NOTE NOTE NOTE NOTE NOTE NOTE NOTE NOTE NOTE NOTE NOTE

On your computer, you might see the Windows 95/98 taskbar displayed at the bottom of the screen. On the computer used to write this book and capture the screens for its figures, the taskbar has been hidden to avoid complicating the illustrations. You can hide your Windows taskbar by choosing Start ➤ Settings ➤ Taskbar, and choosing Auto Hide. The taskbar will appear only when you point to the bottom of your screen.

The indicator on the left side of the status bar shows the current state of the program. Ready indicates that you can perform any action. Other indicators include Edit, when you're editing a cell; Enter, when you're entering new data into a cell; and Point, when you're pointing to a cell while writing a formula.

The right side of the status bar displays the current state of several toggle keys, including CAPS when Caps Lock is on and NUM when Num Lock is on.

Using AutoCalculate to Get a Quick Answer

Excel has a great feature called AutoCalculate that displays the total of the numbers in the currently selected cells. Figure 1.2 shows an example in which five cells, B4:B8, have been selected. The AutoCalculate indicator displays Sum=1168 on the status bar. This is the quickest way to see a total without writing a formula.

But wait, there's more! You can change the calculation that AutoCalculate performs by right-clicking on the AutoCalculate indicator and selecting an arithmetical operation from its shortcut menu. Otherwise, choose None to turn it off. You can see the AutoCalculate shortcut menu in Figure 1.2.

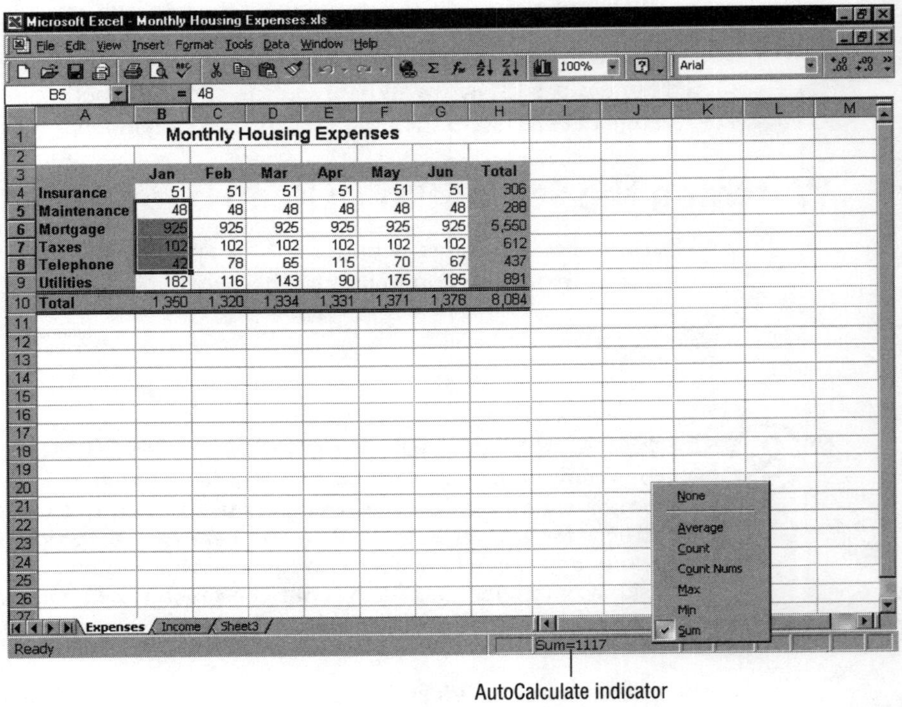

FIGURE 1.2: The AutoCalculate feature displays the sum of the selected cells.

Working with Cells

When you select a cell, that cell is then the *active* cell and is enclosed in a thick border. Its row and column will appear sculpted in the row and column headings to help you identify its position in the worksheet. Its contents, if it has any, are shown in the Formula bar. You can enter data only in the active cell.

You can select a cell in several ways, but here are the three you'll use most often (others are discussed in Skill 3):

- Click the cell with the mouse.
- Move to the cell with the keyboard arrow keys.
- Choose Edit ➤ Go To (or press F5 or Ctrl+G) to open the Go To dialog box, enter the address you want to go to in the Reference field, and click OK. This is especially handy when you want to go to a distant location, such as M1205.

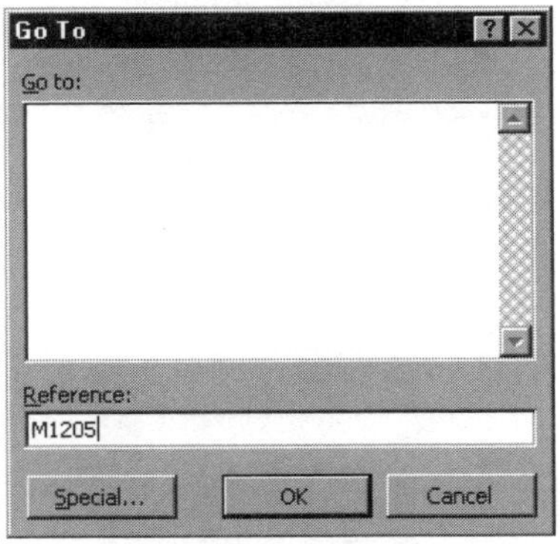

To select multiple cells (a range), drag over the cells with your mouse. You can also use the Shift+arrow key method if you like to keep your hands on the keyboard. A range's address is defined by its upper-left and lower-right cells, such as A1:D9. To deselect a range, simply select another cell.

Entering Data and Formulas into a Cell

Earlier I mentioned that there are a total of 65,536 cells in a worksheet. I'll use that number shortly to show you how to enter a formula in a cell. But first you need to know the following about data entry (Skill 2 explains more):

- You can enter a bit more than 32,000 text characters in a cell; a formula can be a maximum of 1024 characters.

- To cancel your data entry before you press Enter, press Esc, which will leave the cell unchanged.

- To cancel an action after you've already made it, choose Edit ➤ Undo or click the Undo button on the toolbar. Using the Undo drop-down list, you can undo any of the most recent 16 changes you've made in Excel. Choose Edit ➤ Redo or click the Redo button to undo the effects of the Undo command.

- You can erase the contents of a cell by selecting the cell and pressing Delete or by choosing Edit ➤ Clear ➤ Contents (see Skill 3).
- When entering numbers or formulas, you don't have to worry about how they look on the display, because you can format a cell to make a number appear just about any way you want to see it (see Skill 6).

Now, let's calculate how many cells are in a worksheet. We'll use this example again later.

1. Click the Sheet1 tab to make it active. Select cell A1, which is always a good place to start.
2. Type **65536** and press Enter to move to the cell below. (See the section "Moving Around in Excel" later in this skill to learn why the selection moves when you press Enter.)
3. In cell A2, type **256** and press Enter.
4. In cell A3, type the formula **=A1*A2** and press Enter (be sure to include the equals sign—it's important).

Cell A1 contains the number of rows in a worksheet, and cell A2 contains the number of columns in a worksheet. You begin a formula in Excel with the equals sign; the asterisk denotes multiplication. This formula, then, multiplies the number of rows by the number of columns, and presto—it displays the result as 16777216 in cell A3. That's 16 million-plus cells, probably a few million more than you'll ever need! (You will find much more information about writing formulas in Skills 4 and 5.)

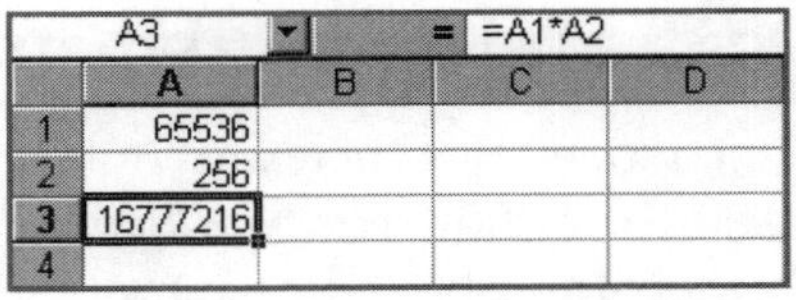

Editing a Cell

Let's revise the formula in cell A3 of our example to calculate the total number of cells in a new workbook:

1. Double-click cell A3 to edit its contents within the worksheet.

2. Press End to place the insertion point at the end of the formula, and then type ***3**.
3. Press Enter to put the revised formula back into the cell

Now the formula results in 50331648—that's 50 million cells in each new workbook. Wow.

TIP TIP TIP TIP TIP TIP TIP TIP TIP TIP TIP TIP TIP TIP TIP TIP TIP TIP TIP TIP TIP TIP TIP TIP TIP TIP

The ability to process formulas that contain numbers or to reference other cells and display the results instantly is the heart of Excel's power.

To get another taste of Excel's power, try this. Enter a different number in cell A1 or A2 and watch the result of the formula in A3. It might have changed too quickly for you to notice, but its result is different now, right?

Excel recalculates a formula when the data it references change, and it will do this for *every* formula in every worksheet in the workbook, as well as in any other open workbooks! When you have created a workbook with thousands of cells containing data and formulas, you will really appreciate Excel's power.

Enhancing a Cell

Skill 6 will show you the many ways you can change the *display* of a cell without affecting its contents. Here's a quick look at one way of using the worksheet from the previous example:

1. Select cells A1:A3—click cell A1 and drag to cell A3.
2. Right-click anywhere within the selected cells, and then select Format Cells from the shortcut menu to open the Format Cells dialog box, as shown in Figure 1.3.
3. Click the Number tab. As you make choices here, watch the Sample field to see how numbers will be displayed.
4. In the Category list of numeric formats, select Number.
5. Click the Use 1000 Separator check box, and set Decimal Places to 0, as shown in Figure 1.3.
6. Click OK.

Notice that the numbers greater than one thousand in cells A1 and A3 are displayed with a comma to separate the thousands. However, if you select either of those cells and then look on the Formula bar, you'll see that the number within the cell does not contain a comma. Only the display of the number has changed.

Other enhancements you'll read about in Skill 6 include fonts, cell colors and patterns, styles, alignment of entries within their cells, and changing the width of columns.

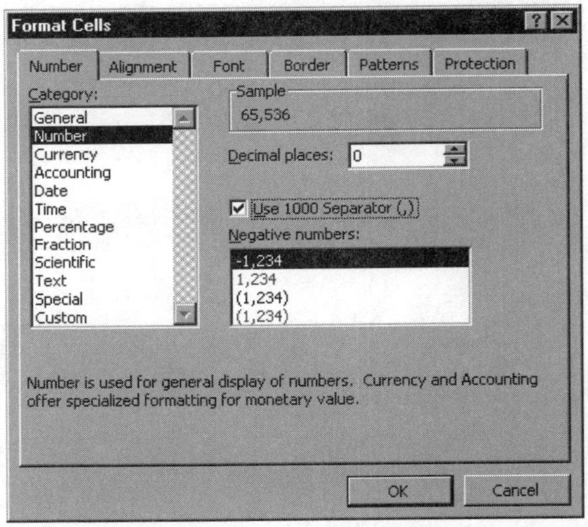

FIGURE 1.3: You can change the way Excel displays numbers by applying a numeric format, which does not affect the value of the numbers themselves.

NOTE NOTE NOTE NOTE NOTE NOTE NOTE NOTE NOTE NOTE NOTE NOTE NOTE NOTE NOTE

While playing with the numbers, you may find that a cell displays not the number but only pound signs: #######. The problem is that the column is not wide enough to display the number (or the numeric result of the formula) in the numeric format you have chosen. To fix this, you can change the format, widen the column, or use a smaller font. You can read about the display of large numbers in Skill 3.

Moving around in Excel

As you've seen, Excel worksheets are big—really, really big. The part you see on the screen is only a very small piece of a worksheet. To go to another part of any of the worksheets, all you need to do is select a cell in that area. In most cases, you can use your mouse, your keyboard, or a command.

Moving Cell by Cell

To move from one cell to another:

- Press one of the arrow keys.
- Click the arrow at either end of a scroll bar to scroll the window in the direction of the arrow. You can then select a cell.
- Make a selection, press Scroll Lock on your keyboard, and use the arrow keys to scroll the worksheet window without affecting the selection. When you're finished, be sure to press Scroll Lock again to turn it off.
- If your mouse has a scrolling wheel, such as Microsoft's IntelliMouse, you can use the wheel in the usual ways to scroll up or down through the window.
- Press Enter. You can disable this feature—or change the direction in which the selection moves—by choosing Tools ➤ Options to open the Options dialog box and then clicking the Move Selection after Enter check box and selecting a direction.
- First, select the range of cells in which you want to edit data. Pressing Enter moves the selection down a cell, but only within that range. From the bottom of one column, the selection will move to the top of the next. Press Shift+Enter to move up a cell, or press Tab or Shift+Tab to move a column to the right or left.

Moving Screen by Screen

To move a screen at a time:

- Press Page Down or Page Up.
- Click within a scroll bar outside the scroll box.
- Drag a scroll box to move to that relative position in the occupied worksheet. If row 100 is the last occupied row, dragging the scroll box halfway down the vertical scroll bar displays the portion of the worksheet around row 50.

NOTE NOTE NOTE NOTE NOTE NOTE NOTE NOTE NOTE NOTE NOTE NOTE NOTE NOTE

When you drag a scroll box, a ScrollTip tells you exactly which row or column will be displayed when you stop scrolling.

Moving between Worksheets

In addition to clicking the Sheet tab to open a worksheet, you can press Ctrl+Page Up or Ctrl+Page Down to move between sheets. If you've added more sheets to a workbook, you'll find that there isn't enough room to display more than about a half-dozen sheet tabs at one time. But you can use the four tab-scrolling buttons to the left of the sheet tabs to display more tabs.

The two outside buttons display the sheet tabs starting from the first sheet or the last sheet in the workbook. The two inner buttons display one more sheet tab in the chosen direction.

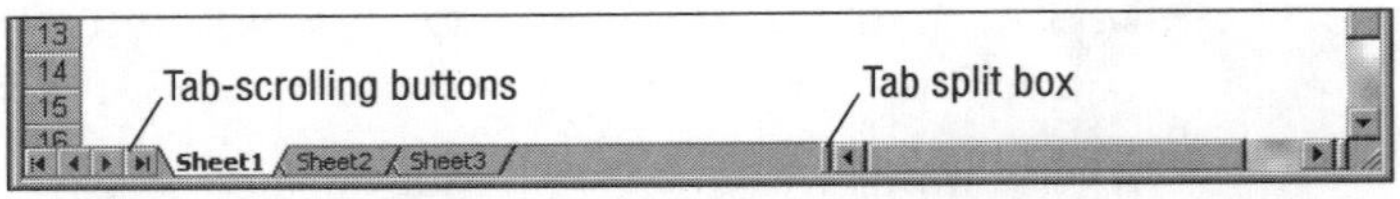

You can also show more or fewer sheet tabs by dragging the tab split box either left or right. Double-click it to display the default number of sheet tabs.

If there are many worksheets in use in the workbook and scrolling through the tabs would be a bit of a pain, right-click a tab-scrolling button to display a list of all the worksheets in the workbook. Click one, and you're there.

Moving in Large Jumps

You'll probably most often use the Go To dialog box (see Figure 1.4) to move in large jumps. (Choose Edit ➤ Go To to open the Go To dialog box.) Simply type the address you want to go to into the Reference field, and click OK. Otherwise, you can select one of the named ranges in the workbook (cells that you have named for convenience, as discussed in Skill 3), as well as the last four addresses from which you chose the Go To command (a quick way to return to places you've been).

Another way to go to and select an address or named range is with the Name Box on the left side of the Formula bar. Select the box, type a range name or cell address, and press Enter. You can also open its drop-down list of range names (if there are any ranges in the workbook) and select one.

Here are several other neat ways for getting to places fast:

- Press Home to move to the beginning of the current row.
- Press Ctrl+Home to move to cell A1 in the current worksheet.

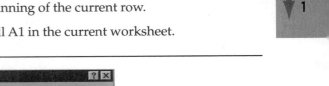

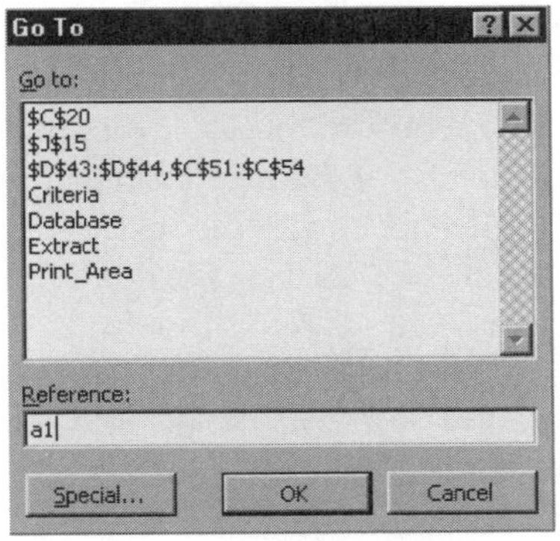

FIGURE 1.4: In the Go To dialog box, you can select or type the name or address you want to go to.

- Press Ctrl+End or End and then Home to move to the cell in the last occupied row and column of the worksheet. (This method will show you the farthest extent of the occupied worksheet.)
- Press Ctrl+arrow key or End, and then click an arrow key to move as far as possible in the given direction, based on whether cells in that row or column are occupied. Play with this one both while the active cell is occupied and while it's unoccupied to see how it works. You can also double-click one of the four edges of the active cell's selection border to get a similar result.
- Press End and then press Enter to move to the last occupied cell in the current row.

Moving between Workbooks

You can work with multiple workbooks at the same time in Excel, just as you can work with multiple documents in Microsoft Word. Switching between workbooks is really just a matter of switching between windows:

- If the other workbook is visible on the screen, click within it.
- Select a workbook from the Window menu.
- Press Ctrl+F6 to switch to the next window.

Using the Toolbars

A new feature in Excel 2000 is the Personal toolbar, which is installed by default. In one row, the Personal toolbar combines buttons from the Standard toolbar and the Formatting toolbar. Of course, there isn't enough room to display all the buttons from both these toolbars, so Excel displays those you use the most. Thus, the Personal toolbar is constantly changing, depending on how you work.

If you need a button that isn't displayed, simply click the More Buttons button to display the rest of the buttons normally found on the Standard or Formatting toolbars. Figure 1.5 shows the results of clicking the More Buttons button at the end of the Standard toolbar portion of the Personal toolbar. Notice that the Personal toolbar includes two More Buttons buttons—one in the middle and one at the far right. Figure 1.6 show the list of buttons that is displayed when you click Add or Remove Buttons. To add or remove a button, simply click it. If you want to reset the toolbar to its original (default) state, click Reset Toolbar.

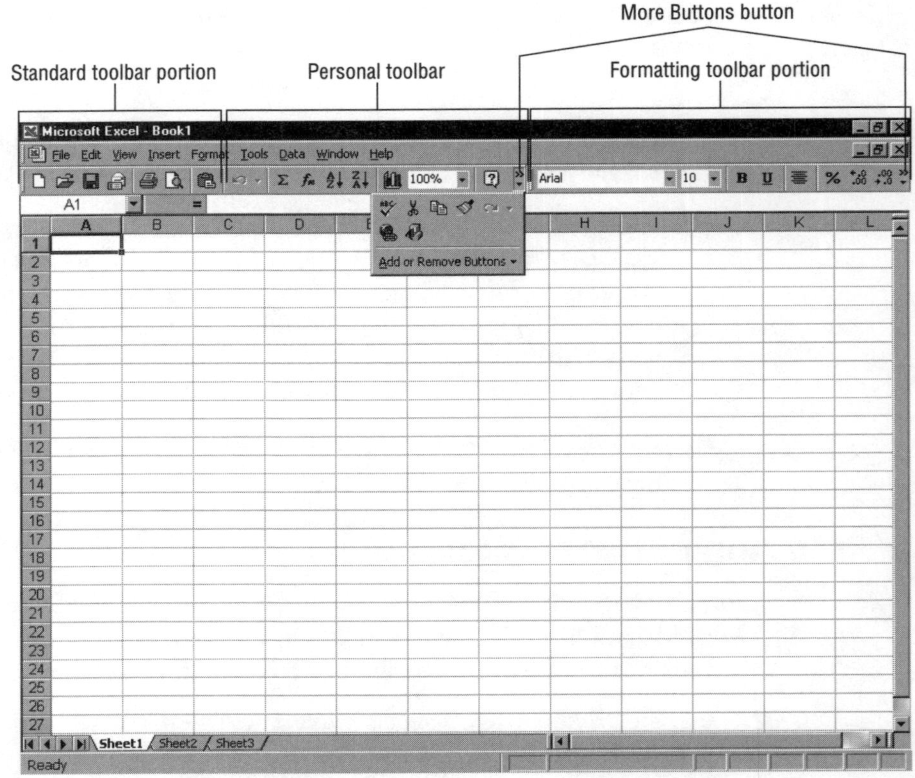

FIGURE 1.5: The Personal toolbar

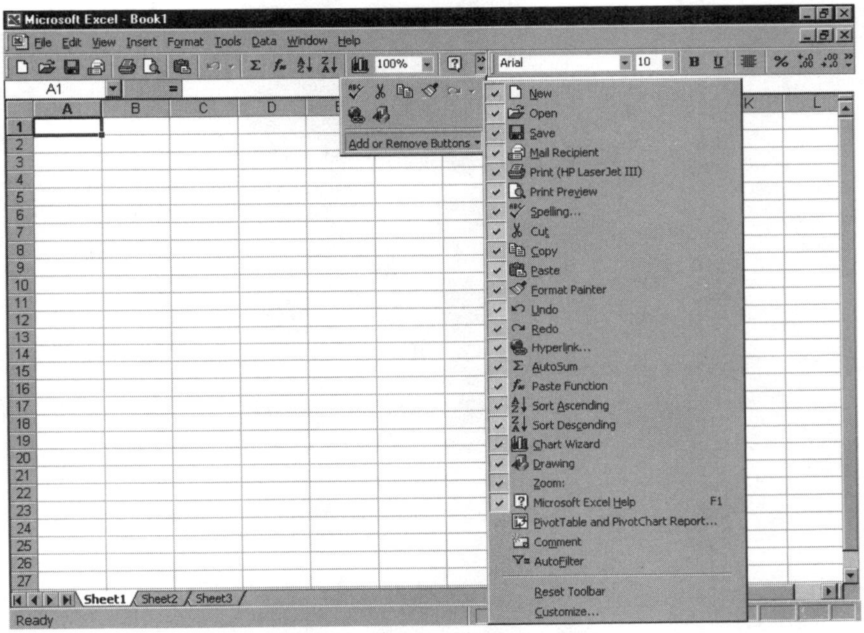

FIGURE 1.6: The results of clicking the Add or Remove Buttons button

I used the Personal toolbar while writing this book, and all the figures and graphics show the Personal toolbar. Of course, my Personal toolbar displays those buttons that I have most recently used, so it will look different from yours. You can, however, choose to display the Standard and Formatting toolbars in two rows, as they appeared in previous versions of Excel. To do so, follow these steps:

1. Right-click anywhere on the Personal toolbar to open the Customize dialog box, and then click the Options tab, as shown in Figure 1.7.
2. Clear the Standard and Formatting Toolbars Share One Row check box.
3. Click Close.

Besides the Standard and Formatting toolbars, Excel has 12 other toolbars. Choose View ➤ Toolbars to display the list shown in Figure 1.8.

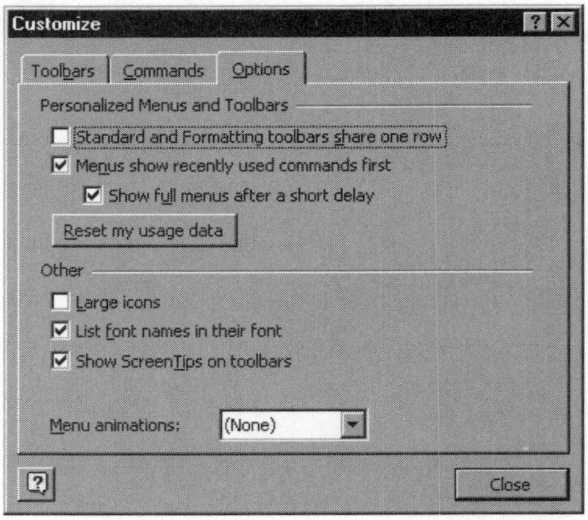

FIGURE 1.7: The Options tab of the Customize dialog box

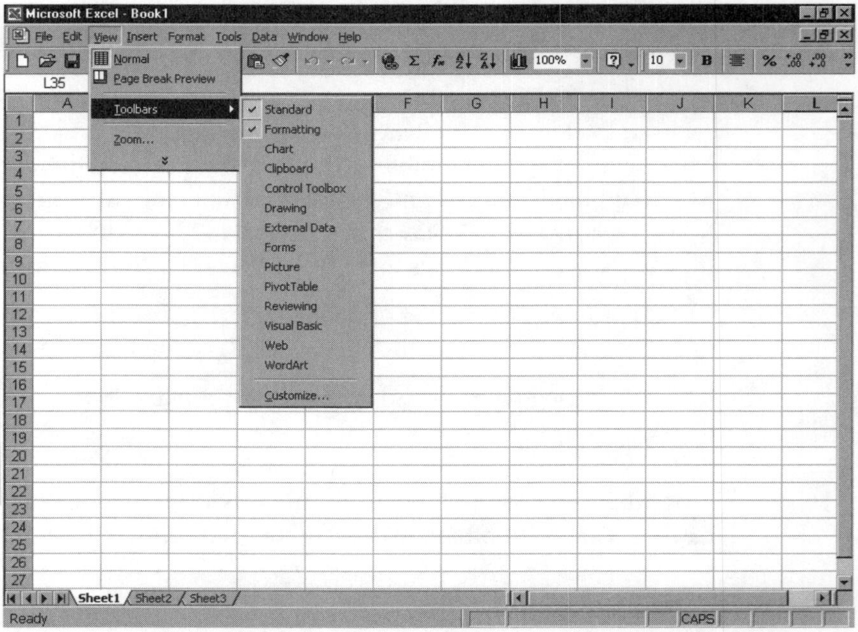

FIGURE 1.8: Click the name of a toolbar to display it or hide it.

NOTE NOTE NOTE NOTE NOTE NOTE NOTE NOTE NOTE NOTE NOTE NOTE NOTE NOTE

In Skill 14, you'll learn how to use the Customize dialog box to create your own toolbars with buttons that suit your work habits.

By default, toolbars appear beneath the menu bar, but you can place them anywhere on the screen and adjust their shape. Simply point to the toolbar's handle on the left side of the toolbar and drag it where you want it. If you drag the toolbar to an edge of the screen, the toolbar will "dock" against that edge. Otherwise, you can change the shape of the toolbar and its position within the window to suit your work habits.

When a button has a drop-down palette of choices, like the Borders and Fill Color buttons on the Formatting toolbar, you can tear off the palette and keep it available on the screen. Just drag its border away from the toolbar. The palette has its own Close button.

Using the Menus

NEW

As you work, Excel 2000 also personalizes your menus to reflect the commands you most recently used. By default, Excel displays short menus. To see all the commands on a menu, hold down the mouse button after you open a menu, or click the More Buttons button at the bottom of a menu. Figure 1.9 shows the short File menu, and Figure 1.10 shows the long File menu.

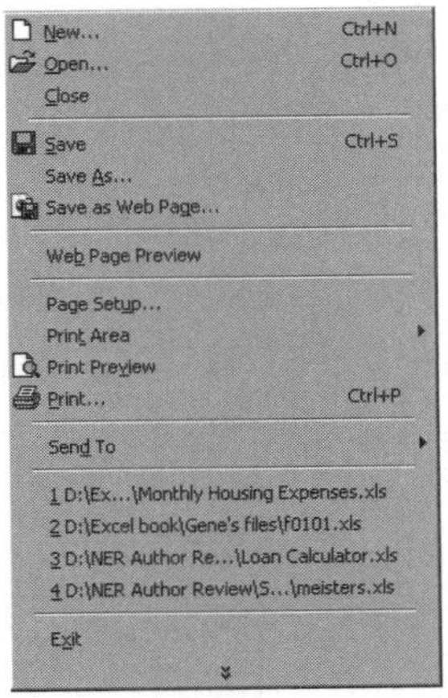

FIGURE 1.9: The short File menu

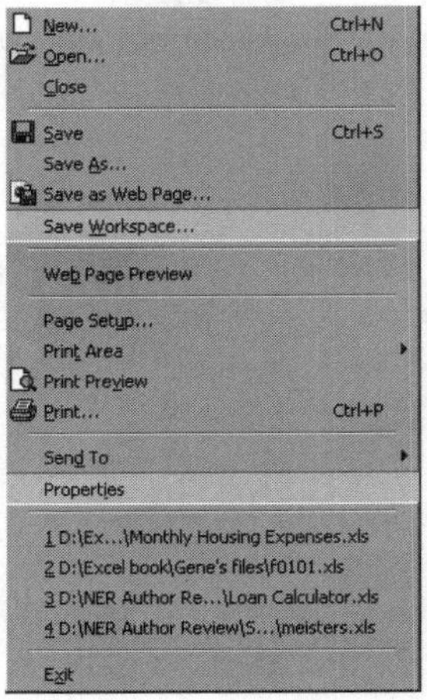

FIGURE 1.10: The long File menu

To reset your menus to their default state, follow these steps:

1. Choose Tools ➤ Customize to open the Customize dialog box.
2. Click the Options tab.
3. Click Reset My Usage Data.
4. When Excel asks if you're sure you want to do this, click Yes.
5. Click Close.

Getting Help

Its abundance of online help is one of the reasons people like to use Excel, especially new users. In Excel 2000, you can get help in three main ways:

Office Assistant A quirky, animated character that answers your questions.

Help topics Countless pages of information about Excel, which you can access through a table of contents or an index or by asking questions of the Answer Wizard.

World Wide Web If you have access to the Internet, you can tap into Microsoft's online help at various Web sites.

You'll also find help in a variety of other places and styles:

- Point at the name of a button on the toolbar to display a descriptive ScreenTip.
- To see a ScreenTip about an item on the Excel screen or a command on its menus, choose Help ➤ What's This (Shift+F1) and then click the item or command.
- To get help on an option in a dialog box, click the question mark in the upper-right corner and then click the option. A ScreenTip describes that option. Most dialog boxes also have a Help button that explains how to work with their settings.

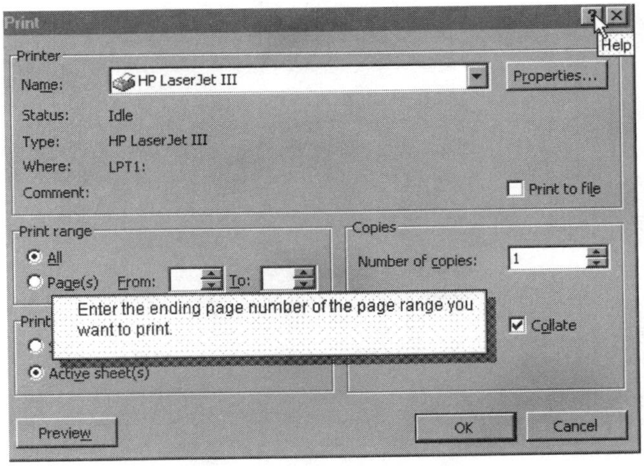

Accessing the Office Assistant

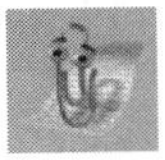

Excel and the other programs in Microsoft Office extend their online help capabilities with the Office Assistant. This perky, user-friendly, always-at-the-ready, "Yes Sir!" kind of help system goes a big step further in the world of online help. Some will say that it goes way too far, but you can decide for yourself.

TIP TIP TIP TIP TIP TIP TIP TIP TIP TIP TIP TIP TIP TIP TIP TIP TIP TIP TIP TIP TIP TIP TIP TIP TIP

While you're trying out the Assistant, you might do your co-workers a favor by turning down your computer's speakers! Alternatively, you can clear the Make Sounds check box on the Options tab of the Assistant's Options dialog box. This change affects the Assistant in all other Microsoft Office applications on your computer.

You access the Assistant for the first time by choosing Help ➤ Show Office Assistant. After you access the Assistant from the Help menu, you can click the Office Assistant button on the toolbar for future help.

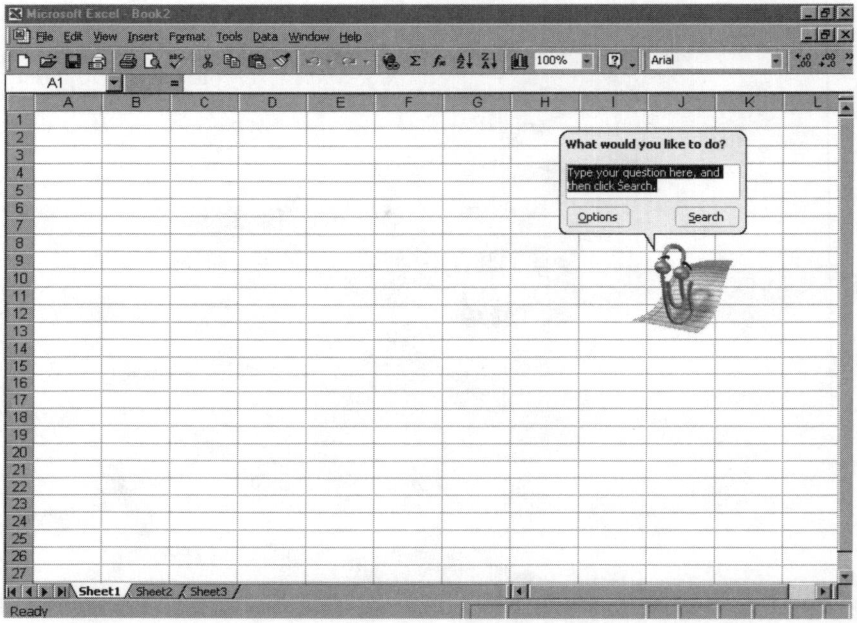

Once you've gotten over the animation of the Assistant, you'll find several ways to get help:

Ask a Question Type your question (be concise) and click the Search button. The Assistant will present you with several suggested help topics that may answer your question. Clicking one will bring up the relevant help screen. For example, try "How do I widen a column?" or "How do I use the Assistant?"

Tips While you're working in Excel, you may see a light bulb appear in the Assistant from time to time. Click the bulb to display a helpful tip about what you're doing. If the Assistant isn't open, you'll see the light bulb in the Office Assistant button on the Standard toolbar. Click the button to open the Assistant, and then click the light bulb to get the tip.

Wizards When a Wizard is helping you perform a task in Excel (Wizards are discussed a little later), you can have the Assistant stand on the side and kibbitz with explanations and helpful tips.

Relevant help When the Assistant is open, you can click it to have it offer help about the current task. When you're performing a task for the first time, the Assistant displays a light bulb. Clicking the light bulb or the Assistant displays relevant help topics.

The Office Assistant is an interesting and lively way to get help while you're working in Excel. If your Assistant gets annoying, you can adjust or disable many of its features. Simply click the Assistant, click the Options button to open the Office Assistant dialog box, and choose the Options tab.

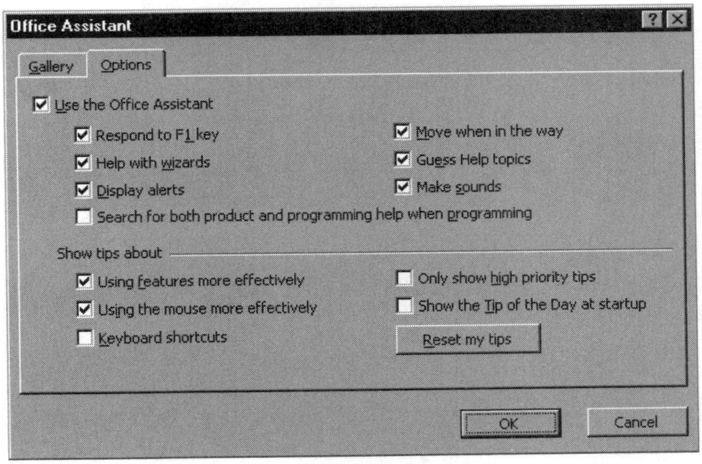

You can then fine-tune the Assistant to suit your needs (but don't you dare peek at the Gallery tab, or you'll twiddle away as much time as I did…just kidding). You can also right-click the Assistant and then click Hide on the shortcut menu to hide the Assistant.

Using Help Topics

You can access the main body of help, shown in Figure 1.11, by pressing F1, which sidesteps the Assistant.

TIP TIP TIP TIP TIP TIP TIP TIP TIP TIP TIP TIP TIP TIP TIP TIP TIP TIP TIP TIP TIP TIP TIP TIP TIP

If the F1 key displays and hides the Office Assistant, click the Office Assistant, click the Options button to open the Office Assistant dialog box, clear the Respond to F1 Key check box, and then click OK.

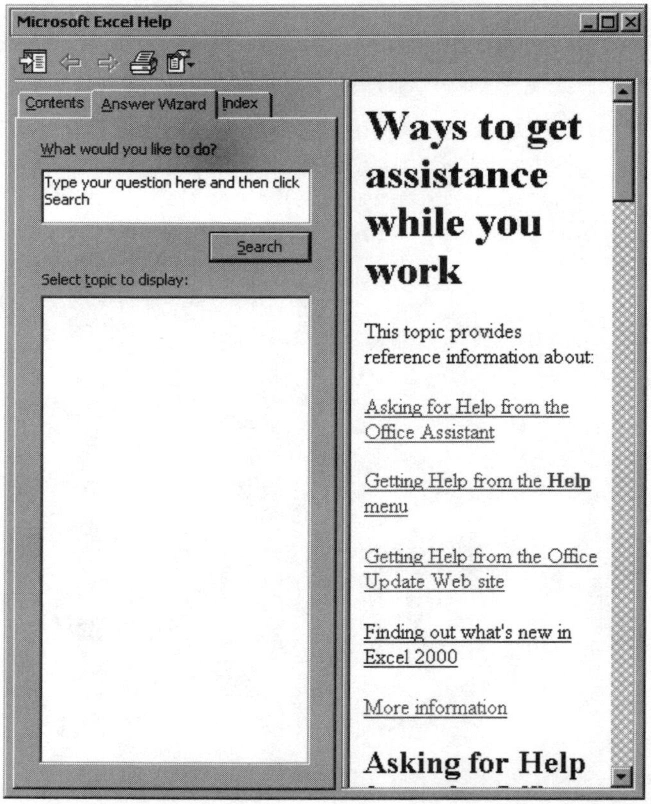

FIGURE 1.11: You can display the Help window by pressing F1.

The Help window opens in the size and shape in which it was last used. Here are a couple of ways to adjust the views of the Help window to get the most out of the Help feature.

- Click the Maximize button so that the Help window covers the entire screen.
- Choose Window ➤ Arrange, select Tiled, and then click OK to display the Help and workbook windows side by side.

If multiple Excel windows are open, choosing Arrange tiles all of them. The Help window has three tabs:

Contents Displays a table of contents of all the available help topics in Excel.

Answer Wizard Lets you find a topic by typing a question.

Index Displays a list of topics related to a word that you enter. Double-click one of them to display help on that topic.

Click the Hide button to hide the tabs and view the entire Help window.

Finding Help on the World Wide Web

If you're connected to the Internet's World Wide Web (would you admit it if you weren't?), Excel can find helpful information for you on Microsoft's Web sites. Choose Help ➤ Office on the Web to open your Web browser and access the Microsoft Office site.

Calling on Wizards to Lend a Hand

Excel is a huge program with lots and lots of features. The Wizards help you with some of the more common tasks that can seem rather complex the first time you use them (or each time if you rarely perform the tasks).

A Wizard is simply an automated question-and-answer session that walks you through the steps to complete a task; you'll also find Wizards in the other programs in Microsoft Office. A Wizard explains what is required at each step, prompts you for your response, and then moves on to the next step.

Some Wizards appear automatically—for example, when you choose Insert ➤ Chart. In this case, the Wizard guides you through the steps that are required to create a chart based on your worksheet.

To find other Wizards and *add-ins* (optional accessory programs), choose Tools ➤ Add-Ins. Once the add-ins are selected and installed, you can find them under the appropriate menus. For example, the Template Wizard is on the Data menu after it is installed.

This skill has introduced you to many of the Excel features that you will use on a daily basis. I hope that you've also begun to tinker with any features or odds and ends that pique your interest. The best way to learn about Excel is to read and experiment.

Skill 2 explains how to work with various types of data in Excel and introduces some features that assist you in creating your spreadsheet.

Are You Experienced?

Now you can...

☑ Open and close Excel

☑ Understand workbooks, worksheets, and cells

☑ Understand the Formula bar and status bar

☑ Use AutoCalculate to show a total of numbers

☑ Edit a cell

☑ Enter data and formulas into a cell

☑ Move around in a worksheet

☑ Jump to other worksheets

☑ Use the Personal toolbar and menus

☑ Use the Office Assistant

☑ Get help

☑ Use Wizards

SKILL 2

Understanding and Entering Data

- Distinguishing text and values
- Entering text
- Entering numbers
- Entering formulas
- Entering dates and times
- Using Excel tools to enter data quickly and accurately

This skill will help you with the common task of entering data of various types in Excel.

Understanding the Difference Between Values and Text

In general, Excel accepts two types of data: values and text. As a rule, if an entry you make is not a value, Excel treats it as text.

Entering Values: Numbers, Formulas, and Dates

A value is any datum that has significance beyond the characters you type, such as a numeric value. Excel aligns most values, such as numbers and dates, with the right side of their cells. To see how Excel displays values, you can enter the following values in a new worksheet:

Numbers Enter **14.5** in cell A1. This is a numeric value that you can include in a formula.

Formulas Enter the formula **=22+A1** in cell A2. The result will be 36.5.

Dates Enter the formula **=A4** in cell B4. Now enter **12/31/99** in cell A4. The display will show 12/31/99, but look at the result of the formula in B4—36525. The appearance of cell A4 didn't fool the formula in B4. The result shows that an underlying number represents the date in A4. The "Entering Dates and Times" section, later in this skill, explains how Excel handles dates.

TIP TIP TIP TIP TIP TIP TIP TIP TIP TIP TIP TIP TIP TIP TIP TIP TIP TIP TIP TIP TIP TIP TIP TIP TIP

The way Excel formats dates, times, and currency depends on the Windows 95/98 Regional Settings, which you'll find in the Windows Control Panel.

Delete the formula in B4, and the worksheet you just created should look like the one shown here.

	A	B
1	14.5	
2	36.5	
3	This is a value	
4	12/31/99	
5		

Only certain characters are allowed when you are creating a value, as discussed in the section "Entering Numbers" later in this skill. Entering text is a lot simpler, because there are really no rules to follow.

Text: Anything That Is Not a Value

Excel checks each entry you make and determines its type. If it is not a value, it is text—whether you intended that or not! Excel aligns text entries with the left side of their cell. To see how Excel displays text entries, you can enter the following in a worksheet:

Plain text In cell C1, enter **This is cell C1**. In C2, enter **123 Main St.** Both of these are text entries, even though they include numeric characters. You can tell that Excel does not consider an entry numeric in a couple of ways. If Excel left-justifies an entry in its cell, it's likely a text entry. If you include the cell address in a formula in another cell, such as =C3+1 in the above example, watch what happens. The result #VALUE! indicates that Excel cannot find a valid result because you can't add text (C3) and numbers.

Invalid formulas Enter **22+A1** in cell C3. Because the equals sign is missing, Excel takes this entry as plain text even though it looks like a formula.

Invalid dates Enter **12/42/99** in cell C4. Excel knows that December 42, 1999, is an invalid date and enters it as text. Notice how the "date" is left-justified in its cell.

Now your worksheet should look like this:

	A	B	C	D	E
1			This is cell C1		
2			123 Main St.		
3			22+A1		
4			12/42/99		
5					

Entering Text

Text entries might include column and row headings (Jan, Feb, Mar, Widget 1, Widget 2, and so on); report titles (Expense List for Analytical Dept.); cell identifiers (principal, interest, term); and small paragraphs of descriptive text.

Forcing an Entry to Be Text

If the text you are entering can be taken as a value, Excel will treat it that way. For example, suppose you're entering three cell identifiers that include a person's name and a year: Mark 99, Fred 99, and Jan 99. The first two will be taken as text, but Excel will take the third as the date January 1, 1999, and treat it as such.

You can force Excel to take an entry as text by preceding the entry with an apostrophe, such as `'Jan 99`.

Making Long Text Entries

A cell can hold more characters than you will ever want to enter, but the default column width in Excel is only about eight characters (in the standard, default font size).

A text entry that is longer than its column is wide will overhang its cell and appear to extend outside the cell. But it only does so on the display—it's still contained within its cell.

There's nothing wrong with this overhanging text, and you will frequently make entries that overhang. But you need to watch one thing: An entry in a cell next to the long text will cut it off at that cell, so the extended entry no longer overhangs. The worksheet shown here has the same long text entry in cells A1 and A3. But there's also an entry in B3, which truncates the text in A3.

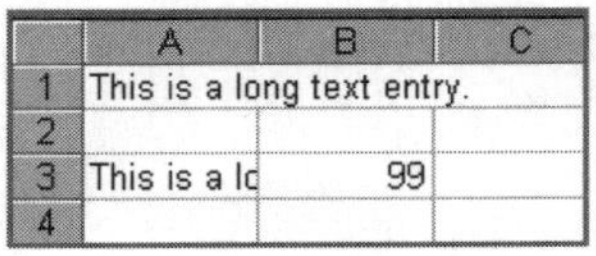

If a long text entry is "trapped" by adjacent entries and cannot overhang its cell, you can fit it within its cell in two ways:

- Use a smaller font.
- Widen its column.

Both methods are discussed in Skill 6. Another nifty way to handle a long entry is to force it to appear on two or more lines within the same cell. Follow these steps:

1. Click in an empty cell.
2. Type some text.
3. Hold down Alt and press Enter.
4. Type some more text.

Notice that all text is inside the cell and that the row height changes to accommodate additional lines.

NOTE NOTE NOTE NOTE NOTE NOTE NOTE NOTE NOTE NOTE NOTE NOTE NOTE NOTE NOTE

If you select a range of cells to print, any overhanging text that extends outside that range will not appear on the printout if you print with the Selection option. Be sure either to include all columns over which the text extends or to print with the Active Sheets option, which will print anything that appears on all selected worksheets. Skill 8 discusses these and other printing issues.

Entering Numbers

You have to pay a bit more attention when you're entering numbers and other values. If you don't, you might end up making a text entry that happens to *look* like the value you intended, and you might not catch the problem.

For example, if you mix text characters within a number, you will usually end up with a text entry. If you enter **125 lbs,** Excel treats the entry as text. Labels (such as lbs, dollars, and so on) must not be in the same cell as a numeric value if you intend to perform calculations based on the value. Put labels in an adjacent cell or in the column or row heading.

Including Formatting Characters

You can include some nonnumeric characters in a number. If you preface a number with a currency symbol, such as $, or include a thousands separator, such as a comma, Excel knows what to do with those characters and treats the entry as a number. It applies the appropriate numeric format to the cell to make it look the way you entered it. To see how this works, enter **$1,234** in a cell, and then compare the display of that cell with what's actually in it by clicking the cell to make it active and then looking at the Formula bar.

If you append a percent sign (%) to a number, Excel divides the number by 100, making it a percentage, and applies a numeric format to it so that it looks like a percentage. For example, enter **15.8%** in a cell and then write a formula in another cell that multiplies a number by the cell that contains the 15.8%. In this case, Excel leaves the percent sign in the cell; as long as it is there, the number that precedes it will be handled as a percentage.

Entering Large Numbers

Unlike a long text entry, a numeric entry (whether a number or the result of a formula) must fit within the width of its cell; it will *not* overhang the cell. Instead, Excel will accommodate a number that is too long for the cell width by expanding the width of the column (up to a maximum width of about 12 characters), as long as the column width has not already been adjusted. Otherwise, Excel will display the number in a numeric format style that makes it fit within the current width of the cell.

For example, on a new worksheet, enter the number **1234567890** in cell A1, and you'll see that Excel widens column A so that the entire number is displayed. Now see how Excel displays the number when it cannot widen the column:

1. In the column heading, point to the dividing line between columns A and B so that the pointer changes to a double-headed arrow.
2. Drag the column edge to the left just a character or two to shrink column A.
3. Release the mouse button, and you'll see that Excel must now change the way the number is displayed in order to fit it within the new width of the column.

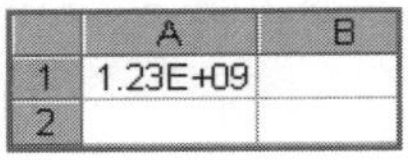

If Excel is using its typical default font size, the number should be displayed as 1.23E+09 (if it's not, try adjusting the column width until it is). Excel chose the Scientific format to display this number, which allowed it to "fit" within its column width.

NOTE NOTE NOTE NOTE NOTE NOTE NOTE NOTE NOTE NOTE NOTE NOTE NOTE NOTE NOTE

If you apply a specific format to a cell, Excel will *not* change it to a different format when the number is too large to fit within its cell.

Try making column A a lot narrower, leaving it only a few characters wide. You'll see that when a column is too narrow to display a number, Excel displays only pound signs instead of the number.

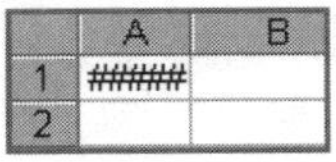

At this point, you can widen the column to display the number as you entered it or apply a smaller font to the cell.

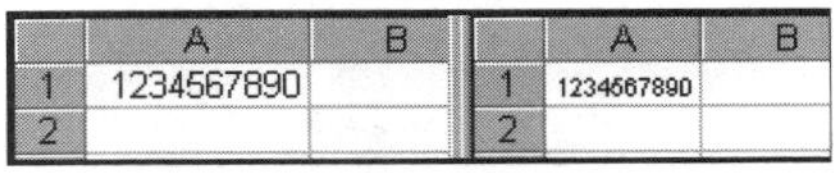

Entering Formulas and Text Values

Skill 4 discusses formula writing in detail, but I'll talk about some issues here in the context of the types of data you can enter.

The data in a formula can consist of numbers, text values, functions, or cell addresses that you combine with arithmetical operators. The operators include the usual + and –, with the asterisk (*) for multiplication and the forward slash (/) for division.

Excel calculates the formula as soon as you enter it and displays the result on the screen.

NOTE NOTE NOTE NOTE NOTE NOTE NOTE NOTE NOTE NOTE NOTE NOTE NOTE NOTE NOTE

A formula *must* begin with an equals sign (=) for Excel to recognize it as such. Otherwise, your "formula" will be taken as plain text, with no resulting value. You can preface a formula with + or –, but Excel will add an = to the beginning of the formula anyway.

A text value, or text string, is really a formula that produces a text value for a result. You can do some slick tricks when you start combining text values within formulas; the process is called *concatenation*.

To create a simple text value, enclose it in quotation marks and treat it as a formula:

```
="This is a text value"
```

To concatenate this with other text, use the ampersand (&):

```
="This is a text value "&"and so is this."
```

The result of this formula is the sentence:

```
This is a text value and so is this.
```

If you enter your name in cell A1, either as plain text or a text value, this formula would make sense:

```
="My name is "&A1
```

Give it a try. Note that the cell reference is not enclosed in quotes, because it is the contents of that cell that you are referencing.

Skill 5 discusses some of the functions you can use to manipulate text values.

Entering Dates and Times

You can enter dates or times in any style that suits you, such as:

```
1999, 31st of December
```

However, you will usually want to enter them in a style Excel recognizes so that you can:

- Perform date or time arithmetic, such as subtracting one date from another to determine the number of days between them.
- Sort a range of cells based on their dates in one of the columns.
- Find all records in a database that have a date greater than a specified date.
- Fill a column with dates that are one week apart.

TIP

Pressing Ctrl+; (semicolon) enters the current date, and pressing Ctrl+: (colon) enters the current time. These are especially handy because, unlike the NOW() function (which updates to the current date and time whenever the file is opened), the date and time are static and never change when entered this way.

Entering Dates and Times That Excel Recognizes

The easiest way to enter a date or a time is to use a style that Excel recognizes. For the date December 31, 1999, and the time 3:30 PM, this small worksheet shows the valid styles (although other styles are understood, they are converted to one of the styles shown here). When you don't include the day, Excel assumes the first of the month; when you don't include the year, Excel assumes the current year.

	A	B	C
1	12/31/99	31-Dec-99	
2	31-Dec	3:30 PM	
3	Dec-99	15:30	
4			
5			
6			

Remember, when you're entering a date or time, do *not* preface it with an equals sign; Excel will assume that you are entering a formula, such as 12 divided by 31 divided by 99.

NOTE NOTE NOTE NOTE NOTE NOTE NOTE NOTE NOTE NOTE NOTE NOTE NOTE NOTE NOTE

The date and time styles that Excel recognizes are determined in part by the choices you make in the Windows 95/98 Control Panel's Regional Settings tool under the Date and Time tabs.

When you enter dates or times in an "approved" style, Excel actually performs a shortcut that lets you avoid several steps, as discussed next.

Understanding Excel's System of Chronology

Excel represents dates with whole numbers and times with fractions. It begins with the date January 1, 1900, and refers to it as a 1. January 2 of that year is a 2, and so on. Therefore, January 1, 1901, is 367 (or 367 days after January 1, 1900), January 1, 1950, is 18,264, and January 1, 2000 is 36,526. This makes it easier for Excel to use dates in calculations. You can calculate the number of days an employee has worked, calculate vacation time, amortize a loan, and more.

A time in Excel is calculated as a fraction of 24 hours; so midnight is 0.0, 6:00 AM is 0.25, noon is 0.50, and 11:59 PM is something like 0.999. So January 1, 2000, 6:00 PM is represented as 36,526.75. Just remember that the time fraction is letting you know how much of the day has passed (noon is .50 or half way through the 24-hour day). Calculating date and time numbers is simple enough—if you're a computer! Excel includes a variety of functions for calculating the correct number for a date or time, some of which are discussed in Skill 5. For example, you can use =DATE(99,12,31) to enter that date or =NOW() to enter the current date and time.

It's easy to see how you can perform date arithmetic when numbers represent the dates. To calculate the date that is one day after December 31, 1999, simply add 1 to it, producing the number 36526. The second trick is to make that number appear as a date.

Applying a Date or Time Format

When you enter the date 12/31/99 into a cell, Excel actually does two things:

- Keeps track of the date's number, 36525.
- Applies a numeric format to the cell to make it look like a date.

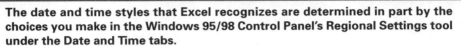

To select the date or time format you want, follow these steps:

1. Choose Format ➤ Cells to open the Format Cells dialog box, as shown in Figure 2.1.
2. Click the Number tab.
3. Choose Date or choose Time in the Category list.
4. Select a format from the Type list.
5. Click OK.

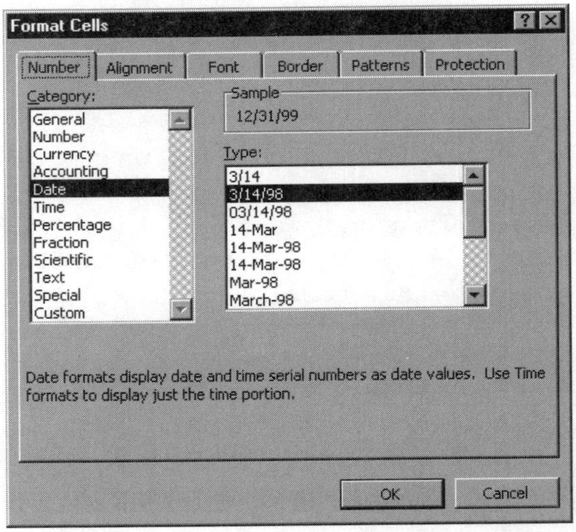

FIGURE 2.1: Applying a date format via the Format Cells dialog box

To view all the tabs in the Format Cells dialog box, Excel must be in Ready mode (in other words, you can't be editing the cell).

You'll find a variety of date and time formats, and you're free to design your own custom formats, too, as discussed in Skill 6.

Using AutoFill and Custom Lists

Excel includes a variety of tools for helping you enter data. The first one I'll discuss is AutoFill, which can enter a sequence of data at the touch of a button.

Actually, that should be at the touch of your mouse. You create an AutoFill sequence by dragging the *fill handle* over the cells you want to fill. The fill handle is the small black box in the lower-right corner of either the active cell or the selected cells. When you point to it, the mouse pointer changes to crosshairs.

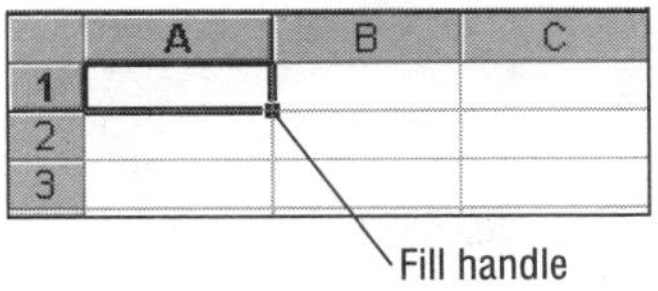

NOTE NOTE NOTE NOTE NOTE NOTE NOTE NOTE NOTE NOTE NOTE NOTE NOTE NOTE NOTE

If you don't see a fill handle, choose Tools ➤ Options to open the Options dialog box, click the Edit tab, and then click the Allow Cell Drag and Drop check box. Click OK and you're ready to go.

AutoFill creates cell entries in a selected range based either on the "seed" entry in the first cell of that range or on the first and any consecutive filled cells. For example:

- Placing a 1 in the first cell of the selected range and placing a 3 in the next cell produces 5, 7, 9, and so on in the following cells of the selected range. Placing a 1 in the first cell and a 5 in the next cell produces 9, 13, 17, and so on.
- The text seed entry Widget 1 produces Widget 2, Widget 3, and so on.
- The seed entry Jan produces Feb, Mar, and so on.
- The seed entry Qtr 1 produces Qtr 2, Qtr 3, Qtr 4, Qtr 1, and so on, and the seed entry Qtr 1 and the next entry Qtr 3 produce Qtr 1, Qtr 3, Qtr 1, and so on.

Excel comes with several ready-made AutoFill custom lists, such as the days of the week and the months of the year. It's easy to create your own as well, as you'll see in the section "Working with Custom Lists" later in this skill.

Filling a Range from One or More Seed Values

AutoFill can create a sequence from just about any numeric entry or text entry that has a numeric prefix or suffix. To see how this works, click the New button on the Standard toolbar to open a blank worksheet, and follow these steps:

1. Enter **Week 1** in cell A1.
2. Select cell A1 if it isn't already selected.

3. Point to the fill handle in the lower-right corner of the cell; the mouse pointer will change to crosshairs.
4. Drag the fill handle straight down to select as many rows as you want to fill. A small window appears by the mouse pointer and displays the exact cell entry that will be created if you stop dragging.
5. Release the mouse button, and Excel completes the sequence.

These steps produced the sequence Week 1, Week 2, and so on. Let's try a few more. Make the following seed entries in the same worksheet in the cells indicated:

- B1 **Qtr 1**
- C1 **1st Quarter**
- D1 **1/1/99**
- E1 **Jan-99**

Now repeat steps 2 through 5 for each of the cells B1 through E1. Your worksheet should look like the worksheet in Figure 2.2.

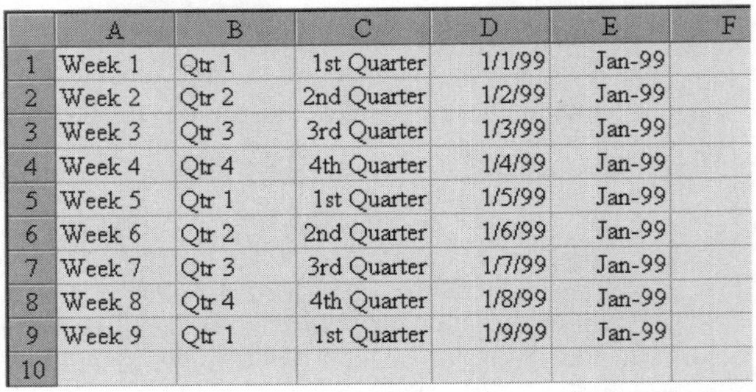

	A	B	C	D	E	F
1	Week 1	Qtr 1	1st Quarter	1/1/99	Jan-99	
2	Week 2	Qtr 2	2nd Quarter	1/2/99	Jan-99	
3	Week 3	Qtr 3	3rd Quarter	1/3/99	Jan-99	
4	Week 4	Qtr 4	4th Quarter	1/4/99	Jan-99	
5	Week 5	Qtr 1	1st Quarter	1/5/99	Jan-99	
6	Week 6	Qtr 2	2nd Quarter	1/6/99	Jan-99	
7	Week 7	Qtr 3	3rd Quarter	1/7/99	Jan-99	
8	Week 8	Qtr 4	4th Quarter	1/8/99	Jan-99	
9	Week 9	Qtr 1	1st Quarter	1/9/99	Jan-99	
10						

FIGURE 2.2: AutoFill lets you create a sequence based on a seed entry that contains a number.

TIP TIP TIP TIP TIP TIP TIP TIP TIP TIP TIP TIP TIP TIP TIP TIP TIP TIP TIP TIP TIP TIP TIP TIP TIP TIP TIP

The sequences based on quarters, such as Qtr 1, rely on AutoFill's ability to recognize that a year contains four quarters.

Now try a multiple seed AutoFill, in which you use your seed entries to determine the increments of the sequence. Make the following entries on a blank worksheet (you can use Sheet2 in the current workbook). This time we'll fill across the rows:

- A1 **1**
- B1 **3**
- A2 **1/1/99**
- B2 **1/8/99**
- A3 **Jan-99**
- B3 **Jan-00**

Now select all the seed entries, A1:B3, and drag the fill handle for that range across the worksheet to column H. Release the mouse button, and your worksheet should look like the worksheet in Figure 2.3.

NOTE NOTE NOTE NOTE NOTE NOTE NOTE NOTE NOTE NOTE NOTE NOTE NOTE NOTE NOTE

Regardless of how you enter Jan 99 or Jan 00, Excel inserts a hyphen between the month and the year.

	A	B	C	D	E	F	G	H	I	J	K	L
1	1	3	5	7	9	11	13	15				
2	1/1/99	1/8/99	1/15/99	1/22/99	1/29/99	2/5/99	2/12/99	2/19/99				
3	Jan-99	Jan-99	Jan-99	Jan-99	Jan-99	Jan-99	Jan-99	Jan-99				
4	Jan-00	Feb-00	Mar-00	Apr-00	May-00	Jun-00	Jul-00	Aug-00				
5												

FIGURE 2.3: When you enter incremental seed entries, AutoFill continues the sequence.

Using AutoFill to Create a Series

You can create any kind of series you can think of using the AutoFill feature. To see just one example, follow these steps:

1. Click the New button on the Standard toolbar to open a blank workbook.
2. Type **3/31/99** in cell A1 and press Enter.
3. Type **6/30/99** in cell A2 and press Enter.
4. Drag the mouse over both cells to select them.

5. Drag the fill handle down several rows and release the mouse button to create the series.

	A	B
1	03/31/99	
2	06/30/99	
3	09/30/99	
4	12/31/99	
5	03/31/00	
6	06/30/00	
7	09/30/00	
8	12/31/00	
9	03/31/01	
10	06/30/01	
11	09/30/01	
12		

You can also create a series in multiple columns or rows by placing a seed entry in two or more cells. To do so, follow these steps:

1. Type **1-99** in cell C1, **1-00** in cell D1, and **01-2001** in cell E1.

WARNING WARNING WARNING WARNING WARNING WARNING WARNING WARNING

If you do not enter the full year for 2001, Excel assumes that 1-01 is January 1 of the current year.

2. Drag the fill handle for cell C1 down one cell to create Feb-99 and repeat for the remaining seed entries.
3. Select the cells C1 to E2 and then drag the fill handle down to create all three series simultaneously.

C	D	E
Jan-99	Jan-00	Jan-01
Feb-99	Feb-00	Feb-01
Mar-99	Mar-00	Mar-01
Apr-99	Apr-00	Apr-01
May-99	May-00	May-01
Jun-99	Jun-00	Jun-01
Jul-99	Jul-00	Jul-01
Aug-99	Aug-00	Aug-01
Sep-99	Sep-00	Sep-01
Oct-99	Oct-00	Oct-01
Nov-99	Nov-00	Nov-01
Dec-99	Dec-00	Dec-01

NOTE NOTE NOTE NOTE NOTE NOTE NOTE NOTE NOTE NOTE NOTE NOTE NOTE NOTE NOTE

Excel automatically formats the month and year to an alphanumeric format. If you want the dates to appear numerically, select that format in the Format Cells dialog box.

Using Other AutoFill Tricks

Dragging the AutoFill handle lets you perform some other tasks as well.

- To create a multiple seed sequence in decreasing values, select the seed values and drag up or to the left, but *past the beginning of the selection* to avoid erasing the cells. For instance, if cells A12:A13 contain the numbers 1 and 2, you can select those cells and drag the fill handle up to A1 to create a decreasing sequence to –10.
- To erase a range of cells, select a range and drag the fill handle *inside* the range; when you release the mouse button, the cells are erased. For example, create a series in cells A1:B10. With the series still selected, drag the fill handle up to row 6. Release the mouse button and the cells in A6:B10 will be erased.
- To insert cells, hold down the Shift key while you drag the fill handle (for more information, see Skill 3).
- To display a shortcut menu of choices, drag the fill handle while holding down the right mouse button and then release the button.

Working with Custom Lists

The second way that AutoFill can create a sequence is from existing lists of data. Several lists are built into Excel. To display two of those lists, follow these steps:

1. In cells A1:D1 of a blank worksheet, enter **Jan**, **January**, **Mon**, and **Monday**.
2. Select those cells.
3. Drag the fill handle down a dozen or so rows and release the mouse button.

Now you know that the days of the week and the months of the year are ready-made lists.

Excel makes it easy for you to create your own lists, which can consist of just about anything—the names of the planets of our solar system, inventory items, the departments of your company, and so on. To create a custom list, follow these steps:

1. Choose Tools ➤ Options to open the Options dialog box, shown in Figure 2.4.

2. Click the Custom Lists tab.
3. Select NEW LIST in the Custom Lists window.
4. In the List Entries window, enter your custom list items (such as the names of the planets in our solar system, as shown in Figure 2.4). Press Enter after typing each item.
5. When you're finished, click Add and then click OK.

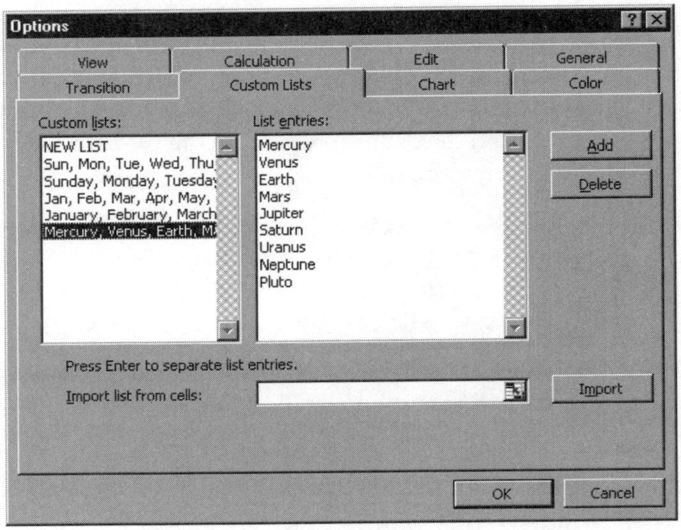

FIGURE 2.4: The Custom Lists in the Options dialog box contains the sequences for the AutoFill feature.

When you want to use this new list, enter one of the items from your list in the worksheet and use that item as a seed value to fill the cells in an adjacent row or column. AutoFill will find the item in one of its lists and continue the sequence based on that list.

Adding a Custom List to AutoFill from the Worksheet

If the sequence you want to create is already in the worksheet, you can import it into Custom Lists. Follow these steps:

1. Highlight the list by dragging the mouse over the items.

2. Click Tools ➤ Options to open the Options dialog box.
3. Click the Custom Lists tab.
4. Click the Import button to add the list.
5. Click OK.

You can also import worksheet elements without first selecting the list. Follow these steps:

1. Click Tools ➤ Options to open the Options dialog box.
2. Click the Custom Lists tab.

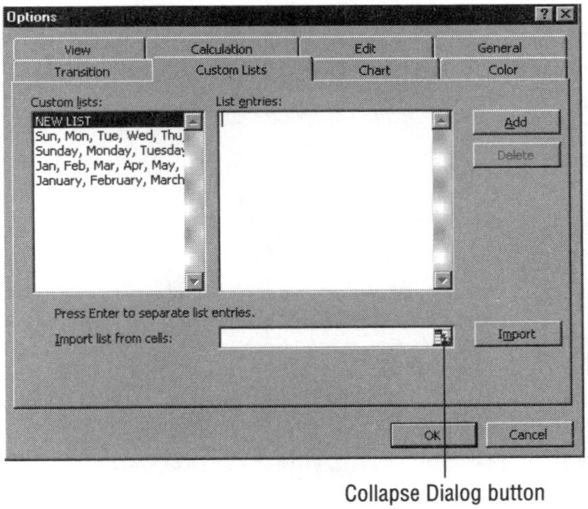

3. Click the Collapse Dialog button in the Import List from Cells text box to open the Options – Import List from Cells dialog box in the worksheet.

4. Select the list elements in the worksheet, and then click the Collapse Dialog button again to return to the Options dialog box.
5. Click the Import button to add the list, and then click the OK button to return to the worksheet.

Filling a Range with a Series

You can fill a selected range with a series of numbers or dates (which we know are actually just formatted numbers) by choosing Edit ➤ Fill and then choosing Down, Right, Up, and Left to copy the first entry in the selected range to the other cells in the selection.

You have still another way to fill a range with a series. Choose Edit ➤ Fill ➤ Series to open the Series dialog box (see Figure 2.6), which offers some useful options and both complements and extends the AutoFill feature discussed in the previous section.

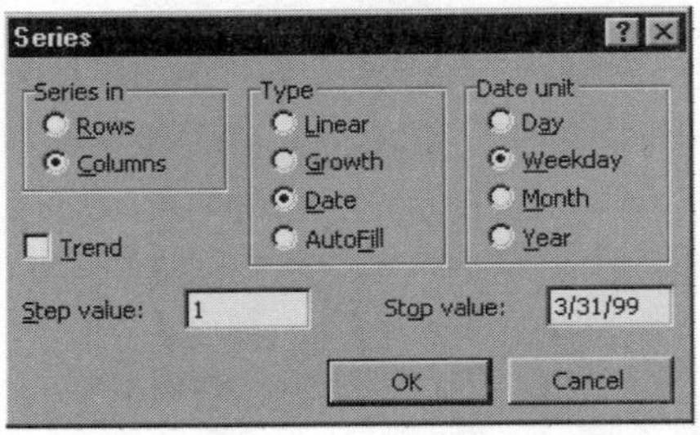

FIGURE 2.5: Use the Series dialog box to fill a range of cells with a variety of series.

Using the Series dialog box, you create a series based on the following:

- The value in the first cell of the selected range that you want to fill serves as the starting value for the series.
- The Step Value is the amount by which each cell in the series will be incremented (or decremented if you enter a negative number) from the cell before it.
- The Stop Value is the highest value (or lowest if decrementing) you want the series to attain.

The other choices in the Series dialog box let you define the type of series that will be created. Series In determines whether the fill will proceed by rows or columns. The Type options let you specify the type of series to create:

Linear The step value is added to (or subtracted from) one cell to fill the next cell.

Growth A cell is multiplied by the step value to fill the next cell.

Date The cells are filled by dates, based on your choice in the Date Unit options.

AutoFill The range of cells is filled following the same rules as the AutoFill feature, discussed in the previous section

NOTE NOTE NOTE NOTE NOTE NOTE NOTE NOTE NOTE NOTE NOTE NOTE NOTE NOTE NOTE

If you first select a range of data, you can use the Trend option in the Series dialog box to replace that data with data that will produce either a linear or best-fitted curve, depending on whether you selected the Linear or Growth fill types. If you don't want to overwrite your data, copy it to another range, and use that data for the Series command.

Entering Data with AutoComplete and Pick List

Excel's AutoComplete and Pick List features are wonderful tools for entering repetitive data quickly and consistently. The best way to understand these tools is to use them in a short example.

Letting AutoComplete Do Your Typing

First, we need to create a column of sample data. For this example, we'll use the months of the year. Follow these steps:

1. In cell A1, enter **January**.
2. Select A1, drag the fill handle down to A12, and release the mouse button to let AutoFill create the months of the year in cells A1:A12.

Now you have a column of data. In the real world, your data might be a customer list that fills hundreds or thousands of rows, with many of the entries being repeated throughout, such as cities, states, product names, and so on. Let's continue entering new data and repeating existing entries in the column.

3. Select the first blank cell beneath the data, which in this case is A13.
4. Enter **February**, but type slowly and watch the cell as you do.

   As soon as you type the F, the AutoComplete feature looks in the column above, sees that only one entry begins with the letter *F*, and completes your entry for you. At this point, you have four options:

   - Accept this suggested entry by pressing Enter or selecting the next cell.

- Continue typing slowly and see if AutoComplete finds another matching entry based on the additional characters you type.
- Continue typing to complete the entry, ignoring the AutoComplete suggestion.
- Press F2 for edit mode, and revise the AutoComplete suggestion to create a new entry.

5. Complete this cell entry and move down to A14.
6. Watch the cell and type **J**. No AutoComplete suggestion is made, because several entries in the cells above begin with that letter.
7. Type **u**; still no suggestion.
8. Type **n**, and now Excel suggests the only entry to match those letters—June.

You can accept this entry, knowing that it is spelled exactly like the earlier entry in the column, including the case of the letters.

Selecting Data from a List

Another way to enter data in a cell without typing it is to select it from a list that is built from the cells above it. You can display the list in two ways:

- Right-click the cell, and choose Pick from List from the shortcut menu.
- Press Alt+down arrow.

Excel alphabetizes the Pick List entries so that it is easy to find the one you want.

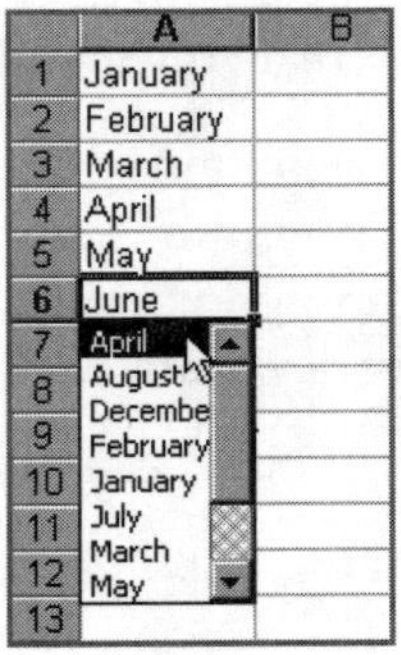

Here are a few rules to keep in mind when you are ready to use the AutoComplete and Pick List features:

- AutoComplete and Pick List look only at the column above or below and therefore won't be of any help when you're entering data across rows. There can be no blank cells between the active cell and the data above.
- AutoComplete and Pick List work only for text entries, not for numbers (including dates) or formulas.

To disable these features (they might slow to a crawl if you have thousands of unique entries in a column), follow these steps:

1. Choose Tools ➤ Options to open the Options dialog box.
2. Click the Edit tab.
3. Clear the Enable AutoComplete for Cell Values check box.
4. Click OK.

Keeping Your Spelling Accurate

With Excel's spell-checking capabilities, the spelling in your worksheets can be just as accurate as the spelling in your word-processing documents. In fact, when you're using the Microsoft Office 2000 suite, Excel and the other Office applications all share the same spelling dictionaries.

You can correct misspelled words in Excel in two ways:

- Choose Tools ➤ Spelling to find errors anywhere in the active workbook.
- Let the AutoCorrect feature automatically correct common typing errors as you make them.

Checking Spelling in the Workbook

Before you begin spell checking, you can select the part of your workbook that you want to check:

- Select only a single cell if you want Excel to spell check the entire active sheet, including all text cell entries, cell comments, embedded text or drawn objects, and charts.
- Select multiple sheets to spell check them all (click the first sheet's tab, hold down Shift, and then click the last sheet's tab).

- Select cells or objects first, if you want Excel to spell check only those elements.

If you run spell-check while you are editing the text in a cell or object, Excel checks only that text.

To begin spell checking, choose Tools ➤ Spelling, click the Spelling button on the Standard toolbar, or press F7. If no suspected misspellings are found, Excel displays a dialog box reporting that the spell checking is finished.

If Excel finds a misspelled word (or rather, a word that is not in the spell checker's dictionary), Excel display the Spelling dialog box (see Figure 2.6).

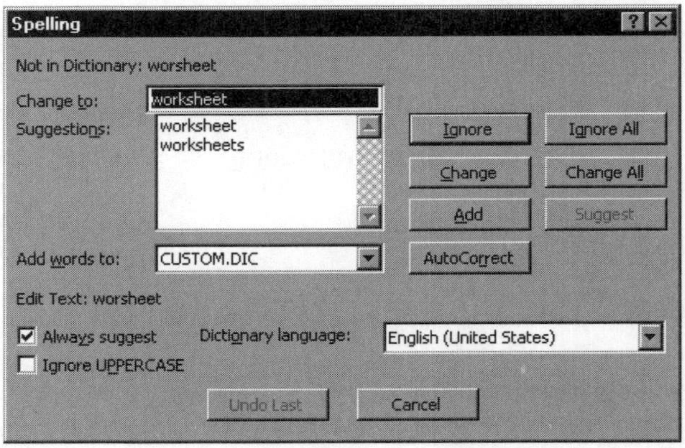

FIGURE 2.6: The Spelling dialog box displays a suspected misspelled word and offers a list of suggested replacements.

NOTE

When you have not selected any cells or objects, the spell checker proceeds row by row from the current cell to the end of the sheet and will continue from the beginning of the sheet at your request.

If the Word Is Spelled Correctly

The spell checker flags many words that are actually correct, especially names or uncommon technical or medical terms. When the suspect word is correct, you can do any of the following:

- Click Ignore to bypass this word and continue spell checking; if the suspect word appears again, Excel flags it again.

- Click Ignore All to bypass all occurrences of the suspect word during this spell-checking session.
- Click Add to add this word to the dictionary (by default, this is the CUSTOM.DIC dictionary file). In the future, Excel will recognize that the word is spelled correctly.

If the Word Is Misspelled

If the word in question is incorrect, you can either type the correct spelling in the Change To field or select a word in the Suggestions list. You then have several options:

- Click Suggest to display a list of suggestions for that word.
- Click Change to replace the misspelled word with the word in the Change To field.
- Click Change All to correct all occurrences of the misspelled word.
- Click AutoCorrect to add this word to the AutoCorrect list. In the future, AutoCorrect will automatically replace the misspelled word with the correct word.

Letting AutoCorrect Fix Errors As They Occur

The AutoCorrect feature in Excel is also found in the other Microsoft Office 2000 applications. It watches as you type and automatically replaces a word it finds in its built-in list with an alternate. The list of words (which is shared by other Office applications) can include:

- Commonly misspelled words, such as "adn" for "and" and "teh" for "the"
- Abbreviations for words that you enter frequently so that, for example, when you type **wdc**, AutoCorrect replaces it with "Washington, D.C."

To turn this feature on and off and access its list of words, choose Tools ➤ AutoCorrect to open the AutoCorrect dialog box, as shown in Figure 2.7.

Before you try this feature, choose Tools ➤ AutoCorrect to verify that AutoCorrect is enabled—the Replace Text as You Type check box should be checked. Choose OK or press Enter to close the AutoCorrect dialog box.

To see what AutoCorrect can do, click a cell and type the sentence below exactly as it is spelled. Watch the results on the screen as you do:

```
Teh poeple saw the sohw at tje cafe.
```

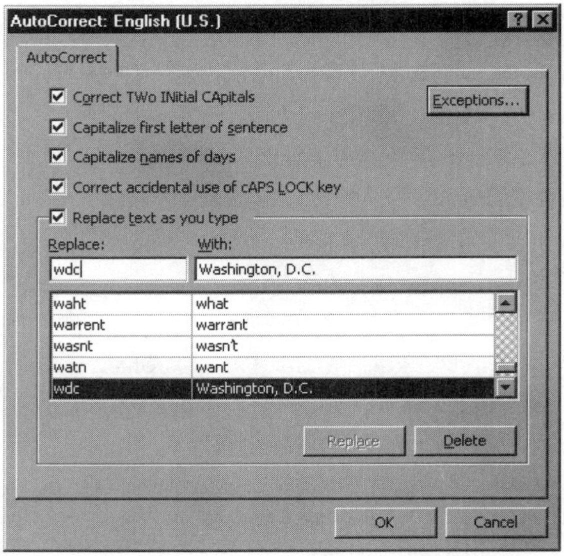

FIGURE 2.7: The AutoCorrect dialog box lets you turn the feature on or off and add to or revise its list of words.

While you type merrily away, AutoCorrect silently picks up after you. Not bad, wouldn't you say?

To add an abbreviation to the list to speed your typing, follow these steps:

1. Choose Tools ➤ AutoCorrect to open the AutoCorrect dialog box.
2. Type the abbreviation in the Replace field.
3. Type what the abbreviation stands for in the With field, and then click Add. You'll see both entries appear in the list.
4. Click OK.
5. Return to the worksheet and type the abbreviation you just added. Press the spacebar or press Enter, and watch how quickly AutoCorrect replaces your abbreviation with its spelled-out equivalent.

The AutoCorrect dialog box has several nifty options. For example, check the Correct TWo INitial CApitals check box, and if you type **SPokane**, Excel changes it to Spokane.

Because there are no absolutely fixed rules of capitalization, you can create a list of words or abbreviations whose capitalization style will be ignored by AutoCorrect. In the AutoCorrect dialog box, click Exceptions to open the AutoCorrect Exceptions dialog box, and enter your terms in the Don't Correct field.

Are You Experienced?

Now you can...

- ☑ **Distinguish between text and value cell entries**
- ☑ **Enter text**
- ☑ **Enter numbers**
- ☑ **Enter formulas**
- ☑ **Enter dates and times**
- ☑ **Use AutoFill and the Edit ➤ Fill ➤ Series command**
- ☑ **Create a custom list**
- ☑ **Fill a range using a series**
- ☑ **Enter data with AutoComplete and Pick List**
- ☑ **Check spelling**
- ☑ **Use AutoCorrect**

SKILL 3

Working with Cells, Ranges, and Worksheets

- Selecting ranges
- Copying and moving cells
- Clearing cell contents, formats, and comments
- Expanding and contracting the workbook
- Taking advantage of range names
- Using the Find and Replace commands

Just about all your work in Excel will involve some piece of the workbook, such as a cell, a range, a column, a row, a sheet, or multiple sheets. This skill shows you how to put these pieces together.

Selecting Ranges

A *range* is any combination of cells that you select, generally so that you can enter data or include the cells in a command or formula. In a broader sense, whenever you move about in the workbook, you are selecting a range, because the cell or range on which you stop is the selected, or active, cell.

In Excel, you can work with two types of ranges:

Single sheet or 2-D A group of adjacent cells that are contiguous (within a rectangle) in a single worksheet, such as B5:D25. This is the type of range you work with most frequently.

Multisheet or 3-D A range that spans multiple sheets, usually contiguous, in the workbook so that the same 2-D range is referenced on each sheet. For example, you could define a range on Sheet1 to Sheet4, which includes the cells in A5:F15 on each sheet. You refer to that range as Sheet1:Sheet4!A5:F15.

You can also work with a *noncontiguous* range, which consists of multiple ranges.

TIP TIP TIP TIP TIP TIP TIP TIP TIP TIP TIP TIP TIP TIP TIP TIP TIP TIP TIP TIP TIP TIP TIP TIP TIP

Not all commands, such as Insert ➤ Rows, accept a noncontiguous range.

Selecting a Single-Sheet Range

Watch the Name box when selecting a range of cells; it displays the number of rows and columns you are selecting. When you are selecting entire rows and columns, a small window near the mouse pointer displays the number of rows or columns you are selecting. You'll also find that the row and column headings for a selected range take on the appearance of pressed buttons, which helps to define the extent of the range.

You can select a single-sheet (2-D) range in several ways, some of which I mentioned in Skill 1:

- Click a corner cell of the range and then Shift+click the diagonally opposite corner.
- Click and drag over the range from corner to corner with your mouse.

- Choose Edit ➤ Go To (press F5 or Ctrl+G), and enter the range you want to select in the Go To dialog box. (See the "Selecting with Edit ➤ Go To" section, later in this skill.)

- Select one corner of the range, hold down Shift, and then use the arrow keys to select the rest of the range.

- Click once within a column or a row heading to select an entire row or column.

- Click and drag over the headings or use Shift+click to select a range of rows or columns.

- To select data in a single column or row, select one cell at the top or bottom (or left or right if selecting a row) of the data. Then hold down Shift and double-click one side of the active cell (watch for the mouse pointer to turn into an arrow) to select all contiguous cells in that direction. With the keyboard, press Ctrl+Shift and an arrow key to select the contiguous cells in that direction.

- Select a range name from the Name box at the left of the Formula bar or by choosing Edit ➤ Go To. (Range names are discussed in the "Taking Advantage of Range Names" section, later in this skill).

- To select the occupied range that surrounds the active cell, which is called the current region, press Ctrl+Shift+* (asterisk), or choose Edit ➤ Go To ➤ Special (which is discussed a little later). In Figure 3.1, I selected a cell within the range A1:D5 and then pressed Ctrl+Shift+*. The unoccupied columns and rows that surround the occupied range define the current region.

WARNING WARNING WARNING WARNING WARNING WARNING WARNING WARNING

When pressing Ctrl+Shift+*, you cannot use the asterisk on the numeric keypad.

	A	B	C	D	E	F	G	H	I	J	K	L
1	X	X	X	X		X						
2	X	X	X			X						
3		X		X		X						
4		X	X	X		X						
5		X	X	X		X						
6						X						
7	X	X	X	X	X	X						
8												

Sample.xls

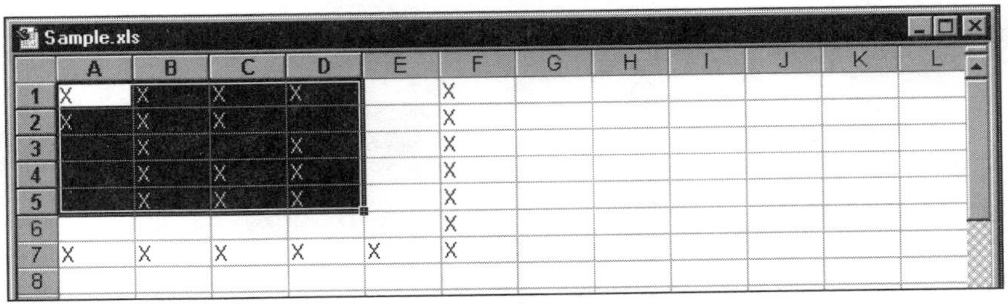

FIGURE 3.1: You can select the current block of data by pressing Ctrl+Shift+*.

Skill 9 discusses the other commands for selecting cells whose formulas depend on (or *reference*) the current cell or cells on which the active cell's formula depends.

Selecting a Multisheet Range

On occasion you might want to select a range that includes more than one sheet, for example, to include in a report. To select a multisheet (3-D) range on contiguous sheets, first select the 2-D range on the first worksheet of the range, such as A5:F15. Then hold down Shift and click the Sheet tab for the last sheet of the range, such as Sheet3.

TIP

Use the Ctrl+click method to select noncontiguous sheets.

In this example, the three Sheet tabs are highlighted, and the word *[Group]* appears next to the filename in the workbook's title bar. This indicates that you're now selecting the same range on a group of worksheets.

After you select multiple sheets, just about any action you take affects the same 2-D range on each sheet. For example, if you enter data in a cell in one sheet, the same data is entered in the same cell in all sheets in the group. Likewise, if you erase the contents of a cell, the contents of that cell are erased in all selected sheets.

To copy the cells from a 2-D range on the current sheet to the same range in all the other sheets in the group, choose Edit ➤ Fill ➤ Across Worksheets to open the Fill Across Worksheets dialog box, and then choose which cell components to copy:

All Copies all aspects of a cell.

Contents Copies only the contents of a cell.

Formats Copies only the formatting of a cell, for example, alignment, number style, and so on.

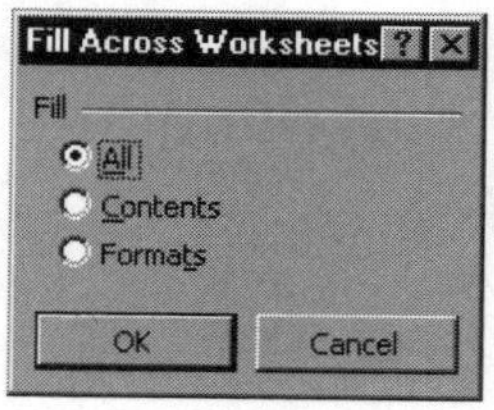

When you want to dissolve the worksheet group, you can:

- Select a sheet that is not part of the group.

- Shift+click the active Sheet tab.
- Right-click one of the Sheet tabs in the group, and choose Ungroup Sheets from the shortcut menu.

WARNING WARNING WARNING WARNING WARNING WARNING WARNING WARNING

Don't forget to ungroup the sheets when you no longer want to affect them all. Otherwise, as you continue to work in what you think is only one worksheet, Excel assumes the group is still active and continues to duplicate your actions in all the other sheets. For example, if you delete a row in one sheet, it will be deleted in all the other sheets in the group.

Selecting a Noncontiguous Range

To select multiple noncontiguous ranges, select the first range, hold down Ctrl, and then select the next range. You can continue to select ranges as long as you hold down Ctrl. You can create noncontiguous 3-D ranges as well, just by clicking a Sheet tab while holding down Ctrl.

To type a reference to multiple ranges in a formula or a dialog box, include the sheet name, and separate each range with a comma. Here's an example:

```
=SUM(A1,D10:M30,Sheet2!A5:B10,Sheet2!M20:N20)
```

The result is the same whether you type the references or select them in the worksheet.

Selecting with Edit ➤ Go To

Choosing Edit ➤ Go To is a fast way to access any location in the workbook (see Skill 1). The range that you choose is selected after you click OK.

The Go To command also offers some powerful options, which you can access by clicking the Special button in the Go To dialog box. Figure 3.2 shows the options in the Go To Special dialog box.

For example, if you select the Constants option, only numbers or text is selected; cells that contain formulas will not be included. You can even fine-tune the Formulas option by selecting from its four options: Numbers, Text, Logicals, and Errors. For example, choose Numbers to select only formulas that produce numeric results.

You can select the Blanks option to select only blank cells within the occupied portion of the worksheet. The Current Region option is equivalent to the Ctrl+Shift+* combination that I mentioned earlier. Take some time to experiment with the other options for this very useful command.

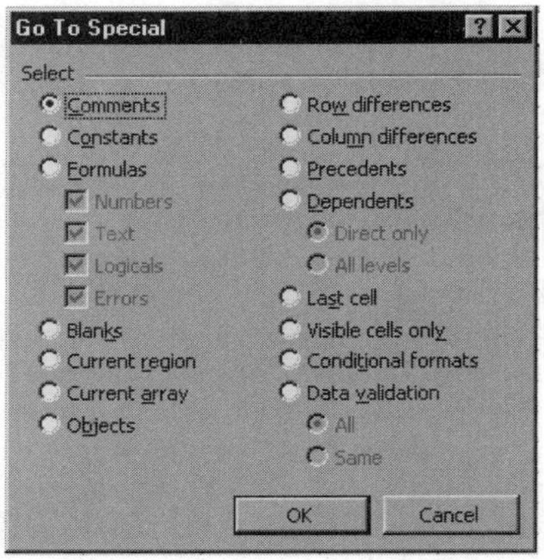

FIGURE 3.2: The Go To Special dialog box sets the options for the Go To command.

Copying and Moving Cells

You can copy or move a cell or a range from its source to a destination (target) in many ways. Sometimes the method you choose is a function of convenience; at other times, you need to use a specific method to get the results you want.

When you copy or move a cell, everything associated with that cell ends up in the target cell, including the data within the source cell and any cell properties associated with it, such as a numeric format or color.

NOTE NOTE NOTE NOTE NOTE NOTE NOTE NOTE NOTE NOTE NOTE NOTE NOTE NOTE NOTE

When you copy or move cells, the target cells are overwritten by the incoming cells whether the source cells are empty or occupied. So use caution when you are shifting cells around the workbook, and don't forget that the Edit ➤ Undo command (Ctrl+Z) can undo as many as 16 of the most recent changes you've made. See the "Using Edit ➤ Paste Special" section later in this skill for ways to control which aspects of a source cell get put onto the target cell.

Copying and Moving with Drag and Drop

Sometimes the fastest way to perform a task in Excel is to use your mouse. *Drag and drop* refers to the process of dragging an object, such as a selected range, with the mouse and then dropping it elsewhere by releasing the mouse button.

If you find that your fingers and Excel don't work well together, you can disable the drag-and-drop feature. Choose Tools ➤ Options to open the Options dialog box, click the Edit tab, and clear the Allow Cell Drag and Drop check box.

Using the mouse to copy or move cells is efficient when the target range is within easy reach. But if you end up having to spend five minutes dragging around the worksheet looking for the destination cell, use Edit ➤ Copy and Paste and Edit ➤ Cut and Paste instead. These methods also enable you to paste the source cell(s) into multiple target cells, such as a single cell into an entire range of cells.

Doing the Drag and Drop

Whether you're copying or moving a single cell or a range, follow these steps:

1. Think about where the target area is in relation to the source cell(s) so that once you start it will be a straight shot to complete the job.
2. Select the source cell or cells.
3. To move a cell, point to any edge of the selection; the mouse pointer will change to an arrow, as shown here:

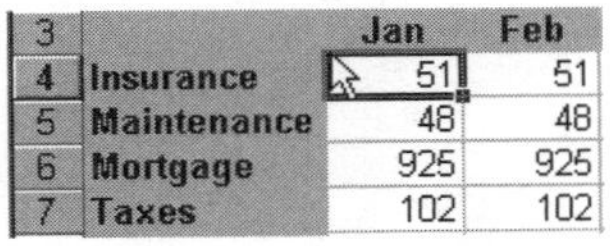

3 Jan Feb
4 Insurance 51 51
5 Maintenance 48 48
6 Mortgage 925 925
7 Taxes 102 102

4. Hold down the mouse button and drag the range to the target location (see the next section for various mouse and key combinations). An outline of the range moves along with the mouse pointer as you drag, along with a helpful window that displays the cell that will be the target if you should release the mouse button. When you are dragging a range of cells, the target cell will be the upper-left cell of the range.
5. Position the source range over the range where you want it, and release the button.

NOTE NOTE NOTE NOTE NOTE NOTE NOTE NOTE NOTE NOTE NOTE NOTE NOTE NOTE NOTE

If data is already in the target range, Excel warns you that you are about to overwrite it. This may or may not be a problem, as long as you know that the existing data will be overwritten. If you're the confident type, you can turn off these warnings. Choose Tools ➤ Options to open the Options dialog box, click the Edit tab, and clear the Alert before Overwriting Cells check box.

Drag-and-Drop Methods

Let's look at some of the drag-and-drop techniques you can use to move or copy cells:

Copy Drag while holding down Ctrl to copy the source data to a new location; a small + will appear next to the mouse pointer to indicate that you are copying and not moving.

Move Drag the selection to move the source data to a new location.

Insert Drag while holding down Shift to move the source data into new cells inserted at the destination. The rectangle changes to a vertical or horizontal bar as you move the pointer to indicate whether the insertion will move rows down or columns to the right. If you want to copy and insert, hold down both the Shift and Ctrl keys while you drag.

Shortcut menu Drag while holding down the *right* mouse button instead of the left one. When you release the button, you can choose the operation you want to perform from the shortcut menu.

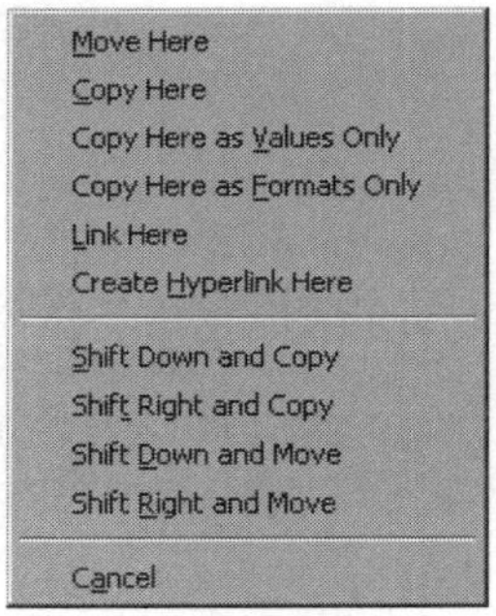

Worksheet To copy or move data to another worksheet, hold down the Alt key and use any of the above methods. Then drag the selection to another worksheet tab to activate that sheet and drop the data in place.

Workbook Dragging data to another Excel workbook is no different from moving or copying it within the same worksheet. As long as you can see both workbook windows on the screen, just drag from one to the other. See Skill 13 for more about arranging windows.

Other applications You can use drag and drop to exchange data between Excel and other applications that use Windows *object linking and embedding*, or OLE. This timesaving technique is discussed later in this skill in the section "Exchanging Data with Other Applications."

Knowing What Happens When You Move or Copy

Regardless of whether you move data or copy data, the resulting destination range looks exactly the same, because both moving and copying transfer everything from the source range to the destination range.

After a copy operation, the source range will still look exactly the same. After a move, however, the source cells will be empty, and their formatting will be set to the defaults for the worksheet.

Effects on Formulas

Moving and copying have different effects on other aspects of the workbook, especially on formulas (you can read about the effects of moving and copying formulas in Skill 4):

- When you copy a formula cell, any cell references in the formula adjust to their new location in the worksheet.
- When you move a formula cell, none of its references changes.
- When you move cells that are referenced by a formula, the formula adjusts its references and "follows" the cells to their destination.
- When you copy cells that are referenced by a formula, the formula does not follow them; it still refers to the source cells.

Dangers of Moving

A formula will be "broken" and will refer to #REF! if you move another cell onto a cell it references, in effect "destroying" that reference. For example, the formula

```
=SUM(A1:A5)+B5/2
```

looks like this after you move another cell onto cell B5:

```
=SUM(A1:A5)+#REF!/2
```

The reference to cell B5 is now gone. To fix this problem you can, of course, resort to the Undo command. Or you can edit the formula and replace the reference to #REF!.

Copying and Moving with Edit ➤ Copy/Paste

When you want to copy or move cells to a distant location, or when the source range is too big to drag around the worksheet, you can use the commands on the Edit menu. The process is the same as in most Windows applications. To copy data, follow these steps:

1. Select the data you want to copy.

2. Choose Edit ➤ Copy (Ctrl+C) or click the Copy button on the Standard toolbar. You'll see a moving border around the source range, which is meant to remind you that a copy is in process and to show you what is being copied. If you are moving the data, chose Edit ➤ Cut (Ctrl+X) or click the Cut button on the Standard toolbar.

3. Select the target range (the next section discusses the different shapes and sizes of the source and target ranges).
4. Press Enter to paste the data one time; the moving border around the source range will disappear.

Choose Edit ➤ Paste (Ctrl+V) or click the Paste button on the Standard toolbar to paste the data while keeping the source range selected so that you can paste the selected range over and over. When you're finished pasting, press Esc to clear the moving border from the source range

If you want the pasted data to be inserted as new cells in the target range, choose Insert ➤ Copied (or Cut) Cells. The data already in the target range will be pushed aside and new cells inserted for the incoming data (this process is the same as using the Shift+drag method of copying or moving, which was discussed earlier).

TIP

You can also use the Copy/Cut and Paste method to copy or move portions of a cell's contents. While editing a cell (or by using the Formula bar), select the characters you want to copy—for example, by dragging over them—and choose Edit ➤ Copy (Ctrl+C). Then either paste the data into another part of the cell contents, or finish editing the current cell and then edit another cell and paste the data into it.

Using the Clipboard Toolbar

The Clipboard temporarily stores information such as text, values, and formatting. In the past, you could cut or copy to the Clipboard and then paste the information somewhere else. The only drawback was that the Clipboard could store only one piece of information at a time. The next time you copied or cut information, the previous Clipboard contents were replaced by the newest information.

NEW

In Excel 2000, the Clipboard can contain as many as 12 cut or copy operations, and you can select the operation(s) you want to paste from the Clipboard toolbar. The Clipboard toolbar displays after you copy more than one cell or range. You can also display the Clipboard toolbar by right-clicking a toolbar and selecting Clipboard from the shortcut menu. Pointing to an item on the Clipboard toolbar displays a ScreenTip that describes the contents.

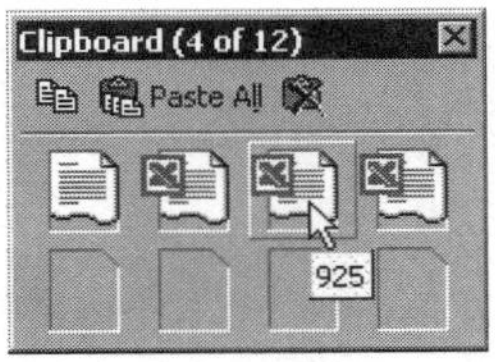

This new Clipboard is extremely handy when you need to copy multiple ranges of information. Before, this would have been a tedious process of selecting the information, moving to the new location, pasting the information, selecting the next piece of information, moving to the next location, pasting the information… you get the picture.

To see how the Clipboard works, follow these steps:

1. Create a list of 12 items in Column A.
2. Select the first four items, and choose Edit ➤ Copy to move the items to the Clipboard.

3. Select the next four items, choose Edit ➤ Copy, and repeat until all the items are on the Clipboard toolbar.
4. Click the Sheet2 tab, click cell A1, and click the first pasted object on the Clipboard toolbar. Repeat for all of the pasted objects, placing them in columns C and E.
5. Click Close to close the Clipboard toolbar.

You can also use the Clipboard toolbar to do the following:

- Copy a new cell or range.
- Paste all Clipboard items at once.
- Clear the contents of the Clipboard.

NOTE NOTE NOTE NOTE NOTE NOTE NOTE NOTE NOTE NOTE NOTE NOTE NOTE NOTE NOTE

If you don't use the clipboard by pasting an entry from it on three consecutive occasions, the clipboard will not display until selected. To display the Clipboard toolbar, right-click any toolbar and select Clipboard.

Copying Blocks of Various Dimensions

The shape and size of the source and destination blocks affect the results of the copy (or move) operation. When you choose Edit ➤ Copy or Edit ➤ Cut to place the source data onto the Clipboard, the target range can be:

- A single cell, which will serve as the upper-left cell of the pasted data
- A selected range, the same size and shape as the source range

If you choose Edit ➤ Copy but not Cut, the target can also be a selected range that can hold two or more of the source ranges. This option gives you the flexibility to copy a source range of one size to a target range of a larger size. Figure 3.3 shows how to do this. I copied the range A1:B3, which consists of 6 cells, to range F5:G13, which consists of 18 cells.

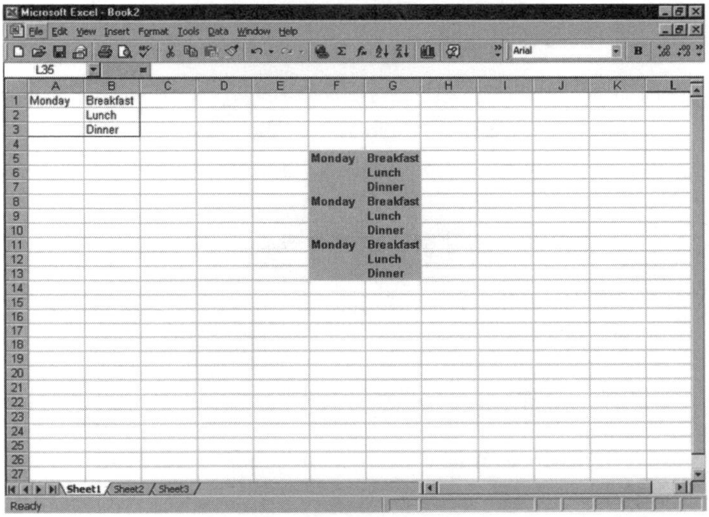

FIGURE 3.3: You can copy data to a target range that has a different size or shape than the source range.

Using Edit ➤ Paste Special

You use the Paste Special dialog box to select from several options that affect the paste operation. To open it, choose Edit ➤ Paste Special:

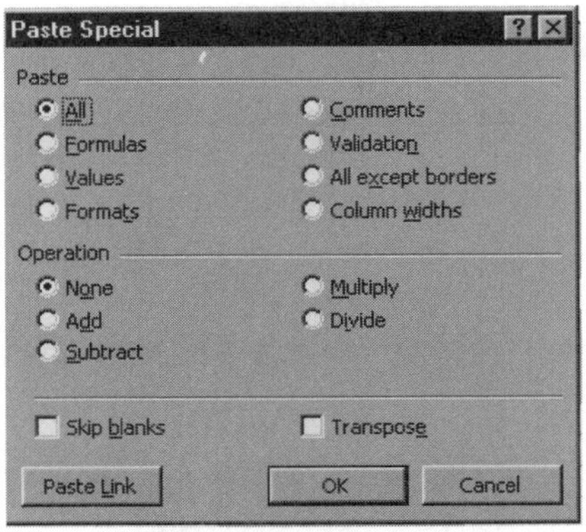

You can choose which components of the source cells to paste into the target cells from the group of options in the Paste section:

All Pastes all aspects of a cell; this is the default and works just like the Edit ➤ Paste command.

Formulas Pastes only the cell contents as they appear in the source range, without any attached comments or cell formatting such as shading, fonts, or borders.

Values Pastes only the cell contents, but if the cell contains a formula, pastes only the results of the formula. In other words, the formula =2+3 would result in the number 5 in the target cell. By copying formulas with this option, you can take a "snapshot" of the formulas by retaining only their results in the target range.

Formats Pastes only cell formatting into the target range.

Comments Pastes only cell comments (or cell notes) into the target range; see Skill 9.

All Except Borders Pastes everything except cell borders.

The two options at the bottom of the dialog box affect the target range in this way:

Skip Blanks Normally, a blank cell in the source range overwrites the target cell. Select this option to exclude empty cells in the source range from the paste operation.

Transpose If you want to make a column of data into a row, or vice versa, select this option. If the source range is more than a single column or row and also contains formulas, you probably won't be happy with the result, because the formulas will no longer refer to the same data (see Skill 4).

NOTE

The options in the Operation section in the Paste Special dialog box are discussed in Skill 4, and the Paste Link button is also discussed in Skill 4.

Exchanging Data with Other Applications

One of the nice things about Excel is that it gives you several ways to share data with other Windows applications. The method you use depends on what you plan to do with the data afterward.

Sharing Unlinked Data

You can copy or move data between Excel and another Windows program in the usual Windows way:

1. Select the source data and choose Edit ➤ Copy (or Cut to move the data).
2. Switch to the target program and select the location where the data should go.
3. Choose the target program's Edit ➤ Paste command. Windows pastes the data into the target program as editable text (when possible), and you can use the data as though you had created it there.

For example, when you copy a single cell from Excel to Microsoft Word, the result will either be the exact contents of the source cell or, if that cell is a formula, the result of the formula. When you copy a range of cells, Word creates a table of the same size.

You can also transfer a picture of the source data, which will show the source's formatting that is not otherwise supported in the target. You can't edit the data in the picture, however. To transfer a picture of the data source, follow these steps:

1. In Excel, select the data, and choose Edit ➤ Copy or Cut.
2. In the target application, choose Edit ➤ Paste Special. Figure 3.4 shows the Paste Special dialog box for Microsoft Word.

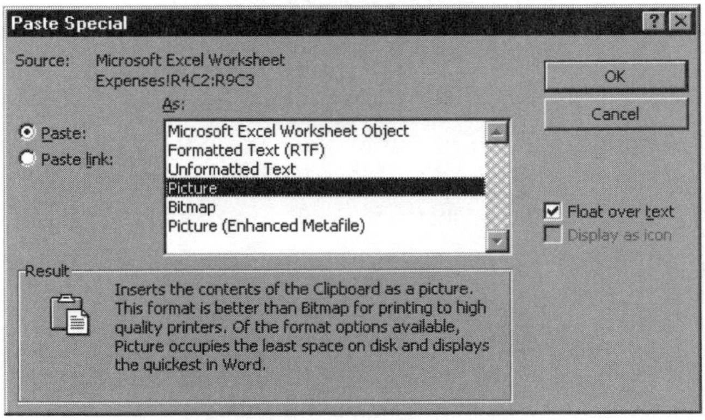

FIGURE 3.4: Use the Paste Special dialog box in Microsoft Word to paste data from other applications in several formats.

3. Select the Paste option (Paste Link is discussed a little later), and choose Picture from the As list.
4. Click OK to paste the selection into the document in the other application.

Embedding Data

You can exchange objects, such as data, charts and pictures, between Excel and any other Windows program that supports OLE (object linking and embedding). The difference between *embedding* an object and simply pasting it, as discussed in the previous section, is that you can edit embedded data within the program in which it was created. For example, if you embed an Excel worksheet in a Word document, you can later edit that worksheet in Word, using the toolbars and menu items from Excel.

To embed an object in Excel, follow these steps:

1. Select the source data you want to embed in the other program.
2. Choose Edit ➤ Copy.
3. Select the target location in Excel.
4. Choose Edit ➤ Paste Special to open the Paste Special dialog box, and select Paste.
5. Choose one of the items in the As list that has the word *object* in it, such as *Microsoft Excel Worksheet Object*.
6. Click OK.

You can also embed an object by dragging it to the other application; hold down Ctrl if you want to copy and not move it.

The result of pasting an embedded object looks just like the Picture discussed in the previous section. However, there's a big difference in the way you edit each of the objects. You can modify an embedded object in two ways:

- Double-click it or right-click it, and choose Document Object ➤ Edit from the shortcut menu. This lets you edit the object within the current worksheet while using the menus and tools of the object's source application.
- Right-click the object, and choose Document Object ➤ Open, which opens this object's source application and loads the object into it; you can then edit it as usual. When you are finished, save the object, choose File ➤ Close and Return to *document*, and return to the first application. You'll see that your changes now appear in the object.

When you edit a picture, though, you use a drawing or painting program such as Windows Paint. You also work with an image of the source, and not the actual source document.

Linking Data

You can also exchange data between Excel and another program by creating a *link*. Any change you make in the data in the source document is reflected in the linked object in the target document.

The process of creating a link is much the same as creating an embedded object, as discussed above in "Sharing Unlinked Data." The only difference is that in the Paste Special dialog box you select the Paste Link option. Then, whichever format you choose in the As list is created with a link back to the source data.

Although both linked and embedded objects will be updated when the source document changes, there is one major difference between the two: the data for a linked object does not actually reside in the target document. Instead, a pointer to the data (the link) keeps track of the source data and displays it in the target.

Although you may not need to, you can edit a linked object just as you can edit an embedded object—double-click it, for example. In general, though, having a linked object in a program implies that you want to stay in touch with changes made to the source file for that object, without having to make those changes yourself.

NOTE NOTE NOTE NOTE NOTE NOTE NOTE NOTE NOTE NOTE NOTE NOTE NOTE NOTE

To view the sources for any linked objects in a workbook, choose Edit ➤ Links. This command is discussed in Skill 4.

Finally, because pasting a link doesn't actually bring any data into the target document, you can't take that document off your computer and expect it to stay updated to the source of the link. If you need to be portable, embed the data.

Clearing Cell Contents, Formats, and Comments

Pencils will always have their erasers, hammers their claws, authors their editors, and computers their Delete and Backspace keys. Excel also gives you several ways to clean up after yourself.

To clear all or part of the selected cells without removing the cells from the worksheet, choose Edit ➤ Clear, and then choose one of the following commands:

All Erases all aspects of a cell, including its contents, formatting, attached cell comment, and hyperlink.

Formats Clears only the formats that have been applied to the cell (resets them to the worksheet defaults), but leaves the other cell attributes untouched.

TIP

Here's a quick way to clear only the cell formatting. Select a blank, unformatted cell and click the Format Painter button on the Standard toolbar (the little paintbrush). Then select the target cells, and their formats will be reset to those of the source cells—the worksheet default formats.

Contents Erases only the contents of a cell (same as pressing the Delete key).

Comments Clears only the cell comment, if one was attached to the cell.

Keep in mind that these commands work on any cells you've selected, which could be entire rows, columns, or all the cells in the worksheet. And don't forget the Edit ➤ Undo command.

Expanding and Contracting the Workbook

Even though your worksheets will always have precisely 65,536 rows and 256 columns, you are free to delete or insert rows and columns as your work progresses. Data will never be pushed off the edge of the worksheet when you insert new cells. Instead, Excel will alert you that it cannot shift occupied cells off the worksheet and cancels the procedure.

Deleting Cells from the Worksheet

When you choose Edit ➤ Delete, you can actually delete (remove) selected cells from the worksheet. The cells below move up to take their place, or the cells to the right move left to fill in the gap.

WARNING

When you delete a cell (such as A1) that a formula references (such as =A1), the formula will now display #REF!—indicating its reference has been broken. You'll have to edit the formula to fix or erase the reference. When you delete an entire row or column, be careful that you don't also lose unrelated data that occupies the same row or column, but is off the screen. You can avoid this problem by placing data on its own worksheet when possible.

The results of choosing Edit ➤ Delete depend on what you select before choosing it. For example, if you select one or more contiguous rows (or columns) by clicking in their headings, choosing Edit ➤ Delete removes them all without prompting you. The rows below move up (or the columns to the right move left) to take their place.

If you select one or more cells instead of entire rows or columns, Excel displays the Delete dialog box, which is shown below. If you choose Entire Row or Entire Column, the result will be as described above. To delete only the selected cells, you choose how you want the gap filled, either by having the cells below them move up or the cells to their right move left.

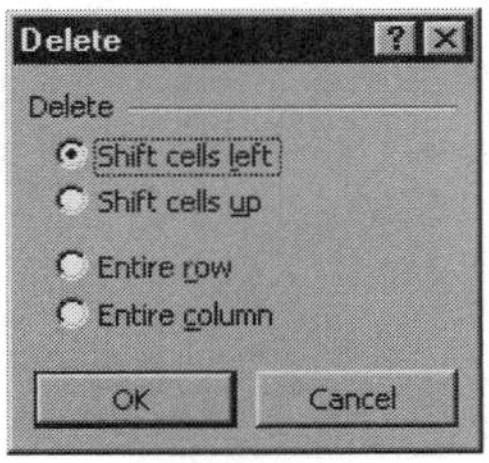

NOTE NOTE NOTE NOTE NOTE NOTE NOTE NOTE NOTE NOTE NOTE NOTE NOTE NOTE

The cells that take the place of the deleted ones are essentially moved to the new location. Formulas that had referenced them will now reference them in their new location. See Skill 4 for more on this topic.

Inserting Cells in the Worksheet

To insert a row in the worksheet, you can either select the entire row by clicking the row heading or select any cell in that row. Then choose Insert ➤ Rows (or right-click any cell in that row and choose Insert from the shortcut menu). The new rows push all existing rows down to make room for themselves. You can also choose Insert ➤ Cells to open the Insert dialog box and choose Entire Row.

When you insert cells in the worksheet, they take on the formatting of the cells within which they were inserted. If you shift the cells down, they acquire the formatting of the cells above; if you shift the cells right, they acquire the formatting of the cells to the left. If that's not what you want, choose Edit ➤ Clear ➤ All or Edit ➤ Clear ➤ Formats immediately after the insertion to clear the inserted cells of their formatting.

For example, to insert seven new rows at row 10, select cells in rows 10 through 16 in any column in the worksheet, such as C10:C16. Then choose Insert ➤ Rows. Old row 10 becomes new row 17, and above it are seven new, blank rows.

If you choose Insert ➤ Columns, Excel inserts new columns and moves the selected columns to the right. The number of columns inserted depends on the number of columns you selected.

To insert a range of cells into the worksheet, select the cells where you want the new cells to appear, and choose Insert ➤ Cells to open the Insert dialog box:

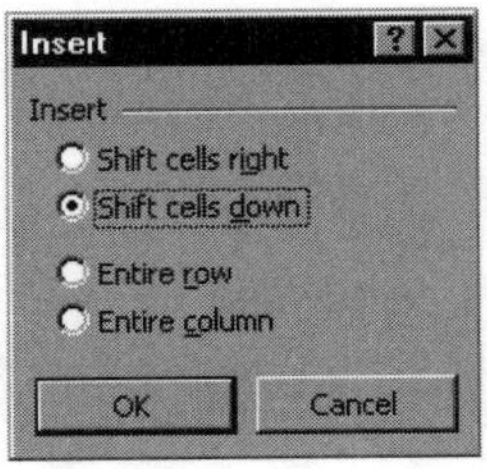

Choose whether you want to move the cells they replace down or to the right.

You can also take advantage of the AutoFill feature (discussed in Skill 2) to insert new cells. Hold down Shift while you drag the fill handle; when you release the mouse button, new cells will be inserted into the worksheet.

As I mentioned earlier, when you choose Edit ➤ Copy (or Cut), the Insert ➤ Copied Cells (or Cut Cells) command is also available. This command, like the Insert ➤ Cells command, lets you choose how the cells inserted from the Clipboard will affect the surrounding cells in the worksheet.

Formulas Adjust to Changes

I will often mention in this book that one of the most helpful aspects of Excel is the work that it does for you. Applying your changes automatically is at the top of the list. In Skills 4 and 5, you will read about referencing cells within formulas. For example, the formula

```
=SUM(B5:B10)*C17
```

adds the values in cells B5 through B10 and multiplies that result by the value in C17.

When you expand or contract the worksheet, these formula references adjust automatically to the change. If you were to add three rows on or above row 5, for example, the formula shown above would look like this:

```
=SUM(B8:B13)*C20
```

If you then deleted rows 9 and 10, the formula would look like this:

```
=SUM(B8:B11)*C18
```

This effect is true for all defined ranges in the worksheet, such as the current print area or the rows or columns you have defined as print titles (these are both discussed in Skill 7). Because Excel takes care of all this housekeeping, you're free to make changes to the worksheet without having to worry about the effects on any defined ranges.

Inserting and Deleting Worksheets

You can also expand and contract the workbook by inserting or deleting worksheets. There is no limit to the number of worksheets you can add to a workbook. Just as when you insert or delete cells, cell references in formulas will adjust to the change as needed.

Deleting Worksheets

To delete sheets from the workbook, select one or more sheets (such as by clicking the first sheet tab and Shift+clicking the last) and then either:

- Choose Edit ➤ Delete ➤ Sheet.
- Right-click one of the selected sheet tabs, and choose Delete from the shortcut menu.

WARNING WARNING WARNING WARNING WARNING WARNING WARNING WARNING

The Edit ➤ Undo command cannot undo the deletion of a worksheet. Therefore, it is always a good idea to save your workbook before making such a major change to it.

Just as when you delete cells, when you delete a worksheet, the existing sheets to its right move left to fill in the gap. Unlike cell addresses, however, the sheet names do not change. If you delete Sheet2, for example, the workbook no longer has a Sheet2.

Inserting New Worksheets

To add new sheets to the workbook, select one or more contiguous sheets and then either:

- Choose Insert ➤ Worksheet to insert a default worksheet, which will look the same as those in a new workbook.
- Right-click one of the selected sheet tabs, and select Insert from the shortcut menu.

The second method opens the Insert dialog box, as shown in Figure 3.5. You can select the type of sheet you want to insert from the available Excel template files, such as Worksheet and Chart.

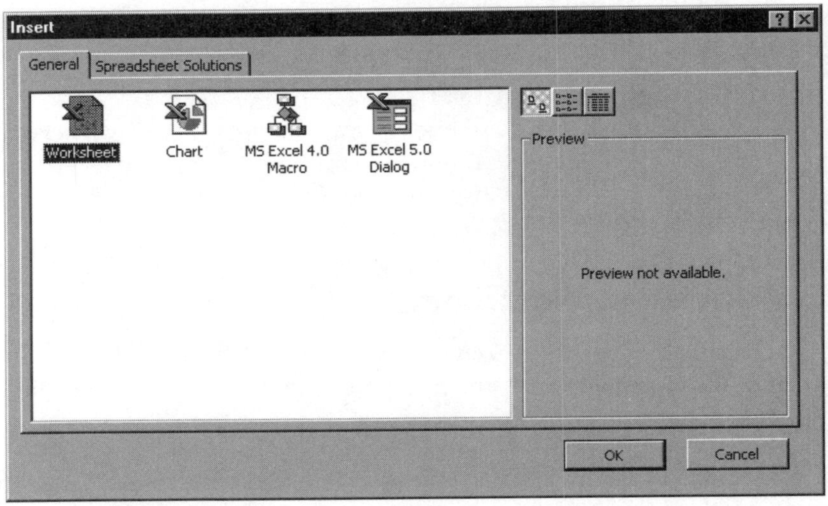

FIGURE 3.5: In the Insert dialog box, choose the type of sheet to insert in the workbook, based on the available templates.

TIP TIP TIP TIP TIP TIP TIP TIP TIP TIP TIP TIP TIP TIP TIP TIP TIP TIP TIP TIP TIP TIP TIP TIP

You can also create your own worksheet template files, as discussed in Skill 7.

Taking Advantage of Range Names

One of the problems with having millions of cells in a workbook is the ease with which you can lose track of the data and formulas you enter into them.

Every time you insert or delete a row or a column, all the addresses change for any data that are below that row or to the right of that column. So when it comes time to edit or print the data in a range, for example, you might not be sure where to find it. But there's a way to keep track of things that can simplify all your range relations in the workbook.

A *range name* is a name you create, such as MyData, that defines a range of cells, such as B10:H25. Once you've defined a name, you can refer to that range by its name instead of its cell coordinates. To add the contents of the cells in the range B10:H25, for example, you could write the formula like this:

```
=SUM(MyData)
```

No matter how that range is moved, expanded, or contracted, the name will still refer to the correct range of cells, wherever they are.

The actual address no longer matters once a range is named. If you want to go to that range, for example, simply choose Edit ➤ Go To and specify the name MyData as the place to go. Better yet, just select the name from the list of range names in the Name box or in the Go To dialog box. It's that simple.

TIP TIP TIP TIP TIP TIP TIP TIP TIP TIP TIP TIP TIP TIP TIP TIP TIP TIP TIP TIP TIP TIP TIP TIP TIP TIP

You can also name a worksheet and thereafter refer to it by that name. Double-click its sheet tab, and enter the new name. One difference between range and sheet names, however, is that a sheet name *replaces* its generic name. With a named range, you can refer to either the name or the address the name represents.

Defining a Name

You don't need to name every possible data area in the workbook, nor should you. In many cases, you can simply define new names as the need arises:

- If you find yourself regularly returning to a data area to update it.
- If you plan to print a range in future sessions with that workbook.
- If several formulas will refer to a cell that contains, for example, an interest rate—name the cell. Perhaps Interest would be a good choice for a name.

Here's how to name a range:

1. Select the range you want to name.
2. Choose Insert ➤ Name ➤ Define to open the Define Name dialog box shown in Figure 3.6.
3. Enter the new name, such as **MyCell**, in the Names in Workbook field.
4. Since you already selected the cells you want to name, you'll see their address displayed as a formula in the Refers To field. However, you can edit that address if you want to change it.

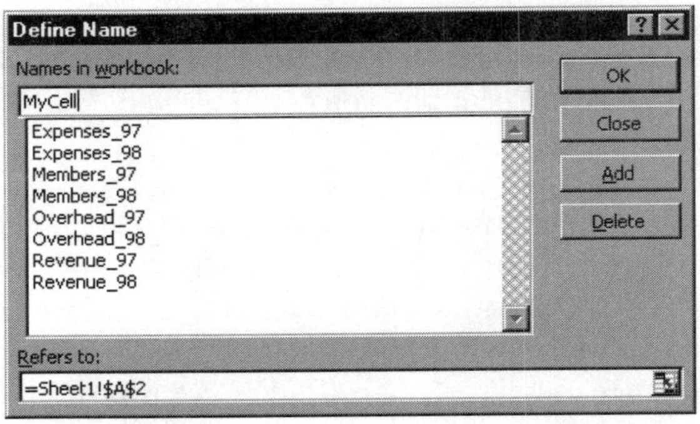

FIGURE 3.6: You define a new name, modify an existing name, or delete a name in the Define Name dialog box.

5. Click the Add button to add this name to the list—or click Close to cancel the operation.
6. Click OK to complete the job.

NOTE

You can also define a new name by selecting the cells you want to name, entering the name in the Name box to the left of the Formula bar, and then pressing Enter.

Here are a few rules of the road when it comes to naming cells:

- A name can be a maximum of 255 characters—but don't press your luck with excruciatingly long names.
- Excel does not allow spaces or most punctuation characters in a name.
- A name cannot look like a cell address, such as *GW1999*.
- You can make names more readable by separating words with an underline and by using uppercase and lowercase letters. Excel retains the case of the letters so that you can make a "one-word sentence" more readable, such as *Total_1999_Data*.
- Excel does not distinguish names by their case, however. If you create the name Sales and later create the name SALES, the new name definition will replace the earlier one.
- Names must be unique within a workbook.

Using Names in Formulas and Commands

Once you've created a name for a range, you'll generally want to use the name instead of the range address. Whenever the address is called for, such as in a dialog box or in a formula, you can enter the name instead.

It's easier to remember a name (such as MyData) than an address (such as B10:H25), and when you reference a name within a formula, the name appears in the formula and serves as a visual cue to the formula's purpose. For example,

```
=SUM(Sheet2!B1:S52)*Sheet1!B10
```

doesn't explain much. However, the formula is meaningful if the two addresses that are referenced are named appropriately:

```
=SUM(BudgetTotals99)*Inflation
```

Plus, when you reference a name, you are much less likely to refer to the wrong location.

Pasting a Name from the List

Here's a problem you may frequently encounter in Excel when you write a formula that references names: the formula results in #NAME?, and you may not realize why Excel didn't recognize one or more of the names. You probably just spelled a name wrong, which Excel lets you do on the assumption that you might create the name later on.

You don't have to type a name into a formula or dialog box, however. Instead, choose Insert ➤ Name ➤ Paste or press F3 to open the Paste Name dialog box and its alphabetized list of all the names in the workbook, which is shown below. Select the name you want and click OK to paste that name into the cell or dialog box as though you had typed it yourself.

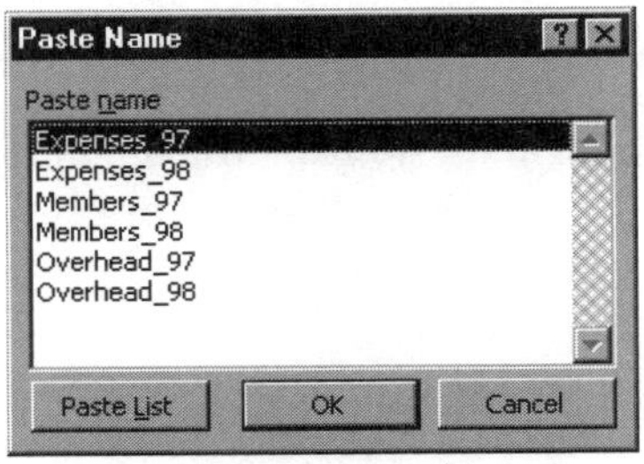

Creating a List of Names

If Excel is in Ready mode when you display the Paste Name dialog box, it contains a Paste List button. Clicking Paste List creates a two-column list in the worksheet, starting at the active cell, of all the names in the workbook (in the first column) and the addresses they define (in the second column).

It's best if you do this in a blank worksheet to avoid the possibility of overwriting any data. This list is static; it does not update automatically as the names or their addresses change. You have to run the command again to update the list.

Having the list of names in a worksheet can be a handy piece of documentation for your workbook. Plus, if you have hundreds of names in a large workbook, you can choose Edit ➤ Find to search through the list for a specific name or address.

TIP TIP TIP TIP TIP TIP TIP TIP TIP TIP TIP TIP TIP TIP TIP TIP TIP TIP TIP TIP TIP TIP TIP TIP TIP TIP

If you want to get a bird's-eye view of your worksheet and the named ranges in it, set the zoom factor to less than 40 percent (choose View ➤ Zoom). All named ranges in the worksheet will be outlined, and each one's name will appear within its outline. It's a great way to step back and take a look at the road map of your worksheet.

Applying Names to Existing Formulas

You don't have to create the names before you incorporate them in your formulas. If you create a name for an already-referenced range, you can have Excel substitute the name for the address within any formulas that use it.

Choose Insert ➤ Name ➤ Apply to open the Apply Names dialog box (see Figure 3.7), select the name or names from the list, and click OK. Excel finds all formulas that reference the name's address and replaces the address with the name.

WARNING WARNING WARNING WARNING WARNING WARNING WARNING WARNING

Incorporating a name into a formula with the Apply command is a one-way street; you can't go back to seeing the address in the formula. See the "For Users of Other Spreadsheets" section later in this skill.

As you'll learn in Skill 4, a formula that references a name and not the address is always absolute. In the Apply Names dialog box, the Ignore Relative/Absolute option is selected by default so that a name will be pasted over its equivalent address in a formula, whether that address is absolute or relative. If you don't want that to happen, clear this option; the name will then be pasted only if it replaces an absolute reference.

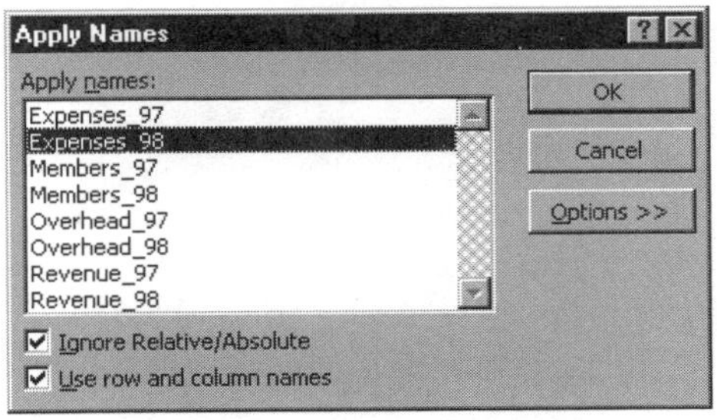

FIGURE 3.7: In the Apply Names dialog box, choose one or more range names that you want to substitute for their addresses in formulas in the worksheet.

You won't need to worry about the Use Row and Column Names option or the Options button until you become quite adept with range names.

Defining Multiple Names

Many cells in your worksheets will contain text entries that describe adjacent cells or that serve as titles for rows or columns. You can use these text entries to name cells in one operation.

Figure 3.8 shows a small worksheet with descriptive text labels in cells A1:A5. In this case, we want to name each cell to their right, B1:B5, according to each label.

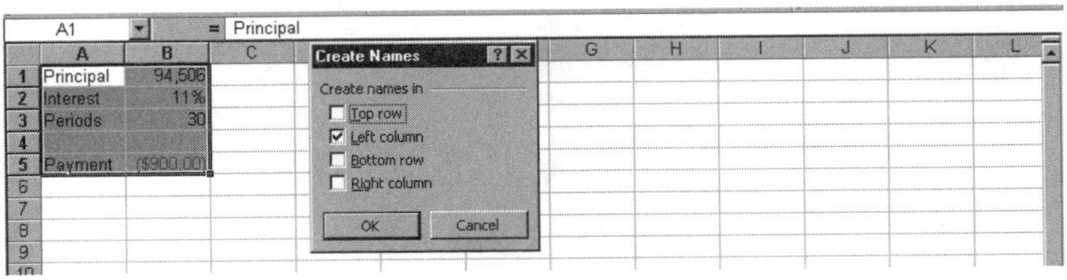

FIGURE 3.8: You can name cells from existing text in the worksheet by choosing Insert ➤ Name ➤ Create.

To do so, select the two-column range A1:B5 and choose Insert ➤ Name ➤ Create. In the Create Names dialog box, which is also shown in Figure 3.8, click the Left Column check box and click OK.

Each cell in column B is now named after the label to its left so that B1 is named Principal and B2 is named Interest

Modifying or Deleting a Name

To change the address that a name defines, choose Insert ➤ Name ➤ Define. In the Define Name dialog box, select the name you want to change and edit its range address in the Refers To field. Click Add or OK to finish the job. Any formulas that reference that name will now refer to its new range.

NOTE NOTE NOTE NOTE NOTE NOTE NOTE NOTE NOTE NOTE NOTE NOTE NOTE NOTE NOTE

If you modify only the name itself, you create a new name that references the same range.

To delete a name, select it in the Define Name dialog box and click the Delete button. A formula that already references that name will result in #NAME?.

You can edit the formula and delete or change the now defunct name reference, or you can create the name again, and the formula will once more have a valid reference.

For Users of Other Spreadsheets

If you've worked with earlier DOS or Windows versions of Lotus 1-2-3 or Quattro Pro, you will find a few major differences in the way Excel handles range names:

- When you edit a formula that references a name in Excel, the name does *not* revert to its underlying address—the name remains the same.
- When you delete a name in Excel, formulas that reference that name do *not* revert to the underlying cell address; they continue to reference the name, but display #NAME? as their result.
- When you use a range name reference in a formula in Excel, it is always an absolute reference, whereas in Lotus 1-2-3 and Quattro Pro, the reference is relative unless you specifically make it absolute.
- When you define a new name for a range that a formula already references, the name does *not* appear in the formula automatically. You must choose Insert ➤ Name ➤ Apply to insert that name in a formula, as discussed earlier in this skill.

NOTE NOTE NOTE NOTE NOTE NOTE NOTE NOTE NOTE NOTE NOTE NOTE NOTE NOTE NOTE

If you want Excel to treat range names closer to the manner of these other spreadsheet programs, choose Tools ➤ Options to open the Options dialog box, click the Transition tab, and then click the Transition Formula Entry check box. You can experiment to see if you prefer this mode, but in general, if you're using Excel, you should get used to the way it handles range names.

Using the Find and Replace Commands

You find and replace data in Excel in much the same way that you find and replace data in any Office application. To search for data in a workbook, choose Edit ➤ Find (or press Ctrl+F). To find and replace data, choose Edit ➤ Replace (or press Ctrl+H). A few aspects of the process are unique to Excel, however.

Before you begin a search, do one of the following:

- Select a single cell to look for the data throughout the current worksheet.
- Select a range to search only those cells.
- Select all the worksheets you want to search.

Finding Characters in Cells and Comments

To find characters in cells or comments, choose Edit ➤ Find to open the Find dialog box:

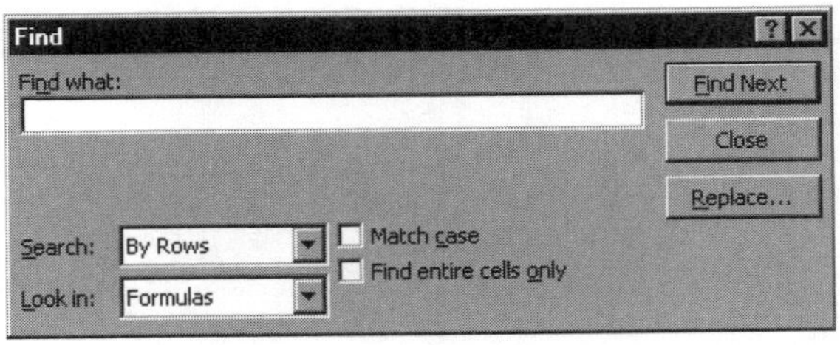

In the Find What field, you enter the characters you want to find. You can include wildcards to search for any characters (*) or any individual character (?), just as you can when specifying filenames.

The Look In drop-down list offers the following three choices, which determine what will be searched:

Formulas All cells

Values Only nonformula cells or the results of formulas

Comments Only cell comments

You can make the search more specific by clicking the following check boxes:

Match Case The case of characters must match exactly. For example, searching for *sum** finds "summary" but not "Summary" or "SUM."

Find Entire Cells Only The complete contents of a cell must match the characters in the Find What field.

You can also set the direction of the search by choosing either By Rows (the default) or By Columns from the Search drop-down list.

TIP TIP TIP TIP TIP TIP TIP TIP TIP TIP TIP TIP TIP TIP TIP TIP TIP TIP TIP TIP TIP TIP TIP TIP TIP

To search in the opposite direction, hold down Shift when you click Find Next.

Replacing Characters That Are Found

If you want to replace the characters that are found, you can either click the Replace button in the Find dialog box or choose Edit ➤ Replace to open the Replace dialog box:

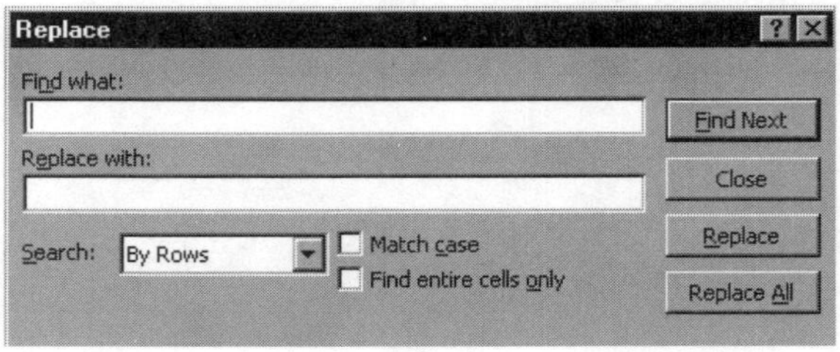

In the Replace With field, enter the characters that you want to appear in place of the characters that match the Find What field. Leave this field blank to erase the found characters.

You won't find the Look In list, because the Replace command essentially uses only the Formulas option to look inside cells, and it doesn't look in cell notes.

You can run the replace process in two ways:

- To find and replace cell-by-cell, click the Find Next button. As each cell is found, you can either click the Replace button to replace the characters in the cell or click Find Next to skip that cell and continue the search.
- Click the Replace All button to process all found cells in one step. Be sure of the results before you do this, and keep your mouse ready to jump to the Undo button.

Are You Experienced?

Now you can...

☑ Select and name a range

☑ Copy and move cells

☑ Clear and delete cells

☑ Insert and delete rows and columns

☑ Find and replace data

SKILL 4

Writing Formulas

- Building a formula
- Referencing cells in the same workbook
- Referencing cells in natural language formulas
- Copying formulas and moving precedent cells
- Referencing cells in other workbooks
- Recalculating formulas manually
- Calculating with Edit ➤ Paste Special

The rows and columns of an Excel worksheet are great for entering data, but it is Excel's powerful mathematical capabilities that bring your worksheets to life. This skill shows you how to work with formulas in Excel and how to tap into its massive computing powers.

Building a Formula

To begin a formula in Excel, always start with an equals sign (=). Then build the formula with any of the following pieces:

Value Numeric (114.8) or string ("hello")

Cell Address B10, A5:B10, Sheet2!B15, or a range name (My_Cell)

Function SUM, AVERAGE, COUNT, LEFT, IF, LOOKUP, and so on

Operator +, –, *, /, ^, >, =, and so on

Parentheses To control the left to right order of precedence in the formula, such as =(A15+B3)*2

Filename Such as [Sample.xls] to create a linking formula to that file

Spaces, tabs, or hard returns Can be included to make your formulas more readable

As I mentioned in Skill 1, when a cell contains a formula, you will see the result of the formula displayed for that cell. If you select the cell, you'll see the formula within the Formula bar.

TIP TIP TIP TIP TIP TIP TIP TIP TIP TIP TIP TIP TIP TIP TIP TIP TIP TIP TIP TIP TIP TIP TIP TIP TIP

If you enter a formula in a cell and see the formula instead of its result, be sure you prefaced the formula with an equals sign (=). Also, remember that you should never include an equals sign *within* a formula unless you are specifically creating a logical formula (for more on this, see Skill 5).

Including Values

You create a formula in Excel much as you would with a calculator. Simply build the formula from left to right, connecting values with operators. For example, you might want to add up the money you spent over several days on a trip:

```
=28.5+7.25+38.4+31.75
```

When you press Enter, the formula's result is displayed in that cell.

TIP TIP TIP TIP TIP TIP TIP TIP TIP TIP TIP TIP TIP TIP TIP TIP TIP TIP TIP TIP TIP TIP TIP TIP TIP TIP

Most of your formulas will not (and should not) include numbers. Instead, they should refer to other cells that may contain numbers. These cells are often called *variables* because their contents can vary (change), while a formula's reference to them does not change (although the formula's result will change). This technique makes it easy to update the data in your worksheet without having to edit the formulas themselves.

When you want to include text within a formula, be sure to enclose the text within quotation marks. If cell A5 contains a number, such as 27.5, you could write the following formula in another cell:

```
="The amount in cell A5 is "&A5
```


The result would look like this:

```
The amount in cell A5 is 27.5
```

You use the ampersand (&) to concatenate, or join, text in a formula. In this case, the result of the formula is text, not a number. Excel decided, quite logically, that when you combine text and a number in this way, the result cannot be a valid number and must therefore be text.

TIP TIP TIP TIP TIP TIP TIP TIP TIP TIP TIP TIP TIP TIP TIP TIP TIP TIP TIP TIP TIP TIP TIP TIP TIP TIP

You can manipulate text in different ways with Excel functions. You'll learn about some of them in Skill 5.

Reliving Math 101: Operators and the Order of Precedence

Remember when you had to memorize the order of precedence for mathematical operators (such as + and –)? Well, the same concepts apply to the operators in Excel, which are the glue that joins the other components of a formula. When a formula includes multiple operators, Excel evaluates the formula from left to right. An order of precedence among the operators determines which operation between a pair occurs first. For example, the formula

```
=7+4*3
```

equals 19, not 33, because multiplication has precedence over addition.

NOTE NOTE NOTE NOTE NOTE NOTE NOTE NOTE NOTE NOTE NOTE NOTE NOTE NOTE NOTE

The rules of precedence are followed throughout the world of math and computers, although you may find slight differences for some of the less common operators, such as the ampersand.

Table 4.1 shows the operators you can use in Excel and their ranking in the order of precedence. An operator above another in the list is evaluated first. When two operators share the same ranking, such as multiplication and division, Excel evaluates them from left to right.

TABLE 4.1: Excel's Operators

Operator	Description
:	Reference operator (as in A1:C3)
,	Argument separator
–	Negation (as in –2)
%	Percent sign
^	Exponentiation
* and /	Multiplication and division
+ and –	Addition and subtraction
&	Text concatenation
>, <, > =, < =, < >	Comparison operators (greater than, less than, greater than or equal to, less than or equal to, not equal to)

Without an established order of precedence, you can find several answers for a formula, depending on the order in which you evaluate its operators. To see Excel's order of preference in action, open a blank worksheet and follow these steps:

1. In cell A1, type **=2+3^2**.
2. In cell A2, type **=1+4*3**.
3. In cell A3, type **=4+1*3**.
4. In cell A4, type **=10–8/2**.

Your formulas should have yielded the answers 11, 13, 7, and 6. You can circumvent the usual flow of calculations, however, with a pair of parentheses.

Using Parentheses to Change the Order of Precedence

When you enclose part of a formula within a pair of parentheses, Excel evaluates that part as an independent unit. The result it produces is used in the normal, left-to-right flow of calculations. Follow these steps to see how parentheses change the result of a formula:

1. In cell B1, type **=(2+3)^2**.
2. In cell B2, type **=(1+4)*3**.
3. In cell B3, type **=(4+1)*3**.
4. In cell B4, type **=(10–8)/2**.

This time, your formulas should have yielded the answers 25, 15, 15, and 1.

An opening parenthesis in a formula must always have a closing parenthesis. If not, Excel will catch the discrepancy and offer to fix the problem or let you complete the parentheses yourself. If you choose to fix it, Excel highlights a portion of the formula that may need a balancing parenthesis, as shown below (it's a bit of a guess on Excel's part though, because *you* are the one who must determine where they belong).

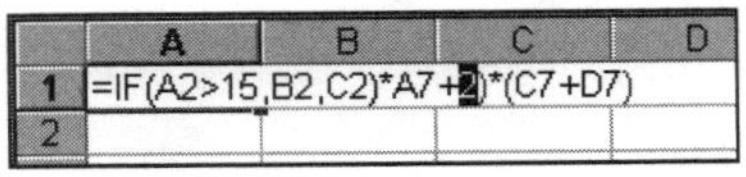

Excel can help you keep track of parentheses while you're working on a formula. As you enter a balancing parenthesis or move the insertion point through the formula and come to a parenthesis, Excel shows the pair of parentheses (briefly) in bold. Keep an eye out for this visual cue, and you're not likely to get out of balance.

Recognizing Error Results

Unfortunately, you can goof up a formula in lots of ways. Fortunately, Excel can warn you in a number of ways that you may be in trouble and can help you determine just what's wrong.

Here's a list of the common error results Excel returns when you enter a formula that Excel can't evaluate:

The column isn't wide enough to display the number; either widen the column, shrink the font, or change the numeric format.

#DIV/0! Dividing by zero is invalid; note that a blank cell has a value of zero.

#N/A Data is "not available," usually because your formula is referencing an NA function or value (for more information, see Skill 5).

#NAME? The formula references a name that is unknown to Excel.

#NUM! The formula is using an invalid number, such as when the second argument is less than the first in the RANDBETWEEN function.

#REF! A cell reference is no longer valid; perhaps you deleted that cell or moved another cell onto it.

#VALUE! The formula contains an invalid operator or argument; perhaps it is trying to add a text value to a numeric one.

NOTE NOTE NOTE NOTE NOTE NOTE NOTE NOTE NOTE NOTE NOTE NOTE NOTE NOTE

Choosing Tools ➤ Auditing is a great way to track the source of a formula's error result. You'll learn about auditing in Skill 9.

Making Your Formulas More Readable

A formula can be a maximum of 1024 characters. I hope that your formulas never need to approach that length. Nevertheless, a complex formula can easily grow lengthy and become particularly difficult to write or, especially, to revise later. Here are some techniques you can use to make your formulas easier to create and interpret.

TIP TIP TIP TIP TIP TIP TIP TIP TIP TIP TIP TIP TIP TIP TIP TIP TIP TIP TIP TIP TIP TIP TIP TIP TIP

You can use Excel's built-in Range Finder to make your formulas more readable when they contain range references. We'll look at this in the "Referencing Cells in the Same Workbook" section, later in this skill.

Use Parentheses to Clarify Your Intent

Even when a formula does not require parentheses, you may want to include them to clarify your intent. You can group sections of the formula within parentheses, which helps document the intended flow of calculations.

For example, the formula

```
=Sheet2!C15*D25+A25-A30-A35
```

is not all that long, but isn't it easier to read when it looks like this:

```
=(Sheet2!C15*D25)+(A25-A30-A35)
```

The added parentheses do *not* change the order of calculation here. They simply break the formula into more bite-sized pieces.

Include Spaces

You can place space characters within a formula, which might make it more readable, and doing so doesn't affect the formula.

```
=Sheet2!C15*D25    +A25-A30-A35
```

Split a Long Formula into Multiple Lines

To break a formula into several lines in its cell, press Alt+Enter to insert a linefeed. You could then make the formula from the example above look like this:


```
=Sheet2!C15*D25
+A25-A30-A35
```

Break a Long Formula into Multiple Cells

You can make a long formula much easier to handle if you break it into several cells. You can create components of the formula in separate cells and then tie them all together with another formula.

For example, you could split the formula used earlier into several cells in this way:

Cell A1 =Sheet2!C15*D25

Cell A2 =A25–A30–A35

Cell A3 A1+A2

You could use any cells for these components. The final formula that produces the desired result (cell A3) could be in some other part of the worksheet; it need not be right next to the cells it references.

Display Formulas, Not Their Results

When you are staring at a worksheet full of numbers, you really can't tell which are simply values and which are formulas. Here's a quick way to make the formulas stand out:

1. Choose Tools ➤ Options to open the Options dialog box:
2. Click the View tab.
3. In the Window Options section, click the Formulas check box.
4. Click OK.

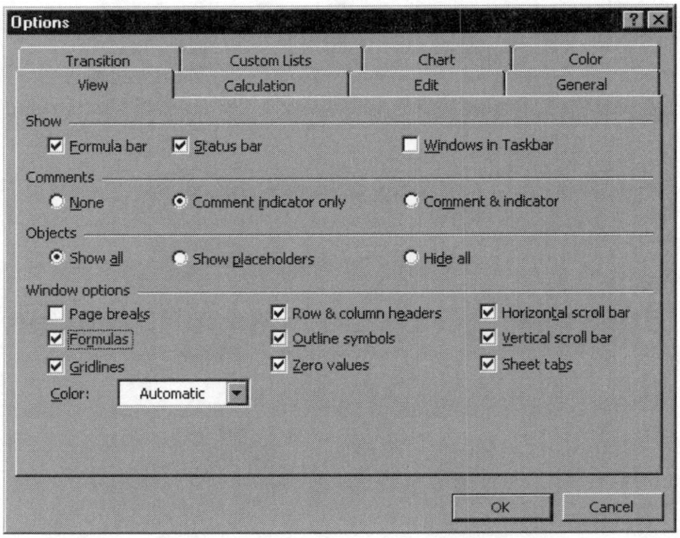

Now the formulas, rather than their results, are displayed in the worksheet. Excel widens columns to show more of each formula, although some may still appear truncated. (But frequently that's all you'll need to get an idea of where the formulas are.)

You can choose either view as needed; press Ctrl+` (the grave accent found to the left of the 1 key, not an apostrophe) to switch between seeing the formula and seeing the result of the formula.

Referencing Cells in the Same Workbook

Most of the formulas you write in Excel will refer to one or more of the millions of cells in the current workbook. A formula depends on the cells it references, and any changes you make to those cells affect the formula's result.

NOTE NOTE NOTE NOTE NOTE NOTE NOTE NOTE NOTE NOTE NOTE NOTE NOTE NOTE NOTE

Referenced cells are called *precedent* cells. You can trace the chain of precedents and dependents by choosing Tools ➤ Auditing, as discussed in Skill 9.

Entering Cell References

You can refer to cells in a formula in several ways. To reference an individual cell, simply type the cell's address, as in this example:

```
=25+A3-B2+12
```

TIP TIP TIP TIP TIP TIP TIP TIP TIP TIP TIP TIP TIP TIP TIP TIP TIP TIP TIP TIP TIP TIP TIP TIP TIP TIP TIP

Excel automatically updates the addresses of all cell references in a formula when you insert or delete cells in the worksheet. In the above example, if you inserted two rows at row 1, the formula would reflect the change and now reference A5 and B4 instead of A3 and B2.

To reference a range of cells, define the range by specifying its upper-left and lower-right corners:

```
=SUM(B5:D9)
```

This formula sums the 15 cells in the rectangle whose corners are B5 and D9.

To reference multiple ranges, separate one from the next with a comma:

```
=SUM(B5:D9,F5:H9,I9,3.14)
```

This formula sums the three cell references and the number 3.14.

If the cell resides on another sheet in the same workbook, be sure to include that sheet's name in the address. To refer to cell B2 on Sheet3, the formula used above would look like this:

```
=25+A3-Sheet3!B2+12
```

The exclamation mark (!) at the end of the sheet name tells Excel that the cell being referenced is on a sheet other than the one that contains the formula. If the formula resides on the same sheet, the sheet name is understood.

If the sheet is named, be sure you reference that name. If the name has a space in it, you must enclose the name in single quotation marks:

```
=25+A3-'My Sheet'!B2+12
```

To reference the same range on multiple consecutive sheets—a *3-D range*—specify the first and last sheet, separated by a colon. The formula

```
=SUM(Sheet1:Sheet3!A1:B3)
```

adds the cells in the range A1:B3 on Sheet1, Sheet2, and Sheet3 (this assumes that those three sheets still have their default names, of course).

Pointing to a Cell or Range

In many cases, you may prefer to *point* to the cell or cells you want to reference in the formula instead of manually typing in the cell addresses. Pointing to and clicking the cell you want to reference displays its address in the formula, as though you had typed it there.

NOTE NOTE NOTE NOTE NOTE NOTE NOTE NOTE NOTE NOTE NOTE NOTE NOTE NOTE NOTE

In order to point to a cell, the insertion point must be positioned so that the formula can accept an address—for example, when the insertion point follows an operator.

For example, when you enter the formula =25+ in a cell and the insertion point is to the right of the plus sign, you can point to and click another cell to reference it within the formula. (Watch for the indicator on the left side of the status bar to display Point). You can then continue adding operators and references to the formula.

You can point to a range of cells by using the Shift+arrow key method. You can also reference noncontiguous ranges and 3-D ranges, as described in Skill 3, and you can point to a cell or range of cells in another sheet.

Using the Range Finder

When a formula contains many cell references, it can look like nothing more than a long string of letters and numbers and give no clues as to what or where all the cells it references may be. Excel's immediate solution to this problem is the Range Finder. You'll see its effects when you edit a formula that contains references to cells or range names. To run the Range Finder, click the cell to display the formula in the Formula bar, and then click anywhere within the formula.

Figure 4.1 shows a formula being edited that contains three range references:

```
=25+SUM(A4:A8)+SUM(B10:D13)+15+10+MyCell
```

The Range Finder performs two tasks when you change a formula:

- Each cell reference in the formula appears in a different color, so it's easy to discern one reference from another. Colors are repeated when there are more than a few references in one formula.
- The cells in the worksheet for each reference are surrounded by a border of the same color as the reference in the formula.

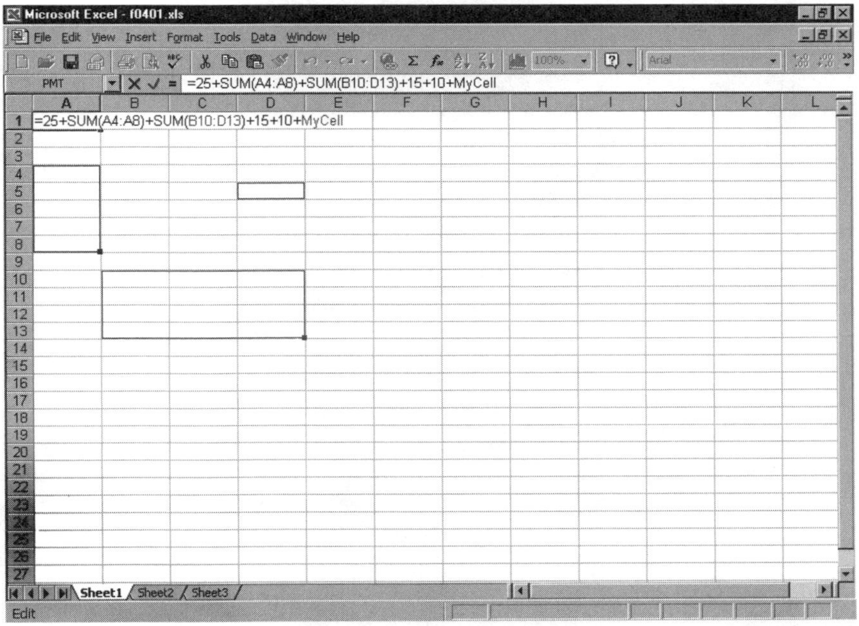

FIGURE 4.1: Cell references within formulas come alive with the Range Finder.

Suddenly the cell references seem to jump out of the formula and associate themselves with the actual ranges in the worksheet. Although Figure 4.1 doesn't show the actual colors, you can duplicate this formula in your worksheet to see the real thing (you'd also need to name a cell MyCell in order to mimic the formula).

The Range Finder not only helps you distinguish one reference from another, but it also lets you modify those references by changing the size or position of a range's border in the worksheet:

- To change the dimensions of a range reference, drag the handle in the lower-right corner of a range's border.
- To move a range reference, point to any edge of a range border (the mouse pointer will change to an arrow) and drag the border to a new position.

You can also edit the formula in the usual ways, such as by typing or pointing.

Referring to a Range Name

A range name is simply a name that describes the address of a single cell or range of cells, as discussed in Skill 3. A name makes it easy to reference a cell or range because you don't have to remember the exact cell address—you simply need to remember the name.

To reference a range name in a formula, you can enter the name instead of the actual cell address. Better yet, select the name from the list of all names in the workbook by clicking the down arrow in the Name box. When you reference a range name in a formula, the actual name—not the cell address—appears in the formula. However, if you reference a cell address that also happens to be named, only the cell address appears in the formula. Either way, the formula produces the same result.

NOTE NOTE NOTE NOTE NOTE NOTE NOTE NOTE NOTE NOTE NOTE NOTE NOTE NOTE NOTE

Seeing the name in a formula can be an advantage. It helps you decipher the meaning of the formula (assuming the name for the range is somewhat relevant, of course) and also ensures that you're referencing the exact range you want. No matter how its address might change as you insert or delete cells in the workbook, the name will always follow the range and define the correct cells.

If you have formulas that reference addresses that are now named, such as

```
=C17*Y95
```

you can replace the addresses in the formulas with their names. Choose Insert ➤ Name ➤ Apply, as discussed in Skill 3. The result is a more readable formula that might look like this:

```
=Pressure*Temperature
```

Here's a quick and easy way to name a range:

1. Highlight the range.
2. Click in the Name box, type a range name, and then press Enter.

Dealing with a Circular Reference

Suppose you write a formula in cell A6 that adds the cells above it in A1:A5, but you accidentally write the formula this way:

```
=SUM(A1:A6)
```

Because the formula refers to its own cell, you've created a *circular reference*, which Excel is unable to evaluate in its normal course of worksheet recalculation. Unless you are specifically designing a worksheet to include a circular reference, you can assume that any you encounter need to be fixed—either delete the circular cell reference or modify it so that it refers to another cell.

NOTE NOTE NOTE NOTE NOTE NOTE NOTE NOTE NOTE NOTE NOTE NOTE NOTE NOTE NOTE

A circular reference can be direct, as in this case where the formula actually refers to its own cell. It can also be indirect, where the formula refers to itself only by referencing another formula, which in turn refers to the circular one (possibly via many other formulas).

When you try to enter a formula that creates a circular reference, whether you do so intentionally or not, Excel immediately notifies you of the potential problem by displaying a warning dialog box. If you click OK, Excel will do the following:

- Enter the formula into the cell.
- Open the Help window to information about circular cell references. When you close or minimize the Help window, the Circular Reference toolbar is displayed to help you track the source of the circular reference.
- Display the Circular indicator on the status bar, which shows the address of the offending formula.
- Not recalculate the formula, since the normal mode of recalculation has no way to deal with (resolve) the circular reference.

Figure 4.2 shows the worksheet that was described above, the Circular Reference toolbar, and the Circular indicator on the status bar.

You can also see a formula tracer arrow running from A1 to A6. This was created by clicking the Trace Precedents button on the Circular Reference toolbar while cell A6, the formula, was selected. The arrow runs through all the cells that the formula references.

The dot in cell A6 indicates that the formula is dependent on its own cell; hence, the circular reference.

TIP TIP TIP TIP TIP TIP TIP TIP TIP TIP TIP TIP TIP TIP TIP TIP TIP TIP TIP TIP TIP TIP TIP TIP TIP

You'll learn more about tracing precedent and dependent cells in Skill 9.

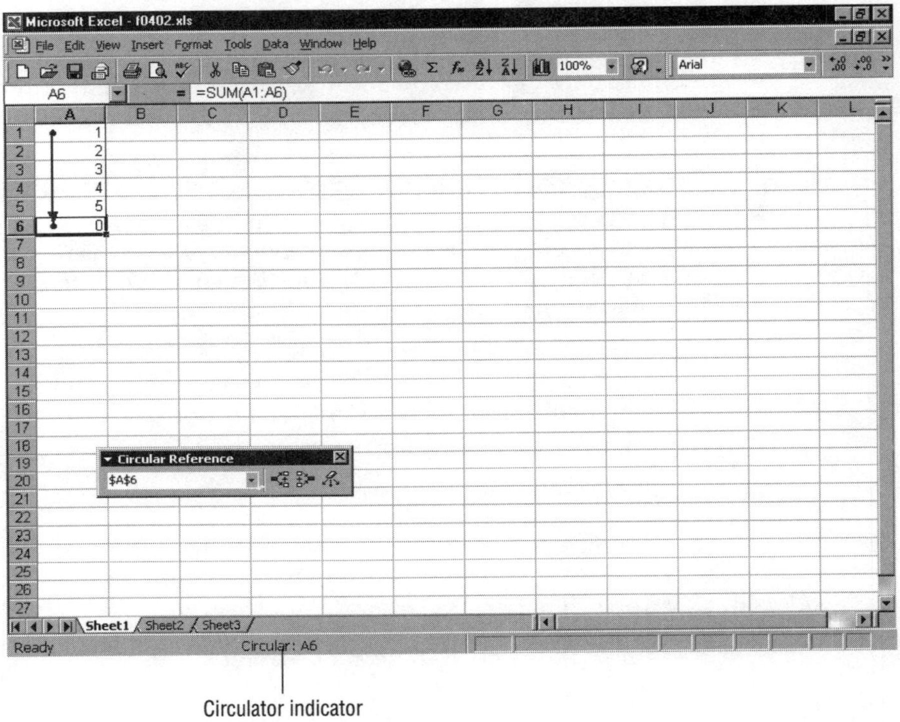

FIGURE 4.2: A formula with a circular reference, the Circular Reference toolbar, and the precedent and dependent arrows

Referencing Cells in Natural Language Formulas

So far you've seen how you can write a formula that refers to other cell addresses, such as =A5*B16, and to range names, such as =A5*Interest. You can also reference cells in another way. Using *natural language formulas*, you can refer to row and column labels (text entries) within the worksheet instead of cell addresses or range names.

In Excel 2000, natural language formulas are not enabled by default. To turn on this feature, follow these steps:

1. Choose Tool ➤ Options to open the Options dialog box.

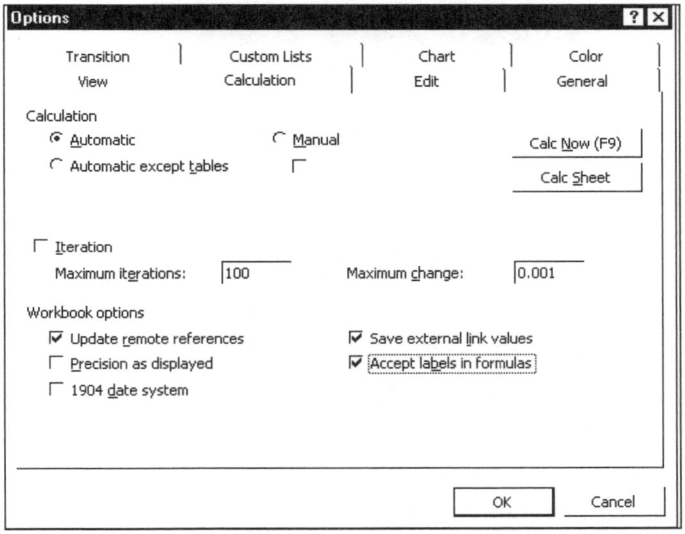

2. Click the Calculation tab, and check the Accept Labels in Formulas check box.
3. Click OK.

The worksheet in Figure 4.3, which is quite typical in its layout, is a perfect candidate for writing natural language formulas. You can use the column titles in row 3 and the row titles in column A to identify any of the data cells in the worksheet.

	A	B	C	D	E	F	G	H	I	J
1		Monthly Housing Expenses								
2										
3		Jan	Feb	Mar	Apr	May	Jun	Total		
4	Insurance	51	51	51	51	51	51	306		
5	Maintenance	48	48	48	48	48	48	288		
6	Mortgage	925	925	925	925	925	925	5,550		
7	Taxes	102	102	102	102	102	102	612		
8	Telephone	42	78	65	115	70	67	437		
9	Utilities	182	116	143	90	175	185	891		
10	Total	1,350	1,320	1,334	1,331	1,371	1,378	8,084		
11										

FIGURE 4.3: You can reference cells in formulas by referring to their row and column titles.

For example, the amount in January for Utilities is 182; the total of expenses for January is 1,350; the total for Utilities is 891; the difference between Utilities in January and in February is 66; and January's Utilities are about 20 percent of the Total Utilities. Here is how you would write natural language formulas for these:

```
=Jan Utilities
=Total Jan
=Total Utilities
=Jan Utilities-Feb Utilities
=Jan Utilities/Total Utilities
```

All it takes are unique column and row titles. In the formula, you separate one label from another with a space to define the intersection. If a row or column label consists of more than one word, you can enclose it in single quotation marks in the formula to make the reference more readable.

Here are a few other points to keep in mind when you work with natural language formulas:

- Ranges expand and contract as usual, so you can insert more rows without damaging any of the existing references.
- If you change a column or row title, formulas that reference those titles update accordingly.
- Be sure that column and row titles are unique, or you could run into trouble without even realizing it.
- When Excel finds more than one possible intersection for the titles you reference, it will prompt you to specify exactly which cell you mean.
- A formula cannot reference column and row titles that are on another worksheet.
- A natural language reference is a relative one; you can make it absolute by prefacing it with a dollar sign, just as you can with cell addresses in formulas (this topic is discussed in the next section).

To disable this feature, follow these steps:

1. Choose Tool ➤ Options to open the Options dialog box:
2. Click the Calculation tab, and clear the Accept Labels in Formulas check box.
3. Click OK.

Copying Formulas and Moving Precedent Cells

When you copy a formula, such as with the Edit ➤ Copy and Paste commands, any cell references in the formula adjust their addresses to the copied formula's new location in the workbook. These addresses in the formula are called *relative* addresses.

Understanding How Relative References Adjust

You can think of a relative address as not really referring to a specific cell, but rather to that cell's position relative to the formula. For example, in this simple formula that resides in cell A1,


```
=B3
```

the cell reference actually refers to the cell that is *one column to the right and two rows down.*

If you copy the formula from cell A1 to C15, the cell reference adjusts and still refers to the cell that is one column to the right and two rows down, so now it reads:

```
=D17
```

A range address adjusts in the same way. Therefore, this formula in cell A1

```
=SUM(B3:D10)
```

changes to

```
=SUM(D17:F24)
```

when the formula is copied from cell A1 to C15.

Applying Absolute References That Do Not Adjust

You can also create an *absolute* cell reference in a formula, and it will not change when the formula is copied. To create an absolute reference, preface both its column and row with a dollar sign ($):

```
=$B$3
```

You can copy this formula to any cell, and it will always reference cell B3.

NOTE NOTE NOTE NOTE NOTE NOTE NOTE NOTE NOTE NOTE NOTE NOTE NOTE NOTE

A reference to a range name is always absolute and never adjusts when the formula is copied. On the other hand, a natural language reference, as discussed in the previous section, is a relative one that you can make absolute with a preceding dollar sign.

A mixed reference contains both relative and absolute portions of the address:

```
=$B3
```

When you copy this formula, only the row reference adjusts.

You can use F4 to create absolute or mixed references. When you are editing a formula and the insertion point is on an address, pressing F4 once makes the reference absolute. You can press F4 once or twice more to make a mixed reference.

Here are a few rules to keep in mind while copying or moving formulas to other worksheets:

- You can copy a formula with relative or absolute addresses to another worksheet.
- If you don't include a sheet address in a formula reference, Excel assumes that the sheet portion of the address is relative. If you copy the formula =$A$1 from Sheet1 to Sheet3, for example, the formula will refer to $A$1 on Sheet3.
- If you include the sheet name in the reference, however, Excel takes that as an absolute reference to that sheet. You don't need to, nor can you, preface the sheet name with a dollar sign.
- When you move a formula to a cell in the same or in another worksheet, its cell references will not change, no matter what type of reference was used.

Moving Precedent Cells

When you move a cell, such as by choosing Edit ➤ Cut and Paste, a formula that contains a reference to that cell "follows" the cell to its new location. It does not matter whether the reference was absolute or relative.

For example, the formula

```
=A1+$A$1
```

would look like this

```
=B5+$B$5
```

if you moved cell A1 to B5.

When you move a precedent cell to another worksheet, a formula that references it will follow it to that new sheet and update its reference accordingly.

Finally, when you *copy* a precedent cell, the formula that refers to it will still refer to the same cell afterward—the copy is ignored.

Referencing Cells in Other Workbooks

Just as you can write a formula that refers to a cell on another worksheet, you can do the same with cells in another workbook. Writing this type of *external* reference in the *primary* workbook's formula creates a link to the cells in the *source* workbook.

By using workbook-linking formulas, you avoid having to duplicate data in one workbook that already exists in another. In fact, you can reference data in *many* workbooks; as a result, linking formulas vastly expand Excel's calculating abilities. Figure 4.4 shows an example of how you can take advantage of linking formulas. In the upper portion of the screen is the monthly housing expenses workbook from Figure 4.3, this time named *123 Main St.*

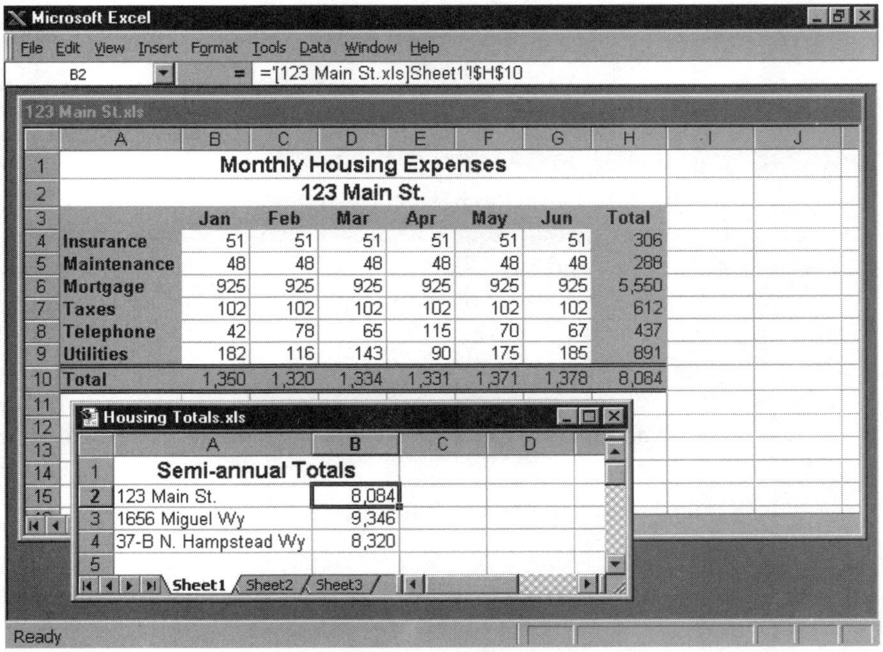

FIGURE 4.4: Linking formulas let you easily access data in other workbooks.

Imagine that you have several other housing workbooks and that you want quick access to their totals. Those files might be sent to you by others, for example, or reside elsewhere on your network or anywhere on the Internet.

The workbook in the lower portion of the screen in Figure 4.4 does the job. It simply lists the houses in column A; to the right of each one is a linking formula that references the cell containing the totals in the appropriate expenses workbook. For example, here is the formula in B2, which can also be seen in the Formula bar in Figure 4.4:

```
='[123 Main St.xls]Sheet1'!$H$10
```

NOTE NOTE NOTE NOTE NOTE NOTE NOTE NOTE NOTE NOTE NOTE NOTE NOTE NOTE

When you reference a range of cells in another workbook, such as with the SUM function, Excel actually stores all the values of that range in the primary workbook. Referencing a huge range could consume a lot of memory or disk space. That's when you might want to clear the Save External Link Values check box in the Calculation tab of the Options dialog box. Choose Tools ➤ Options to open the Options dialog box.

Specifying the Filename

A linking formula is essentially the same as any other formula, except that it includes a filename in a cell reference. The name is enclosed in square brackets, followed by the reference to the sheet (required) and cells in that file. For example, the linking formula in cell B2 in Figure 4.4 references cell H10 on Sheet1 in the source workbook 123 Main St. It doesn't matter if that file is open and in memory or only on disk.

If the source file is not open and does not reside in the same folder as the primary workbook, be sure to include the path to that file, such as `='C:\Houses\ [123 Main St.xls]Sheet1'!H10`. You must enclose the path and sheet reference within single quotation marks and enclose the filename in brackets. Even without the path, when the filename has a space in it, you must enclose it in single quotation marks.

Typing the Filename Link

To write a linking formula, you can begin the formula and then type the linking reference, although this can be tedious if you have to include the path to the file.

TIP TIP TIP TIP TIP TIP TIP TIP TIP TIP TIP TIP TIP TIP TIP TIP TIP TIP TIP TIP TIP TIP TIP TIP TIP

If you can't remember the file's name or location when you are typing a formula link to a file that is not open, enter an invalid filename in the formula and press Enter. You can then use the File Not Found dialog box to locate and select the correct filename.

Pointing to the File

If the workbook whose cells you want to reference is open, there's a much easier way to create the link. Simply point to the cells in the other workbook, just as you do when referencing cells in the active worksheet. Excel creates the linking reference for you in the formula.

Creating Links over the Internet

You can also create a linking formula that references a workbook residing on the Internet or your intranet, using the transfer protocols HTTP or FTP (as always, this assumes you already have a connection available). On a good day, you won't notice any difference when you link to a file on your local hard disk, on your network, or on the Internet. On a bad day, of course, a modem connection to a busy site on the Internet could really slow down a link to a large workbook.

You specify a Net link much as you would a local link, except that the path to the source file will be over the Internet, as in this example:

```
='http://www.domain.com/rentals/[123 Main St.xls]Sheet1'!$H$10
```

You can either type in the full path and name or, if the source workbook is open, point to the cells you want to reference.

NOTE NOTE NOTE NOTE NOTE NOTE NOTE NOTE NOTE NOTE NOTE NOTE NOTE NOTE NOTE

When dealing with workbooks on the Internet, don't confuse linking formulas with hyperlinks. You can click a hyperlink to open the target workbook, whereas a linking formula simply brings in data from the target workbook for the formula to evaluate. Creating hyperlinks and other Internet topics are discussed in Skill 10.

Keeping Links Current

When you open a workbook containing linking formulas to one or more workbooks that are not open, Excel will ask you if you want to update the results of those formulas with whatever data is in the other files. Generally you will want to click the Yes button and let Excel update the results of the linking formulas.

WARNING WARNING WARNING WARNING WARNING WARNING WARNING WARNING

If you change the data in the source workbook when the target workbook isn't open, the linking formulas won't be updated and your data won't be accurate.

However, if there are many links in the workbook or many links to sites on the Internet that could take a lot of time to access, you may not want to wait while the formulas are updated. If you're working on your portable computer away from your network connection, the source files may simply not be available.

In these cases, you can select No and not have the formulas updated. Just realize that the results displayed for any linking formulas will be from the last time they were updated and, therefore, may no longer be accurate.

NOTE NOTE NOTE NOTE NOTE NOTE NOTE NOTE NOTE NOTE NOTE NOTE NOTE NOTE

Formulas that link to open workbooks are evaluated during the normal course of formula recalculation, which by default is whenever you change any data to which the formulas refer.

You can update the results of linking formulas at any time by choosing Edit ➤ Links to open the Links dialog box (see Figure 4.5), which was mentioned in Skill 3 in relation to creating object links between Excel and other Windows programs.

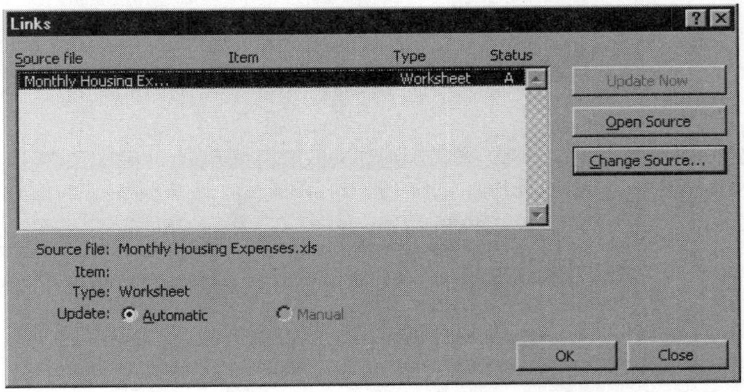

FIGURE 4.5: The Links dialog box lets you update, open, or change the source workbooks for linking formulas in the active workbook.

The Source File list shows the source files for all the linking formulas in the active workbook (as well as the source for object links to other programs). Its options include:

Update Now Recalculates all formulas that link to the files you selected in the Source File list. This is called a manual update.

Open Source Opens the selected source files.

Change Source Lets you replace the selected source filename with another filename, which you would do if the source file were moved or renamed.

Update Is set by default to Automatic so that linking formulas are evaluated when you open the workbook. Choose Manual if you want Excel to update the links only when you click the Update Now button in this dialog box. To make this choice, you must first clear the Update Remote References check box on the Calculation tab in the Options dialog box.

TIP TIP TIP TIP TIP TIP TIP TIP TIP TIP TIP TIP TIP TIP TIP TIP TIP TIP TIP TIP TIP TIP TIP TIP

Suppose that workbook A links to workbook B and that workbook B links to workbook C, and that all of them are closed. If you open C, update its data, save the file, and then open workbook A (but not B), the results in that workbook may not be accurate. You must first open workbook B, update its links to C, save it if it is not a local file, and then open workbook A and update its links.

Recalculating Formulas Manually

By default, Excel recalculates formulas in all open workbooks whenever the data they reference change. This happens automatically, so under normal conditions your formulas are always up-to-date and correct.

When you have hundreds or thousands of formulas in open workbooks, the recalculation time may be longer than the blink of an eye that Excel usually requires. In that case, Excel displays the Calculate indicator on the status bar, and when you stop working for a moment, Excel takes that opportunity to recalculate the formulas. The presence of the Calculate indicator means that some formulas are not yet up-to-date.

You can turn off the automatic recalculation feature if it's too distracting or perhaps to avoid the stress on your less-than-state-of-the-art computer. To turn off the automatic recalculation feature, follow these steps:

1. Choose Tools ➤ Options to open the Options dialog box.
2. Click the Calculation tab.

3. In the Calculation section, click the Manual button.
4. Click OK to return to the worksheet.

Now when data changes, formulas will not automatically recalculate. The Calculate indicator on the status bar reminds you that not all formulas in the workbook are up-to-date.

NOTE NOTE NOTE NOTE NOTE NOTE NOTE NOTE NOTE NOTE NOTE NOTE NOTE NOTE NOTE

By default, when you select Manual, you also select the Recalculate before Save check box. This means that Excel will update all your formulas before it saves the workbook.

To recalculate formulas in all open workbooks while working in Manual mode, do either of the following:

- Choose Tools ➤ Options to open the Options dialog box, click the Calculation tab, and then click the Calc Now button.
- From the worksheet, simply press F9.

To recalculate only the formulas on the active worksheet, do either of the following (doing this partial-workbook recalculation does not remove the Calculate indicator from the status bar):

- Choose Tools ➤ Options to open the Options dialog box, click the Calculation tab, and then click the Calc Sheet button.
- From the worksheet, press Shift+F9.

TIP TIP TIP TIP TIP TIP TIP TIP TIP TIP TIP TIP TIP TIP TIP TIP TIP TIP TIP TIP TIP TIP TIP TIP TIP

You can also press F9 while you're editing a formula to display the result of only that formula. If you want to keep only this result, you can press Enter; otherwise, press Esc to bring back the formula. You can also recalculate a piece of a formula by selecting that piece and pressing F9. Again, be sure to press Esc if you want to keep the formula and not its current result.

Calculating with Edit ➤ Paste Special

After you copy data to the Clipboard with the Edit ➤ Copy command, you can choose Edit ➤ Paste Special to perform arithmetic between the data you are pasting and data that are already in the worksheet.

Figure 4.6 shows the Paste Special dialog box. By default, the None option in the Operation section is selected. This means that no arithmetic is performed when the data are pasted, and the new data overwrite any data already in the worksheet.

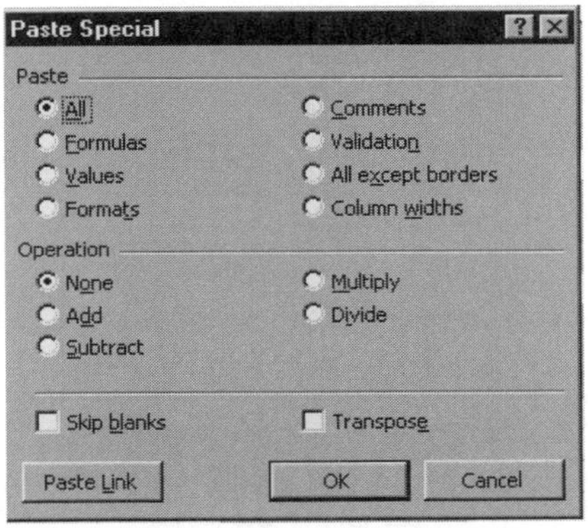

FIGURE 4.6: Choose Edit ➤ Paste Special, and use the Paste Special dialog box to perform arithmetic between the pasted data and the data already in the worksheet.

NOTE NOTE NOTE NOTE NOTE NOTE NOTE NOTE NOTE NOTE NOTE NOTE NOTE NOTE NOTE

Along with the arithmetical options, you can also use the other options in the Paste Special dialog box, which were discussed in Skill 3.

To perform arithmetic between each incoming (pasted) cell and the cell it overwrites, choose one of the other Operation options:

Add Both data items are added together.

Subtract The pasted data are subtracted from the cell data.

Multiply Both data items are multiplied.

Divide The cell data are divided by the pasted data.

This command is a handy way to perform arithmetic on existing data without having to create formulas elsewhere in the worksheet. Figure 4.7 shows a quick example using the housing expenses workbook used earlier in this book.

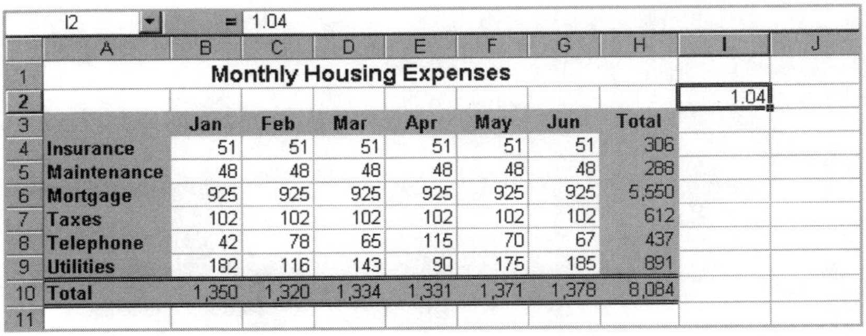

	A	B	C	D	E	F	G	H	I	J
1		Monthly Housing Expenses								
2									1.04	
3		Jan	Feb	Mar	Apr	May	Jun	Total		
4	Insurance	51	51	51	51	51	51	306		
5	Maintenance	48	48	48	48	48	48	288		
6	Mortgage	925	925	925	925	925	925	5,550		
7	Taxes	102	102	102	102	102	102	612		
8	Telephone	42	78	65	115	70	67	437		
9	Utilities	182	116	143	90	175	185	891		
10	Total	1,350	1,320	1,334	1,331	1,371	1,378	8,084		
11										

FIGURE 4.7: Using the Paste Special dialog box, you can combine two groups of data with arithmetic.

You can also use the Paste Special dialog box as a fast way to replace a range of formulas with their results. For example, if you entered data via formulas, you could eliminate the formulas when you were done, leaving only their results. To do so, follow these steps:

1. Choose Edit ➤ Copy to copy the formula range to the Clipboard.
2. Select the first cell of that range.
3. Choose Edit ➤ Paste Special to open the Paste Special dialog box.
4. Click the Values option, and then click OK.

The formulas are overwritten by their results.

Suppose your housing expenses worksheet contained proposed or budgeted expenses for the coming year, but you realize that you forgot to factor in an expected 4 percent increase due to inflation. Follow these steps to use the Paste Special command to increase each data item by 4 percent in one operation.

1. Enter **1.04** into any blank cell in your worksheet, such as I2 in Figure 4.7. (This is just a temporary entry; we'll delete it after the task is done.)

2. Copy that cell to the Clipboard by choosing Edit ➤ Copy or clicking the Copy button on the Standard toolbar.
3. Select all the data cells in the worksheet (for example, B4:G9 in Figure 4.7).

4. Choose Edit ➤ Paste Special to open the Paste Special dialog box, and select the Multiply option.
5. Click OK.

You would not want to select any of the formula cells in this case, because they also would have been increased by the 1.04 value. For example, the formula in cell H4 in Figure 4.7, which adds the Insurance row for all months, looks like this before the Paste Special operation

```
=SUM(B4:G4)
```

and would look like this afterward:

```
=(SUM(B4:G4))*1.04
```


The result would be too large by 4 percent.

You need to change the format of the data to reflect that most of the numbers now include decimal places.

1. Select all the data and formulas (in Figure 4.8, cells B4:H10).

2. Click the Comma Style button on the Formatting toolbar to apply that numeric format to these cells.
3. With the cells containing data and formulas (B4:H10 in Figure 4.7) still selected, choose Format ➤ Column ➤ AutoFit Selection to expand the columns to accommodate the wider numbers.
4. Select the cell in which you entered 1.04 (for example, I2 in Figure 4.7), and press Del to remove that temporary value.

Your worksheet should look like the one in Figure 4.8. Each cell value was multiplied by the value in the Clipboard, 1.04.

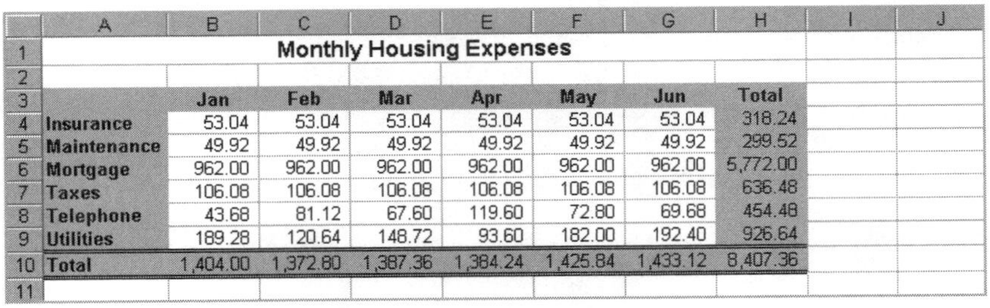

	A	B	C	D	E	F	G	H	I	J
1			Monthly Housing Expenses							
2										
3		Jan	Feb	Mar	Apr	May	Jun	Total		
4	Insurance	53.04	53.04	53.04	53.04	53.04	53.04	318.24		
5	Maintenance	49.92	49.92	49.92	49.92	49.92	49.92	299.52		
6	Mortgage	962.00	962.00	962.00	962.00	962.00	962.00	5,772.00		
7	Taxes	106.08	106.08	106.08	106.08	106.08	106.08	636.48		
8	Telephone	43.68	81.12	67.60	119.60	72.80	69.68	454.48		
9	Utilities	189.28	120.64	148.72	93.60	182.00	192.40	926.64		
10	Total	1,404.00	1,372.80	1,387.36	1,384.24	1,425.84	1,433.12	8,407.36		
11										

FIGURE 4.8: After selecting the Multiply option in the Paste Special dialog box, each datum has been multiplied by the value that was in I2.

Working Backward with the Goal Seek Command

The Tools ➤ Goal Seek command helps you solve a mathematical formula "backward," by finding a value that makes a formula result in an amount you specify. It's quite a powerful tool when you have a complex worksheet with many intertwined formulas.

Here's a typical example of how you can use Goal Seek. Suppose you want to buy a house and will be borrowing money at 9 percent annual interest. The bank that's loaning you the money believes that the maximum monthly payment you can afford is $900. How much house does that buy?

You can use the PMT function to find the payment amount on a loan. (The PMT function is discussed in Skill 5.) Its required arguments look like this:

```
=PMT(interest,periods,pv)
```

In our example, we know the interest rate is 9 percent, and we can assume the number of periods is 30 years. What we need to find is the present value of the money to be borrowed (the principal).

Figure 4.9 shows a small worksheet and the Goal Seek dialog box that will answer this question. The values needed for the PMT arguments have been entered in cells B1:B3. Here's the actual formula in B5:

```
=PMT(B2/12,B3*12,B1)
```

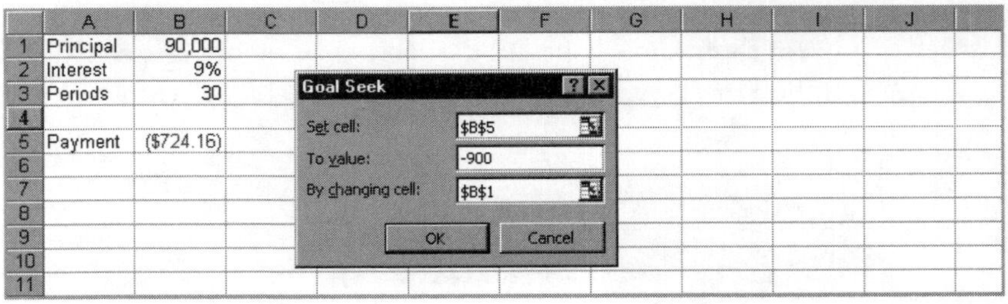

FIGURE 4.9: Use the Goal Seek tool to make a formula result in the amount you specify.

The principal amount in B1 is what we need to know. I entered a guess of $90,000, which returned a payment of $724.16 from the formula in B5. I could keep playing with the principal amount, increasing it or decreasing it until the formula produced a payment of exactly $900, but here's the easy way to do it.

1. Choose Tools ➤ Goal Seek to open the Goal Seek dialog box, as shown along with the worksheet in Figure 4.9.
2. In the Set Cell field, enter the address of the formula whose result you want to change—**$B$5** in this case.
3. In the To Value field, enter the result you want the formula to produce, which in this example is **–900**.

NOTE NOTE NOTE NOTE NOTE NOTE NOTE NOTE NOTE NOTE NOTE NOTE NOTE NOTE NOTE

You need to enter a negative value because the PMT function returns a negative value when calculating the payment for paying down a loan.

4. In the By Changing Cell field, enter the address of the principal—**$B$1** in this example.
5. Click OK and, in less than an instant, a suggested solution is displayed in the Goal Seek Status dialog box, and the number it offers has been placed in the cell containing the principal (B1 in this example):

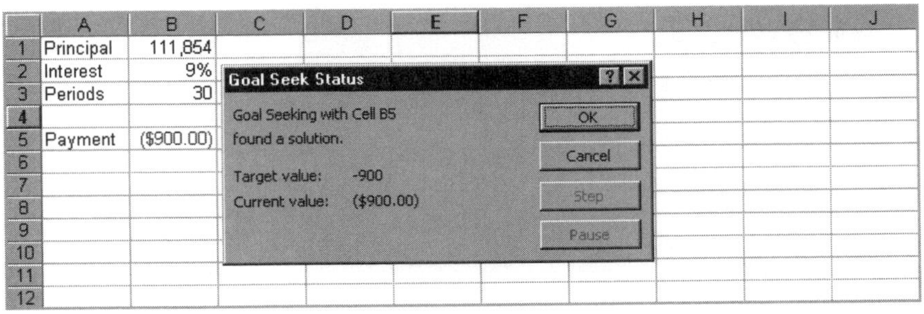

6. Click OK to accept the solution (111,854 in this example).

In many cases, there may be multiple solutions that would satisfy the criteria you specify for the Goal Seeker. Therefore, start with a value in the changing cell (B1 in this example) so that Goal Seek has a better guess at what result you expect to attain.

Are You Experienced?

Now you can...

- ☑ Write a formula using numbers, cell addresses, and operators
- ☑ Reference cells in the current or another workbook
- ☑ Create natural language formulas
- ☑ Write formulas that link to other workbooks
- ☑ Link to workbooks on the Internet
- ☑ Copy and move formulas
- ☑ Use manual recalculation
- ☑ Calculate using the Paste Special dialog box
- ☑ Use Goal Seek to solve for an unknown

SKILL 5

Calculating with Functions

- Finding help for functions
- Writing functions with their arguments
- Using the AutoSum tool
- Exploring popular functions from a variety of categories
- Using the Paste Function command
- Using the Formula Palette

If you're new to using Excel, the term *function* may be a bit intimidating, but you may have used functions without being aware of doing so. For example, if you've used the SUM formula in Word to total the cells in a table, you were using a function. In Excel, a function is simply a shortcut for a series of calculations.

Similar to the SUM formula in Word, the SUM function in Excel adds one or more cells or values. For example,

```
=SUM(A1:B5,C20,C25;3.14)
```

returns the total for all numeric values in the range A1:B5, all the numeric values in cells C20 and C25, and the number 3.14. It serves as a shortcut for writing the following tedious formula

```
=A1+A2+A3+A4+A5+B1+º
```

Excel includes hundreds of functions that perform a variety of operations. To access all of them, you need the Analysis ToolPak. Choose Tools ➤ Add-Ins to open the Add-Ins dialog box. If Analysis ToolPak is not checked, you'll need to install it. (You'll need the CD from which you installed Excel.)

Getting Help with Functions

Typically, you will probably never use more than a few dozen functions. I suggest that you learn how to get the most out of those and worry about the others when you need them. Once you're experienced with several functions, you'll find it easy to pick up new ones, especially when you take advantage of the following Excel tools.

The first is the Paste Function dialog box (choose Insert ➤ Function to open it), which lets you choose a function from a list of all functions in Excel and describes the syntax and usage for each one.

After you select a function in the Paste Function dialog box, the Formula Palette steps you through the process of entering the function arguments. (Arguments are explained in the next section, and the section "Getting Assistance in Selecting and Entering Functions," later in this skill, discusses the Paste Function dialog box and the Formula Palette in detail.)

You should also take advantage of Excel's extensive Help system, which provides a description, syntax, and examples of just about every function. You can access Help in several ways:

- Choose Help ➤ Microsoft Excel Help, and then click the Index tab. In the Type Keyword field, type **function** to display a list of functions. Double-click a function to display an explanation of what it is and does in the pane on the right, as shown in Figure 5.1. If you know the function name, you can type it in the Type Keyword field and go directly to the topic.

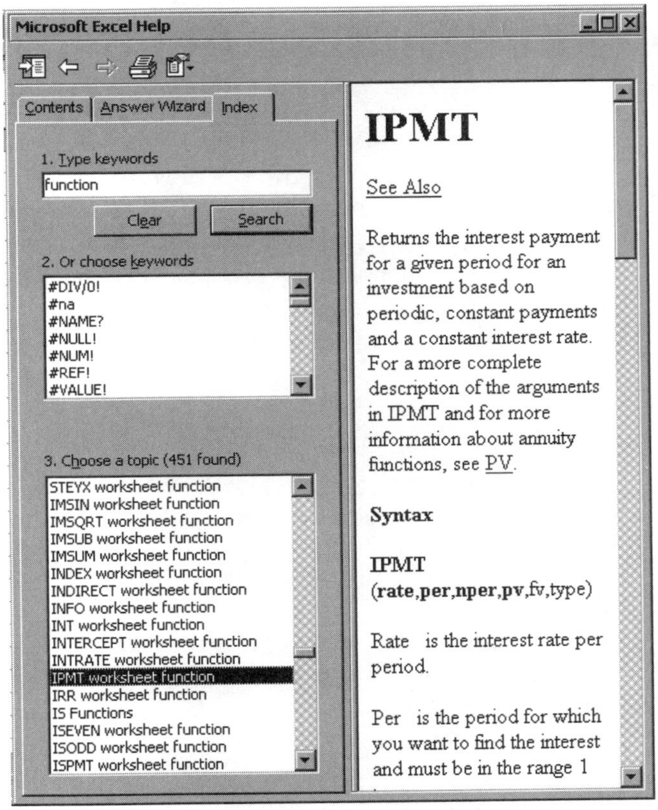

FIGURE 5.1: This Help screen describes the IPMT function.

- In Microsoft Excel Help, click the Contents tab, and then click the plus sign next to Creating Formulas and Auditing Workbooks. Browse through some of the function-related topics, such as Using Functions and Worksheet Function Reference. Clicking a topic in the left pane displays it in the right pane.

- Click the Answer Wizard tab, and in the What Would You Like to Do field, type a task, for example, "Calculate a mortgage payment," and then click the Search button or press Enter.
- In the Paste Function dialog box, select a function category, select a function from the list, and press F1 to display that topic in Microsoft Excel Help.

Dealing with Function Arguments

The function name is always followed by a pair of parentheses. Most functions also require one or more *arguments*, or *parameters*, within the parentheses, which define the scope of the function. Some functions take several arguments; some are required, and some are optional. You separate arguments with a comma.

An argument may consist of a number, text, a cell reference that returns a number or text, a cell in another workbook, a keyboard, and so on. *List* can be one or more arguments, each separated by a comma.

For example, the function

```
=NOW()
```

returns the current date and time and takes no arguments. The function

```
=SUM(A1:B5,C20,C25,199)
```

requires at least one argument and returns the sum of the numbers in those arguments. In this case, the function adds the numbers in three ranges plus the number 199.

An argument that is a range of cells, such as A1:B5, will automatically expand or contract as you insert or delete rows within that range. For example, if you insert two rows at row 2, the formula above would then reference A1:B7. Here's a function that takes two different types of arguments:

```
=CELL("format",A1)
```

Its first argument must be a keyword. In this example, the keyword "format" returns the numeric format of the cell that is referenced, such as G for General. The second argument must be a cell address, range name, or a natural language cell reference (as discussed in Skill 4). For more information about the CELL function, see the "Using Information Functions" section later in this skill. The CELL function does *not* automatically update when the cell it references changes, for example, when you apply a different numeric format to that cell. However, the function is updated at the next automatic recalculation for other formulas or when you press F9 to recalculate manually.

An argument can also consist of a formula or another function, so you can *nest* functions within functions. The only requirement is that the result of the nested formula or function be of the correct type for that argument. For example, the formula

```
=SUM(A1,B1,DATE(96,12,31))
```

contains a nested DATE function, whose resulting value would be used as one of the arguments for SUM. Keep an eye on those parentheses when you have functions within functions.

Now we'll take a look at a variety of functions that illustrate the scope of Excel's power.

Quick Totals with AutoSum

Since summing cells with the SUM function is such a common task, Excel provides the AutoSum tool for doing the job with the click of a button. Here's how quick and easy summing can be.

Figure 5.2 shows the housing expenses worksheet that we've looked at in earlier skills. In Figure 5.2, however, it lacks the formulas in column H and row 10 for the totals. Here's how AutoSum can insert the formulas for you:

	A	B	C	D	E	F	G	H	I
1		Monthly Housing Expenses							
2									
3		Jan	Feb	Mar	Apr	May	Jun	Total	
4	Insurance	51	51	51	51	51	51		
5	Maintenance	48	48	48	48	48	48		
6	Mortgage	925	925	925	925	925	925		
7	Taxes	102	102	102	102	102	102		
8	Telephone	42	78	65	115	70	67		
9	Utilities	182	116	143	90	175	185		
10	Total								
11									

FIGURE 5.2: You can create multiple SUM functions with one click of the AutoSum button.

1. Select all the data you want to sum and include the blank cells in the adjacent column to the right and the row below, which is the range B4:H10.

2. Click the AutoSum button or press Alt+=, its shortcut, and the job is done.

The SUM functions that appear in B10:G10 and H4:H10 are no different from the ones you would get if you had created the functions "by hand." It's just a lot faster to let Excel do the work.

In the previous example, you selected both the data and the blank cells for the SUM functions. That's often the best method, because both you and AutoSum will know exactly what should be done.

But you can let AutoSum determine which cells to sum if you select only the blank cells for the formulas. Select a row of blank cells to sum the data above that row or select a column of blank cells to sum the data in the rows to the left.

Using Math and Trigonometry Functions

The Math and Trigonometry category includes many functions that you find on an everyday scientific calculator, plus many that go far beyond day-to-day calculations.

ABS(number)

This function returns the absolute value of its single numeric parameter, making that number a positive one. Suppose you have two cells A1 and A2; each contains a date, and you want a formula that determines the number of days between the two dates but always returns the result as a positive number. The ABS function does the trick:

```
=ABS(A1-A2)
```

No matter which number is bigger (or which date is the more recent), the result is always positive.

COS(number)

This function returns the cosine of its single numeric argument. COS and the other trigonometric functions work with radians, not degrees. You can take advantage of another Excel function, RADIANS, to convert degrees to radians.

For example, this formula returns the cosine of 45 degrees:

```
=COS(RADIANS(45))
```

PI()

You can probably remember the first 3 or 4 decimal places of pi, but the PI function returns the first 14 and saves you some typing. It takes no arguments, but be sure to append the pair of parentheses.

Here's the formula for finding the volume of a cylinder that is 5 meters in diameter and 8 meters tall:

```
=PI()*(5/2)^2*8
```

INT(number)

The INT function returns the integer portion of its numeric argument, so

```
=INT(PI())
```

returns 3. To produce today's date number without the associated time value, use

```
=INT(NOW())
```


which is also equivalent to the TODAY function.

INT always rounds down to the nearest integer. If you are working with a negative number,

```
=INT(-5.3)
```

returns –6. If you simply want to truncate a number without any rounding, use the TRUNC function:

```
=TRUNC(-5.3)
```

which returns 5.

RAND()

This function is convenient when you need to generate a random number. By itself, it returns a random number greater than or equal to zero and less than one. Generally, you will be multiplying it by some other value to create a larger random number. The formula

```
=100*RAND()
```

returns a random number greater than or equal to zero, but less than 100.

TIP TIP TIP TIP TIP TIP TIP TIP TIP TIP TIP TIP TIP TIP TIP TIP TIP TIP TIP TIP TIP TIP TIP TIP TIP

The RAND function returns a new random number every time the worksheet recalculates. But you can lock in a random value by converting the formula to a number. One way to do so is to edit the formula, press F9 (the Calc key), and then press Enter. To "freeze" a range of RAND formulas, choose Edit ➤ Paste Special to open the Paste Special dialog box, and select the Values options, as discussed in Skill 3.

ROMAN(number,form)

This fun function converts its numeric argument into the equivalent Roman numeral (as a text value), so that the formula

```
="The current year is "&ROMAN(YEAR(NOW()))
```

returns

```
The current year is MCMXCIX
```

in the year 1999.

If you don't include the *style* argument, the Roman numeral appears in the traditional style. If you do include a style number from 1 to 4, Excel uses a more concise version of the Roman numeral. For example, in the year 1999, the formula

```
="The current year is "&ROMAN(YEAR(NOW()),2)
```

returns

```
The current year is MXMIX
```

SQRT(number)

This function returns the square root of its numeric argument and is equivalent to =*number*^0.5. To find the length of the hypotenuse of a right triangle whose two other legs are 3 and 4 units in length, use the formula

```
=SQRT(3^2+4^2)
```

which returns 5. If *number* is not a positive value, the result will be invalid and will return #NUM!. To avoid this situation, use the ABS function to ensure that *number* is positive.

Using Date and Time Functions

In Skill 2, you learned how to enter and format dates and times in Excel so that you can later sort them or perform date arithmetic with them. Here are some of Excel's functions that help you enter or manipulate dates and times.

DATE(year,month,day)

This function takes three numeric parameters: the year (from 1900 through 9999), month, and day. It returns the appropriate Excel value that represents that date. For example,

```
=DATE(99,12,31)
```

displays the date 12/31/99 with the underlying date value of 36525.

NOTE NOTE NOTE NOTE NOTE NOTE NOTE NOTE NOTE NOTE NOTE NOTE NOTE NOTE NOTE

You can use either a two-digit or four-digit year number, such as 99 or 1999. For the year 2000 and beyond, you can use either a three-digit or four-digit year, such as 100 for the year 2000 and 200 for the year 2100 (if that begins to look a little odd, stick with four-digit years). If you're already planning for the next millennium, you have to use a four-digit number for years 3000 and beyond.

For example, you have a worksheet in which dates are entered in three parts in columns A, B, and C. A day is in A2, a month is in B2, and a year is in C2. You can use the Date function to build a complete date in D2:

```
=DATE(C2,B2,A2)
```

	A	B	C	D	E
1	Day	Month	Year	Date	
2	31	12	1999	12/31/99	
3					

YEAR(serial_number)

This function looks at its numeric argument as a date value and returns the year that corresponds to that date. The formula

```
=YEAR(36187)
```

returns 1999 because 36187 is the date number for the date January 27, 1999. If that is also the current date, the formula

```
=YEAR(NOW())
```

returns 1999.

You can also use the functions MONTH and DAY to return the month and day of the numeric argument.

NOW()

This function returns the current date and time, based on your computer's internal clock. At noon on December 31, 1999, this function returns 12/31/99 12:00, with the underlying date and time value of 36525.5.

Like the other date and time functions, NOW is updated only when the worksheet recalculates, so you won't see a new date or time updated continuously.

TIME(hour,minute,second)

This function takes an hour, a minute, and a second as its parameters and returns an Excel time value, formatted as a time. For example:

```
=TIME(18,30,0)
```

returns the time value for 6:30 PM.

TIP TIP TIP TIP TIP TIP TIP TIP TIP TIP TIP TIP TIP TIP TIP TIP TIP TIP TIP TIP TIP TIP TIP TIP TIP

Remember from Skill 2 that Excel counts time as a fraction of 24 hours, so time values run from 0 (midnight) to 0.99999 (11:59:59 PM).

The functions HOUR, MINUTE, and SECOND return those components of their single numeric arguments, so the formula

```
=HOUR(0.75)
```

returns 18 because 0.75 is the time value for 6:00 PM.

WEEKDAY(serial_number,return_type)

This function returns a number that represents a day of the week. Its first argument is a date number and is required. The formula

```
=WEEKDAY(DATE(99,12,31))
```

returns 6 because December 31, 1999, is a Friday.

By default, the WEEKDAY function counts days from Sunday (1) to Saturday (7). You can use its optional second parameter to change the day numbering. Enter a 2 to count from Monday (1) to Sunday (7) or a 3 to count from Monday (0) to Sunday (6).

TIP TIP TIP TIP TIP TIP TIP TIP TIP TIP TIP TIP TIP TIP TIP TIP TIP TIP TIP TIP TIP TIP TIP TIP TIP TIP

This function's result is simply a number, not a day of the week or a date value. If you want the day of the week displayed for a date, create a custom numeric format for that cell, as described in Skill 6.

Using Text Functions

You can't add one text item to another, but you can join them by concatenating them with the ampersand, as discussed in Skill 2. Excel has functions that allow you to manipulate text in some interesting ways. Don't forget, if you include text in a formula, you must enclose it within quotation marks.

LEFT(text,number_chars)

This function returns the number of characters in *text*, starting from the left, that you specify in *number*. The following

```
=LEFT("Gordon",5)
```

returns *Gordo*. The RIGHT function works the same way, but returns characters starting from the right of *text*.

The MID function returns characters from anywhere within *text*. You specify the starting point and how many characters you want, so

```
=MID("Gordon",2,3)
```

returns *ord*.

TIP TIP TIP TIP TIP TIP TIP TIP TIP TIP TIP TIP TIP TIP TIP TIP TIP TIP TIP TIP TIP TIP TIP TIP TIP TIP

You may be familiar with another spreadsheet program in which the MID function counts the first character in *text* as number 0. In Excel, the first character is number 1.

LEN(text)

This function simply returns the number of characters in *text;* for example:

```
=LEN("Gordon")
```

returns 6.

Here's a way to use the LEN function to truncate each text entry in the range A10:A50 so that the formula's result (a text value) displays the same number of characters as the text entry in cell A1. You could enter the following formula in B10 to produce the correct result and then copy the formula from B11 to B50:

```
=LEFT(A10,LEN($A$1))
```

LOWER(text)

This function simply converts *text* to all lowercase; for example:

```
=LOWER("Gordon S.")
```

returns

```
gordon s.
```

Use UPPER and PROPER to convert to all uppercase or propercase (each word begins with a capital letter).

TEXT(value,format_text)

As described in Skill 2, Excel lets you include numbers within a text value. For example, if cell A1 contains 12345.6, the formula:

```
="Cell A1 contains "&A1
```

returns *Cell A1 contains 12345.6.*

But with the TEXT function, you can convert a number into plain text while also formatting it as specified with the *format* argument. If you rewrote the above formula like this:

```
="Cell A1 contains "&TEXT(A1,"$#,###.00")
```

it would return *Cell A1 contains $12,345.60.*

TIP TIP TIP TIP TIP TIP TIP TIP TIP TIP TIP TIP TIP TIP TIP TIP TIP TIP TIP TIP TIP TIP TIP TIP TIP

The codes for the numeric format argument are the same codes you use to define a custom format, as described in Skill 6.

You can also use the DOLLAR function as a shortcut for transforming a number into text with a currency format with two decimal places.

```
="Cell A1 contains "&DOLLAR(A1)
```

would return *Cell A1 contains $12,345.60.*

Here's a formula that tells you what percentage of the day is done, to two decimal places:

```
=TEXT(NOW()-TODAY(),"0.00%")
```

Using Logical Functions

Each function in this group returns a TRUE or FALSE result, which in computer terms can also be represented by a 1 or a 0. You can create a simple logical formula by including an equals sign or other logical operator to express a comparison within the formula. For example:

```
=(10+5)=16
```

returns FALSE because the expression is not true, while:

```
=100>99
```

returns TRUE.

IF(logical_test,value_if_true,value_if_false)

IF is a powerful function that has many uses. Its result will be either the *value_if_true* or *value_if_false* argument, depending on whether the value, or *condition,* is true or false. For example:

```
IF(3>2,5,10)
```

returns 5 because the condition 3 > 2 is true. The following formula:

```
=IF(TODAY()=DATE(99,1,1),"Happy New Year","")
```

returns a greeting on January 1, 1999; otherwise, it returns an empty, or null, result (represented by a pair of quotation marks with nothing between them).

TIP TIP TIP TIP TIP TIP TIP TIP TIP TIP TIP TIP TIP TIP TIP TIP TIP TIP TIP TIP TIP TIP TIP TIP TIP

You don't have to wait for New Year's Day to test this formula's true condition. After you enter it in the cell, edit it and change the = to another logical operator, such as < >, for not equal to. Then you'll see the true argument used as the result.

You can be even more specific by nesting IF functions within IF functions, up to seven levels deep:

```
IF(condition1,true1,IF(condition2,true2,false2))
```

This formula says "if condition1 is true, return true1; otherwise, evaluate the second IF function, and if condition2 is true, return true2; otherwise return false2."

Some functions in the Information category also return results of TRUE or FALSE. For example, these three functions:

```
=ISBLANK(A1)
=ISNUMBER(A1)
=ISTEXT(A1)
```

return TRUE if cell A1 is blank, contains a number, or contains text. Otherwise, each displays FALSE.

Using Financial Functions

Excel has dozens of financial functions that can calculate the monthly payment on a loan, the depreciation allowance, the yield of a Treasury bill, or the effective interest rate. Many of these functions are part of the Analysis ToolPak add-in that I mentioned at the beginning of this skill.

NOTE NOTE NOTE NOTE NOTE NOTE NOTE NOTE NOTE NOTE NOTE NOTE NOTE NOTE

In most financial functions that include an interest rate, you enter the interest rate as the per-period rate. If the function calculates the monthly payment on a loan, for example, you enter the interest as 1/12 of the annual rate. If the payments are to be made quarterly, you use one-fourth of the annual rate.

PMT(rate,nper,pv,fv,type)

This function calculates the payment due to pay down a loan or build up a savings account; the last two arguments are optional.

Here's how to find the payment amount for a loan of $50,000 (*pv*) at 11 percent annual interest to be paid back monthly over 5 years (*nper*):

```
=PMT(11%/12,5*12,50000)
```

It returns –1087.12, the monthly payment amount, which includes both interest and principal. Both the interest and the term are calculated on a monthly basis.

If you omit the *type* argument or enter a 0 for it, the payment is calculated as being made at the end of each period. Enter a 1 if the payment is to be made at the beginning of the period. The *fv* argument is the future value that you want the payments to result in after the final payment. If you omit *fv* (as in the preceding example), it is assumed to be 0.

PPMT(rate,per,nper,pv,fv,type)

This function calculates the principal portion of a payment; the IPMT function calculates the interest portion and takes the same arguments. When both are used with the same arguments, their total should equal the result of the PMT function.

In the *per* argument, enter the period for which you want to calculate the principal. For a loan, the first period would have very little principal, and the last period should be just about all principal. As in the PMT function, the *fv* and *type* arguments are optional.

Use the following functions to calculate the principal and interest portions of the first monthly payment from the example for the PMT function:

```
=PPMT(11%/12,1,5*12,50000)
=IPMT(11%/12,1,5*12,50000)
```

The principal is –628.79, and the interest is –458.33, for a total payment of –1087.12.

EFFECT(nominal_rate,npery)

This function calculates the annual effective yield of a nominal rate of interest, given the number of compounding periods per year. When the annual interest rate is 5 percent and the interest is compounded monthly, the effective rate is

```
=EFFECT(5%,12)
```

which returns 5.12%. This means that compounding 5 percent interest monthly yields an annual rate of 5.12 percent. To calculate the nominal interest rate given the effective rate, use:

```
=NOMINAL(0.0512,12)
```

which returns 5.00%.

SLN(cost,salvage,life)

The straight-line depreciation function returns the amount of depreciation for an asset based on its cost, its salvage value at the end of the depreciation period, and the life of the asset.

Here's a formula to calculate the annual depreciation of a $10,000 asset over 5 years; it will have a salvage value of $1,500 at the end of its life:

```
=SLN(10000,1500,5)
```

This returns $1,700. If you multiply that by 5 you get $8,500 in total depreciation, the difference between the cost and the salvage.

TBILLYIELD(settlement, maturity, pr)

This function calculates the yield on a Treasury bill. The *settlement* argument is the date you buy it, *maturity* is the date on which the bill matures, and *price* is the amount you paid per $100 of face value.

If you buy a $10,000 T-bill for $9,650 on January 1, 1999, and it matures on June 30, 1999, your yield is:

```
=TBILLYIELD(DATE(99,1,1),DATE(99,6,30),96.50)
```

which returns 0.0725, or 7.25 percent. Excel also includes the TBILLPRICE function, which calculates a T-bill's discount price, and the TBILLEQ function, which calculates its bond-equivalent yield.

Using Database Functions

Excel has a group of database functions that perform their operations selectively, on just the data that matches the criteria you specify. Each function name begins with a D and includes operations such as DSUM, DCOUNT, and DAVERAGE.

NOTE NOTE NOTE NOTE NOTE NOTE NOTE NOTE NOTE NOTE NOTE NOTE NOTE NOTE NOTE

To use a database function, the data on which it operates must be laid out as an Excel database, or list. Each column of data must have a unique column title over it and contain the same type of data, and each row is considered a separate "record." Plus, you should understand how to write the criteria needed to perform a query on the database. All these are discussed in Skill 12.

All the database functions have the same syntax, such as:

```
=DSUM(database,field,criteria)
```

The three arguments are:

Database The database range whose data will be the source of the function's operation, including the column titles row and the data beneath it.

Field The column number within the database range (a field) on which the function should operate; the first column of the range is number 1.

Criteria The range that contains your criteria, which the function uses to select the rows (records) in the database on which it will operate.

Figure 5.3 shows a simple example of a database function that illustrates how they all work (the two key ranges in the figure are shaded). The database is in the range D1:E9, and the criteria reside in G1:G2. The DSUM function in cell B1 looks like this:

```
=DSUM(D1:E9,2,G1:G2)
```

	A	B	C	D	E	F	G	H	I
1	**Total for Nutmeg:**	**20**		Name	Amount		Name		
2				Sugar	4		Nutmeg		
3				Nutmeg	5				
4				Sugar	4				
5				Cinnamon	3				
6				Nutmeg	5				
7				Nutmeg	5				
8				Sugar	4				
9				Nutmeg	5				
10									

FIGURE 5.3: A DSUM database function (B1) works on a database (D1:E9), operating on only those rows that match the criteria (G1:G2).

Its column reference, 2, refers to the second column in the database, column E.

Therefore, the function looks for each record that matches the criteria ("Nutmeg" in the data's Name column) and sums the value found in the second column for that record. The total is 20. If you change the word in G2 to Sugar, the function returns 12.

TIP

The text in cell A1 in Figure 5.3 is actually a formula that includes the criteria cell G2 and looks like this: ="Total for "&D2&":". This is a good example of why text formulas are so handy—when you change the criterion to Sugar, for example, the formula automatically updates its result to *Total for Sugar.*

The SUBTOTAL function is also used with a worksheet database, but does not take criteria. It's a powerful tool that you will generally use in conjunction with the Data ➤ Subtotals command, which is discussed in Skill 12.

Using Information Functions

These functions return information about data, cells, and Excel. They're handy tools for revealing underlying structure that might not otherwise be seen.

CELL(info_type,reference) and INFO(type_text)

You can choose from several types of information for the type argument in both the CELL and INFO functions. Figure 5.4 shows several examples of these formulas. The formulas themselves are displayed in column C, and their results are shown in column D.

	A	B	C	D	E	F	G	H
1	5.50%		=CELL("address",A1)	$A$1				
2			=CELL("filename",A1)	D:\Excel book\Gene's files\[f0504.xls]Sheet1				
3			=CELL("format",A1)	P2				
4			=CELL("type",A1)	v				
5			=CELL("width",A1)	8				
6								
7			=INFO("directory")	D:\Excel book\Gene's files\				
8			=INFO("memavail")	1048576				
9			=INFO("osversion")	Windows (32-bit) 4.10				
10								

FIGURE 5.4: The functions CELL and INFO return information about the workbook, its contents, and its environment.

To see a list of the available arguments you can use, look up the CELL and INFO functions in Excel's Help system.

COUNTBLANK(range)

This function is a quick way to find out how many blank cells are in a range. It's similar to the COUNTA function, which returns the count of the nonblank cells in the range.

IS*function* name(value)

Several functions begin with IS and return a logical result, either TRUE or FALSE. The IS functions allow you to test cells or data to find out something about them (look up one of them in Excel's Help system to see a list of all of them).

The ISBLANK function, for example, takes a cell address or range as its argument and returns TRUE if the cell is blank or FALSE if it is not blank. The result is TRUE if one or more cells in a referenced range are blank.

The ISNUMBER function returns TRUE if its argument is a number (or a cell address that contains a number) and FALSE if it is anything else.

TIP TIP TIP TIP TIP TIP TIP TIP TIP TIP TIP TIP TIP TIP TIP TIP TIP TIP TIP TIP TIP TIP TIP TIP TIP

Although you can mix text and numbers in many formulas, that won't work for IS functions. If you enter text that looks like a number in a cell, such as ="123.4", the ISNUMBER function returns FALSE.

The ISERR function is a good one for testing the results of formulas that might return an error, such as division by zero or an invalid address. This formula

```
=IF(ISERR(A1/A2),0,A1/A2)
```

checks the result of dividing A1 by A2. If that result is an error, the IF condition is TRUE and Excel returns a 0. If the division does not produce an error, the division is performed and Excel returns its result.

NA()

This function returns the value #N/A, which stands for "not available." You can also enter that value directly in a cell to get the same result. The function or the value can serve as a placeholder, indicating that you don't yet have the necessary data for a cell.

Any formula that refers to that cell also returns #N/A. So if you see that result popping up anywhere in the workbook, remember that somewhere at least one datum or formula is not yet available.

TIP TIP TIP TIP TIP TIP TIP TIP TIP TIP TIP TIP TIP TIP TIP TIP TIP TIP TIP TIP TIP TIP TIP TIP TIP

In Skill 9, you can read about tracking down the source of #N/A and error-related results.

Using Lookup and Reference Functions

Instead of performing some advanced calculations with their arguments, the Lookup and Reference functions simply pick up a result from either a list of arguments or a range of cells in the worksheet.

CHOOSE (index_num,value1,value2,...)

This function returns one of the items in *list*, as determined by the *index* number. The first item in *list* is at position 1, the second is 2, and so on. If cell A1 contains the number 3, the formula

```
=CHOOSE(A1,"Jim","Chris","Fran","Suzanne","Jeremy")
```

returns *Fran*.

> TIP TIP TIP TIP TIP TIP TIP TIP TIP TIP TIP TIP TIP TIP TIP TIP TIP TIP TIP TIP TIP TIP TIP TIP TIP
>
> **If the index value is greater than the number of items in the list or less than or equal to 0, the formula results in #VALUE!.**

CHOOSE can also select a range reference, as in this formula:

```
=SUM(CHOOSE(MONTH(NOW()),A1:A10,B1:B10,C1:C10, D1:D10,...))
```

The SUM function sums one of the ranges listed, depending on the current month number. In March, for example, the MONTH(NOW()) portion returns 3, so CHOOSE would select the third range and the formula would be equivalent to

```
=SUM(C1:C10)
```

VLOOKUP(lookup_value,table_array,col_index_num,range_lookup)

You can look up an item in a range of cells with VLOOKUP. It's a handy way to find a result based on varying input values for *lookup_value* and *table_array*, which can be numeric or text arguments (or cells that contain numbers or text, of course).

VLOOKUP looks in the first column of *table_array* for the largest value that is not greater than *lookup_value* and returns the contents of the cell to the right of it in the column specified by *index_num*. The HLOOKUP function is essentially the same, but it looks in the first row of *lookup_value* and then goes down the rows to find the item.

> TIP TIP TIP TIP TIP TIP TIP TIP TIP TIP TIP TIP TIP TIP TIP TIP TIP TIP TIP TIP TIP TIP TIP TIP TIP
>
> **You might want to try out Excel's Lookup Wizard the first few times you use the Vlookup function. It walks you through the process of specifying the range, the index number, and the column. Choose Tools ➤ Wizard ➤ Lookup; if you don't see Lookup on the menu, you'll need to choose Tools ➤ Add-ins and select the Lookup Wizard in the Add-ins dialog box.**

One thing to keep in mind when you're using either of these functions is that if the data in the first column of *range* (or in the first row for HLOOKUP) is not sorted in ascending order (A to Z, 1 to 10), the function will not be able to look up a value and will return #N/A.

In the event that the first column (or row) is unsorted, you can include a 0 (or FALSE) as a fourth parameter to the VLOOKUP or HLOOKUP function to specify exact matches only. This consideration is especially important when the first column of *lookup_value* has text and not numbers as the items to look up, because with text, generally only an exact match makes any sense.

You can use VLOOKUP to create tax tables and other lookup tables. Figure 5.5 shows a sample tax calculation table (a very simplified one). You enter the salary earned in cell B1 (for example, 32,500) and the number of exemptions in B2 (for example, 3). In cell B3, the formula

```
=VLOOKUP(B1,B6:G11,B2+1)
```

performs the calculation.

	A	B	C	D	E	F	G	H	I
1	**Income**	32,500							
2	**Exemptions**	3							
3	**Tax Due**	4,070							
4					**Exemptions**				
5		**Income**	1	2	3	4	5		
6		30,000	4,350	4,200	4,050	3,900	3,750		
7		31,000	4,360	4,210	4,060	3,910	3,760		
8		32,000	4,370	4,220	4,070	3,920	3,770		
9		33,000	4,380	4,230	4,080	3,930	3,780		
10		34,000	4,390	4,240	4,090	3,940	3,790		
11		35,000	4,400	4,250	4,100	3,950	3,800		
12									

FIGURE 5.5: The VLOOKUP function looks up the value in the first column of the table and returns the result from that row.

It looks up the largest salary in the first column (B) of the range (B6:G11) that is not greater than the value in B1 (this is 32,000). The formula then looks across that row for the column number that matches B2 plus 1 (4), which is column E. It then returns the value found there (cell E8): 4,070. In this case, 1 was added to the column number in the formula because we would not want an exemption of 1 to return a value from the very first column of the range.

Getting Assistance in Selecting and Entering Functions

Excel offers several ways to help you find, decipher, and use any of its hundreds of functions. It will give you a quick reminder about the arguments that are needed in a function or take you through the whole process of selecting a function and entering each of its arguments.

Pasting the Function Arguments

Here's a neat trick when you've used a function before but still need a quick reminder. Type a function in a cell (either alone or within another function or formula), but before you enter any of the arguments, press Ctrl+Shift+A. This pastes the names of the arguments into the function to remind you of what is needed.

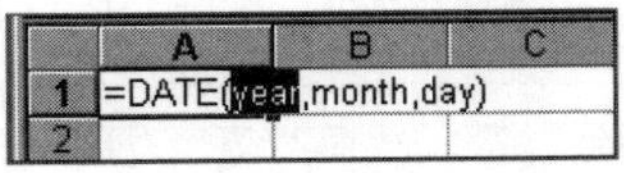

For example, in cell A1 type **=DATE** and then press Ctrl+Shift+A. You'll see the argument names appear in the function in their proper order. You can then either delete them or overwrite each one with the actual arguments.

Finish the DATE function in cell A1 so that it will be available for the example in the next section: **=DATE(99,12,31)**.

Using the Paste Function Command, the Formula Palette, and the Office Assistant

The Paste Function dialog box, along with help from the ever-watchful Office Assistant, makes it a snap to find the right function and use it correctly. Even experienced Excel users benefit when they pop up the Paste Function dialog box for a quick reminder on the exact spelling, syntax, and arguments for one of Excel's hundreds of functions.

You can use the Paste Function dialog box to:

- Find a function in a list of functions that are arranged alphabetically within categories.
- Get immediate help from the Office Assistant on selecting and using a function.
- Get more assistance while entering the arguments for the function.

Finding a Function

When you want to use a function but aren't quite sure of its spelling, syntax, or the types of arguments it takes, or if the function you think you need even exists, the Paste Function command and Office Assistant can lend a hand.

In the previous section, you entered a DATE function into A1 that returned the date 12/31/99. Here's the formula you want to create now in cell B1, shown here on two lines for clarity:

```
=IF(A1=TODAY(),"Happy New Millennium!",
"Still "&ABS(TODAY()-A1)&" days to go")
```

Select cell B1 and, with the Office Assistant open, either choose Insert ➤ Function (Shift+F3) or click the Paste Function button on the toolbar to open the Paste Function dialog box, as shown in Figure 5.6.

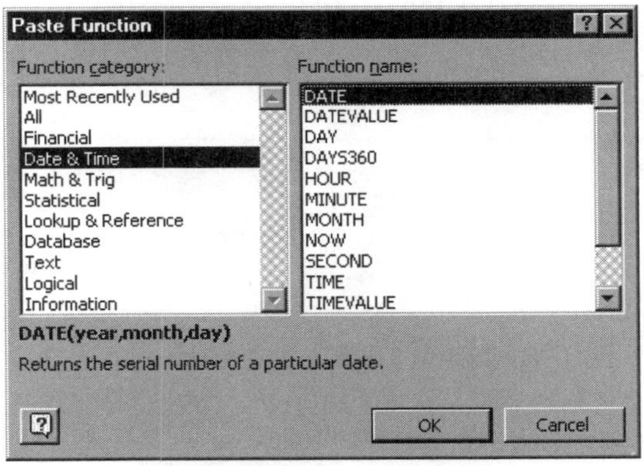

FIGURE 5.6: The Paste Function dialog box displays a list of all the functions in Excel, arranged alphabetically by category.

You can now find the function you want in several ways:

- The Office Assistant will ask if you want help choosing a function. Click Yes in its dialog box, and you'll have two choices. You can click the Help on Selected Function button to display help on the currently selected function. If you're not sure which function you want, enter a description of what you would like and let the Office Assistant suggest a few functions. (They will appear in the Paste Function dialog box under a category called Recommended.)

- Select a category in the Function Category list on the left side of the Paste Function dialog box, and then select a function from the Function Name list. The syntax and a description of the currently selected function appear beneath the lists, which may be all the reminding you need in order to choose the right one.
- Select the Most Recently Used category, which lists only the functions you've selected from the list within the not-too-distant past.

For this example, select the Logical category in the Paste Function dialog box, choose the IF function from the Function Name list, and then click OK. Now another dialog box opens that will help you enter the arguments for the function, as discussed in the next section.

Entering Arguments in the Formula Palette

Selecting a function from the Paste Function dialog box opens the Formula Palette dialog box, in which you enter each argument for the function. Figure 5.7 shows this for the IF function.

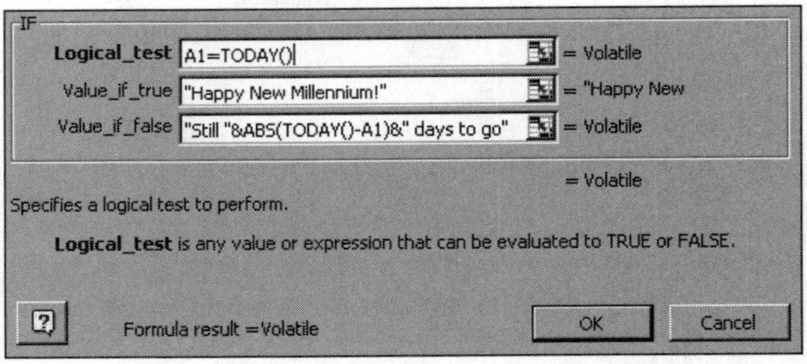

FIGURE 5.7: The Formula Palette dialog box for entering the arguments for a function

All the arguments for the function are listed with an edit field next to each one. As you select a field to enter an argument, you'll see a description of it in the lower part of the dialog box. You'll also see the formula being constructed in the Formula bar as you enter each argument.

When you are finished with the arguments and click OK, they are placed into the function in the cell. A comma is entered automatically between each one, and quotation marks surround any textual arguments. This is a lot easier than trying to enter all the arguments in one formula while keeping track of their order in the function and of the commas, parentheses, and quotation marks. Remember there's a Help button in the dialog box, which takes you directly to the help screen for the function in question.

TIP TIP TIP TIP TIP TIP TIP TIP TIP TIP TIP TIP TIP TIP TIP TIP TIP TIP TIP TIP TIP TIP TIP TIP TIP TIP

You can also access the Formula Palette for an existing formula by selecting the cell and clicking the Paste Function button or pressing Shift+F3.

Now let's get to work entering the arguments for the IF function that was shown earlier.

1. In the Formula Palette dialog box for the IF function, select the field for the first argument, logical_test.
2. Type **A1** into the field or click cell A1 in the worksheet (you can move the Formula Palette dialog box, if necessary). Notice that the result of this argument is displayed to its right. The result says TRUE because this is the conditional portion of the IF function, and so far the condition is true (not zero).
3. Type an equals sign after A1 in the field.
4. Enter the function **TODAY()**. Notice that the result displayed to the right of this field is now Volatile, meaning that there is no firm result at this point.
5. In the second argument field, value_if_true, enter the text value **Happy New Millennium!**.
6. In the third argument, value_if_false, enter the following somewhat long formula.

```
"Still "&ABS(TODAY()-A1)&" days to go"
```

Note that there is a space after *Still* and before *days to go*. Watch those quotation marks; in this case Excel won't know where you want them to go.

7. Click OK to enter this formula in B2, and you're done.

If your computer's clock thinks the current date is anything except 12/31/99, the formula's result is its FALSE statement. For example, if the current date is 3/31/99, the formula displays

```
Still 275 days to go
```

You can change the date in the function in A1 to today's date to see the IF function's result change to the TRUE statement.

NOTE NOTE NOTE NOTE NOTE NOTE NOTE NOTE NOTE NOTE NOTE NOTE NOTE NOTE NOTE

If you happen to be doing this exercise on New Year's Eve at the turn of the millennium—turn off your computer and take the rest of the day off!

Are You Experienced?

Now you can...

- ☑ Find help for functions
- ☑ Write functions with their arguments
- ☑ Use the AutoSum tool
- ☑ Explore popular functions from a variety of categories
- ☑ Use the Paste Function command and the Formula Palette

SKILL 6

Enhancing the Look of Your Work

- Changing the look of cells
- Applying formats to numbers
- Creating your own numeric formats
- Aligning entries in their cells
- Applying fonts
- Applying borders to cells
- Filling a cell with a pattern or color
- Creating a worksheet background
- Applying formats conditionally
- Using the AutoFormat command
- Working with styles
- Setting column widths and row heights

So far in this book you've learned how to enter and manipulate data, write formulas, and use Excel functions and tools to make your work fast and accurate.

Now we'll switch to what goes on "outside" the cells in the worksheet and explore some ways that you can change the look of your work without actually changing the data that's inside the cells. In Skill 13, you'll learn how to change the overall look of Excel.

Changing the Look of Cells

Excel includes a variety of features and tools that you can use to change the look of cells in a worksheet. None of them changes the data within the cells (except for one, and you'll be warned), so you're free to apply or remove these enhancements as your designs (or fickleness) dictate. In this section, I'll introduce you to these features and tools, and then in later sections of this skill, I'll discuss each in detail and give you step-by-step instructions for using them to customize your worksheets.

NOTE

As I mentioned in Skill 3, you can remove only the formatting from the selected cell or range by choosing Edit ➤ Clear ➤ Formats.

Changing Cell Formats

You use the Format Cells dialog box to make many changes in the appearance of a cell. After you select the cells you want to affect, you can access this dialog box in the following ways:

- Choose Format ➤ Cells (or press Ctrl+1).
- Right-click a selected cell, and choose Format Cells from the shortcut menu.

The Format Cells dialog box has six tabs that you use to do the following:

Number Apply a numeric format so that a number is displayed with a specific number of decimal places, for example, or as a percentage, a date, or a time.

Alignment Align an entry horizontally or vertically within its cell or at an angle; wrap a long text entry within its cell; merge multiple cells into one.

Font Change the font, size, and style for a cell or for only some characters in a cell.

Border Apply borders in several styles around any side of a cell or range.

Patterns Change the interior color or pattern of a cell.

Protection Lock or unlock a cell to prevent or allow editing or hide a cell's formula. To lock or hide a cell the worksheet must be protected. All the details are in Skill 9.

You can apply several of these cell attributes by clicking buttons on the Formatting toolbar, including font, alignment, cell borders and fill color, and font color.

Adding a Background to a Worksheet

You can choose a graphical image to serve as the background for a worksheet; choose Format ➤ Sheet ➤ Background to open the Sheet Background dialog box, and then select an image from the folder that stores your picture files. You have probably seen this technique used to good (and bad) effect while browsing the World Wide Web.

Applying Conditional Formatting

To specify the cell color, border, and font that will be applied only when the cell contents meet certain criteria, choose Format ➤ Conditional Formatting to open the Conditional Formatting dialog box. For example, you can change a cell's fill color to red when the cell contains a negative value, or you can surround the cell with borders when its value equals zero.

Using AutoFormat

You'll often build worksheets that are laid out with row and column titles to the left of and above the data you enter and with formulas to the right of and below the data. You can format such worksheets all at once so that, for example, the row and column titles are in a bold font, the data area is shaded, and the formula cells are displayed with two decimal places by choosing Format ➤ AutoFormat and then selecting a sheet format in the AutoFormat dialog box.

Applying Styles

Instead of applying numerous individual formats to a cell, you can apply them all at once with a style. A style is a named collection of formats, such as font, color, or numeric type. To apply one of Excel's built-in styles or to create or apply a style of your own design, choose Format ➤ Style, and make a selection in the Style dialog box

Creating and applying styles is a great convenience, but the really neat trick happens when you change the definition of an existing style. Any cells in the workbook to which you've already applied that style take on the new look.

Adjusting Column Width and Row Height

You can expand or contract the columns and rows in a worksheet to suit your design needs or the size of the cell entries; you can even hide specific rows and columns from view altogether. Choose the Column and Row commands on the Format menu, or use your mouse to drag columns and rows to a new size.

Copying a Format Quickly

In Skill 3, you learned how to use the Paste Special dialog box. You can use its Formats option to paste only the cell attributes (enhancements) of a source range into a target range. This is a fast way to duplicate the look of one cell in others.

In Skill 3, you also learned about a shortcut for doing this—the Format Painter button. Simply select a cell or range that has the look you want, click the Format Painter button, and select the target cells. To format multiple target ranges, double-click the Format Painter button; click it again or press Esc when you're done with it.

TIP TIP TIP TIP TIP TIP TIP TIP TIP TIP TIP TIP TIP TIP TIP TIP TIP TIP TIP TIP TIP TIP TIP TIP TIP TIP

If you plan to continue to incorporate the look of a particular cell into other cells, create a style based on that cell, as described in "Working with Styles" later in this chapter.

Applying Formats to Numbers

A cell's numeric format determines the way Excel displays a number in that cell. You can choose from variety of formats, each with its own set of options. Plus, you can create your own customized formats.

Choosing a Format

By default, a cell's numeric format is set as General. Consequently, a number is displayed much as you enter it—without separators between thousands or monetary symbols such as the dollar sign, and with only the number of decimal places that you enter or that are returned by a formula in the cell.

To change a cell's numeric format, follow these steps:

1. Select the cell.
2. Choose Format ➤ Cells to open the Format Cells dialog box.

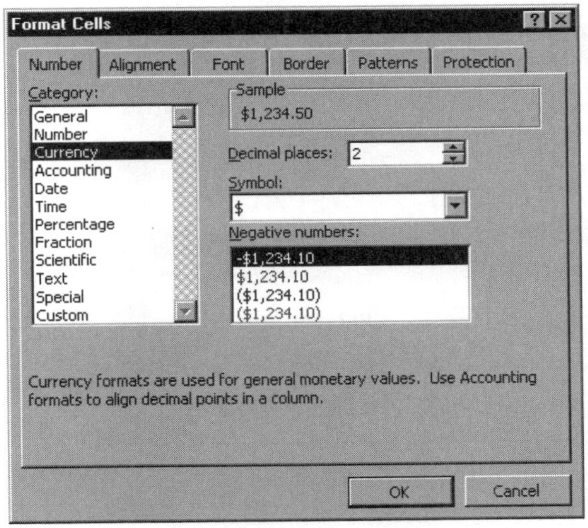

3. Click the Number tab.
4. Select a category from the Category list, and then select from the options on the right.
5. Click OK to apply those formats to the selected cell.

TIP

If you include some formatting characters (such as a currency symbol, comma, or percent sign) when you enter a number, Excel automatically formats the cell in that style. For example, if you enter the number $1,234.56, Excel applies the Currency format with two decimal places.

As you choose formats or options in the Format Cells dialog box, watch the Sample field. It shows you the effect that format will have on the number in the active cell. Table 6.1 shows a sample of each of the numeric formats.

TABLE 6.1: The Numeric Formats

Format	Options	Number	Result
General		12345.678	12345.678
Number	2 decimal places; comma	12345.678	12,345.68
Currency	2 decimal places; currency symbol	12345.678	$12,345.68
Accounting	2 decimal places; currency symbol	12345.678	$12,345.68
Date	In the m/d/y style	35795.75	12/31/97
Time	In the h:m AM/PM style	35795.75	6:00 PM
Percentage	2 decimal places	0.253	25.30%
Fraction	Up to one digit (_)	22.375	22 3/8
Scientific	2 decimal places	=PI()*10000^2	3.14E+08
Text	(shows cell contents as entered)	=PI()*10000^2	=PI()*10000^2
Special	Phone Number	8005551212	(800) 555-1212
Special	Social Security number	123456789	123-45-6789
Custom	#,### ?/? "pounds"	12345.678	12,345 2/3 pounds

A numeric format has no effect on the cell contents, so feel free to experiment and see how various formats affect the display of a number.

As I mentioned in Skill 2, if you apply a numeric format that makes a number too wide for its cell, Excel automatically widens the column as needed. But it cannot do so if the column's width has already been set manually. In that case, the number is displayed as pound signs (#####), and you can choose a more compact format, widen the column, or apply a smaller font.

To quickly change the way decimals are formatted in a selected cell, simply click the Increase Decimal or Decrease Decimal button on the Formatting toolbar.

Watch Those Decimal Places

One hazard of specifying the number of decimal places in a numeric format is the rounding that occurs to the display of the number—but not to the actual number within the cell. Who cares, as long as it looks nice, right? Well, here's what can happen.

Suppose you have ten cells, each containing the number 9.6, that you then format to show no decimal places. The format automatically rounds the display to zero decimal places, so each cell displays the number 10. If you sum those cells, however, the total is only 96. Fascinating.

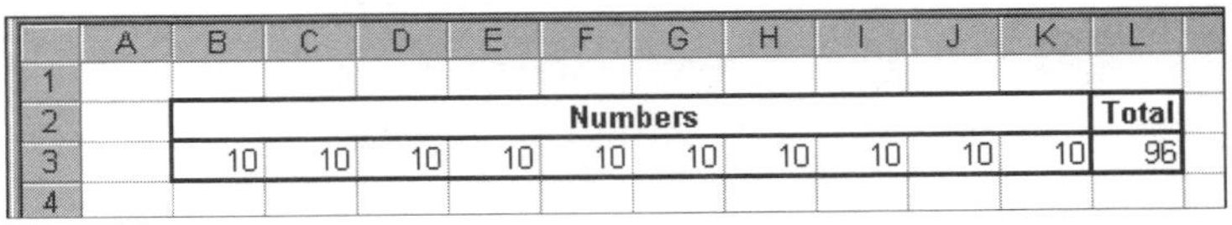

A B C D E F G H I J K L
1
2 Numbers Total
3 10 10 10 10 10 10 10 10 10 10 96
4

You can fix this problem in these ways:

- Format the numbers to show the actual number of decimal places they contain.
- If you don't want any decimal places, enter them that way, and you won't have to change the cell format.
- Use the ROUND function to round each number to the appropriate number of decimal places, such as =ROUND(9.6,0), which would result in the number 10.

In addition, you can fix this problem by using the Options dialog box. Follow these steps:

1. Choose Tools ➤ Options to open the Options dialog box.

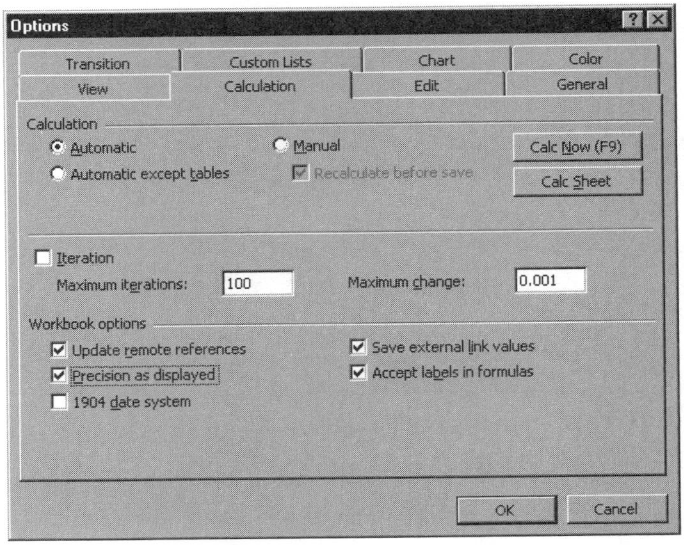

2. Click the Calculation tab.
3. In the Workbook Options section, check the Precision As Displayed check box to change all numbers in the workbook so that the number of decimal places each one contains will match the cell's numeric format.
4. Click OK.

When you enable Precision As Displayed, a cell's content matches its display. For example, if a cell's format displays no decimals, the number within the cell loses all its decimal places.

WARNING WARNING WARNING WARNING WARNING WARNING WARNING WARNING

Enabling this option actually changes all numbers in the workbook to match their displayed formats. New entries are also adjusted to match the cell formats you apply. You must clear the Precision As Displayed check box to disable it.

Creating Your Own Numeric Formats

If you just can't find an appropriate numeric format in the Format Cells dialog box, don't complain—create your own. You can customize a format in a remarkably wide range of styles. The easiest way to do this is to start with one of the built-in formats that looks something like the one you want to build.

To illustrate the process, let's create the Custom format shown earlier in Table 6.1, which displayed the number:

```
12345.678
```

like this:

```
12,345 2/3 pounds
```

Open a blank worksheet, and follow these steps:

1. Enter **12345.678** in a cell, and press Enter.
2. Choose Format ➤ Cells to open the Format Cells dialog box.
3. Click the Number tab.
4. Choose the Fraction category, and then choose *Up to one digit (1/4)* from the Type list.
5. Select Custom from the Category list. Figure 6.1 shows how the Format Cells dialog box now appears.

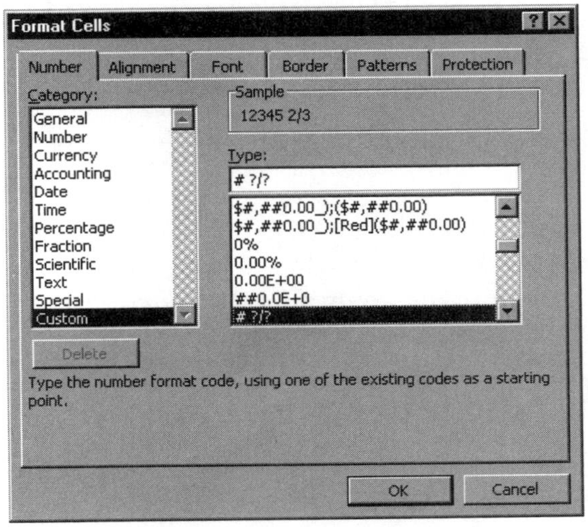

FIGURE 6.1: The Format Cells dialog box while creating a Custom format

As Figure 6.1 shows, Excel now presents you with a list of predesigned custom formats. In this case, Excel selected a custom format that incorporates the Fraction style:

```
# ?/?
```

which is also displayed above the list of custom formats in the Type field. You can expand on this format to build the new one.

TIP TIP TIP TIP TIP TIP TIP TIP TIP TIP TIP TIP TIP TIP TIP TIP TIP TIP TIP TIP TIP TIP TIP TIP TIP

In a later section in this skill, you'll read about many special formatting codes you can include in a custom format.

6. Edit the custom format in the Type field. First, we want to display a comma between thousands, which is represented by a comma as we might expect. To represent number placeholders, use the pound sign. So in this case, edit the codes to look like this: **#,### ?/?**.
7. To display text within a format, enclose it in quotes. For this example, add the text so that the resulting format codes look like this: **#,### ?/?" pounds"** (there's a space before the letter *p*).

8. That's it. The Sample field in the dialog box should be showing you how the format will look. If it's as you expected, click OK to return to the worksheet.

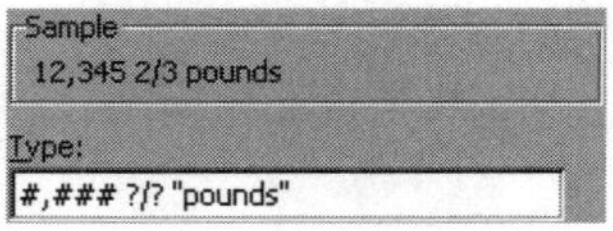

Back in the worksheet, Excel should have automatically widened the column to display the number in this new format. If not (perhaps because you already set the width of the column manually), choose Format ➤ Column ➤ AutoFit Selection to widen the column as much as needed.

Reusing Custom Formats

Each format you design appears in the Custom format list for that workbook, right below the others that come with Excel. Once your custom format is on the list, you can select it as you would any other format and apply it to any cell in the current workbook.

To transfer one of your custom formats to another workbook, follow these steps:

1. Select a cell, and use the Format Cells dialog box to apply the custom format to the cell.
2. Choose Edit ➤ Copy.
3. Open the other workbook, select the cell to which you want to copy the custom format, and choose Edit ➤ Paste.

In the process, Excel adds your format to the list of custom formats in that workbook. To copy all your formats, copy an entire worksheet to the destination workbook. (You can then delete the new worksheet if you want only its custom formats.)

In the process of designing a format, you may end up creating several "drafts" of it (we do learn from our mistakes). To avoid confusion, you can delete any of your not-quite-ready-for-prime-time custom formats from the Custom format list. In the Format Cells dialog box, select the format and click Delete.

Using Custom Format Codes

You define a custom format with special codes. As you saw in the earlier example, the process can be quick and easy. There are codes for all sorts of numeric styles, including codes that display leading and trailing zeros, a currency symbol, a percent sign, dates and times, and plain text.

NOTE NOTE NOTE NOTE NOTE NOTE NOTE NOTE NOTE NOTE NOTE NOTE NOTE NOTE NOTE

If you want to take advantage of the huge variety of custom format possibilities, be prepared for a dizzying learning curve, at least at first. After all, we're discussing computers, and when the method of working with the computer involves "codes," you can expect the process to be confusing.

General Format Codes

Here are some codes that affect the display of numbers in a custom format:

Code	Effect
#	Digit placeholder if the digit exists in the number.
0	Digit placeholder; if no digit exists, displays a zero.
, (comma)	Places a comma between thousands.
. (period)	Places a decimal point in the format.
%	Multiplies the display of the number by 100 and appends the percent sign.
"text"	Text enclosed within quotation marks is displayed in the format.

Here are a few examples to illustrate these codes:

Format	Cell Entry	Display
00.0	3	03.0
000	5.25	005
#,###	5432	5,432
#,###	3	3
###	5.25	5
###.#	5.25	5.3
###.00%	5.25	525.00%

Date and Time Codes

To create a date or time format, you include codes for the day, month, and year or the hours, minutes, and seconds. Repeating the code letter, such as *mmm* or *mmmm*, displays a longer style of month, such as *Jan* or *January*.

TIP TIP TIP TIP TIP TIP TIP TIP TIP TIP TIP TIP TIP TIP TIP TIP TIP TIP TIP TIP TIP TIP TIP TIP TIP TIP

If the *m* code follows an hour, such as *h:m*, Excel treats it as minutes; otherwise, Excel treats it as month.

Here are some codes you can include in a date or time format:

Code	Effect
m, mm, mmm, or mmmm	1, 01, Jan, or January
d, dd, ddd, or dddd	1, 01, Sun, or Sunday
yy or yyyy	99 or 1999
am/pm, am/pm, or a/p	Time is shown in a 12-hour format, followed by one of these am/pm indicators.
h or hh	1 or 01
m or mm	1 or 01
s or ss	1 or 01

Here are some examples of date and time formats for the date December 31, 1999, and the time 3:00 PM:

Format	Display
mm/dd/yy	12/31/99
dddd, mmmm d, yyyy	Wednesday, December 31, 1999
"On a "dddd" in "mmmm	On a Wednesday in December
"Due by "h:mm	Due by 15:00
"Due by "h:mm am/pm	Due by 3:00 pm

The Four Sections of a Custom Format

Each custom format can consist of as many as four sections separated by semicolons. From left to right, each of the sections affects the following types of cell entries: positive numbers, negative numbers, zero values, and text.

The custom format example shown earlier used just one section:

```
#,### ?/?" pounds"
```

which therefore applies to positive and negative numbers, as well as zero values. If the format has two sections, the first section handles both positive numbers and zeros, and the second section handles negative numbers.

TIP TIP TIP TIP TIP TIP TIP TIP TIP TIP TIP TIP TIP TIP TIP TIP TIP TIP TIP TIP TIP TIP TIP TIP TIP TIP

If you include only three semicolons in a custom format, the contents of the cell will not be displayed; you've created a "hidden" format. You can still see the cell contents in the Formula bar, however, and you can still edit the cell.

In the process of revising and expanding the format, you can include any of the other sections, as well. To skip over a section while putting in another, include only its semicolon.

Let's expand this format so that:

- When the cell contains a negative number, the format displays the number followed by "[Error <0!]".
- When it contains a value of zero, it displays "No weight".

```
#,### ?/?" pounds";-#,### ?/?" [Error <0!]";"No weight"
```

As you can see, a custom format can quickly grow long and involved, and this example is just a short custom format!

TIP TIP TIP TIP TIP TIP TIP TIP TIP TIP TIP TIP TIP TIP TIP TIP TIP TIP TIP TIP TIP TIP TIP TIP TIP TIP

For easy access to the custom formats you expect to use in other workbooks, store them in a "library" workbook. As you experiment with custom formats and create one that you like, apply it to a cell and copy that cell to the library workbook.

Aligning Entries in Their Cells

By default, a cell's horizontal alignment within its cell is set to General, so that:

- Text is left-aligned.
- Values (numbers, numeric results of formulas, and so on) are right-aligned.
- Error values (such as #DIV/0!) and logical values (such as TRUE) are centered.

To change a cell's alignment, follow these steps:

1. Select the cell.
2. Choose Format ➤ Cells to open the Format Cells dialog box.
3. Click the Alignment tab, and select the options you want.
4. Click OK.

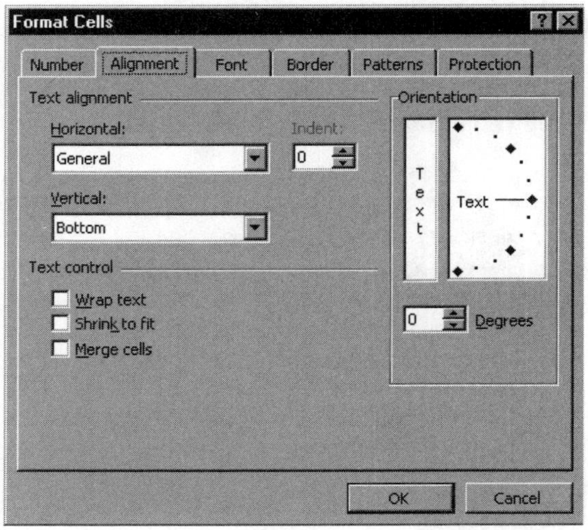

In the Alignment tab, you have the following options (subsequent sections give you the details about how to use each one):

Horizontal Aligns entries within the width of their cells.

Vertical Aligns entries within the height of their cells (on the bottom, by default).

Orientation Aligns entries vertically within the worksheet or at an angle you specify.

Wrap text Wraps text to fit within its column width.

Shrink to fit Reduces the font size of the selected cell so that its contents fit within the cell's width. If you change the column width, the font size changes accordingly. This alignment option does not actually change a cell's font size; it simply shrinks the displayed size.

Merge cells Combines the selected cells into one cell. This is a convenient tool for designing the layout of your worksheet.

WARNING WARNING WARNING WARNING WARNING WARNING WARNING WARNING

When you select the Merge Cells option, data in all cells is erased, except for the upper-left cell of the range.

Aligning Entries Horizontally

To change the way text is aligned within the width of its cell, click the down arrow and select one of the Horizontal options, or click the appropriate button on the Formatting toolbar. If you choose General, the cell will have the default alignment, as discussed earlier. Choosing one of the other horizontal alignments aligns *all* types of data within the cell in that manner:

Clicking the Align Left button or choosing the Left (Indent) Horizontal option aligns an entry with the left edge of the cell. In the Indent box, you can also specify the number of characters (from 1 to 15) by which to indent the entry, which is one way to build indented lists in the worksheet without using multiple columns (you can also use the Decrease Indent and Increase Indent buttons on the toolbar).

Clicking the Center button or choosing the Center Horizontal option centers an entry in the cell.

Clicking the Align Right button or choosing the Right Horizontal option aligns an entry with the right edge of the cell.

Selecting the Fill Horizontal option repeats the entry to fill the width of the cell.

Selecting the Justify Horizontal option wraps a long text entry within the width of the cell, and the row's height expands as needed. The text aligns with both the left and right edges of the cell.

Selecting Center Across Selection merges the cells in each selected row into one cell in that row and then centers the left cell entry within the selected columns.

WARNING WARNING WARNING WARNING WARNING WARNING WARNING WARNING

Don't confuse Center Across Selection with the Merge and Center button on the Formatting toolbar. Their effects can be the same under some conditions, but Merge and Center erases all data in the selected cells except for that in the upper-left cell. Experiment with these options to see how they behave.

Figure 6.2 shows some examples of these alignments, as well as the Wrap Text option.

- Cells A2:A4 show Left, Center, and Right alignments on text entries that fit within their cells.
- Cells D2:D4 show the effects of the same alignments on long text entries that overhang their cells.

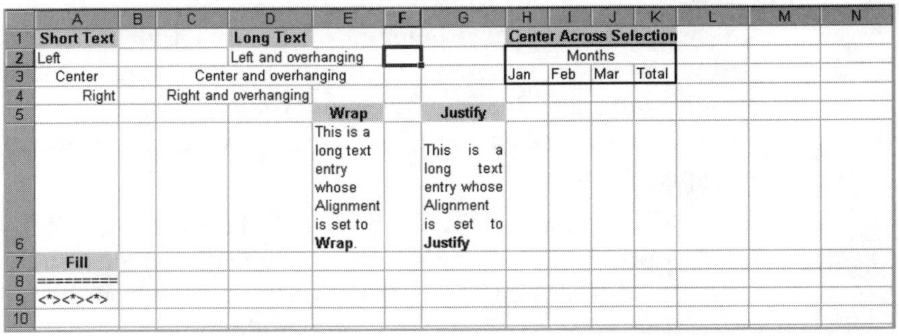

FIGURE 6.2: The effects of the Horizontal and the Wrap Text options in the Alignment tab of the Format Cells dialog box

- Cell H2 contains the word *Months*, which is shown serving as a title for the month names in columns H through K. It was centered over those columns by selecting H2:K2 and choosing the Center Across Selection option. If the widths of those columns change, the title will still remain centered over them.
- Cell E6 contains a long text entry that shows the effect of the Wrap Text option. Instead of the text overhanging its cell, it wraps within the width of the cell and expands to multiple lines, increasing that row's height. You can use Wrap Text with any of the other alignment options.
- Cell G6 shows the effect of the Justify option on a long text entry. It automatically wraps the text and aligns it with both edges of the cell.
- Cell A8 contains a single equals sign (=), and cell A9 contains the three-character entry <*>. I applied the Fill option to each, which repeats the entry (text or numeric) to fill the width of the column.

Aligning Entries Vertically

The Vertical option on the Alignment tab in the Cell Formats dialog box has a drop-down list that includes four options:

- Top aligns an entry with the top of the cell (see cell A2 in Figure 6.3).
- Bottom, the default, aligns the entry with the bottom of the cell (see cell B2 in Figure 6.3).
- Center places the entry in the vertical center of the cell (see cell C2 in Figure 6.3).

- Justify spreads rows of text evenly throughout the height of the cell (see cell D2 in Figure 6.3).

In Figure 6.3, I increased the height of row 2 so that the effect of each alignment is easy to see. You can also use these options with the Horizontal alignment options.

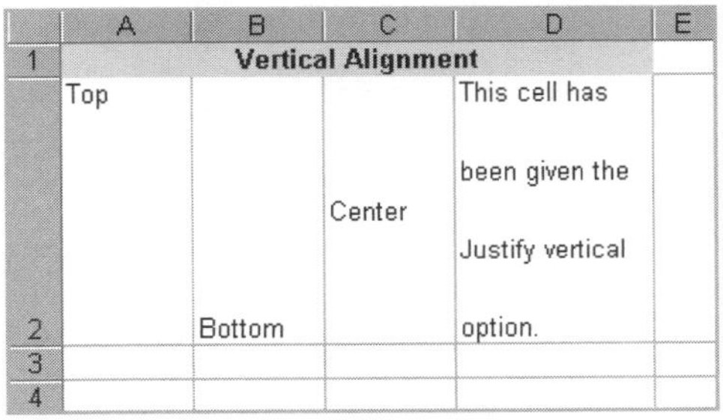

FIGURE 6.3: The effects of the Vertical alignment options

Changing the Orientation

Figure 6.4 shows examples of the Orientation options in the Alignment tab of the Format Cells dialog box. You use these options to orient a cell entry either vertically or at an angle within its cell.

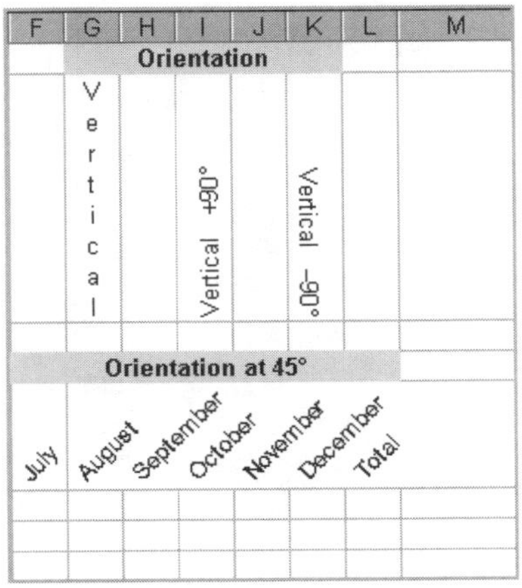

FIGURE 6.4: The effects of the Orientation options

To set a cell's orientation at an angle, you can either enter a specific angle in degrees in the Degrees box or drag the arrow in the angle gauge up or down. A positive angle (0 to 90 degrees) orients a cell entry from bottom to top, and a negative angle (0 to 90 degrees) orients it from top to bottom.

A row's height will expand as needed to fit the width (running vertically or at an angle) of the entry. You may have to experiment to find the best way to display some cells vertically while leaving others in their default orientation.

Applying Fonts

You can change the font (or its size or attributes) that a cell displays in two ways:

- Select the cell and change its font; Excel applies the new font to all characters within the cell.
- Select a portion of the cell's contents, and apply a new font to the selection; Excel applies the new font only to the selection.

To apply a font, follow these steps:

1. Select the cells or characters whose font you want to change.
2. Choose Format ➤ Cells to open the Format Cells dialog box.

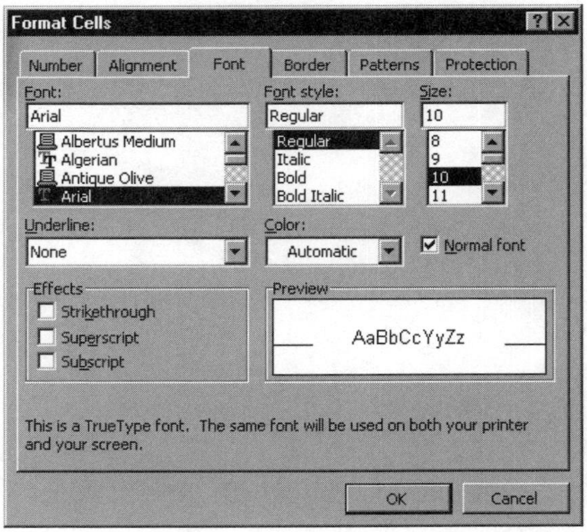

3. Click the Font tab.

4. Select a font, a style, size, and any other options you want.
5. Click OK to close the Format Cells dialog box and apply the font to your selection.

If you're familiar with other Office applications, you'll notice that the Excel Font tab is similar to the Font tab in them, and it works in the same way. As you make your choices, watch the Preview field to see the results.

You can also use the buttons on the Formatting toolbar to select a font or size from the two drop-down lists or to underline a font or change it to bold or italic.

In the Font tab, use the Color drop-down list to select a color for the characters within the cell (use the options on the Patterns tab to change the color or pattern of the cell's background). You can also click the Font Color button on the Formatting toolbar to set this attribute.

NOTE NOTE NOTE NOTE NOTE NOTE NOTE NOTE NOTE NOTE NOTE NOTE NOTE NOTE NOTE

If the Standard and Formatting toolbars are sharing a row, click the More Buttons button on the right side of the toolbar, and select the Font Color button.

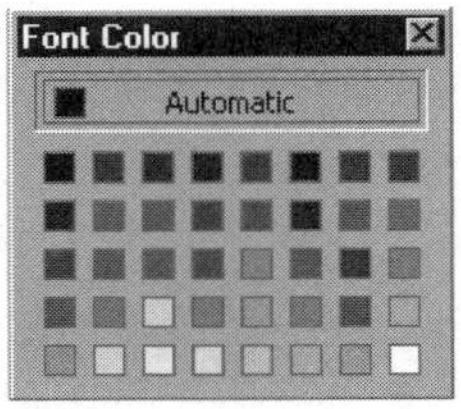

The Font Color button has a palette that you can "tear off" the toolbar and leave displayed over the worksheet. Just drag the palette by its title bar (the title bar will change colors when you point to it) to pull it away from the toolbar. Use it as needed, and when you're finished, click the palette's Close button.

In the Font tab, you can select the Normal Font option as a quick way to reset the selection's font to the one used by the Normal style, which is the default style that Excel applies to all cells in the workbook (see "Working with Styles" later in this chapter).

TIP TIP

To set the default font for all new worksheets and workbooks, choose Tools ➤ Options to open the Options dialog box, and click the General tab. Select a font and size in the Standard Font and Size fields. The changes won't take effect until the next time you start Excel.

CREATING A BULLETED LIST IN A WORKSHEET

Here's a quick-and-easy way to create bulleted lists in your worksheets. The TrueType font called Wingdings includes several characters that can serve as bullets:

1. Type the letter **l** (as in lady), a space, and some text in a cell.
2. Select only that l.
3. Apply the Wingdings font (using the steps earlier in this section). (You might want to choose a smaller font size than that used in the rest of the cell.)
4. Press Enter to enter the text into the cell.

As shown here, the letter *l* is displayed as a solid, round bullet, and other characters create different types of bullets. You can make the bullet smaller or larger by selecting it in the cell and changing its font size.

	Sample.xls							
	A	B	C	D	E	F	G	H
1								
2	**Justification for this data**						Character	Wingdings
3	• Inflation of 4% annually						l	●
4	• Personnel to increase 3% annually						m	○
5	• Interest rates to remain flat						n	■
6	• Competition not expected for 18 months						o	□
7							u	◆
8							w	•

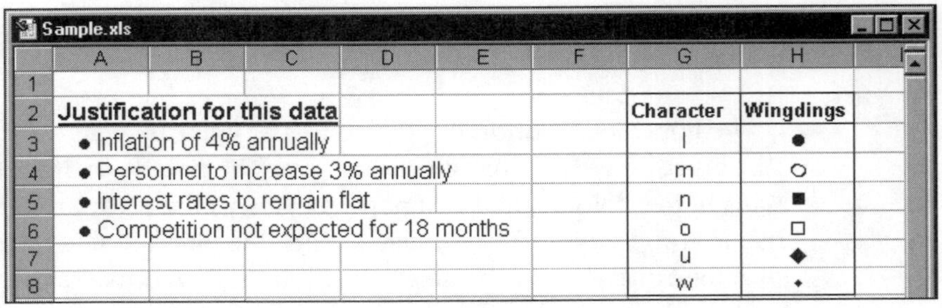

Applying Borders to Cells

You can apply a border to any side of a cell or a selected range with the options in the Border tab in the Format Cells dialog box, which is shown in Figure 6.5. To apply a border, follow these steps:

1. In your worksheet, select a cell or a range to which you want to apply a border.
2. Choose Format ➤ Cells to open the Format Cells dialog box.
3. Click the Border tab.
4. From the Color drop-down list, select a color.
5. In the Style box, select a line style, click one of the Border buttons to select a line style, or choose one of the presets.
6. Click OK.

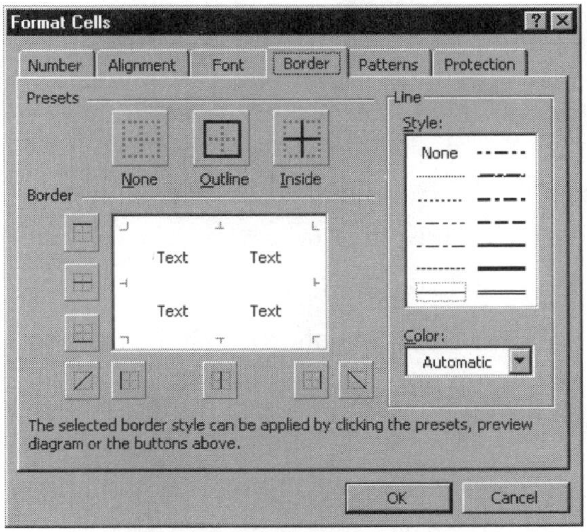

FIGURE 6.5: Use the options in the Border tab to add lines to the edges of a cell or range.

As you can see, you can format a border in myriad ways. Here are a few ideas to get you started:

- To apply a heavy line around the outside edge of the selected cell or range, click the heavy line in the Style options, and then click the Outline button.
- To enclose a range in a border and also draw vertical lines along its columns, click the Outline button, and then click the center vertical line button. To draw horizontal lines within a range of cells, click the center horizontal line button.

NOTE NOTE NOTE NOTE NOTE NOTE NOTE NOTE NOTE NOTE NOTE NOTE NOTE NOTE NOTE

The range must be more than one row or column to have inside, vertical, and horizontal available.

- To draw a vertical line along the left side of a column, select only the cells in that column where you want the line, and click the left edge of the diagram.
- To draw a diagonal line across each selected cell to make it appear crossed out, click one of the diagonal buttons.

To erase a border from one of the Border locations, click that line in the diagram, or click the None button and then click a border you want to erase.

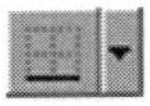

You can also use the Borders button on the Formatting toolbar to apply borders to a cell or range. Follow these steps:

1. Select the cell or range.
2. Point to the Borders button.
3. Click a Border button from the drop-down palette.

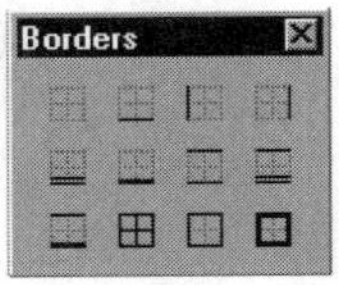

The Borders palette contains several ready-made border configurations. The first one is empty of borders, and clicking it erases any borders already applied to the selected cells. You can experiment to see where each one draws lines in a range and the style of line that is used.

If you want to keep the Borders palette available while you work, drag its title bar to a handy location on your worksheet. When you're finished with it, click the Close button.

Filling a Cell with a Pattern or Color

You can change a cell's background color or pattern using the options in the Patterns tab in the Format Cells dialog box, as shown in Figure 6.6. To apply a pattern or a color, follow these steps:

1. Select the cell or range to which you want to apply a pattern or a color.
2. Choose Format ➤ Cells to open the Format Cells dialog box.
3. Click the Patterns tab.
4. Select a color from the Cell Shading palette.
5. Click the down arrow to open the Pattern drop-down list, and select a pattern.
6. Click OK.

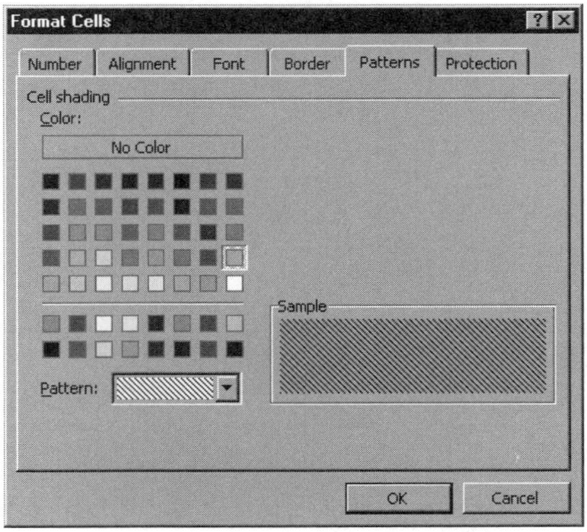

FIGURE 6.6: Use the Patterns tab in the Format Cells dialog box to change the color or pattern of a cell's background.

TIP

After you finish adjusting colors and return to the worksheet, you may wonder why some cells no longer display their contents. It's probably because you've set the background to the same color as the font for those cells.

Creating a Worksheet Background

If you've browsed the World Wide Web, you've seen a background image on countless Web pages. You can also add a background image to a worksheet. Follow these steps:

1. Open the worksheet to which you want to add a background image.
2. Choose Format ➤ Sheet ➤ Background to open the Sheet Background dialog box:

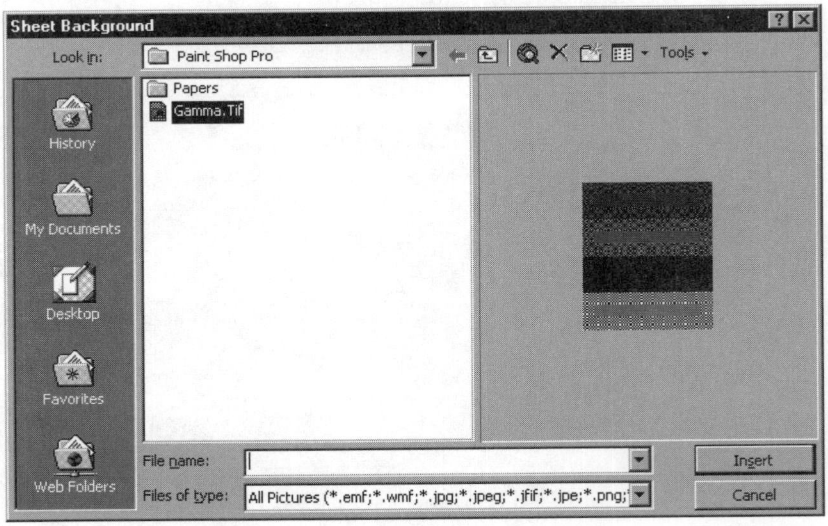

3. Select a graphic file that has one of the following filename extensions: BMP, GIF, JPEG, TIF, or WMF formats.
4. Click Insert to tile the image so that it fills the entire background of the worksheet.

Now, no matter how you change the worksheet window size, the tiled background will fill it. Of course, this is one of those features that, in order to be put to good effect, relies on our good judgment, taste, artistic sensibilities, and lack of a wild imagination.

Applying Formats Conditionally

You can apply a conditional format to cells to make them stand out in the worksheet when they or other cells contain data that meet your criteria. You define the criteria under which the formatting will go into effect, and then you choose any of three formats (Font, Border, or Patterns), which will appear on the cell only when the criteria are met. Typically, you use conditional formatting when you prepare a worksheet that others will use to enter data. You might, for example, want all cells that need information to be in one particular color.

TIP TIP TIP TIP TIP TIP TIP TIP TIP TIP TIP TIP TIP TIP TIP TIP TIP TIP TIP TIP TIP TIP TIP TIP TIP TIP

You can also set criteria by choosing Data ➤ Validation and limiting the kind of data that can be entered in a cell. See Skill 13.

To see how this works, let's specify that if a cell contains a negative number, the cell's background will be red, and if the cell's value is larger than the value in another cell, the cell's background will be yellow. Figure 6.7 shows the Conditional Formatting dialog box with the settings that we'll end up with.

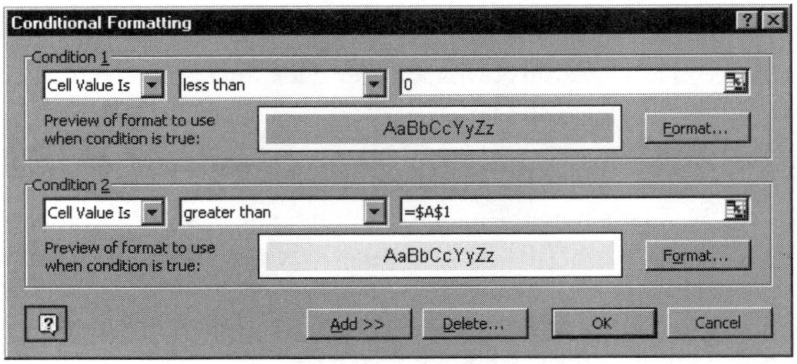

FIGURE 6.7: In the Conditional Formatting dialog box, you specify the criteria and format to apply to a cell.

To apply conditional formatting, follow these steps:

1. Open a blank worksheet, and in cell A1, enter **100**, which will serve as the comparison number for the conditional format.
2. Select cell B1, and choose Format ➤ Conditional Formatting to open the Conditional Formatting dialog box.
3. From the drop-down list on the left side of the dialog box, select Cell Value Is to base the criterion on the contents (or results of a formula) in the current cell. The other option is Formula Is, which lets you write a logical formula that will determine whether the condition is true or false.
4. In the second field's drop-down list, select Less Than.
5. Enter **0** in the third edit field so that this criterion will be true if the selected cell's value is less than zero.
6. Now click the Format button to open the Format Cells dialog box and select the format that will be applied when the condition is true.
7. Click the Patterns tab, select red as the cell's background color, and click OK.
8. Back in the Conditional Formatting dialog box, click Add to create a second condition (you can create a maximum of three).
9. For this condition, select Cell Value Is in the first field, and select Greater Than in the second field.
10. Select the third field and click in cell A1. This enters the formula =$A$1 in this field so that the condition will be true if the current cell's value is greater than the value in A1 (which is currently 100).
11. Click the Format button, click the Patterns tab, select yellow as the color, and click OK.
12. Finally, click OK in the Conditional Formatting dialog box.

To see how the new formatting works, enter a number greater than 100 in the current cell (B1). The cell's background should turn yellow. Enter a number less than 100 but greater than or equal to zero, and the yellow should be replaced by the cell's normal background color (white by default). If you enter a negative number, the cell should turn red.

TIP TIP TIP TIP TIP TIP TIP TIP TIP TIP TIP TIP TIP TIP TIP TIP TIP TIP TIP TIP TIP TIP TIP TIP TIP

The format chosen for the conditional formatting will override a cell's normal format as long as the condition is true. As soon as that is no longer the case, the cell's normal format will once again be displayed.

Using the AutoFormat Command

Suppose you want to enhance the look of a range of cells that will serve as a worksheet report or table. Figure 6.8 shows just such a worksheet after all the formatting was added.

	A	B	C	D	E	F	G	H	I
1	Monthly Housing Expenses								
2									
3		Jan	Feb	Mar	Apr	May	Jun	Total	
4	Insurance	51	51	51	51	51	51	306	
5	Maintenance	48	48	48	48	48	48	288	
6	Mortgage	925	925	925	925	925	925	5,550	
7	Taxes	102	102	102	102	102	102	612	
8	Telephone	42	78	65	115	70	67	437	
9	Utilities	182	116	143	90	175	185	891	
10	Total	1,350	1,320	1,334	1,331	1,371	1,378	8,084	
11									

FIGURE 6.8: A worksheet with added formatting

SKILL 6

You might increase the font size for the column and row titles, apply a color to the totals, change the numeric format for the data or totals, or add borders around the range. That could be a tedious job if you had to hand-select each part of the table range and apply the appropriate formatting. Here's how to cut down on the work:

1. Select the table range, including its column and row titles and totals in the last row and column.
2. Choose Format ➤ AutoFormat to open the AutoFormat dialog box, (see Figure 6.9), and click the Options button.
3. Use the scroll bar to view all the available formats.
4. When you find a format that you like or that is close enough to what you need, select it and click OK.

The range you selected is formatted to look like the AutoFormat you chose. You are free to add more enhancements to the range as needed; the AutoFormat command simply added multiple formats in a single operation.

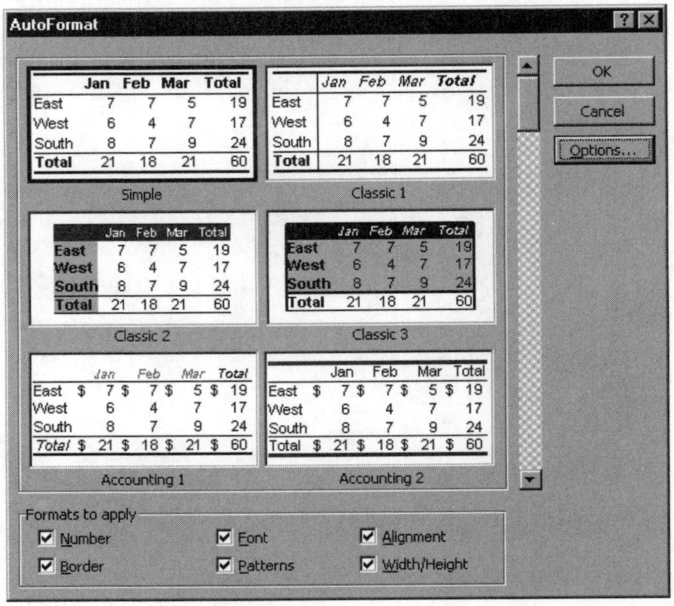

FIGURE 6.9: The AutoFormat dialog box

NOTE NOTE NOTE NOTE NOTE NOTE NOTE NOTE NOTE NOTE NOTE NOTE NOTE NOTE NOTE

If you have already applied some formatting to the cells in the table, you can still use AutoFormat while leaving those enhancements unchanged. Click the Options button in the AutoFormat dialog box and clear the check boxes for the enhancements that you do not want to change. Watch the Sample window to see the effects (or lack of effects).

Working with Styles

When you want to duplicate the look of a cell in other cells in the workbook, you can create a *style*, which is a named collection of cell formats. Two big advantages are associated with using styles:

- A style contains several formats, such as font, numeric format, and cell color. When you apply a style to a cell, the cell takes on the look of all those formats in a single operation. Using styles not only saves a lot of time but also ensures that your worksheet will have a nice consistent look.

- If you later change some of the formats in a style, any cells to which you've already applied that style will take on the new look. Once again, styles can save you time and effort.

The process of working with styles includes applying them to cells in the worksheet, revising existing styles, and creating new ones.

Applying a Style

Excel comes with a few styles already built in, such as Comma, Currency, and Percent, which contain just those numeric formats in their definition. You can also apply built-in styles by clicking buttons on the Formatting toolbar.

The built-in style named Normal is a special case; by default, it is applied to every cell in the workbook and defines the underlying look of all cells. You can't delete the Normal style, but you can modify it. Modifying Normal changes the look of every cell in the workbook, except those to which you've already applied another style or individual formats.

Follow these steps to apply a style:

1. Select the cell or range whose look you want to affect.
2. Choose Format ➤ Style to open the Style dialog box.

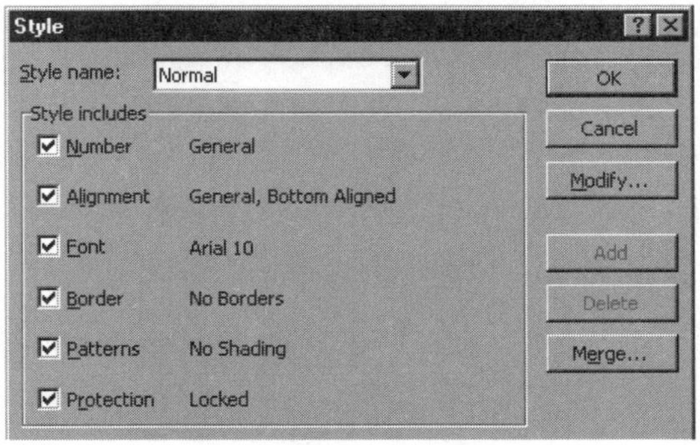

3. Open the Style Name list, and select a style name.
4. Click OK to apply the style.

When you select a style name from the list, the definition of its formatting appears in the Style Includes area. This shows you at a glance what the style contains.

TIP TIP TIP TIP TIP TIP TIP TIP TIP TIP TIP TIP TIP TIP TIP TIP TIP TIP TIP TIP TIP TIP TIP TIP TIP TIP

If the Style list is displayed on your Formatting toolbar, you can select a style from it instead of from the dialog box. It also displays the style of the active cell. See Skill 13 for information about how to add the Style list to a toolbar.

Creating a New Style

Here's the easiest way to create a new style:

1. Select a cell that is already formatted the way you want the style to look.
2. Choose Format ➤ Style to open the Style dialog box.
3. Type a new name in the Style Name field. As soon as you start typing, you'll see that Excel has applied all the formats of the active cell to the new style definition. If you do not want all these characteristics included in the style, clear the check box for those you do not want.
4. To add the style to the list but not apply it to the current cell, click Add and then click Close. To add the style to the list and also apply it to the current cell, click OK.

You can always make more changes to the style definition in the Style dialog box, as discussed in the next section.

Another easy way to create a new style is by copying a cell that already has that style applied to it from another workbook. The copied style becomes part of the current workbook and appears in its Style Name list.

You can also bring all the styles from another *open* workbook into the current workbook. Follow these steps:

1. Choose Format ➤ Style to open the Style dialog box.
2. Click the Merge button to open the Merge Styles dialog box.

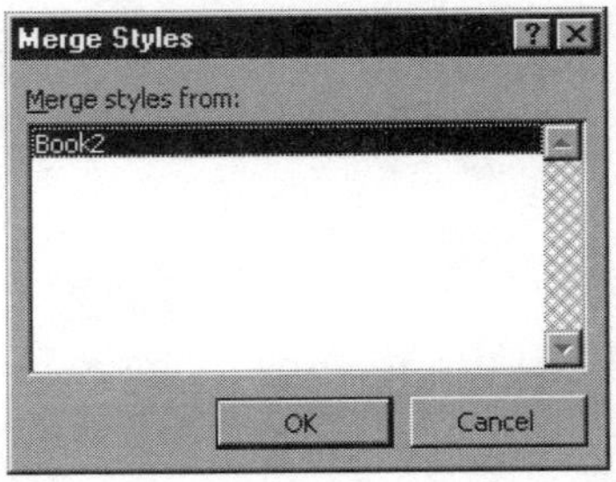

3. Select a workbook name from the list of open workbooks, and click OK.

All the workbook's styles will now appear in the Style Name list in the active workbook.

Modifying or Deleting an Existing Style

To modify the formats for an existing style or for a style you're in the process of creating, follow these steps:

1. Choose Format ➤ Style to open the Style dialog box.
2. Select the style's name in the Style Name list.
3. Click Modify to open the Format Cells dialog box.
4. Adjust the formats you want to change.
5. Click OK.

In the Style dialog box, the Style Includes list of formatting options reflects your changes.

TIP TIP TIP TIP TIP TIP TIP TIP TIP TIP TIP TIP TIP TIP TIP TIP TIP TIP TIP TIP TIP TIP TIP TIP

To exclude a format from a style, clear its check box in the Style dialog box. For example, if you clear the Font check box, a cell's existing font will not be affected when you apply the new style.

You can also modify an existing style by selecting a cell that you want the style to look like and then choosing Format ➤ Style. This time, *type* the name of the style you want to change in the Style Name field, and then click Add. The definition for that style is now based on the formatting of the cell.

Finally, to delete a style from the workbook, select its name from the Style Name list, and click Delete. Any cells to which that style had been applied revert to the Normal style.

Setting Column Widths and Row Heights

You can change the width of columns or the height of rows to suit the look you want for the worksheet. You can even hide columns and rows from view.

Row heights adjust automatically to the tallest entry in the row, whether that's due to a large font or to text that wraps to several lines in a cell. You'll rarely need to change a row height on your own. Columns also adjust automatically when you create a wide numeric cell entry (perhaps due to its format or font size), although they don't contract automatically in response to font changes, as rows do.

Column widths are measured in *characters,* based on the current font size for the default font in the workbook. That's the font in the Normal style. For example, when the default font is TrueType 10-point Arial, the *standard width* for all columns is 8.43.

Row heights are measured in *points,* which is the unit of measurement that expresses the height of fonts. Like column width, the default row height (such as 12.75) is based on the default font.

Setting Column Widths

You can adjust the width of one or more columns by using either your mouse or the Column Width dialog box.

Dragging Columns

To change the column width with the mouse, follow these steps:

1. Select one or more columns that you want to adjust by clicking within the column headings. For example, you can select a noncontiguous range of columns with the Ctrl+click method.

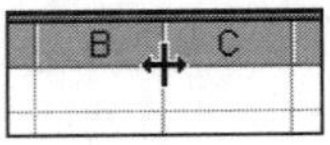

2. Point to the *right* edge of the column heading of one of the selected columns; the pointer changes to a double-headed arrow.
3. Hold down the mouse button and drag the column edge to the left or right to narrow or widen the selected columns. A ScreenTip displays the current width as you drag the column edge.
4. Release the mouse button. All the columns take on the width of the one you adjusted.

Setting the Width Automatically

You can widen or narrow a column to the width of its longest entry. The quickest way to adjust the width of a single column is to point to its right edge in the column heading (the pointer changes to a double-headed arrow) and double-click the column edge. If you want to adjust multiple columns at the same time, select the columns first, such as by dragging across their column headings, and then double-click one of their edges in the column heading. You can also choose Format ➤ Column ➤ AutoFit Selection to adjust column widths automatically. The results depend on whether you select entire columns or only some cells in the columns.

- If you select entire columns, Excel considers the entries in all cells in each column in determining the width of each column (the same result as the double-clicking method).

- If you select only some cells in the columns, Excel considers only the entries in those cells in determining the width of each column.

Specifying a Width

To change column widths to a specific size, follow these steps:

1. After selecting the columns or any cells in the columns, choose Format ➤ Column ➤ Width to open the Column Width dialog box.

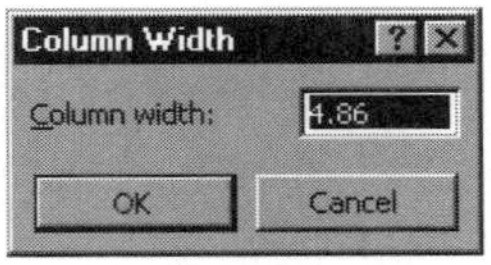

2. Enter a new width in the Column Width field, from 0 to 255.
3. Click OK.

Setting to the Standard Width

The standard width of columns is the default width of all columns in the workbook. To return the selected columns to the standard width, follow these steps:

1. Select the columns or cells in those columns, and choose Format ➤ Column ➤ Standard Width to open the Standard Width dialog box.

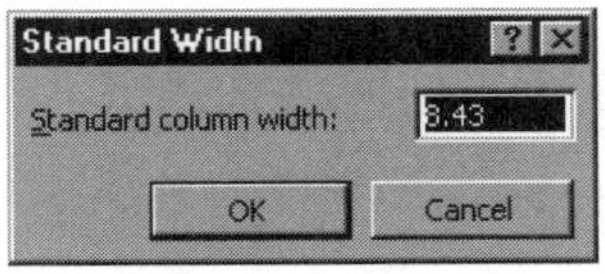

2. Click OK.

Changing the Standard Width

To change the default column width for all columns in a worksheet or workbook, follow these steps:

1. Select a single cell to change the standard width of all columns in the current worksheet, except those that you've changed manually. Or click the Select All button (located where the row and column headings intersect) to select all columns and reset their widths, including those you've set manually.

2. Now select any other sheets in the workbook that you want to affect.
3. Choose Format ➤ Column ➤ Standard Width to open the Standard Width dialog box.
4. Enter a new width in the Standard Column Width field.
5. Click OK.

The width of any new columns you insert on those sheets will also be the revised standard width.

TIP TIP TIP TIP TIP TIP TIP TIP TIP TIP TIP TIP TIP TIP TIP TIP TIP TIP TIP TIP TIP TIP TIP TIP TIP

If you want every new workbook to have the revised standard column width, create a new workbook, change its standard width for every column in every sheet in it, and save the workbook as a template named Book.xlt in the XLStart folder, which you'll find in Excel's program folder. Skill 7 discusses the start-up templates.

Setting Row Heights

The procedure for setting the height of one or more rows is similar to the procedure for setting column widths. First, select one or more rows, and then do one of the following:

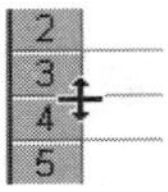

- Point to one row's *bottom* edge in its row heading and watch for the pointer to change to a double-headed arrow, this time pointing up and down. Drag that edge up or down to make the rows shorter or taller.
- Point to the bottom edge of one of the selected rows, and double-click to change the row heights to match their tallest entries.
- Choose Format ➤ Row ➤ AutoFit to change the row heights automatically; rows that are empty are set to the standard height. Remember, the default font in the Normal style determines the standard height of rows.
- Choose Format ➤ Row ➤ Height to open the Row Height dialog box, enter a specific height in points in the Row Height field, and click OK.

Again, if you haven't specifically set a row's height, it automatically grows taller or shorter, depending on the tallest cell entry in that row (such as a large font or a text entry wrapped within its cell).

Hiding Columns, Rows, and Sheets

You can hide rows, columns, and worksheets from view without actually deleting them. You might want to hide parts of a worksheet before you print it, for example, or to remove some clutter to make it easier to enter data.

You might also want to hide portions of a workbook when other people will be using it. Eliminating real estate not only makes it easier for other users to find their way around the workbook, but also reduces the chances of making mistakes.

TIP TIP TIP TIP TIP TIP TIP TIP TIP TIP TIP TIP TIP TIP TIP TIP TIP TIP TIP TIP TIP TIP TIP TIP TIP

Choosing Data ➤ Filter also hides rows from view, but only those rows that match your chosen criteria. This command is a real boon when you're manipulating the data in a worksheet list; it's discussed in Skill 13.

Hiding Rows and Columns

You can hide columns or rows with either the mouse or the Hide command. To hide columns or rows with a mouse, do one of the following:

- Select the column or columns, and drag the right edge in the heading of one of the selected columns to the left, just *past* the next column's edge. The size displayed in the ScreenTip shrinks to zero. Release the mouse button, and those columns disappear from view.
- Select the row or rows, drag the bottom edge of one row up past the next row's edge, and then release the mouse button.

To hide rows or columns with the Hide command, follow these steps:

1. Select the rows or columns you want to hide.
2. Choose Format ➤ Row ➤ Hide, or choose Format ➤ Column ➤ Hide.

Even though you can't see them, you can still access hidden rows and columns in formulas and in most commands. You can even choose Edit ➤ Go To to go to a hidden cell; its contents appear in the Formula bar where you can view or edit them in the usual way.

TIP TIP TIP TIP TIP TIP TIP TIP TIP TIP TIP TIP TIP TIP TIP TIP TIP TIP TIP TIP TIP TIP TIP TIP TIP

To eliminate hidden rows or columns from a range selection, choose Edit ➤ Go To to open the Go To dialog box, click Special to open the Go To Special dialog box, and then click the Visible Cells Only option. The selection then includes only visible cells, which can be especially helpful when printing.

To display hidden rows or columns, select a range of rows or columns that includes the hidden ones, and choose Format ➤ Row (or Column) ➤ Unhide. To unhide only a single row or column, choose Edit ➤ Go To to go to a cell in that row or column, and then choose the Unhide command.

Hiding Worksheets

To hide worksheets, select the sheets you want to hide (click their sheet tabs), and choose Format ➤ Sheet ➤ Hide. The selected worksheets disappear from the workbook. You can still reference the data in the cells in a hidden worksheet, but you can't actually go to that sheet.

To display a hidden sheet, choose Format ➤ Sheet ➤ Unhide, and then choose the sheet from the list of all hidden sheets.

Are You Experienced?

Now you can...

- ☑ **Enhance your worksheet in a variety of ways**
- ☑ **Apply numeric formats to cells**
- ☑ **Set cell assignment**
- ☑ **Change fonts**
- ☑ **Add borders to cells and ranges**
- ☑ **Change cell color or pattern**
- ☑ **Apply a conditional format**
- ☑ **Use AutoFormat**
- ☑ **Use styles to apply formats**
- ☑ **Change column widths and row height**

SKILL 7

Working with Files

- Saving workbooks
- Automatically saving workbooks
- Creating new workbooks
- Opening workbooks
- Sharing workbooks
- Saving or opening a file in another file format
- Working with templates
- Saving the workspace

You'll find that dealing with files in Excel is much the same as dealing with them in other Windows programs. Just remember that an Excel file has an XLS filename extension and is an entire workbook.

Saving Your Workbooks

When you save a workbook the first time, it's important to give your file a meaningful name. Excel will suggest something like Book8.xls, which is not helpful when you try to remember which workbook contains your budget for 1999. In this case, naming your workbook 1999 Budget allows you to retrieve it much more efficiently. To save a workbook the first time, follow these steps:

1. Choose File ➤ Save As to open the Save As dialog box.

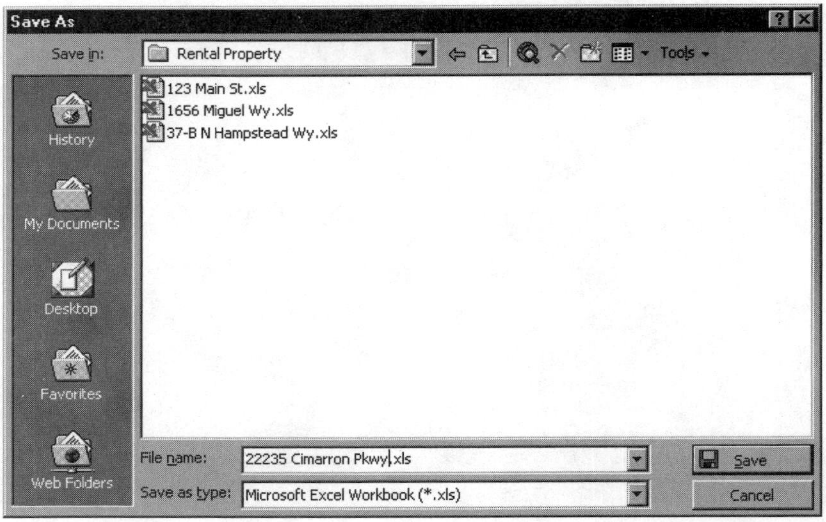

2. In the Save In box, select a folder in which to save your workbook.
3. In the Filename box, enter a filename for your workbook. (Windows 95/98 allows you to use a maximum of 218 characters for the filename, including the complete path to the file, the drive, and the folder.)
4. Click Save.

NEW

In Excel 2000, you can easily save a file as a Web page. Choose File ➤ Save As Web Page to open the following Save As dialog box.

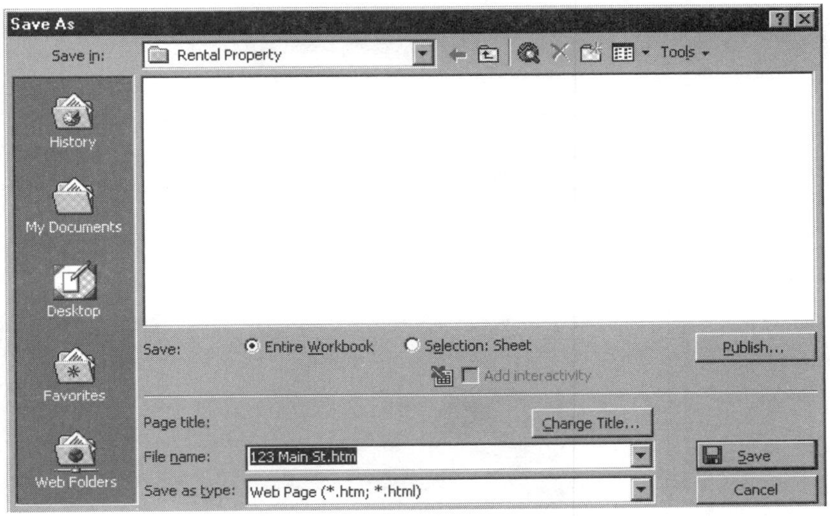

Excel automatically gives your file the HTM extension. In Skill 10, you'll learn how to use this dialog box to save and publish Web pages.

A recently saved copy of your work on disk is your first and often your only defense against power outages, line surges, and gross errors on your part. To save your file while you work and when you're finished editing a file, do one of the following:

- Choose File ➤ Save.
- Press Ctrl+S.
- Click the Save button on the Standard toolbar.

TIP TIP TIP TIP TIP TIP TIP TIP TIP TIP TIP TIP TIP TIP TIP TIP TIP TIP TIP TIP TIP TIP TIP TIP TIP

To save a file that you've already saved but to give it a different name (thus, creating two versions of the same file with different names), choose File ➤ Save As, and follow the steps earlier in this section.

Setting the Default File Type

You can open files from earlier versions of Excel and even from other spreadsheet programs without a problem in Excel 2000. But a workbook that you save in Excel 2000 cannot be opened in earlier versions of Excel because it uses an updated file format.

By default, Excel 2000 saves workbooks in the Microsoft Excel Workbook format. If you find that you're frequently saving your workbooks in another file format, you can change the default format that Excel uses. Follow these steps:

1. Choose Tools ➤ Options to open the Options dialog box, and click the Transition tab.

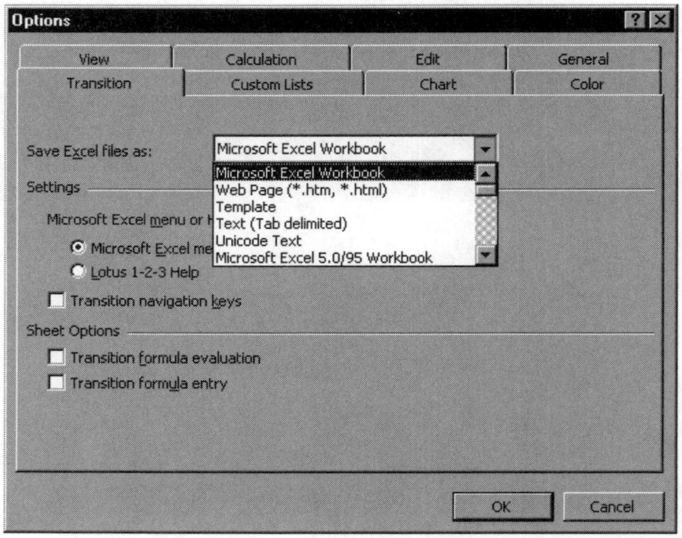

2. In the Save Excel Files As drop-down list box, select another file format.
3. Click OK.

If you want to only occasionally save a workbook to another file format, you can simply select that format in the Save As Type box in the Save As dialog box. The "Saving or Opening a Workbook in Another File Format" section, later in this skill, explains more about this.

Setting File Properties

An Excel file, as well as any other Office file, has properties associated with it. A property is simply some bit of information about a file—its size, who created it, when it was last changed, and so on. To view the properties of an open workbook that you or someone else has saved, choose File ➤ Properties to open the Properties dialog box for that file.

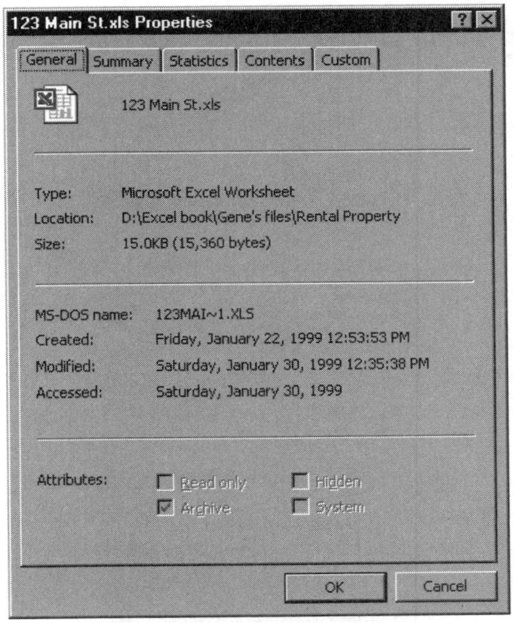

Some of the information in the Properties dialog box is entered automatically when you save a workbook, such as the information on the General tab, and you can't modify it. You can, however, use the Properties dialog box to enter a lot of information that makes it easy to find, organize, and document your files. In addition to the General tab, the Properties dialog box has four other tabs:

Summary Provides a variety of data-entry fields in which you can enter information to describe the purpose and content of the workbook. You can search all these when you open a file; for example, you can search for all workbooks created by a specific author that contain certain keywords. Click the Save Preview Picture check box to save in the workbook file a small image of the first sheet, which you can view in the Open Files dialog box by clicking the Preview button.

Statistics Displays file information that is more Excel oriented than that in the General tab. Here you'll see the date and time that the file was first created and last modified in Excel, the name of the person who last saved it in Excel, and the number of times it has been saved.

Contents Displays the worksheet names that are in the workbook.

Custom Lets you create properties that, when used in many other workbooks, can help you manage large numbers of workbooks or projects.

If you want to be prompted to fill out the Properties dialog box each time you save a workbook, follow these steps:

1. Choose Tools ➤ Options to open the Options dialog box, and click the General tab.
2. Click the Prompt for Workbook Properties check box.
3. Click OK.

Saving Automatically with AutoSave

Based on other lessons we've all learned in life, it's a good idea to save your workbooks to disk frequently. There's just no better feeling than having a recently saved copy of your work on disk. One way to avoid the danger of not saving your work frequently enough is to use Excel's AutoSave add-in (an add-in is an optional accessory program). AutoSave automatically saves the active workbook or all open workbooks at regular intervals.

You still need to choose File ➤ Save before you close a workbook or exit Excel, but AutoSave guarantees that you don't let the entire day pass without ever saving your workbooks! The add-ins listed in Figure 7.1 all come with Excel, although you can choose the ones you want when you install Excel or install an add-in as you find you need it. Many companies other than Microsoft also distribute Excel add-ins, as well.

To load AutoSave, follow these steps:

1. Choose Tool ➤ Add-Ins to open the Add-Ins dialog box.
2. In the Add-Ins Available list, click the check box next to AutoSave Add-In.
3. Click OK.

If you see a prompt that asks if you want to install the AutoSave add-in, click Yes.

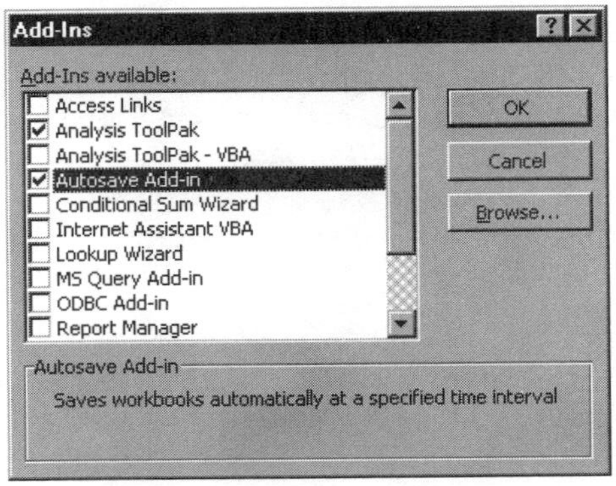

FIGURE 7.1: The Add-Ins dialog box lists the add-ins that you can attach to Excel.

When you return to the workbook, you can check to see that the AutoSave command has been added to the Tools menu, where most add-in commands appear. The check mark next to the AutoSave command indicates that the feature is active.

Once you select an Excel add-in from the Add-Ins dialog box, that add-in loads into memory each time you run Excel until you specifically clear it from the Add-Ins Available list in the Add-Ins dialog box.

To change or verify the AutoSave settings, choose Tools ➤ AutoSave to open the AutoSave dialog box, shown in Figure 7.2.

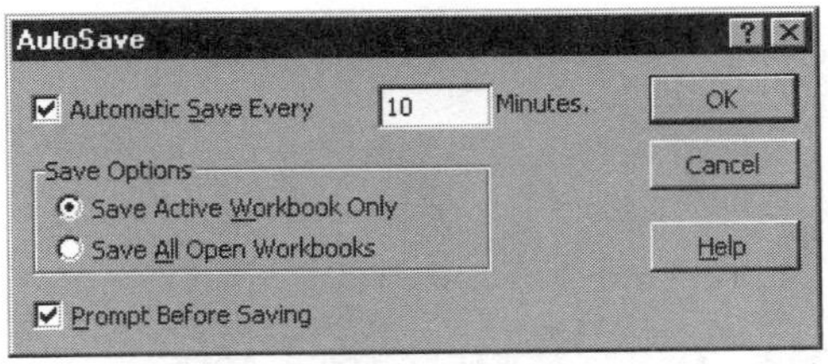

FIGURE 7.2: The AutoSave dialog box lets you specify how often to save your work and which workbooks to save.

In this dialog box, you can:

- Specify the number of minutes between saves (the default of 10 minutes isn't a bad choice).

- Choose whether to save only the active workbook or all open workbooks.
- Tell AutoSave to prompt you before it saves anything. AutoSave saves your workbooks under their current names, as though you chose File ➤ Save. If you have accidentally messed up a workbook, you might not want it saved until you've straightened things out.
- Disable AutoSave by clearing the Automatic Save Every x Minutes check box. The check mark next to the AutoSave command on the Tools menu disappears, indicating that the feature is not active.

Creating New Workbooks

By default, when you first start Excel, Excel displays a new, empty workbook named Book1. When you need them, you can create new, blank workbooks in several ways:

- Click the New button on the Standard toolbar, which opens a new workbook immediately. (Book2 is the name of the second workbook you open.)
- Choose File ➤ New (or press Ctrl+N) to open the New dialog box, and choose an Excel template for the new file (see the "Using Templates" section, later in this skill).
- Click and drag a sheet tab from a worksheet in an open workbook onto Excel's desktop (the blank area behind any windows or icons). Excel removes that sheet from the open workbook and makes it the first worksheet in a new workbook. If you hold down Ctrl while dragging, you will copy the worksheet to the new workbook. You can also right-click a sheet tab, choose Move or Copy from the shortcut menu, and then choose "(new book)" from the drop-down list as the destination.

Opening a Workbook File

In Excel, you can open an existing file in the following ways:

- Click the Open button on the Standard toolbar to open the Open dialog box (see Figure 7.3), select a file, and click OK.
- Choose File ➤ Open to open the Open dialog box, select a file, and click OK.
- Choose File, and then select a filename from those listed near the bottom of the File menu.

TIP

If you want Excel to open a particular workbook every time you run the program, save the workbook in the XLStart folder, which you should find in C:\Program Files\Microsoft Office\Office\XLStart unless you installed Excel on another disk or in a different folder.

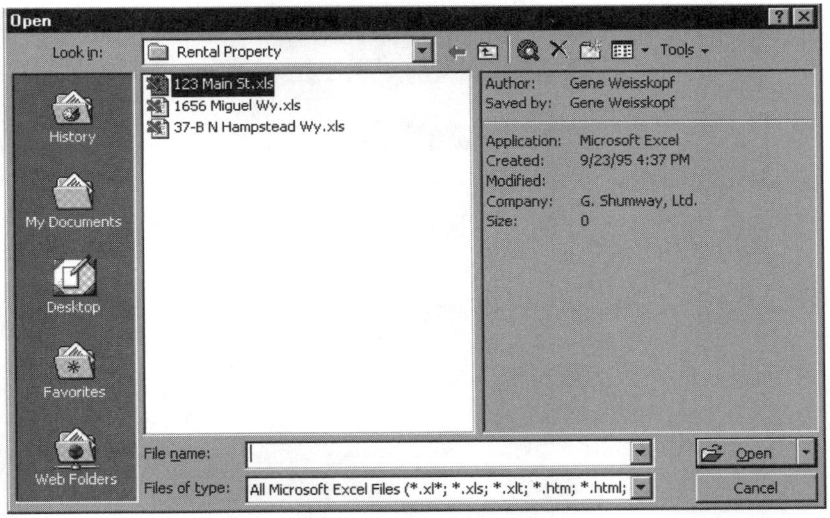

FIGURE 7.3: The Open dialog box offers a variety of tools for working with files.

Finding a File

If you're not sure where a file is (although maybe that's never happened to *you*), Excel offers several ways to find it. First, you can use the Look In list in the Open dialog box to display the files in another drive or folder.

If the current folder has too many files to browse through, you can filter the list of names to limit the display to files that match your entry. Simply type part of a name in the Filename field, and press Enter or click Find Now. You can also select a file type from the Files of Type drop-down list, such as dBASE Files (`*.dbf`), which displays only files that have an extension of `.DBF`.

TIP

You can select a previously used filename or filename filter from the drop-down list for the Filename field.

NEW

With Excel 2000, you have an additional, more powerful way to search for files—the Find dialog box, as shown in Figure 7.4. To open it, in the Open dialog box, choose Tools ➤ Find.

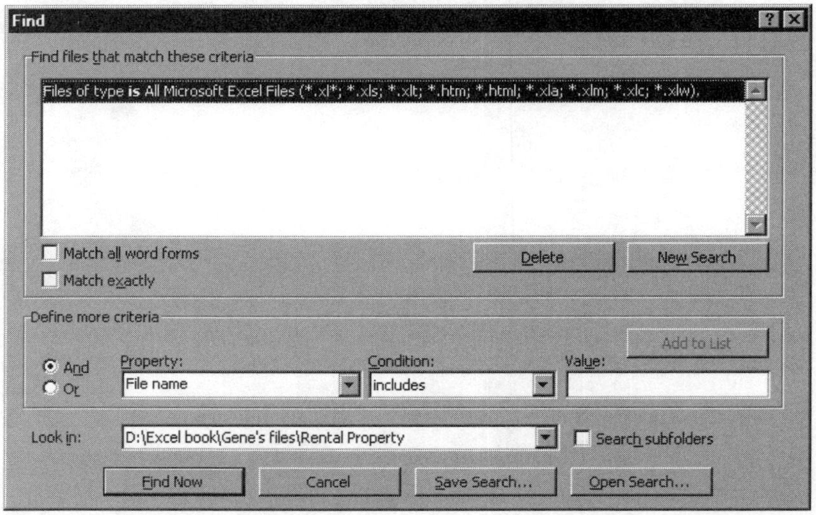

FIGURE 7.4: Use the Find dialog box to define criteria and search for files based on their properties, content, values, and so on.

Let's take a look at the options in the Find dialog box:

- The information displayed at the top of this dialog box, in the Find Files That Match These Criteria section, reflects what you selected in the Files of Type box in the Open dialog box. If this isn't what you want, close the Find dialog box, and make another selection.
- To find all forms of a word in a filename, click the Match All Forms check box. For example, if you enter Budget*.xls, clicking this check box finds all filenames that include Budget, Budgets, and Budgeting.
- To find only a specific word form in a filename, click the Match Exactly check box.

- In the Define More Criteria section, you select the search criteria you want, and then click Add to List:
  - In the Property drop-down list, click the down arrow to see the available properties. The conditions that are available depend on the property you select and include Includes, Begins With, and Ends With.
  - If the Value box is available (not grayed out), you must supply a value. For example, if you select Author in the Property list, the value might be Peter.
- In the Look In box, select the folder(s) to search, and click the Search Subfolders check box to search in subfolders as well.
- To begin your search, click Find Now.
- To save your search criteria, click Save Search to open the Save Search dialog box, enter a name for your search, and click OK.
- To reuse a search that you have saved, click Open Search.

TIP TIP TIP TIP TIP TIP TIP TIP TIP TIP TIP TIP TIP TIP TIP TIP TIP TIP TIP TIP TIP TIP TIP TIP TIP TIP

For help at any time in the Find dialog box, click the Help button (the question mark), and then click the item about which you want more information.

Tips for Working with Files in the Open Dialog Box

Suppose you want to work with an Excel file that someone else created and does not want changed. Instead of using the original document, make a copy of the workbook and open the copy. In the Open dialog box, right-click the filename, and choose Open As Copy from the shortcut menu. To peek at workbooks before you open one, select the file, click the Views down arrow, and choose Preview. This will work only for files whose Save Preview Picture option was selected before they were saved, as discussed earlier in "Setting File Properties."

You can look at the properties for each workbook by choosing Tools ➤ Properties.

NOTE NOTE NOTE NOTE NOTE NOTE NOTE NOTE NOTE NOTE NOTE NOTE NOTE NOTE NOTE

For information about opening a file that is in use on a network, see the next section, "Sharing Workbooks with Other Users." For information about opening a file from the Internet, see Skill 10.

Sharing Workbooks with Other Users

Normally, when multiple Excel users on a network can all access the same workbook at the same time, only the first one to open the workbook is allowed full rights to the file. When you're the only one to have a workbook open, you can share the file with other users so that all can work on it at the same time. To do so, follow these steps:

1. Choose Tools ➤ Share Workbook to open the Share Workbook dialog box, see Figure 7.5.
2. Click the *Allow changes by more than one user at the same time* check box.
3. Click OK.
4. Save the file.

Now, another Excel user can open the workbook, make changes to it, and save it in the usual ways. The names of all users who have the shared workbook open on their computers will appear in the list in the Share Workbook dialog box.

NOTE NOTE NOTE NOTE NOTE NOTE NOTE NOTE NOTE NOTE NOTE NOTE NOTE NOTE NOTE

To share and revise an Excel 2000 workbook, you must be using Excel 2000 and not an earlier version of Excel.

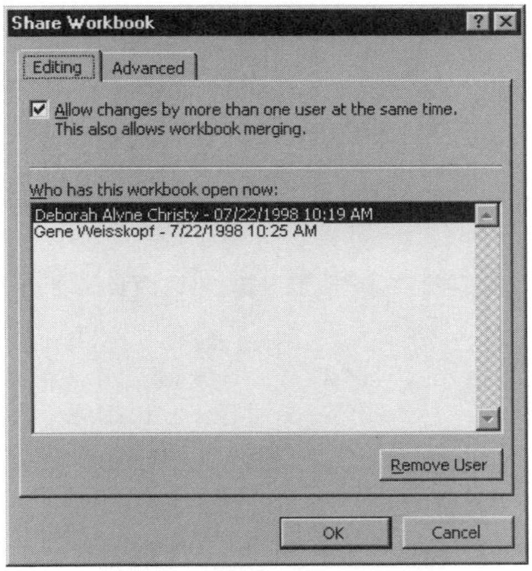

FIGURE 7.5: The Share Workbook dialog box

Opening a File That Is in Use

When multiple users are accessing files on a network, the workbook you try to open may already be in use. If file sharing has not been enabled for that workbook, the File Reservation dialog box will alert you to the conflict:

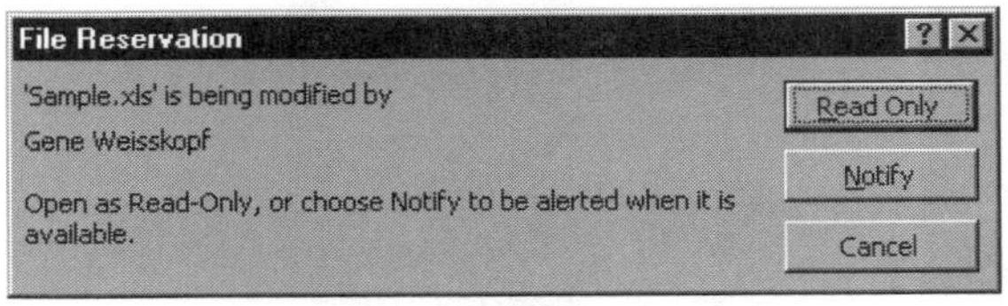

You have three choices:

- Choose Cancel and do not open the file.
- Choose Read Only to open the file with read-only access rights. In order to save it, you need to use File ➤ Save As and save it under a new name or in a new location.
- Choose Notify to open the file as read-only and have Excel let you know when the file is yours for saving.

If you click Notify, you anticipate opening the workbook with full rights to it. When Excel notifies you that the other user is done with the file, you can choose the Read-Write button in the dialog box to gain full access rights.

If you have already made changes to the workbook, you have to decide whether you want to lose your changes and open the file from disk or save your changes (Excel prompts you for a new filename) so that you can then compare your workbook with the version on disk.

Tracking Changes in a Shared Workbook

All users of the shared workbook can make changes to it as though it were their own. But they will all see the changes others have made and saved to disk either when they save their workbooks to disk (the default) or when they have chosen to be notified of those changes automatically. To be notified of changes, follow these steps:

1. Choose Tools ➤ Share Workbook to open the Share Workbook dialog box.
2. Click the Advanced tab.

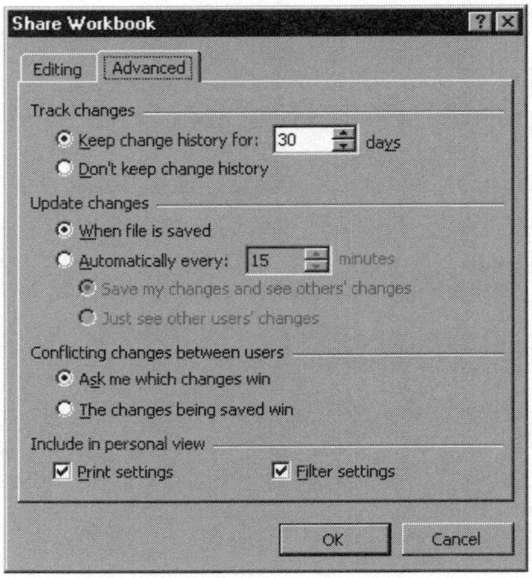

3. In the Update Changes section, click the Automatically Every x Minutes option.
4. Click OK.

When you save a shared workbook (or when you are notified automatically of the changes others have made), a change made by another that does *not* conflict with any changes you have made will appear in your workbook after you save it. (Excel will prompt you with a dialog box to tell you that changes were made by others.)

If a change made by another does conflict with a change you have made, you will be asked to accept either your change or the other one in the Resolve Conflicts dialog box (see Figure 7.6).

Action Number	Date	Time	Who	Change	Sheet	Range	New Value	Old Value	Action Type	Losing Action
1	1/17/99	6:14 PM	Annette Marquis	Cell Change	Cards	J3	2	<blank>		
2	1/17/99	6:14 PM	Annette Marquis	Cell Change	Cards	J3	<blank>	2		
3	1/17/99	6:34 PM	Gini Courter	Cell Change	Cards	J3	1	<blank>		
4	1/17/99	6:50 PM	Annette Marquis	Cell Change	Cards	J3	2	<blank>	Won	3
5	1/17/99	6:52 PM	Annette Marquis	Cell Change	Cards	J3	<blank>	2		
The history ends with the changes saved on 1/17/1999 at 6:52 PM.										

FIGURE 7.6: When changes made by another user conflict with changes you have made, you decide which ones to keep in the Resolve Conflicts dialog box.

When someone else's change to a cell has been made in your copy of the workbook, that cell will have a comment attached to it that explains the nature of the change, the author of the change, and the date and time the change was made (cell comments are discussed in Skill 10). Those comments remain in the worksheet only until you make a change to the worksheet yourself.

You can also keep track of changes that have been made to a workbook since sharing was enabled. To do so, follow these steps:

1. Choose Tools ➤ Track Changes ➤ Highlight Changes to open the Highlight Changes dialog box.
2. Click the Track Changes While Editing check box.
3. Click the List Changes on a New Sheet check box.
4. Click OK.

The result is a new sheet in the workbook named History, on which the changes are listed row by row, with each column representing information about each change, such as the date and time it was made, the author of the change, the cell in which

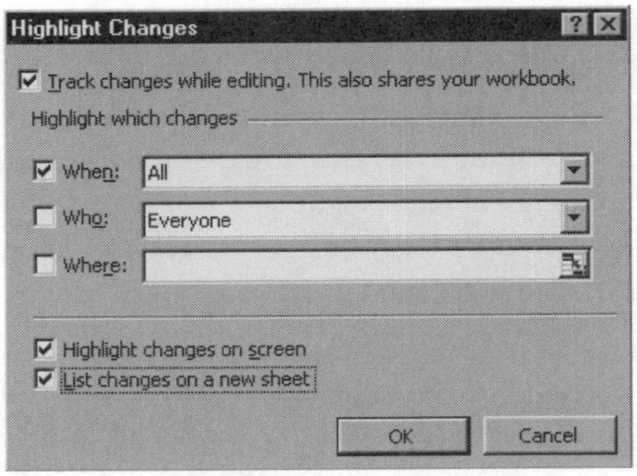

the change was made, and so on. This list of changes is already set up as a filtered list (see Skill 13), so you can display only those rows that meet the criteria you specify. When you save your workbook, the History sheet is removed, but you can create a new one with the Highlight Changes dialog box.

Words of Caution about Sharing Workbooks

The concept of sharing a workbook may seem simple at first if you think of passing one piece of paper around to several co-workers, with each having the authority to override any changes made by the preceding person. At the end of the line, the job is done, and the last person has the ultimate say on which changes ended up on the page.

But that's not the case at all with shared workbooks. The concept is more like making copies of a piece of paper for many co-workers, with all of them then sitting down to work. At some point, you (the one who made the copies in the first place) must look at who made which changes, and decide which of those changes to accept and which to reject. Even with Excel's excellent tracking capabilities, the job of reconciliation can become complex.

Of course, the process would be much more manageable if each Excel user were working on a different worksheet in the same workbook, as opposed to everyone trying to update a number in cell G124, forcing a decision on whose version should be left intact.

When a workbook is being shared, you cannot do any of the following:

- Delete worksheets.
- Delete or insert a range of cells (full rows or columns are allowed).
- Insert or revise charts.

- Insert or revise pictures.
- Work with the drawing tools.
- Merge cells into one cell.
- Apply conditional formatting to cells.
- Apply data validation to cells.
- Work with scenarios.
- Create automatic subtotals.

Saving or Opening a Workbook in Another File Format

Excel can handle files from many programs, including spreadsheets from Lotus 1-2-3, dBASE database files, and earlier versions of Excel. Simply open the file in the usual way, and Excel translates it as needed. Remember that you can filter the list of files that are displayed in the Open dialog box by entering the filter in the Filename field or by selecting a file type from the Files of Type drop-down list.

You can also save an Excel workbook in another file format. Follow these steps:

1. With the workbook open, choose File ➤ Save As to open the Save As dialog box.
2. In the Filename box, enter a filename, but do not type the period or the extension.
3. In the Save As Type list, as shown in Figure 7.7, select a file type. Excel adds the appropriate filename extension.
4. Click Save to save the workbook in the new format.

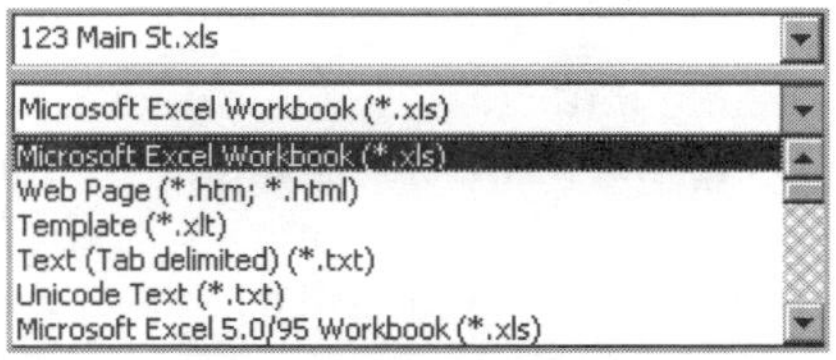

FIGURE 7.7: To save the current workbook in another format, choose the file type from the Save As Type list.

You can save an Excel 2000 workbook file in the format called Microsoft Excel 97-2000 & 5.0/95 Workbook. This allows the resulting file to be opened in Excel 95, Excel 97, and Excel 2000. Although users of earlier versions of Excel won't be able to access the features found only in Excel 2000, they will be able to use the workbook as though it were created in their versions of Excel. However, the caveat is that if they save the workbook, all Excel 2000 features will be lost in the resulting file.

Because there are differences between the various file types, not all the information in the workbook may be saved. For example, your workbook may have several worksheets containing data, but when you save the workbook as a 1-2-3 WK1 file, only the active sheet will be saved, since that file format supports only one spreadsheet. You have to save each of the other occupied sheets to their own files.

If you have many files to convert, you can open multiple files in the Open dialog box by holding down Shift (for contiguous files) or Ctrl (for noncontiguous files) and selecting the files. Then save each file to the new format.

Using Templates

A *template* is a pattern for creating new items. Call it the cookie-cutter school of design, if you will. In the world of computers, a template document is a simple method for maintaining consistency as you design new documents.

Excel has workbook template files, named with an XLT extension, that can serve as the basis for new workbooks. The template might contain formulas, cell colors and borders, numeric formats, and titles and other textual labels. A template lacks only the numbers (that you will enter) to complete the workbook.

NOTE NOTE NOTE NOTE NOTE NOTE NOTE NOTE NOTE NOTE NOTE NOTE NOTE NOTE

Excel comes with several templates that can serve as examples of template design and functionality. Although Excel's templates are interesting, they are involved, and their features may complicate, rather than illuminate, your learning process.

You'll read about creating your own templates later in this section, but here's a way to create an "informal" template without actually creating an Excel template file. Suppose you want to create a workbook for next year's budget, and you have in hand the budget workbook from this year. Follow these steps:

1. Open the file, and save it under a new name.
2. Delete the numbers in it, but not the formulas or other data that will be relevant in the new year.

3. Change its title to reflect a new year.
4. Save it again.

Opening a Workbook Template

To create a workbook based on a template, follow these steps:

1. Choose File ➤ New to open the New dialog box.
2. Click the Spreadsheet Solutions tab:

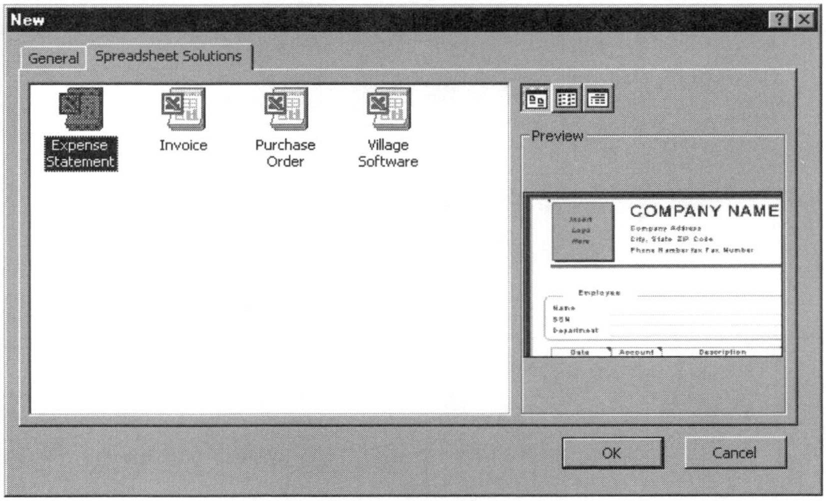

3. Select the template you want, and click OK.

   When Excel opens the template, it gives the template a new name so that you won't accidentally save it under the same name and overwrite the template file. That way, you can use the same template over and over again.

   Excel also displays a toolbar for the template. Click the question mark (Help) to get help on using the template (see Figure 7.8).

4. Enter your data and make any other changes you want to the workbook.
5. Choose File ➤ Save.
6. When Excel prompts you for a new filename, enter a new name, and click Save to save the file. By default, Excel saves the workbook with an XLS extension so that you don't overwrite the original template.

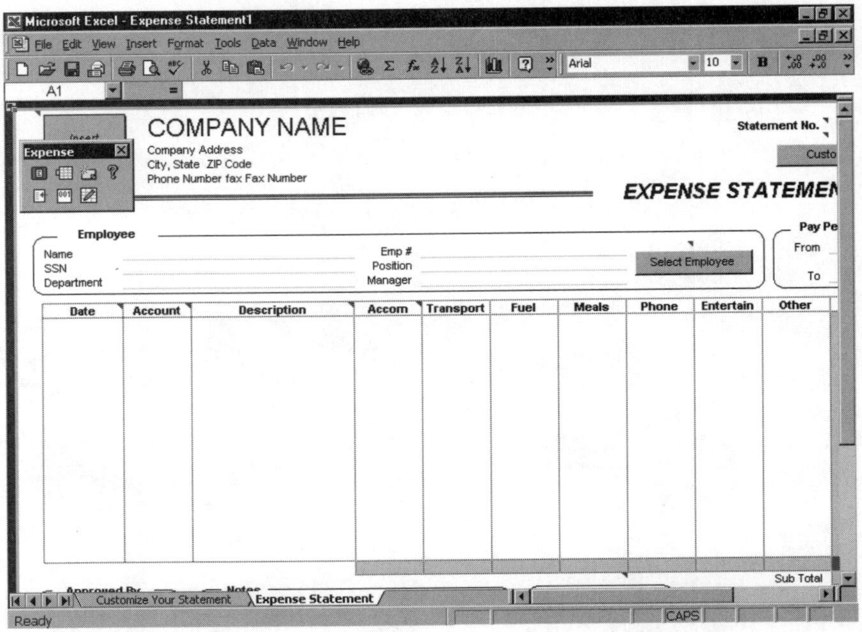

FIGURE 7.8: An Excel Expense Statement template

In many cases, the key to using a template effectively is *not* to make changes to it! At least, don't make changes to the information that was part of the template file. If everyone in your company uses the same Excel template to fill out expense reports, for example, all the reports should look the same and make the same calculations.

Opening a Sheet Template

If you want to insert a template into the current workbook, follow these steps:

1. Right-click the sheet tab before which you want to insert the template.
2. From the shortcut menu, choose Insert to open the Insert dialog box with the Spreadsheet Solutions tab selected.
3. Select a template, and click OK.

NOTE NOTE NOTE NOTE NOTE NOTE NOTE NOTE NOTE NOTE NOTE NOTE NOTE NOTE NOTE

You can choose any template, but if the template contains a dozen worksheets, Excel inserts all of them into the active workbook.

Creating a Workbook Template

It's a snap to create your own templates. Follow these steps:

1. Add the basic information to a workbook, such as a title, column and row titles, formulas, formatting, and so on. If you want to create a single-sheet template, delete all but one worksheet from the workbook.
2. Choose File ➤ Save As to open the Save As dialog box.
3. Choose Template in the Save As Type list.
4. By default, Excel selects the Templates folder.
5. Specify a filename, but don't append the period or an extension after it; Excel appends the XLT.
6. Click Save to finish the job.

The next time you open the New dialog box, the template you added is available on the General tab.

Creating a Default Template

You can create your own default worksheet or workbook template, called an *autotemplate*, by giving it a special name and storing it in Excel's XLStart folder.

To create a worksheet autotemplate, save a single-sheet workbook in the XLStart folder as a template with the name Sheet.xlt. When you later choose Insert ➤ Worksheet, the new default worksheet will be based on the Sheet.xlt template.

To create a default workbook, save a workbook as a template with the name Book.xlt in the XLStart folder. When you click the New button to create a new workbook, the new default workbook will be based on the Book.xlt file.

Revising a Template

To make changes to a template, follow these steps:

1. Choose File ➤ Open to open the Open dialog box.
2. Select the template you want to change, and open it.
3. Make any changes you want, and then choose File ➤ Save to save it.

Saving the Workspace

When you really have Excel running like a champ, you may have several workbooks open, as well as several more windows that contain different views of those workbooks (as described in Skill 14). When 5:00 comes (or 9:30 if you're *really* working hard), you can save the layout of all the windows that are open so that you can open them all again the next morning.

To save your workspace, follow these steps:

1. Choose File ➤ Save Workspace to open the Save Workspace dialog box.
2. Give the file a name to save a list of the workbook filenames, their window positions and sizes, and a list of any other open windows.
3. Click Save.

Excel automatically gives the file an XLW extension and prompts you to save the open workbooks.

TIP TIP TIP TIP TIP TIP TIP TIP TIP TIP TIP TIP TIP TIP TIP TIP TIP TIP TIP TIP TIP TIP TIP TIP TIP TIP

Excel opens a workspace file every time you run the program if you save the workspace in the XLStart folder. Save the actual workbooks in their normal locations, not in XLStart.

Are You Experienced?

Now you can . . .

- ☑ **Save workbooks manually and automatically**
- ☑ **Create new workbooks**
- ☑ **Open workbooks**
- ☑ **Share workbooks**
- ☑ **Save or open a workbook in another file format**
- ☑ **Work with templates**
- ☑ **Save the workspace**

SKILL 8

Printing Your Workbooks

- Specifying what to print
- Paginating print jobs
- Designing the page
- Setting page options
- Setting margins
- Specifying the header and footer
- Setting sheet options
- Using Print Preview

You may not print every worksheet every time you use it, but you'll probably print it at least once. This skill shows you how to select what you want to print, how to set the page layout and print options, and how to preview your printouts.

Specifying What to Print

Printing the current worksheet can be as simple as choosing File ➤ Print (or pressing Ctrl+P) and clicking OK, or clicking the Print button on the Standard toolbar to start the print job immediately. In many cases, though, you may want to specify which part of the workbook to print and set some print options.

NOTE NOTE NOTE NOTE NOTE NOTE NOTE NOTE NOTE NOTE NOTE NOTE NOTE NOTE NOTE

You can set the print options for each sheet in a workbook. For example, when you print Sheet1, you can set the left margin to an inch. You can then print from Sheet2 with half-inch margins without affecting the margin settings for Sheet1.

Printing a Sheet or a Selection

When you choose File ➤ Print (Ctrl+P), the Print dialog box appears, as shown in Figure 8.1. You use this dialog box to choose the part of the workbook to print, the number of copies to print, and the pages to print.

The Print What section in the Print dialog box has three options:

Selection Prints the currently selected range of cells; the selection must be a single contiguous (rectangular) range.

Active Sheet(s) Prints all the data on the selected sheets; this is the default if you have not yet printed the current workbook.

Entire Workbook Prints every sheet in the workbook that contains data.

The printout contains everything that appears on your screen within the chosen print area, including any charts or graphic objects. Therefore, before you print a worksheet or, especially, an entire workbook for the first time, be sure to use the Print Preview tool (discussed later in this skill) to see just what Excel intends to print. For example, if you accidentally entered something into cell BD950, Excel would happily print every column and row on that sheet from A1 to BD950. And you would end up with *lots* of blank pages and perhaps a small headache.

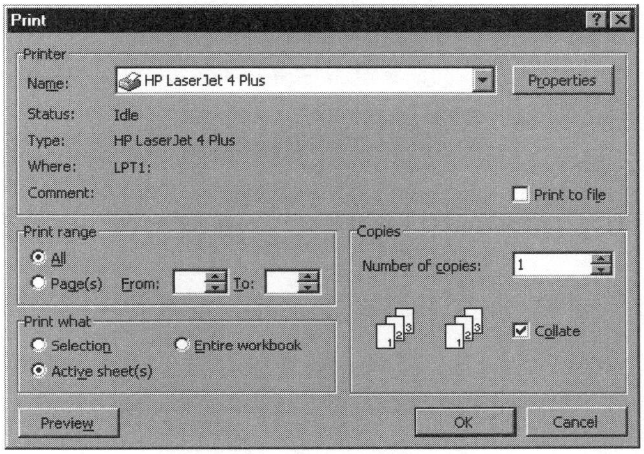

FIGURE 8.1: Use the Print dialog box to select how much and what part of the current workbook to print.

Selecting a Range of Cells to Print

When a page has many occupied ranges, you can choose to print only a single range. Follow these steps:

1. Select the range you want to print.
2. Choose File ➤ Print to open the Print dialog box.
3. In the Print What section, click Selection.
4. Click OK.

When selecting a specific range, be sure to include all the necessary rows and columns. Be especially careful of text that overhangs its cell and extends past the last column of the range. The text that appears outside that last column will not appear in the printout. In that case, you need to include all the columns over which the text extended.

NOTE NOTE NOTE NOTE NOTE NOTE NOTE NOTE NOTE NOTE NOTE NOTE NOTE NOTE NOTE

Avoid the temptation to include extra blank columns or rows to serve as margins. Let Excel's Page Setup options handle the way the data is laid out on the page.

Selecting Multiple Ranges

You can print multiple ranges anywhere in the workbook. Follow these steps:

1. Choose File ➤ Page Setup to open the Page Setup dialog box.

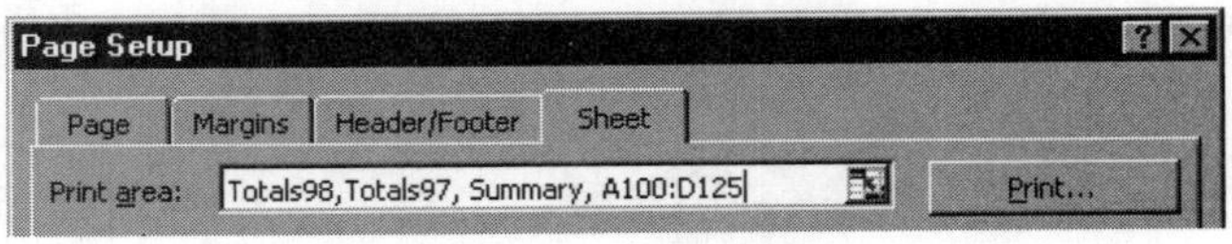

2. Click the Sheet tab.
3. In the Print Area field, enter the ranges you want to print.
4. Click OK.

TIP TIP TIP TIP TIP TIP TIP TIP TIP TIP TIP TIP TIP TIP TIP TIP TIP TIP TIP TIP TIP TIP TIP TIP TIP TIP

In the Print Area field, you can either type cell addresses or point to each range in the worksheet. Separate each range's address from the next with a comma.

TIP TIP TIP TIP TIP TIP TIP TIP TIP TIP TIP TIP TIP TIP TIP TIP TIP TIP TIP TIP TIP TIP TIP TIP TIP TIP

Take advantage of named ranges. If you already named the ranges you want to print, simply click in the Print Area field, press F3, select a range name from the Names list, enter a comma, and press F3 again to select the next name.

The ranges you select are printed in the order in which they appear in the Print Area field. Each range starts on a new page.

Setting the Print Area

You can specify the print area and use it to specify the range that you want to print the next time you print. You might find this convenient for a range that you're currently working in and can therefore select easily, but are not quite ready to print.

To set the print area, follow these steps:

1. Select a single contiguous range.
2. Choose File ➤ Print Area ➤ Set Print Area.

Excel enters dashed page break lines on each side of the selected range (page breaks are discussed a little later in this skill in the section "How Excel Paginates Print Jobs").

You can choose File ➤ Page Setup to see that the range you selected has also been entered in the Print Area field in the Page Setup dialog box.

NOTE NOTE NOTE NOTE NOTE NOTE NOTE NOTE NOTE NOTE NOTE NOTE NOTE NOTE NOTE

The Print Area command actually creates a name (Print_Area) for the range you select. If you redefine the cell address for that name, you also change the Print Area.

Printing Charts and Graphics

When you print an entire worksheet, by default you print all charts and graphics on that sheet. If you select a range to print, you print any charts or graphics within that range.

You can also print a chart from its chart sheet, without any worksheet data. The chart sheet will have print settings specific to that chart. Many of the print settings are the same settings discussed in this skill, but others are unique to charts. You'll learn about printing a chart on its own sheet in Skill 11.

Choosing the Pages and Copies to Print

In the Print Range section of the Print dialog box, you specify which pages to print. By default, All is selected. Click the Pages option to specify the starting (from) and ending (to) pages to print.

TIP TIP TIP TIP TIP TIP TIP TIP TIP TIP TIP TIP TIP TIP TIP TIP TIP TIP TIP TIP TIP TIP TIP TIP TIP

If you use click Preview, the status bar displays the total number of pages in the printout. If you specify a page range, only the selected pages are included in the preview.

In the Print dialog box, you can set the Copies option to a number greater than one to print multiple copies of each page. For example, if you set Copies to **5**, you'll end up with five copies of page 1, followed by five copies of page 2, and so on. If you click the Collate check box, Excel prints one complete set of pages before it prints the next set.

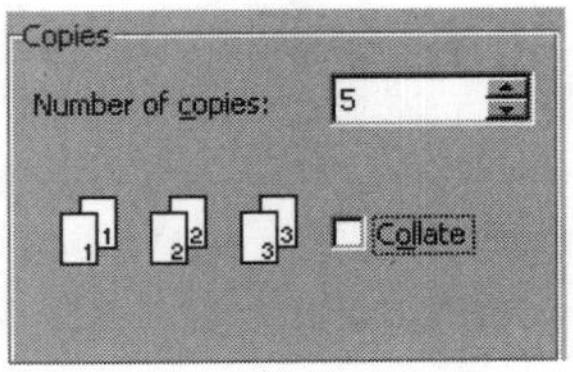

Paginating Print Jobs

Excel lays out the printed page according to the settings in the Page Setup dialog box (choose File ➤ Page Setup). These settings include paper size, margins, header and footer, and so on and are discussed later in this skill in the "Setting the Page Options" section.

When a range of data has too many rows or columns to fit on a page, Excel breaks the range onto multiple pages as needed.

> TIP
> **You can have Excel contract or expand the print range so that it fits on the number of pages you specify. The Scaling options are discussed in the "Setting the Page Options" section, later in this skill.**

When a range has too many rows to fit within the height of one page, Excel prints them all on multiple pages.

When a range has too many columns, by default Excel includes as many as it can fit within the width of the page, such as columns A through F. It prints all the rows in those columns, taking as many pages as needed. Then Excel prints the next group of columns, such as G through K, and all the rows in them. After printing, you can arrange the pages side-by-side to duplicate the layout of the range.

When a range is broken onto multiple pages, you may want to take advantage of the Print Titles option. You designate the rows or columns of cells that you want to serve as column or row titles on each page of the printout. See the "Setting Print Titles" section, later in this skill.

If you want Excel to print all columns of data before all the rows are printed, follow these steps:

1. Choose File ➤ Page Setup to open the Page Setup dialog box.
2. Click the Sheet tab.

3. Click the Over, Then Down option.

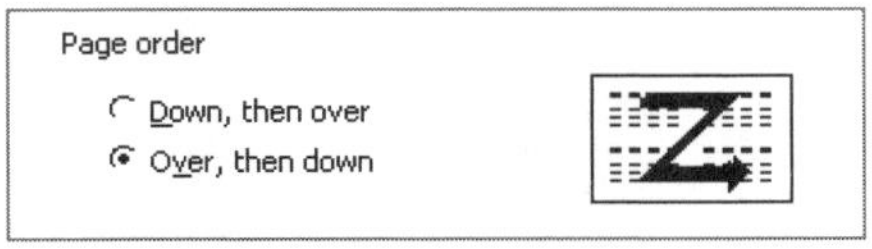

4. Click OK

Excel prints multiple worksheets in the order that they appear in the workbook. Excel prints all the data on the first sheet on as many pages as needed and then starts a new page to print the data on the second sheet.

Excel prints multiple ranges in the order in which you select them. Each range starts on a new page.

Previewing Page Breaks

When you print any part of the workbook, Excel must calculate at which row and column a new page will start in the printout. Afterward, it includes these automatic page breaks within the worksheet as dashed lines that run horizontally and vertically at the appropriate rows and columns. Excel does not break a page *within* a row or a column.

TIP TIP TIP TIP TIP TIP TIP TIP TIP TIP TIP TIP TIP TIP TIP TIP TIP TIP TIP TIP TIP TIP TIP TIP TIP TIP

If you don't see the dashed automatic page break lines on the screen, choose Tools ➤ Options to open the Options dialog box, click the View tab, and then select Page Breaks. You can clear this option at any time if the page break lines are cluttering up the screen.

You can get an even better look at the way Excel will paginate your worksheet by choosing View ➤ Page Break Preview. An example is shown in Figure 8.2, in which a table in the worksheet has been selected as the print range (A1:N26), but it spans more rows and columns than will fit on a single page. I expanded the top and bottom margins so that more page breaks would appear in the worksheet (because fewer rows fit on a page). I also erased many cells so that the page numbers would show up.

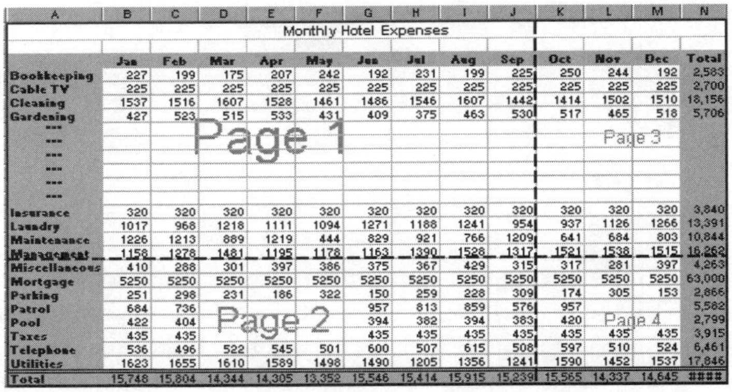

A	B	C	D	E	F	G	H	I	J	K	L	M	N
					Monthly Hotel Expenses								
	Jan	Feb	Mar	Apr	May	Jun	Jul	Aug	Sep	Oct	Nov	Dec	Total
Bookkeeping	227	199	175	207	242	192	231	199	225	250	244	192	2,583
Cable TV	225	225	225	225	225	225	225	225	225	225	225	225	2,700
Cleaning	1537	1516	1607	1528	1461	1486	1546	1607	1442	1414	1502	1510	18,156
Gardening	427	523	515	533	431	409	375	463	530	517	465	518	5,706

Insurance	320	320	320	320	320	320	320	320	320	320	320	320	3,840
Laundry	1017	968	1218	1111	1094	1271	1188	1241	954	937	1126	1266	13,391
Maintenance	1226	1213	889	1219	444	829	921	766	1209	641	684	803	10,844
Management	1158	1278	1481	1195	1178	1163	1390	1528	1317	1521	1538	1515	16,262
Miscellaneous	410	288	301	397	386	375	367	429	315	317	281	397	4,263
Mortgage	5250	5250	5250	5250	5250	5250	5250	5250	5250	5250	5250	5250	63,000
Parking	251	298	231	186	322	150	259	228	309	174	305	153	2,866
Patrol	684	736				957	813	859	576	957			5,582
Pool	422	404				394	382	394	383	420			2,799
Taxes	435	435				435	435	435	435	435	435	435	3,915
Telephone	536	496	522	545	501	600	507	615	508	597	510	524	6,461
Utilities	1623	1655	1610	1589	1498	1490	1205	1356	1241	1590	1452	1537	17,846
Total	15,748	15,804	14,344	14,305	13,352	15,546	15,414	15,915	15,239	15,565	14,337	14,645	####

FIGURE 8.2: Page Break Preview shows exactly where the page breaks will occur during printing.

Here are some more things you should know about Page Break Preview:

- The view of the worksheet is shrunk to 60 percent of the normal view (100 percent), so more rows and columns are displayed (although you can change the magnification by choosing View ➤ Zoom and choosing a percentage).
- The selected print range or ranges are shown on the normal worksheet grid and light background, and the rest of the worksheet is shown in gray so that you can see exactly what will be printed.
- Page breaks are shown as bold dashed lines that stand out clearly.
- Pages are numbered on the worksheet so that you can see the page on which each cell will be printed. In Figure 8.2, you can see that the table will print on four pages—the range A1:J17 will print on page 1, A18:J26 on page 2, K1:N17 on page 3, and K18:N26 on page 4.
- Choose View ➤ Normal to return to the normal view of the worksheet. You can toggle between the two views as needed.

The page breaks in Figure 8.2 are not fixed in stone. If you decrease the top or bottom print margins (in the Page Setup dialog box), the horizontal page break lines move down, and more rows of the table fit on each page.

In Page Break Preview, you can drag a page break to a new position (doing so changes an automatic page break to a manual one; see the next section). If you increase the number of rows or columns on a page by dragging a horizontal page break down or a vertical one to the right, Excel shrinks the size of the font in the printout, if necessary, to comply with the new page break location (see "Setting the Page Options" later in this skill).

You also see the effects on pagination when you insert or delete rows or columns. For example, in Figure 8.2, if you insert a couple of columns at column A, the table moves to the right, causing more of its columns to appear on page 3 with the columns Oct through Total.

Inserting Manual Page Breaks

You can create page breaks manually anywhere in the worksheet to control what appears on any page. In Page Break Preview, a manual page break is a solid line; in Normal view, it is a dashed line, but the dashes are a bit longer than the dashes in an automatic break.

NOTE NOTE NOTE NOTE NOTE NOTE NOTE NOTE NOTE NOTE NOTE NOTE NOTE NOTE NOTE

Unlike automatic page breaks, a manual page break always stays with the row or column on which you created it, even when you insert new columns or rows.

When you insert a manual page break at a row (or column), all the automatic page breaks below that break (or to the right of the column break) adjust their positions to take it into account. That's because each automatic page break is calculated to remain a specific distance from the preceding page break.

Inserting a Page Break

You can create two kinds of page breaks:

- A full page break spans the entire width (or height) of the worksheet and affects all print ranges that may lie in its path.
- A partial page break affects only the print range in which you created it.

To create a full page break, follow these steps:

1. Select the entire row or column that you want to appear first on a new page (click in the row or column heading).
2. Choose Insert ➤ Page Break.

To create a partial page break, follow these steps:

1. Select a print range, as discussed earlier in this skill.

2. Select a single cell of the print range.
3. Choose Insert ➤ Page Break.

The result depends on the location of the cell you selected in the print range:

- Selecting a cell in the first row of the print range creates a vertical page break.
- Selecting a cell in the first column of the print range creates a horizontal page break.
- Selecting a cell within a print range but not in its first row or column creates both a horizontal and vertical page break.

Removing a Manual Page Break

To remove a manual page break, follow these steps:

1. Select a cell directly below a horizontal page break or directly to the right of a vertical page break.
2. Choose Insert ➤ Remove Page Break.

To remove all manual page breaks from the current worksheet, follow these steps:

1. Click the Select All button to select all the cells in the worksheet.
2. Choose Insert ➤ Reset All Page Breaks.

TIP TIP TIP TIP TIP TIP TIP TIP TIP TIP TIP TIP TIP TIP TIP TIP TIP TIP TIP TIP TIP TIP TIP TIP TIP TIP

The Select All button is the blank cell at the intersection of the row and column headings.

Designing the Page Layout

The default settings for the layout of the printed page are defined in the Page Setup dialog box (choose File ➤ Page Setup), and you use this dialog box to change them. The Page Setup dialog box has the following four tabs, and I'll discuss each of them in the next four sections:

Page Sets the paper type, orientation on the page, scaling, and starting page number.

Margins Adjusts the page margins.

Header/Footer Specifies the header or footer that appears on each page.

Sheet Sets the print area for single or multiple ranges, specifies row or column titles to appear on every page, sets the page order, and selects options such as the display of worksheet gridlines.

Your selected printer's features and capabilities also affect the layout of the printed page. To change those settings, click the Options button in the Page Setup dialog box. To select another printer, choose it from the drop-down list in the Print dialog box, and then change the printer's settings by clicking the Properties button next to the printer name.

Setting the Page Options

When you choose File ➤ Page Setup and click the Page tab in the Page Setup dialog box, you'll see the dialog box shown in Figure 8.3.

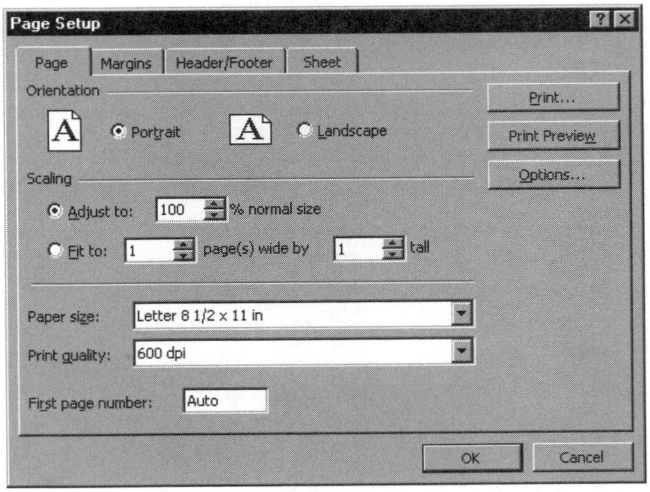

FIGURE 8.3: The Page tab in the Page Setup dialog box

Three options may already be familiar to you from other Windows programs:

Orientation Chooses whether the printout should run across the paper in the narrow direction (portrait, the default) or the wide direction (landscape).

Paper Size Selects the size of the paper that your printer will be using.

SKILL 8

Print Quality Sets the print resolution; in most cases, resolution affects only the way that graphics are printed. A higher resolution produces a higher quality printout, but it usually takes longer to print.

The default setting for the First Page Number option is Auto, which means that the first printed page is numbered 1. But you can specify any starting number here. Let's say you're going to print several workbooks to produce one large report with all the pages numbered consecutively. If the print job you just finished ended with page 72, you would set the First Page Number option for the next print job to 73.

The Scaling options can be real time-savers when you want to adjust the fit of the printout on the paper:

Adjust To Is the default selection and lets you specify a percentage for enlarging or shrinking the printout. Valid numbers range from 10 (that's really tiny) to 400. The default is 100 (percent), at which no scaling is done.

Fit To Lets you specify exactly how many pages you want to use for your printout, including both the number of pages wide and the number of pages tall. Excel does its best to fit your printout within the number of pages you specify.

NOTE NOTE NOTE NOTE NOTE NOTE NOTE NOTE NOTE NOTE NOTE NOTE NOTE NOTE NOTE

Excel ignores manual page breaks when you choose the Fit To option, but accepts them when you set a scaling factor with the Adjust To option.

Suppose the Page Break Preview shows that a printout will take just a tiny bit more than two pages because of the number of rows in the worksheet, but you prefer to use only two pages. Instead of fussing around trying to eliminate a few rows or shrinking the fonts in the worksheet, you can select the Fit To option and specify **1** page wide by **2** pages tall. Excel will fit your spreadsheet on the two pages perfectly.

Setting the Margins

You adjust the margins on the printed page with the Margins tab in the Page Setup dialog box, as shown in Figure 8.4. The representation of a page in the dialog box shows you where each margin appears on the page. When you select a margin setting, such as Left, the corresponding margin line in the diagram is shown in black.

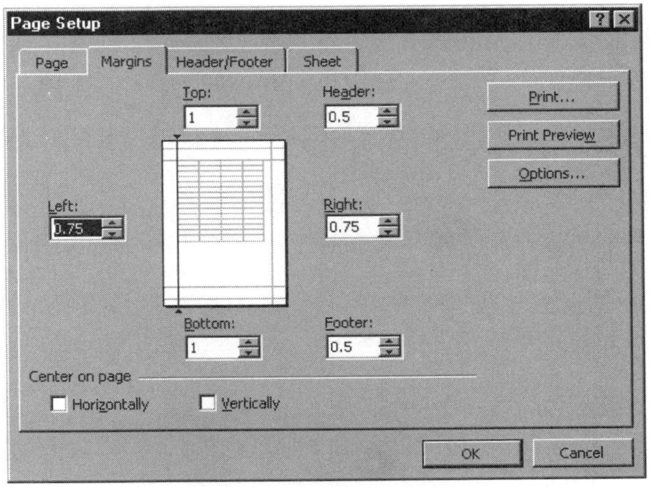

FIGURE 8.4: The Margins tab in the Page Setup dialog box

TIP TIP TIP TIP TIP TIP TIP TIP TIP TIP TIP TIP TIP TIP TIP TIP TIP TIP TIP TIP TIP TIP TIP TIP TIP

You can also set the margins in Print Preview simply by dragging any of the displayed margin lines to a new position. This method is fast and displays the results immediately. See the "Preview to Save a Tree (and Your Time)" section, later in this skill.

The four margin settings—Top, Bottom, Left, and Right—specify how much blank space appears between each of those edges of the printed page and the edge of the printed worksheet. A larger margin means more blank space and less printed area.

The Header and Footer options specify the margin size between the header and the top of the page and the footer and the bottom of the page. Their left and right margins are the same as for the data being printed.

NOTE NOTE NOTE NOTE NOTE NOTE NOTE NOTE NOTE NOTE NOTE NOTE NOTE NOTE NOTE

In most cases, the Header and Footer margins should be smaller than the Top and Bottom margins. Otherwise, the header or footer text might appear on top of the worksheet data in the printout.

In the Center on Page section, you can choose to center the printout on the page horizontally, vertically, or both. This option is a fast way to produce a nicely centered printout without fooling with each margin setting.

Specifying the Header and Footer

The header appears at the top of every printed page, and the footer appears at the bottom. You can use one or both for information such as the report title, the date of the printout, page numbering, or the name of the workbook that produced the printout. Figure 8.5 shows the Page Setup dialog box with the Header/Footer tab selected.

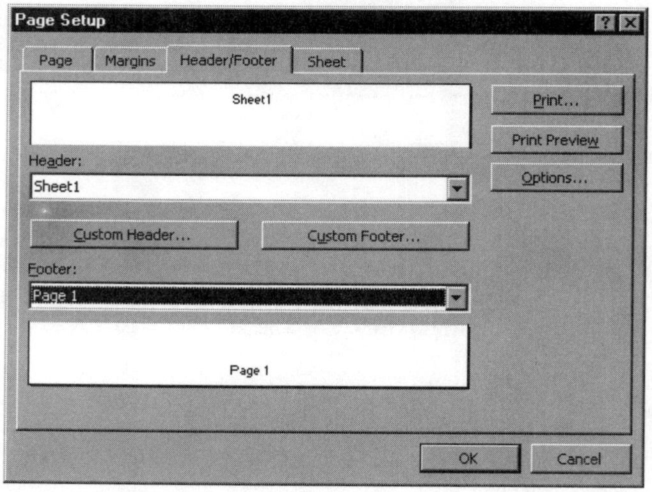

FIGURE 8.5: The Header/Footer tab in the Page Setup dialog box

You can either use a ready-made header or footer or create your own. In Figure 8.5 each field—Header and Footer—has a drop-down list from which you can select one of the built-in headers or footers.

You can include special codes in a header or footer to print such things as the page number, date, time, or filename. The codes are discussed a little later in this skill in the "Entering Special Codes" section.

Creating a Custom Header or Footer

If you want to create your own header or footer, click the Custom Header or Custom Footer button in the Page Setup dialog box. The process is exactly the same for creating either one of them. Figure 8.6 shows the Header dialog box.

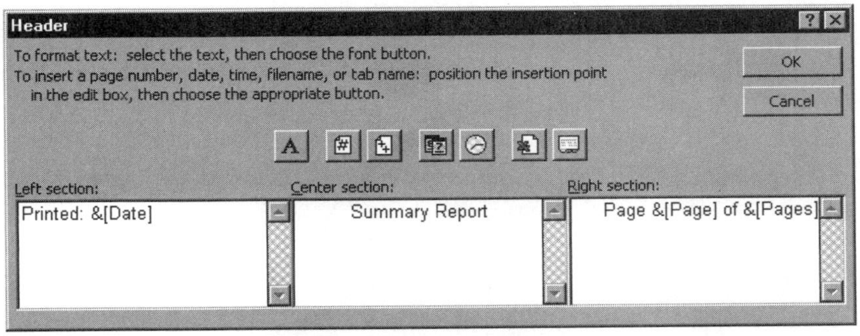

FIGURE 8.6: The dialog box for creating a custom header

TIP TIP TIP TIP TIP TIP TIP TIP TIP TIP TIP TIP TIP TIP TIP TIP TIP TIP TIP TIP TIP TIP TIP TIP TIP

You can use one of the ready-made headers or footers to jump-start your customization. Simply select one before you click the Custom Header or Footer button.

Enter the text you want to appear in the header or footer in any of the three fields:

Left Section Text starts at the left margin.

Center Section Text is centered within the margins.

Right Section Text aligns against the right margin.

Be careful not to enter too much text in a section because it can overwrite the text in one or both of the other sections in the printout. Choosing Print Preview before you print will alert you to any potential problems.

Although the text you enter in any of the three fields wraps to extra lines in the dialog box as needed, Excel still treats each entry as a single, long line. You can press Enter to create a multiline header or footer in any of the three sections.

Entering Special Codes

You can type anything you want into a custom header or footer, but Excel provides several special codes that you can include to print current information, such as the date or page number. You can type these codes, but it's easier to use one of the buttons in the Header or Footer dialog box, as shown earlier in Figure 8.6.

Button	Description
	Formats the font of all or part of the header/footer.
	Prints the current page number.
	Prints the total number of pages in the printout.
	Prints the current date.
	Prints the current time.
	Prints the workbook's file name.
	Prints the worksheet's name.

When you click the Date button, for example, Excel inserts the code

```
&[Date]
```

in the header or footer. When you print your worksheet, Excel substitutes the current date for the code in the printout.

If the date is December 31, 1999, and there are 14 pages in the printout, the custom header in Figure 8.6, earlier in this skill, would look like this when it is printed:

Printed: 12/31/99   Summary Report   Page 1 of 14

Setting the Sheet Options

The Sheet tab in the Page Setup dialog box is shown in Figure 8.7; its options affect what gets printed and the appearance of the output.

Earlier in this skill, we looked at the Print Area field, in which you can enter the range or ranges you want to print, and the Page Order section. Now we'll look at the other Sheet options.

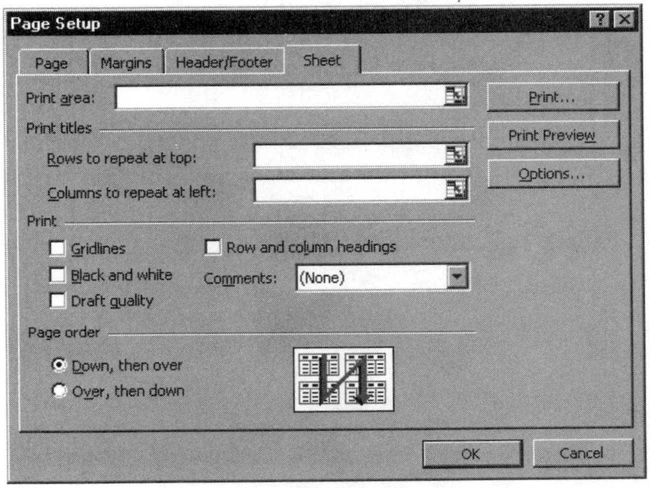

FIGURE 8.7: The Sheet tab in the Page Setup dialog box

Setting Print Titles

Many worksheets are organized around tables of data that have titles above each column and to the left of each row, as in Figure 8.8.

	A	B	C	D	E	F	G	H
1		Monthly Housing Expenses						
2								
3		Jan	Feb	Mar	Apr	May	Jun	Total
4	Insurance	51	51	51	51	51	51	306
5	Maintenance	48	48	48	48	48	48	288
6	Mortgage	925	925	925	925	925	925	5,550
7	Taxes	102	102	102	102	102	102	612
8	Telephone	42	78	65	115	70	67	437
9	Utilities	182	116	143	90	175	185	891
10	Total	1,350	1,320	1,334	1,331	1,371	1,378	8,084

FIGURE 8.8: A worksheet with titles above each column and to the left of each row

But unlike this worksheet, real-world worksheets often have many rows and columns, and real-world printouts require many pages. The problem here is that the titles that identify the data are printed only once—on page 1—and people who look at all the other pages have to guess which data are which.

That's where the Print Titles section of the Sheet tab comes in. In it you specify which rows (or columns) you want to appear at the top (or left side) of each page of the printout.

For example, Figure 8.9 shows a monthly expenses worksheet for a hotel, with a full year of columns and many rows of items. This worksheet is too large to print on a single page, so you use the Print Titles feature to print the row and column headings on each page.

	A	B	C	D	E	F	G	H	I	J
1						Monthly Hotel Expenses				
2										
3		Jan	Feb	Mar	Apr	May	Jun	Jul	Aug	Sep
4	Bookkeeping	227	199	175	207	242	192	231	199	225
5	Cable TV	225	225	225	225	225	225	225	225	225
6	Cleaning	1537	1516	1607	1528	1461	1486	1546	1607	1442
7	Gardening	427	523	515	533	431	409	375	463	530
8	Insurance	320	320	320	320	320	320	320	320	320
9	Laundry	1017	968	1218	1111	1094	1271	1188	1241	954
10	Maintenance	1226	1213	889	1219	444	829	921	766	1209
11	Management	1158	1278	1481	1195	1178	1163	1390	1528	1317
12	Miscellaneous	410	288	301	397	386	375	367	429	315
13	Mortgage	5250	5250	5250	5250	5250	5250	5250	5250	5250
14	Parking	251	298	231	186	322	150	259	228	309
15	Patrol	684	736	761	798	585	787	813	859	576
16	Pool	422	404	398	385	405	390	382	394	383

FIGURE 8.9: You can include the column and row titles on each page of the printout for a wide or long worksheet.

Here's how to print a worksheet so that the column titles and the row titles appear on each page:

1. Choose File ➤ Page Setup to open the Page Setup dialog box, and click the Sheet tab.
2. Select the Rows to Repeat at Top field.
3. In the worksheet, point to any cell that contains a column title.
4. Select the Columns to Repeat at Left field.
5. In the worksheet, point to any cell that contains a row title.
6. Click OK.

Now when you print, every page will have the appropriate titles over each column and to the left of each row, no matter how many pages are in the printout.

You do *not* need to exclude the column or row title cells from the print range. Excel knows that those cells should not be printed twice (once as the title cells and once as the worksheet range being printed).

TIP TIP TIP TIP TIP TIP TIP TIP TIP TIP TIP TIP TIP TIP TIP TIP TIP TIP TIP TIP TIP TIP TIP TIP TIP

To remove the settings for the Print Titles option, delete the row or column references in the Rows to Repeat at Top and the Columns to Repeat at Left fields.

Setting the Print Options

The settings in the Print section in the Sheet tab of the Page Setup dialog box affect the look of the printout.

Gridlines Prints the worksheet gridlines, which can help the reader follow rows and columns of data across the page in a large printout or in one that was printed in a small font.

Black and White Tells Excel that you are printing to a black and white printer. If a worksheet contains colors, Excel handles the colors appropriately.

Draft Quality Speeds printing by omitting graphics from a printout. Charts or graphics in a worksheet take longer to print, so you can print faster by selecting this option. You can then clear this option to include the graphics in the final printout.

Row and Column Headings Prints the worksheet row and column headings so that each item in the printout can be identified by its cell address.

Comments Prints any cell comments in the worksheet. You can choose to print all comments together after the worksheet has printed, or you can print comments in their actual positions within the worksheet (choose View ➤ Comments to display all comments).

TIP TIP TIP TIP TIP TIP TIP TIP TIP TIP TIP TIP TIP TIP TIP TIP TIP TIP TIP TIP TIP TIP TIP TIP TIP

Use the Gridlines, Comments, and Row and Column Headings options in unison to create a printout that helps you document your worksheet.

Preview to Save a Tree (and Your Time)

After you've specify the range to print, set all the various options, and turn on your printer, take a short detour. A few more acres of forest will thank you for it!

Choose File ➤ Print Preview or click the Print Preview button on the Standard toolbar to display on the screen what your printout will look like on paper. You can use this command at any time as you fine-tune the look you want in the printout. You'll also find Print Preview buttons in the Print dialog box and in the Page Setup dialog box.

Print Preview saves you time and paper by helping you avoid faulty or unattractive printouts; it is also an excellent design tool. Print Preview allows you to set options and adjust the print settings while you see the effects immediately on the screen.

Figure 8.10 shows the Print Preview for the worksheet in Figure 8.9. Although you can't edit the data in this view, you can make lots of other (style) adjustments.

The buttons on the preview toolbar perform the following tasks:

Next Displays the next page of a multipage printout; you can also press PgDn. The left side of the status bar shows the total number of pages in the printout (4 in Figure 8.10).

Previous Displays the previous page; you can also press PgUp.

Zoom Toggles between the full-page preview you see in Figure 8.10 and a magnified view that shows more detail. You can also click within the page to toggle between the two views.

Print Closes the preview but opens the Print dialog box, in which you can specify the number of pages to print, the number of copies, and so on, or click OK to send the worksheet to the printer.

Setup Opens the Page Setup dialog box, in which you can adjust any of its settings.

Margins Displays the margin lines on the preview (see Figure 8.10); drag one to a new position to change that margin.

Page Break Preview Closes the preview and returns to your worksheet.

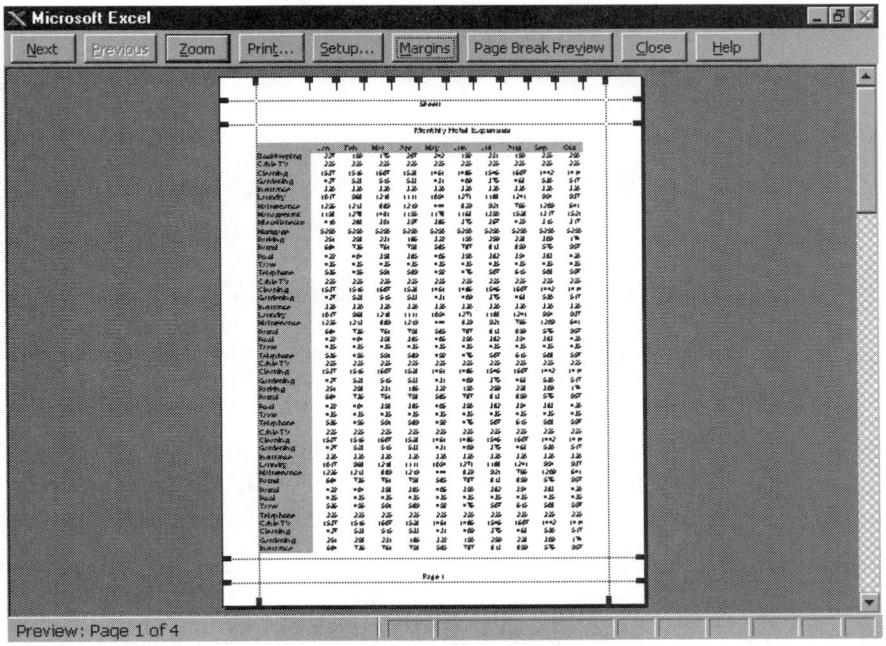

FIGURE 8.10: A print preview shows you what your printout will look like without taking the time or wood pulp to actually print it.

Close Closes the preview and returns to your previous view of the worksheet; you can also press Esc.

Help Opens the help window for Print Preview.

You can also adjust column widths while previewing the printout. In Figure 8.10, you can see small column indicators at the very top of the page being previewed. If you point to one and hold down the mouse button, two vertical dashed lines appear, indicating the width of that column. You can then drag the indicator left or right to make the column narrower or wider.

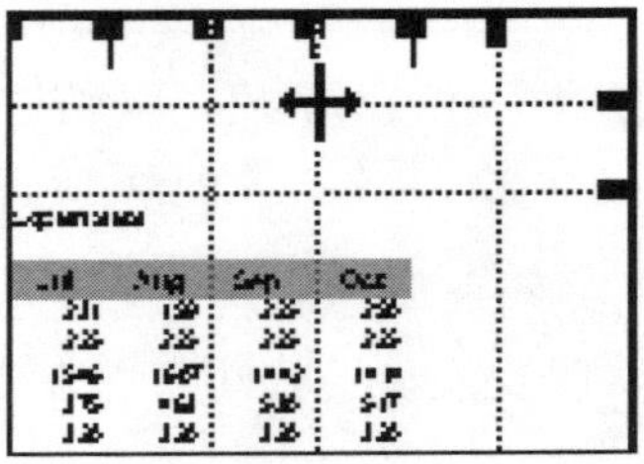

TIP TIP TIP TIP TIP TIP TIP TIP TIP TIP TIP TIP TIP TIP TIP TIP TIP TIP TIP TIP TIP TIP TIP TIP TIP

If you point to a margin line or column indicator and press and hold down the mouse button, you can see the current setting for the margin or the width of the column on the left side of the status bar.

The importance of previewing your printouts before committing them to paper cannot be overemphasized. You'll be amazed at how much time and energy you can save by fine-tuning your worksheets on screen before you send them to the printer.

Are You Experienced?

Now you can...

- ☑ Choose the print range
- ☑ Choose multiple print ranges
- ☑ Paginate your printout automatically and manually
- ☑ Design the page layout
- ☑ Set the print margins
- ☑ Specify headers and footers
- ☑ Create custom headers and footers
- ☑ Use special codes to print the current date and time
- ☑ Print row and column headings on every page of your printout
- ☑ Preview your worksheets before printing

SKILL 9

Keeping Track of Your Work

- Protecting cells and worksheets
- Protecting workbooks
- Hiding information from view
- Attaching comments to cells
- Running an audit
- Creating scenarios

Excel has many tools you can use to build and maintain your workbooks. You can use any of them on an as-needed basis. If you familiarize yourself with their usage in this skill, you can return here when you want to learn more about these tools.

Protecting Cells and Worksheets

Once you've put a lot of work into building a worksheet, you'd probably prefer not to accidentally replace a cell entry or formula with some other entry. Remember, it can take a Sherlock Holmes to discover that a formula was overwritten by a number. For example, when you look at a printout you can't tell the difference between a cell that contains a number and one that contains a formula that results in the same number.

Protecting data and formulas is especially important when more than one person is using a workbook. There are more opportunities for a mistake or for the "too many cooks" syndrome to kick in—each person can make a mistake in a different way!

NOTE NOTE NOTE NOTE NOTE NOTE NOTE NOTE NOTE NOTE NOTE NOTE NOTE NOTE NOTE

OK, so this book is written by someone who has *created* many more spreadsheets than he has ever had to use on a daily basis. The truth is that mistakes made by users can often be traced to the original design of the worksheet. A well-designed worksheet that has adequate safeguards and instructions for the user should leave few opportunities for problems.

By default, each cell and object is locked so that no changes can be made to it. But, also by default, the worksheet is *not* locked, and the cells and objects in it can be freely accessed and changed.

Locking the Entire Worksheet

Until you lock the worksheet, the protection status of individual cells or objects is irrelevant—they can all be changed as needed. To turn on protection for the entire worksheet, follow these steps:

1. Choose Tools ➤ Protection ➤ Protect Sheet to open the Protect Sheet dialog box.
2. By default, the Contents, Objects, and Scenarios check boxes are selected; clear one if you do not want to enable locking for it. (Scenarios are discussed in the "Defining Scenarios for Future Reference" section, later in this skill.)

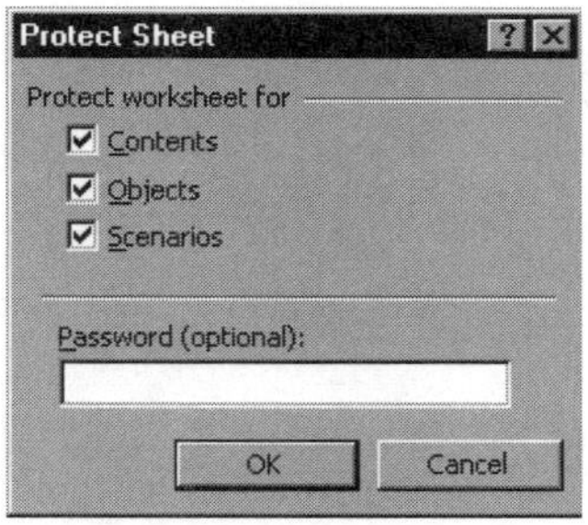

3. If you want, enter a password in the Password field.
4. Click OK.

If you enter a password in the Password field, no one—including you—can remove the worksheet protection without first entering that password. A password can be a maximum of 255 characters, can contain any letters, numbers, or symbols, and is case sensitive (so that "mypassword" and "MyPassword" are different passwords). Whatever you come up with, make it something you can remember, or else you might be locked out of your own sheet.

Once a worksheet has been protected, you have limited access to it. Excel warns you with a dialog box when you try to change any of its protected components. For example, when a worksheet is protected, you won't be able to:

- Change the contents or formats of any locked cells.
- Move a locked cell or object.
- Delete or insert rows or columns.
- Change column widths or row heights.
- Define a name for a range.
- Create a chart or graphic object on the worksheet.

To turn off worksheet protection, choose Tools ➤ Protection ➤ Unprotect Sheet.

Locking Cells and Objects

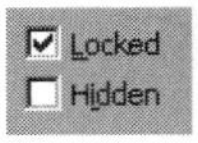

To lock or unlock a cell, follow these steps:

1. Select the cell or range and choose Format ➤ Cells to open the Format Cells dialog box.

2. Click the Protection tab.

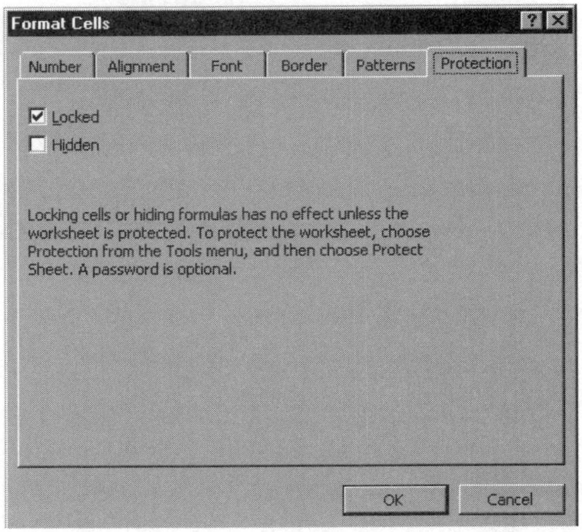

3. Clear or select the Hidden or Locked check boxes.
4. Click OK.

NOTE NOTE NOTE NOTE NOTE NOTE NOTE NOTE NOTE NOTE NOTE NOTE NOTE NOTE NOTE

Selecting Hidden hides the cell contents, so you can't see them on the Formula bar. You can use this option with or without the Locked option. See the section "Hiding Information from View," later in this skill.

The Locked option box is selected by default. Clear this check box if you want to be able to change the cell. You can also lock or unlock charts and other graphic objects on the worksheet. To lock or unlock a chart, follow these steps:

1. Right-click the chart area (generally the area outside the plotted area or the legend), and choose Format Chart Area from the shortcut menu to open the Format Chart Area dialog box.
2. Click the Properties tab.
3. Click or clear the Locked check box.
4. Click OK.

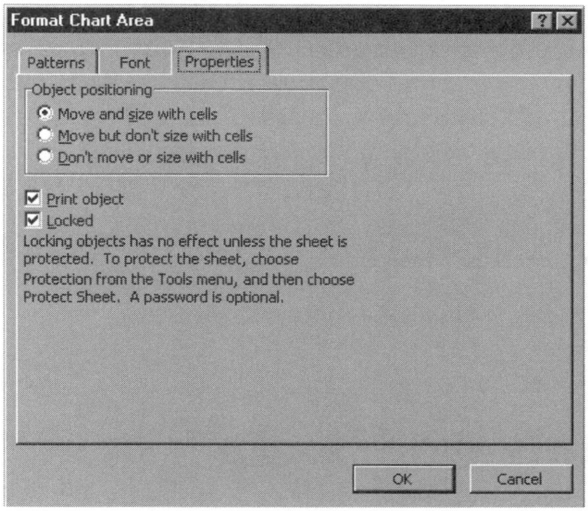

To lock or unlock a graphic object, follow these steps:

1. Right-click the object, and choose Format *Object* (such as AutoShape or Picture) to open the Format *Object* dialog box.
2. Click the Protection tab.
3. Click or clear the Locked check box.
4. Click OK.

TIP TIP TIP TIP TIP TIP TIP TIP TIP TIP TIP TIP TIP TIP TIP TIP TIP TIP TIP TIP TIP TIP TIP TIP TIP

Remember, if you do not enable worksheet protection, all cells or objects on that sheet behave as though they are unlocked.

Unlocking Cells

When you want to give others access to locked cells or objects, you'll need to unlock them. Follow these steps:

1. Open the worksheet.
2. Select the cell, range, or object you want to unlock.
3. Choose Format ➤ Cells to open the Format Cells dialog box, click the Protection tab, clear the Locked check box, and then click OK.

Because there's so little to do in a locked worksheet, it's the perfect place for entering data into unlocked cells and for other routine tasks, such as printing. But how do you find those unlocked cells? Well, if you're the worksheet designer, you should clearly mark unlocked cells so they're easy to find. You might put descriptive titles next to them, give them a background color, or enclose them in borders.

TIP TIP TIP TIP TIP TIP TIP TIP TIP TIP TIP TIP TIP TIP TIP TIP TIP TIP TIP TIP TIP TIP TIP TIP TIP

Excel provides a neat way to find unlocked cells: Press tab in a locked sheet to move to the next unlocked cell; press Shift+Tab to move to the previous locked cell. It can't get much easier than that.

Protecting Workbooks

In the normal course of building and using workbooks, you probably won't need most of the cell, object, worksheet, and workbook protection features. But if you develop and are responsible for workbooks that others use, you will appreciate the ways you can protect *the user* from unseen pitfalls that could damage the workbook. (There, that's the nice way to discuss protection issues.)

You can protect an entire workbook from changes in several ways. You can use *worksheet* protection along with *worksheet* protection, but neither of them is dependent on the other.

Protecting a Workbook after It Is Open

You can offer protection for many aspects of a workbook after it is open and in use. Choose Tools ➤ Protection ➤ Protect Workbook to open the Protect Workbook dialog box:

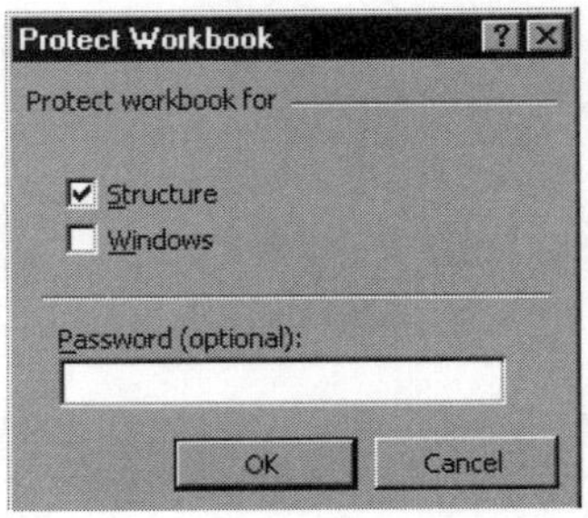

Highlight.
- ANNUAL TOTALS
- Tools
- Properties - enter.

Hidden /apply

: and prevents any changes
e, hide, move, or rename a

windows that display a
closed.

quires that password
n. Like a worksheet pass-
um of 255 characters and is

To turn off workbook protection, choose Tools ➤ Protection ➤ Unprotect Workbook.

Protecting Workbook Files

When you save a workbook, you can apply protection to it that will either prevent or limit access to it in the future. Follow these steps:

1. Choose File ➤ Save As to open the Save As dialog box.
2. Choose Tools ➤ General Options to open the Save Options dialog box.

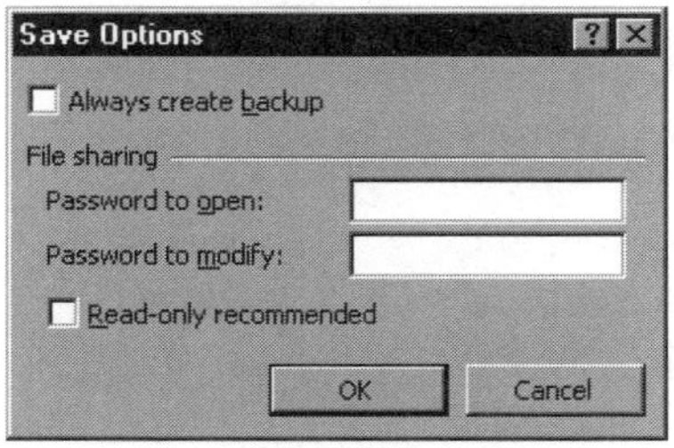

3. Select the options you want.
4. Click OK.
5. Back in the Save As dialog box, click Save to save the file.

You can protect a file in four ways, all of which are disabled by default.

Always Create Backup Option

When the Always Create Backup check box is selected, each time you save the workbook, the previous version already on disk is renamed, thereby giving you a backup copy. For example, if the active workbook is named MyFile.xls, saving it renames the previous version Backup of MyFile.xls.

Password to Open Option

You can specify a password with as many as 15 characters (letters, numbers, or symbols); Excel prompts you to enter the password again for verification as you save the file. A password is case-sensitive.

No one will be able to open or access the workbook without first supplying that password. Nor can anyone create a formula that links to the workbook without the password.

To remove the password from the file, follow these steps:

1. Choose File ➤ Save As to open the Save As dialog box.
2. Choose Tools ➤ General Options to open the Save Options dialog box.
3. In the Password to Open field, delete the password characters.
4. Click OK.
5. Back in the Save As dialog box, click Save.

Password to Modify Option

To limit access to the workbook, enter a password in the Password to Modify field. Anyone who tries to open the workbook will be prompted either to supply the password for full rights to the file or to open it as a read-only file.

If you open the file with read-only rights and then want to save the workbook, you will have to give it a new name so as not to overwrite the original.

Read-Only Recommended Option

This is a very mild, polite form of protection. When a user tries to open a workbook that has the Read-Only Recommended option selected, Excel displays a dialog box that simply *recommends* that the file be opened with read-only access rights. Selecting Yes opens the file as read-only. Selecting No opens it with full access rights.

NOTE NOTE NOTE NOTE NOTE NOTE NOTE NOTE NOTE NOTE NOTE NOTE NOTE NOTE NOTE

To remove any restrictions that have been placed on the file, you must open it with full access rights.

Hiding Information from View

You might want to hide pieces of a workbook from view for reasons of security, such as to hide an important equation. Or you might hide unneeded data or formulas from view to make the worksheet easier to navigate or less cluttered when printed. You can hide the following parts of an Excel workbook:

- Cell display or contents
- Cells that display zero
- Columns or rows
- Graphic objects
- Worksheets
- Windows

In Skill 6, you learned how to apply a custom format (three semicolons) to a cell to hide it from the display. Also in that skill, you learned how to hide columns, rows, and worksheets.

Hiding Cell Contents

Although you can hide the display of a cell with a custom format, to hide the contents of the cell (in the Formula bar) from view, follow these steps:

1. Choose Format ➤ Cells to open the Format Cells dialog box.
2. Click the Protection tab.
3. Click the Hidden check box, and then click OK.
4. Choose Tools ➤ Protection ➤ Protect Sheet to open the Protect Sheet dialog box.
5. Be sure that the Contents check box is selected.
6. Click OK.

A hidden cell is displayed on the screen, as usual, but its contents are not—when you select the cell, the Formula bar appears empty. Double-clicking the cell to edit it also reveals nothing.

WARNING WARNING WARNING WARNING WARNING WARNING WARNING WARNING

Even though you can't see the cell contents when you edit a hidden cell, pressing Del or Backspace will nonetheless erase the contents, and typing a new entry will overwrite the contents. You'll probably find that, in most cases, when a cell is important enough that you hide its contents, you should also lock it, following the steps in the "Locking Cells and Objects" section, earlier in this skill.

To unhide one or more cells, choose Tools ➤ Protection ➤ Unprotect Sheet to turn off sheet protection. All cell contents will be displayed in the normal way. You can then turn off the Hidden option for any cells you want and turn sheet protection back on again, as needed.

Hiding Graphic Objects

Graphic objects in the worksheet—such as charts, drawn images, buttons, or pictures—take up room on the screen and can also slow the process of scrolling through the worksheet. You can mitigate these effects by hiding graphic objects, either partially or fully. To hide graphic objects, follow these steps:

1. Choose Tools ➤ Options to open the Options dialog box.
2. Click the View tab.
3. Click one of the following Options:

   Show All The default; to display all graphic objects.

   Show Placeholders To display charts and pictures in the worksheet as shaded boxes, which show their position and size without slowing worksheet scrolling. Drawn objects, buttons, and other simple graphics are still displayed.

   Hide All To hide all graphic objects.
4. Click OK.

When you print a worksheet that contains graphic objects, the printout matches what you see on the screen.

Attaching Comments to Cells

Just about everyone who has ever used a worksheet has come across the Num Lock Effect. It happens to your brain when you're staring at a cell trying to figure out just what its formula is doing or why another cell contains the number 72 or why some other cell is formatted with zero decimal places when it contains a number with a decimal fraction. After a couple of minutes, the Num Lock Effect begins to set in!

A simple tool can alleviate much of the Num Lock potential. You can attach comments to a cell as a convenient way to leave a description or reminder note about that cell. Here are some situations that might warrant attaching a comment:

- Important formula cells
- Cells that need to be updated regularly
- Any cells around a chart in a worksheet
- Unprotected cells in a protected worksheet

NOTE NOTE NOTE NOTE NOTE NOTE NOTE NOTE NOTE NOTE NOTE NOTE NOTE NOTE NOTE

You can also apply data entry criteria to a cell, which prompts users with a message when they select the cell. See Skill 13.

Attaching Comments to Cells

To pin a comment on the active cell, follow these steps:

1. Choose Insert ➤ Comment or click the New Comment button on the Reviewing toolbar to open a comment box next to the active cell.
2. Enter your note.
3. Click outside the comment box.

NOTE NOTE NOTE NOTE NOTE NOTE NOTE NOTE NOTE NOTE NOTE NOTE NOTE NOTE NOTE

To display the Reviewing toolbar, choose View ➤ Toolbars ➤ Reviewing.

By default, a cell that has a comment attached to it displays a small red triangle in its upper-right corner. When you point to the cell with your mouse, the comment pops up. Figure 9.1 shows a worksheet with a completed comment.

A comment can be as long as you want, but realize that the term *comment* usually doesn't apply to a 5,000-word treatise. Text wraps to a new line as necessary; if you want to force a line break, press Enter.

You can also use the Clipboard to place information in a comment. For example, if you want to refer to a formula that's in the current cell, follow these steps:

1. Select the formula in the Formula bar.
2. Press Ctrl+C (shortcut for Edit ➤ Copy).

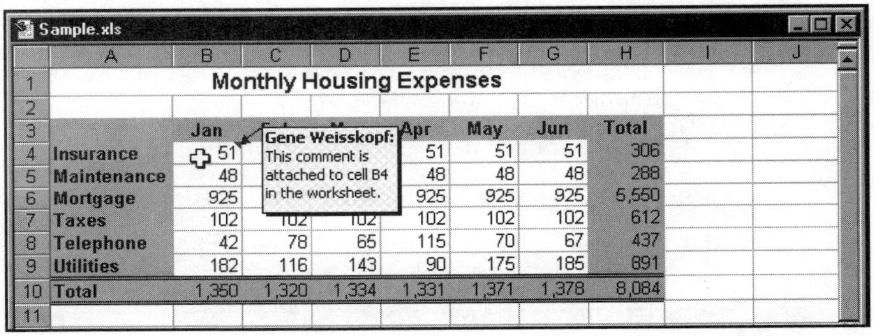

Sample.xls
Monthly Housing Expenses
Jan
Apr
May
Jun
Total
Gene Weisskopf:
This comment is attached to cell B4 in the worksheet.
Insurance 51 51 51 51 306
Maintenance 48 48 48 48 288
Mortgage 925 925 925 925 5,550
Taxes 102 102 102 102 612
Telephone 42 78 65 115 70 67 437
Utilities 182 116 143 90 175 185 891
Total 1,350 1,320 1,334 1,331 1,371 1,378 8,084

FIGURE 9.1: A comment appears next to the cell to which it is attached.

3. Press Esc.
4. Create a new comment for that cell (choose Insert ➤ Comment) or edit an existing one, and press Ctrl+V (shortcut for Edit ➤ Paste) to paste the formula into the comment.

Reading Cell Comments

You can read a cell's comment simply by pointing to the cell. Point outside the comment to close it. But you can also find and display cells in several other ways: To view a comment *without* your mouse, select the cell, press Shift+F10 to display the shortcut menu, and choose Show Comment. To hide the comment, repeat these steps, and choose Hide Comment.

- To view all comments in the worksheet, choose View ➤ Comments, or click the Show All Comments button on the Reviewing toolbar.

- To move to the next or previous comment in the worksheet and display its comment, click the Next Comment or Previous Comment button on the Reviewing toolbar.

Revising a Comment

To edit a cell's comment, do one of the following:

- Right-click the cell, choose Edit Comment from the shortcut menu, and make your changes.
- If you have disabled the Edit Directly in Cell option (on the Edit tab in the Options dialog box), double-click a commented cell to edit the comment.
- If a comment is not hidden, simply click it to select it for editing.
- To duplicate only the current cell's comment in another cell, choose Edit ➤ Copy to copy the comment, select the target cell, choose Edit ➤ Paste Special to open the Paste Special dialog box, click the Comments option, and click OK.

To delete a cell's comment, do one of the following:

- Right-click the cell, and choose Delete Comment from the shortcut menu.

- Select the cell, and click the Delete Comment button on the Reviewing toolbar.
- Select the cell, choose Edit ➤ Clear ➤ Comments.
- Copy another cell onto the commented cell.

Running an Audit

On the surface of a worksheet, you might see only some numbers and text. Behind the scenes, though, may be a web of interconnecting formulas and the cells to which they refer. And those cells may also contain formulas that refer to yet more formulas.

This is truly great stuff, but when you need to figure out the chain of references in a complex relationship of formulas, you may be up against a difficult investigation (a common source of the Num Lock Effect, I mentioned earlier). Fortunately (you knew that was coming), Excel provides some powerful tools for tracing the relationship of formulas, a process known as *auditing*.

Formula Relationships

In Skill 4, you learned about dependent cells and precedent cells:

Dependent cell A formula cell that references a cell so that the formula is dependent on it.

Precedent cell A cell that the formula in the current cell references.

If the formula

```
=SUM(B10:G10)
```

is in cell H10, its precedent cells are in the range B10:G10. For each of those cells, cell H10 (the formula) is a dependent cell.

If a precedent cell, such as B10 or C10, also contains a formula that refers to yet another formula, the first relationship is *direct* (B10 or C10); the second and any other references are *indirect*.

When you want to reveal the chain of precedents or dependents, use the commands on the Tools ➤ Auditing menu. Better yet, choose the Show Auditing Toolbar command and work from that toolbar.

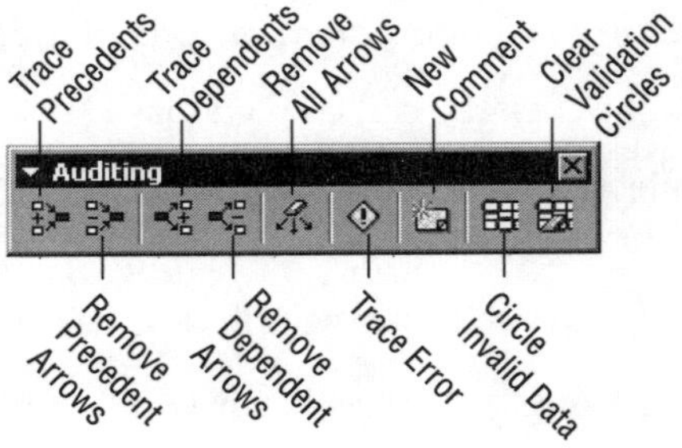

You can then trace precedent and dependent relationships, as well as the source of error results, such as #NAME? or #N/A. Clicking the Circle Invalid Data button on the Auditing toolbar circles all cells whose data are out of range, based on the criteria set for those cells with the Data ➤ Validation command. (For information about validating data, see Skill 13.)

TIP TIP TIP TIP TIP TIP TIP TIP TIP TIP TIP TIP TIP TIP TIP TIP TIP TIP TIP TIP TIP TIP TIP TIP TIP

The only way to display the Auditing toolbar is to choose Tools ➤ Auditing ➤ Show Auditing Toolbar. You cannot display it by choosing View ➤ Toolbars.

Tracing Precedents

Figure 9.2 shows the housing expenses worksheet after tracing precedent cells for the selected cell, H10. Cell H10 contains the formula

```
=SUM(B10:G10)
```

To find all the cells that this formula references directly, click the Trace Precedents button on the Auditing toolbar. A blue arrow points to the formula from the cells that the formula references directly. In Figure 9.2, this arrow runs along row 10, indicating the range B10:G10.

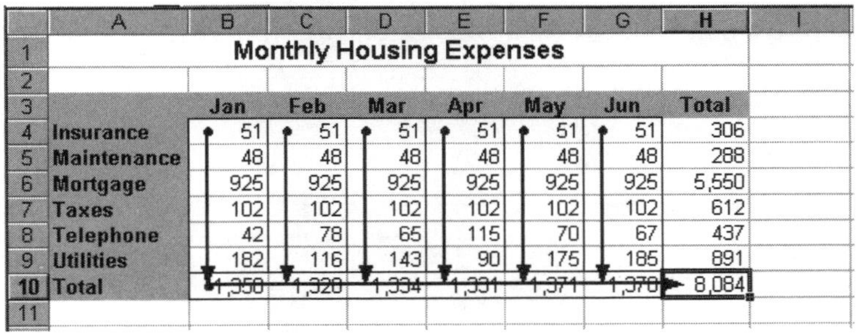

	A	B	C	D	E	F	G	H	I
1		Monthly Housing Expenses							
2									
3		Jan	Feb	Mar	Apr	May	Jun	Total	
4	Insurance	51	51	51	51	51	51	306	
5	Maintenance	48	48	48	48	48	48	288	
6	Mortgage	925	925	925	925	925	925	5,550	
7	Taxes	102	102	102	102	102	102	612	
8	Telephone	42	78	65	115	70	67	437	
9	Utilities	182	116	143	90	175	185	891	
10	Total	1,350	1,320	1,334	1,331	1,371	1,378	8,084	
11									

FIGURE 9.2: Clicking the Trace Precedents button draws an arrow from the cells that are referenced, either directly or indirectly, to the formula in the selected cell.

You can double-click a precedent trace arrow to select the formula cell at one end of it; double-click the arrow a second time to select the range of precedent cells. You can also select all the direct precedent cells by choosing Edit ➤ Go To ➤ Special and selecting Precedents.

To find any cells that the formula references indirectly, click the Trace Precedents button again. In Figure 9.2, the blue arrows running down columns B through G indicate the indirect references. That's because those cells are referenced by each of the SUM formulas in row 10, such as this one in B10:

```
=SUM(B4:B9)
```

If you don't see any arrows at all, be sure that you have selected a formula cell that refers to other cells. Also, choose Tools ➤ Options to open the Options dialog box, click the View tab, and be sure that the Hide All option in the Object section is *not* selected.

You can click the Trace Precedents button to display more and more levels of indirect relationships until you hear a beep, which indicates that there are no more. Figure 9.2 has only two levels of precedent cells.

Tracing Dependents

To find cells that are dependent on the current cell (formulas that refer to it either directly or indirectly), click the Trace Dependents button on the Auditing toolbar. Thinner blue arrows point to the cells containing formulas that reference the active cell. Click the button multiple times to draw arrows to all the indirect references.

To select cells that are dependent on the selected cell, choose Edit ➤ Go To ➤ Special, select Dependents, and then choose either Direct Only or All Levels.

The left side of Figure 9.3 shows a portion of the worksheet in Figure 9.2. Cell G5 is selected, and the Trace Dependents button has been clicked. The resulting two arrows point to the formulas in H5 and G10, which reference this cell directly via their SUM formulas.

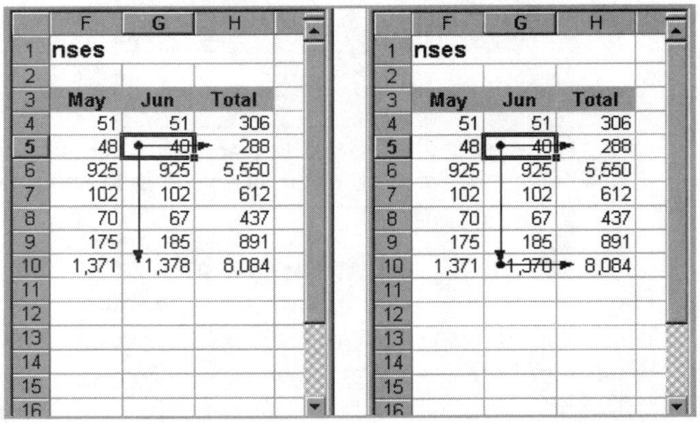

FIGURE 9.3: The Trace Dependents button draws an arrow to formula cells that reference the selected cell, either directly or indirectly, through other formulas.

The right side of Figure 9.3 shows the same columns after clicking the Trace Dependents button a second time. Now it is evident that the formula in H10 is indirectly dependent on G5, via the formula in G10.

Tracing Errors

When a formula returns an error result, the cause might be an invalid formula, such as division by zero that returns #DIV/0!. The error could also be due to the formula referring to another formula cell that is the source of the error. It's even more difficult to track the source of an error when there is a chain of formula references several levels deep.

There's an easy way to trace the source of an error when it lies outside the current cell. Simply select a cell that displays an error result, and click the Trace Error button on the Auditing toolbar. Excel draws a red trace arrow from the cell that is the source of the error, and selects that cell as well, so you can see what needs fixing.

Removing Trace Arrows

After you spend some time auditing formulas, you can end up with lots of trace arrows in the worksheet (undoubtedly another source of Num Lock). You can remove some or all the trace arrows at any time.

To remove just some of the precedent or dependent arrows, select a cell whose arrows you want to remove, and then do one of the following:

- Click the Remove Precedent Arrows button on the Auditing toolbar once for each indirect reference level of arrows you want to remove.

- Click the Remove Dependent Arrows button on the Auditing toolbar once for each indirect reference level of arrows you want to remove.

- Click the Remove All Arrows button to remove all trace arrows from the worksheet.

Trace arrows will disappear on their own when you change a formula that is part of the arrow's path or when you add or delete rows, columns, or cells in the worksheet. If you want to restore the arrows, simply run the audit trace again.

Tracing External References

An audit trace for a precedent, dependent, or error cell can lead to another worksheet or even to another workbook when an external link is involved. A black dashed line running to a worksheet icon indicates that the link crosses over to another worksheet or workbook.

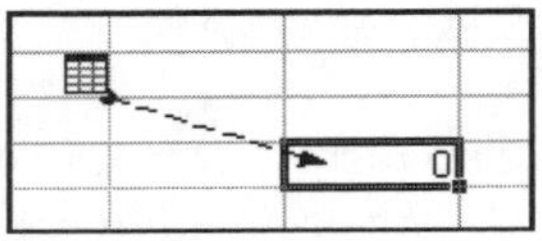

To go to the reference in the other sheet or workbook, point to the black line; when the mouse pointer becomes an arrow, double-click it—just as you would with any trace line. In this case, though, the Go To dialog box will open, listing the sheet or filenames to which a formula in the trace line refers. Select the name you want, and click OK to go to that cell.

NOTE NOTE NOTE NOTE NOTE NOTE NOTE NOTE NOTE NOTE NOTE NOTE NOTE NOTE NOTE

If the reference refers to a different workbook, the workbook must be open in order to go to the referenced worksheet.

Defining Scenarios for Future Reference

Excel's lightning-fast recalculations make quick work of what-if games with data and formulas. For example, what if you change your overhead amount from 10 percent to 8 percent, or what if you change the price you estimate for land from $22,000 to $28,000?

You can manipulate your data for hours and watch the formulas change as you fine-tune the results. However, at some point you may run into the common problem of wanting to return to an earlier version of the game, or a *scenario*. Was overhead set to 8 percent or 9 percent when land was set to $25,000 and lumber was $8,500?

You could build each scenario as a separate worksheet in the workbook, but that would be wasteful and tedious. As always, Excel comes to your aid, this time with the Scenario Manager, which you access by choosing Tools ➤ Scenarios. Using the Scenario Manager, you can name, save, and later recall scenarios for the active worksheet.

TIP TIP TIP TIP TIP TIP TIP TIP TIP TIP TIP TIP TIP TIP TIP TIP TIP TIP TIP TIP TIP TIP TIP TIP TIP

If you're going to do a lot of work with scenarios, customize a toolbar by adding the Scenario list. It lets you create new scenarios and revert to existing ones right from the toolbar. Skill 14 describes how you can create your own toolbars or modify existing ones. To open the Scenario list, choose Tools ➤ Customize to open the Customize dialog box, and click the Commands tab.

Building the Example Worksheet

I'll use the worksheet in Figure 9.4 to illustrate the Scenario Manager. If you want to follow along, you can also create this worksheet.

Cells B2:B3 and E2:E7 contain the values shown. Cells E8:E11 contain formulas that refer to the other cells:

- E8: =SUM(Land:Labor)
- E9: =Subtotal*Overhead_Value
- E10: =Subtotal*Profit_Value
- E11: =SUM(Subtotal:Profit)

	A	B	C	D	E	F
1						
2	Overhead_Value	10%		Land	22,000	
3	Profit_Value	12%		Concrete	5,000	
4				Lumber	8,500	
5				Gyp. board	4,500	
6				Roof	4,000	
7				Labor	38,000	
8				**Subtotal**	82,000	
9				Overhead	8,200	
10				Profit	9,840	
11				**Total**	100,040	
12						

FIGURE 9.4: The sample worksheet for the Scenario Manager. Cells B2:B3 and E2:E7 contain values; cells E8:E11 contain formulas.

I used the text labels in columns A and D to create names in the cells to their right. To name these cells, follow these steps after you create the worksheet:

1. Select A2:B3 and D2:E11 (hold down Ctrl while you select the second range).
2. Choose Insert ➤ Name ➤ Create to open the Create Names dialog box.
3. Click the Left Column check box, and click OK.

You have given the name Overhead_Value to cell B2, Profit_Value to B3, Land to E2, and so on.

Now it's time to create some scenarios and play what-if with the values in the worksheet.

Creating a New Scenario

The simplest way to create the first scenario is to define it after setting up the worksheet with its initial values.

You define a scenario by giving a name to the *changing cells*, which are those cells whose values you want to track. You can later change the values in those cells and then create another scenario name. You can continue to change the data and create new scenario names as needed.

You can revert to one of the named scenarios at any time and replace the values in the changing cells with those that were in effect when that scenario was created. In this way, you can play what-if in one worksheet while keeping track with scenario names.

WARNING WARNING WARNING WARNING WARNING WARNING WARNING WARNING

When you apply a named scenario to the worksheet, the changing cells in the worksheet literally revert to the values that were in them when you defined that scenario. Any changes you might have made since you last named a scenario are lost.

Let's assume that you want to be able to change any of the numbers in the worksheet (B2:B3 and E2:E7) in Figure 9.4 and see the results of the formulas. To create a scenario, you must specify the changing cells that you want the named scenario to track and then define a new name for the scenario. To do this, follow these steps:

1. Select the changing cells, those that you want to change for different scenarios. Using Figure 9.4, select B2:B3 and E2:E7 (remember to hold down Ctrl while you select multiple ranges).
2. Choose Tools ➤ Scenarios to open the Scenario Manager dialog box. This dialog box displays the names of the three scenarios I'll create in this skill.

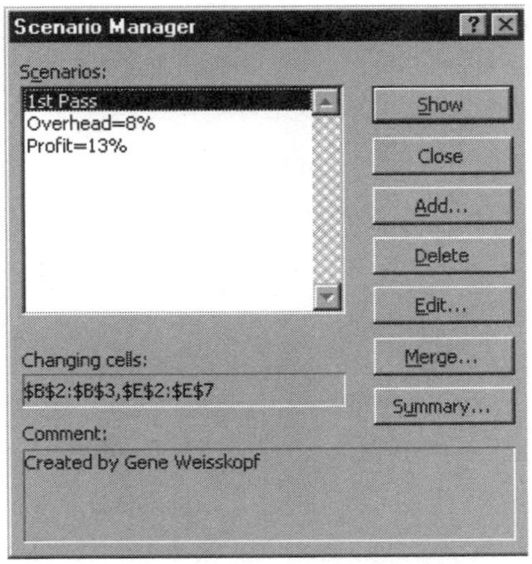

3. Click Add to open the Add Scenario dialog box, in which you create a new scenario.

4. Enter the name **1st Pass** in the Scenario Name field. This name is a convenient way to represent the very first scenario. You can always restore the original data by activating this first scenario.

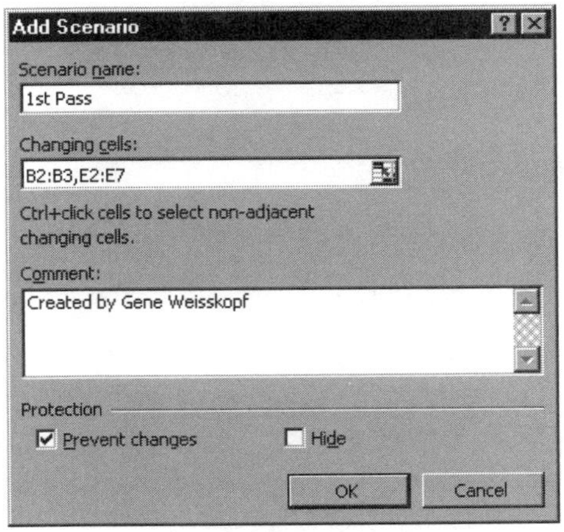

5. The Changing Cells field should already show the ranges you selected in the worksheet, B2:B3 and E2:E7. You can otherwise modify these range addresses as needed.

   The Add Scenario dialog box has three other options, which you can leave as is for this example:

   Comment Enter any comments you think might help describe this scenario.

   Prevent Changes This is selected by default; if you turn on worksheet protection (as described earlier in the "Locking the Entire Worksheet" section), any existing named scenarios cannot be deleted or modified.

   Hide This option hides all named scenarios in the Scenario Manager dialog box when worksheet protection is enabled.

6. Click OK in the Add Scenario dialog box to open the Scenario Values dialog box, which lists each of the changing cells and its current value. If you had not already set those values ahead of time, you could modify them here.

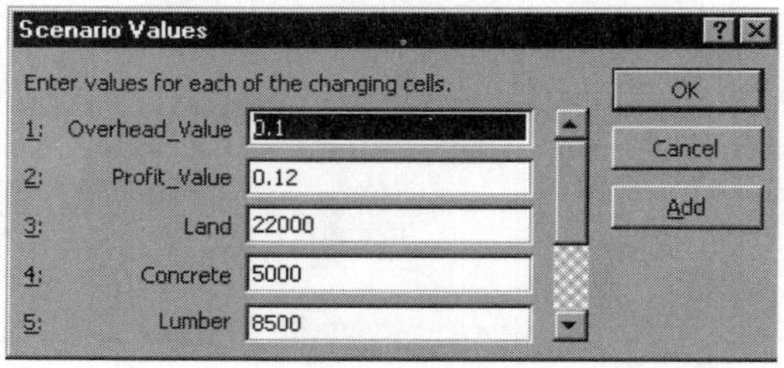

7. The current values are fine, so click OK to return to the Scenario Manager dialog box, where you should see the first named scenario in the Scenarios list.

8. That's it. The first scenario is named, so click Close to complete the job.

TIP TIP TIP TIP TIP TIP TIP TIP TIP TIP TIP TIP TIP TIP TIP TIP TIP TIP TIP TIP TIP TIP TIP TIP TIP

To create a new scenario using the Scenario list on a customized toolbar, enter your values in the worksheet, select all the changing cells, enter a new name in the Scenario list, and press Enter.

There won't be anything different when you're back in the worksheet, but Excel will remember the values that were in the changing cells when you defined this scenario. Later, you'll see how you can bring back those values to "relive" this scenario.

Creating More Scenarios

Once you name that first scenario, you can continue to revise the data in the changing cells and name new scenarios at any time. Let's create two more.

1. Enter **8%** (or without the percent sign, **0.08**) in the cell named Overhead_Value (B2).
2. Select the changing cells for this scenario, which are the same that we used for the first scenario, B2:B3 and E2:E7.
3. Choose Tools ➤ Scenarios to open the Scenario Manager dialog box.

NOTE NOTE NOTE NOTE NOTE NOTE NOTE NOTE NOTE NOTE NOTE NOTE NOTE NOTE NOTE

You can include any cells as the changing cells, but in this example I'll continue to specify the same cells so that each named scenario always tracks the same cells. You might consider creating a name for the changing cells range, B2:B3,E2:E7, so it would be easy to select them all just by selecting that name from the Name box.

4. Click Add to open the Add Scenario dialog box, and enter the new scenario name, **Overhead=8%,** in the Scenario Name field.
5. Click OK here and again in the Scenario Values dialog box because we have already set the values in the changing cells.
6. Now you should see two named scenarios in the Scenario Manager dialog box; click Close to return to the worksheet.
7. To create a third scenario, change the cell named Profit_Value (B3) to **13%**.
8. Select the changing cells B2:B3 and E2:E7.
9. Repeat steps 3 through 6, but this time enter the new scenario name **Profit=13%**.
10. Save the workbook.

With several scenarios named for different data in the changing cells, you can revert to any of them at any time.

Reverting to a Previous Scenario

To revert to a previous scenario, choose Tools ➤ Scenarios to open the Scenario Manager dialog box, select one of the names from the Scenarios list, and then click Show. Watch the worksheet as you do so that you can see the numbers change. Click Close when you want to return to the worksheet.

TIP TIP TIP TIP TIP TIP TIP TIP TIP TIP TIP TIP TIP TIP TIP TIP TIP TIP TIP TIP TIP TIP TIP TIP TIP

If you're using the Scenario list on a customized toolbar, you can revert to an existing scenario simply by selecting its name from the drop-down list.

If you are following along with my worksheet, you will see that if you select the 1st Pass scenario, cells B2 and B3 are reset to 10% and 12%, which are the values they held when you named that scenario.

Don't forget that if you change the data in any changing cells, but don't create a new scenario for them, reverting to another scenario will cause you to lose those changes. To retain the new data when you revert to a previous scenario, create a new scenario name for the changes you've made. You can then always recall that data by selecting that scenario name.

Modifying a Scenario

All the named scenarios for a worksheet appear in the Scenarios list in the Scenario Manager dialog box. You can modify one by selecting it in the list and clicking one of the following options:

Delete Select this option to remove the selected scenario from the list; this does not affect the worksheet in any way.

Edit Select this option to revise the definition for the selected scenario, including its name, the changing cells, and the cells' values.

You can also click Merge to bring the scenarios from another worksheet (either in the current workbook or in another open workbook) into the current worksheet so that their names appear in the Scenario Manager dialog box. When you then switch to any of those scenarios, their changing cells are updated accordingly in the current worksheet.

Creating a Scenario Summary Report

Clicking Summary in the Scenario Dialog box creates a new worksheet in the workbook for the summary report—a great tool for comparing all scenarios in one place.

To create a summary report for the scenario workbook we've been using, follow these steps.

1. Choose Tools ➤ Scenarios to open the Scenario Manager dialog box, and click Summary to open the Scenario Summary dialog box:

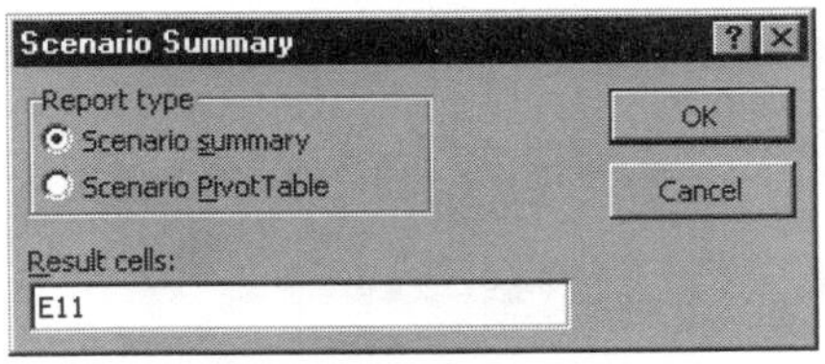

2. Select the Scenario Summary option.
3. Select the Result Cells, and enter the addresses of the formula cells whose results you want to see for each scenario. In this case, cell E11 is the only one you need to see. Realize that the result cells are the key to the whole scenarios scheme—you make changes to the data to see the results in these formulas.
4. Click OK to build the report.

A new worksheet named Scenario Summary is inserted, as shown in Figure 9.5. The report compares the changing cells and result cells for the current worksheet (column D) and in each of the scenarios (columns E through G in this case). It shows you at a glance how each scenario affects the "bottom" line of this worksheet (or at least the bottom line that is the focus of your interest).

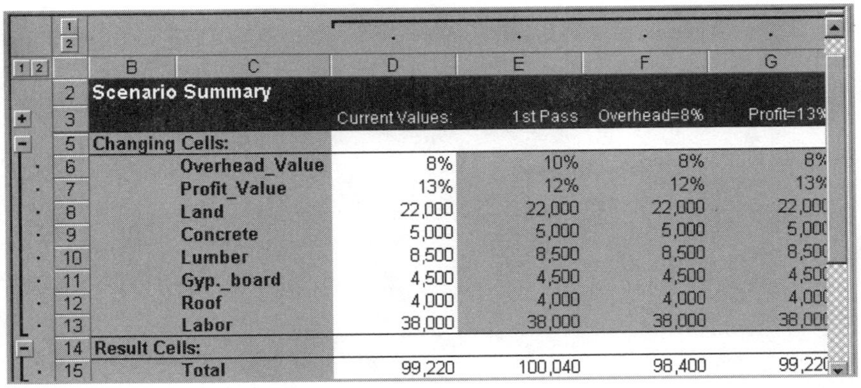

	B	C	D	E	F	G
2	Scenario Summary					
3			Current Values:	1st Pass	Overhead=8%	Profit=13%
5	Changing Cells:					
6		Overhead_Value	8%	10%	8%	8%
7		Profit_Value	13%	12%	12%	13%
8		Land	22,000	22,000	22,000	22,00
9		Concrete	5,000	5,000	5,000	5,00
10		Lumber	8,500	8,500	8,500	8,50
11		Gyp._board	4,500	4,500	4,500	4,50
12		Roof	4,000	4,000	4,000	4,00
13		Labor	38,000	38,000	38,000	38,00
14	Result Cells:					
15		Total	99,220	100,040	98,400	99,22

FIGURE 9.5: The Scenario Summary sheet compares the changing cells and result cells of all the scenarios in the worksheet.

The Scenario Summary sheet is set up as a worksheet outline; you can see the outline's navigation tools to the left of the row headings and above the column headings. You can expand and collapse the three horizontal sections of the outline to show more or less detail. Outlines are discussed in Skill 13. Finally, remember that scenarios won't be of much help if you don't save your workbook.

Are You Experienced?

Now you can...

- ☑ **Lock cells and objects**
- ☑ **Lock worksheets**
- ☑ **Hide information**
- ☑ **Attach comments to cells**
- ☑ **Audit formulas in the workbook**
- ☑ **Create scenarios**

SKILL 10

Working with Excel and the Internet

- Opening files from the Internet
- Saving Excel files as Web pages
- Inserting hyperlinks
- Formatting hyperlinks
- Deleting hyperlinks
- Using the Web toolbar

The limits to the files you can access in Excel don't stop at your computer or your local area network. If you're connected to the Internet, you can access files anywhere in the world, just about as easily as you do from your own hard drive. In this skill, we'll look at Excel's capabilities for dealing with files on the Internet. The ease with which you can open, save, and create HTML files is perhaps one of the most dramatic new features of Excel 2000.

Opening HTML Files from the Internet

As you probably know, a Web page needs to be in HTML (HyperText Markup Language) format in order to be viewed in a Web browser such as Internet Explorer. HTML is simply a language that tells the browser how to display the page. If you want to see what this looks like, open a Web page in Internet Explorer, and then choose View ➤ Source.

TIP TIP TIP TIP TIP TIP TIP TIP TIP TIP TIP TIP TIP TIP TIP TIP TIP TIP TIP TIP TIP TIP TIP TIP TIP

If you're interested in learning more about HTML, I recommend you take a look at *Mastering HTML, 2nd Edition*, by Deborah and Eric Ray, and published by Sybex.

You can open HTML Web pages in Excel, and what you would normally view in your Web browser is loaded into an Excel worksheet. You probably won't do this for just any Web page, but it could be particularly helpful if a page contained a table of data that you wanted to manipulate as real data within the rows and columns of a worksheet.

Figure 10.1 shows a table of gasoline prices that I opened in Internet Explorer. It contains weekly prices for 1996, 1997, and 1998. Figure 10.2 shows the same page open in Excel and saved as an Excel worksheet. Before I captured this figure, I scrolled down the page to find the 1998 prices and then deleted all the cells that showed 1996 and 1997 data.

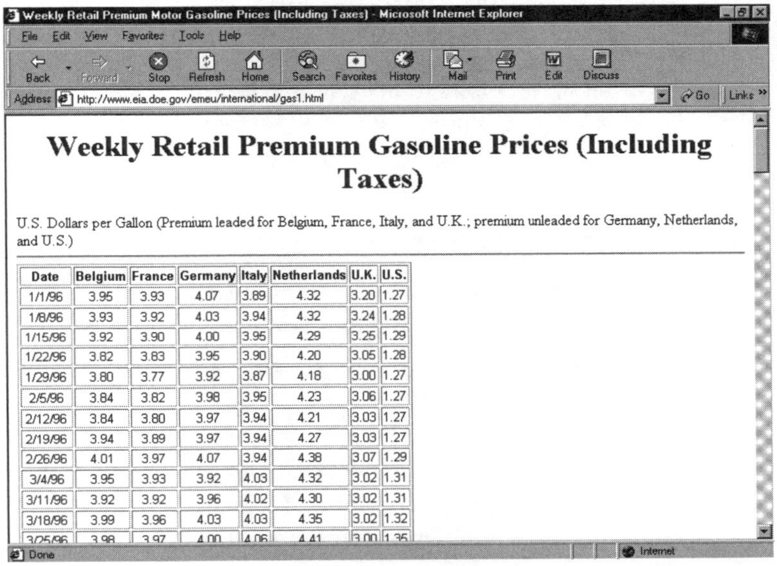

FIGURE 10.1: An HTML page open in Internet Explorer

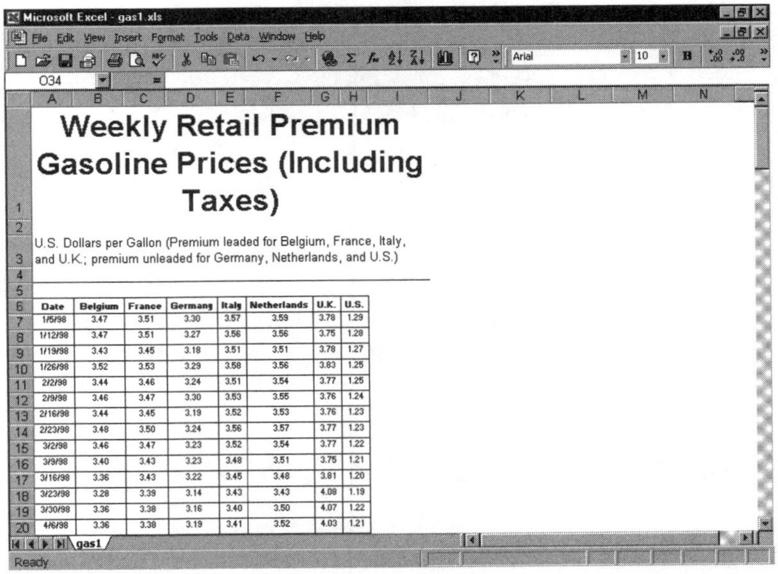

FIGURE 10.2: The page shown in Figure 10.1 open as an Excel worksheet.

SKILL 10

NOTE NOTE NOTE NOTE NOTE NOTE NOTE NOTE NOTE NOTE NOTE NOTE NOTE NOTE NOTE

The Internet-related topics in this book apply equally to intranets, which are local networks that behave just like sites on the Internet, although they are often inaccessible to the world at large. For example, you can browse the Web on an intranet in the same way that you do on the Internet.

To open an HTML file in Excel, follow these steps:

1. Choose File ➤ Open to open the Open dialog box.
2. In the File Name field, enter the URL (*uniform resource locator*; the file's path and name) of the file that you want to open, such as:

   ```
   http://www.eia.doe.gov/emeu/international/gas1.html
   ```

3. Click Open.

If you use a dial-up connection to access the Internet and you're not currently connected, Excel's request for an Internet file will cause Windows to make the dial-up connection. Once that is completed, Excel will open the file.

NOTE NOTE NOTE NOTE NOTE NOTE NOTE NOTE NOTE NOTE NOTE NOTE NOTE NOTE NOTE

If the file you want to open in Excel is in a format that Excel can't easily display as a worksheet, the Text Import Wizard will open. Follow the on-screen instructions to modify the formatting.

Once you've loaded the HTML page into Excel, you can work on the file as a normal worksheet and save it to disk as an Excel file or any other file type that you want. You will have to save it under a new name or to a new location if the Web site does not offer you complete access, for example, if the file opens as Read-Only.

Watch out when you've opened an HTML Web page in Excel. Any hyperlinks in the document will be just as active in Excel as they are in a Web browser. It's all too easy to click a link accidentally, because that's the normal way to select a cell. It's only an inconvenience, though, as the target of the link will most likely be loaded into your Web browser in the usual way.

Saving Excel Files as Web Pages

NEW

Using Excel 2000, not only can you save workbooks and worksheets as Web pages, but you can save them with interactivity. In other words, you can save tables and charts as Web pages, and visitors can manipulate them.

NOTE

Visitors must be using Internet Explore 4 or 5 to view and manipulate interactive pages properly.

To save an Excel workbook or worksheet as a Web page, follow these steps:

1. Open an existing file or create a new one.
2. Choose File ➤ Save As Web Page to open the Save As dialog box.

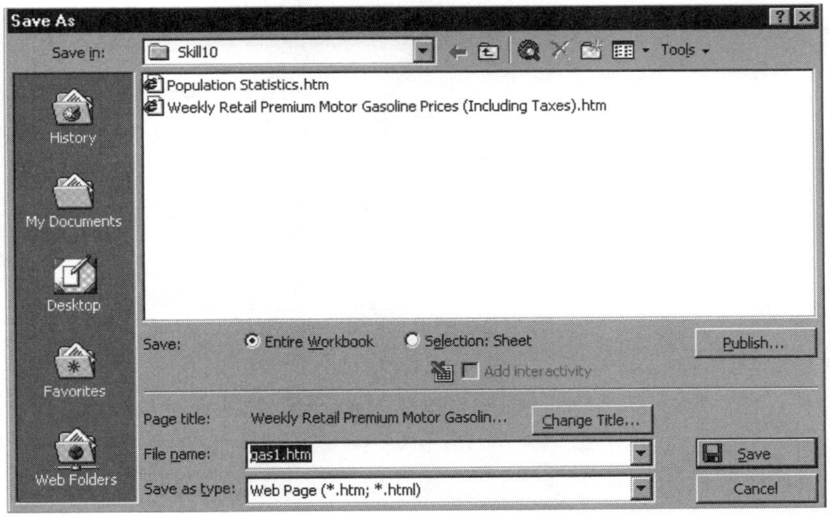

3. Make sure that the file type is correct in the Save As Type box. You can accept the filename that Excel suggests or enter another one in the File Name box.
4. If you want to change the title that Excel suggests for your Web page, click Change Title to open the Set Page Title dialog box, enter a new title in the Page Title field, and click OK.

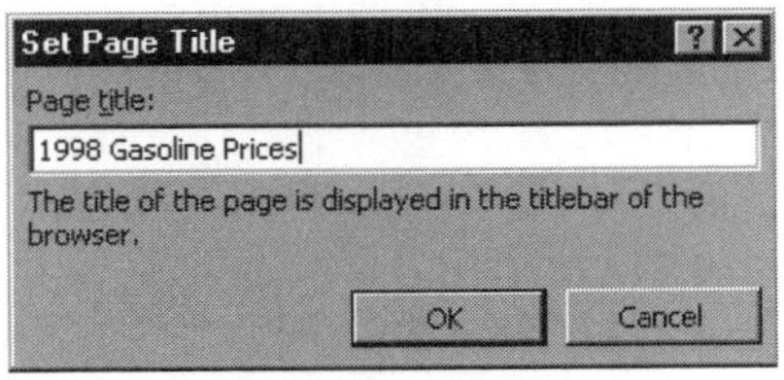

5. Select whether to save an entire workbook or only a selected sheet by clicking the appropriate option button.
6. If you want your visitors to be able to access the interactivity in your workbook or worksheet, click the Add Interactivity check box.
7. Click Publish to open the Publish As Web Page dialog box:

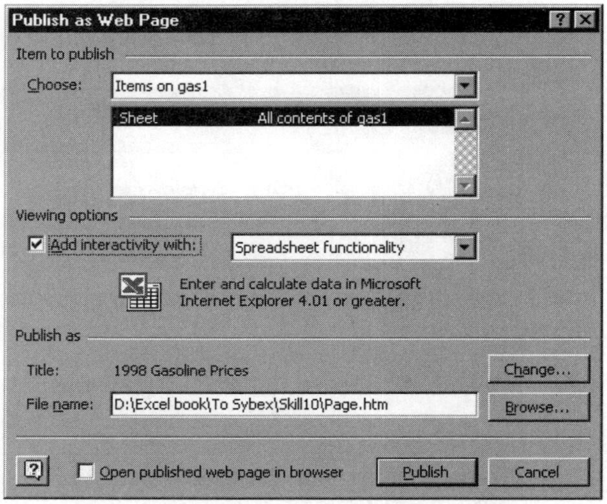

8. Click the Choose drop-down list to specify whether you want to publish previously published items (that is, update data that you've already published), a range of cells, or a worksheet.
9. Click the Add Interactivity With check box, and then choose the type of functionality you want to include. Your choices are Spreadsheet and PivotTable. (See Skill 13 for information about PivotTables.)
10. Click the Open Published Web Page in Browser check box, and then click Publish. Excel saves your file as a Web page and opens it in your browser.

Figure 10.3 shows the Monthly Housing Expenses worksheet saved as a Web page with interactivity and open in Internet Explorer.

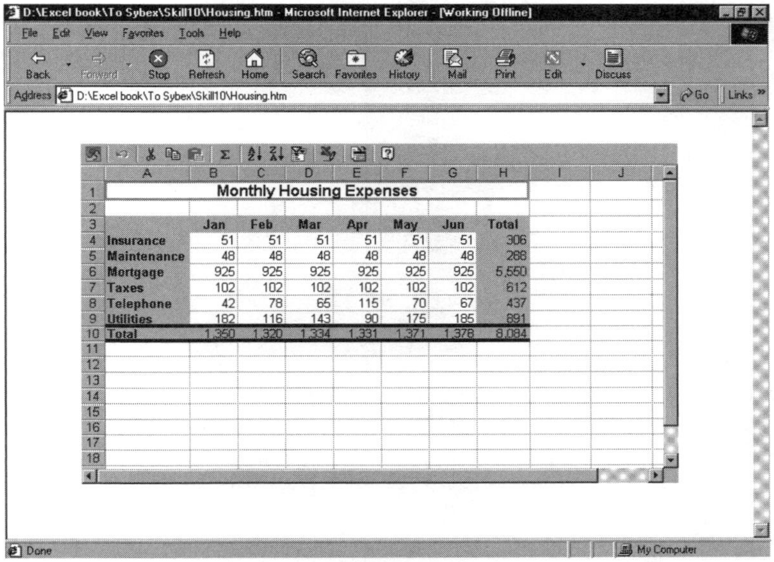

FIGURE 10.3: A Web page created from an Excel worksheet

TIP TIP TIP TIP TIP TIP TIP TIP TIP TIP TIP TIP TIP TIP TIP TIP TIP TIP TIP TIP TIP TIP TIP TIP TIP TIP

While you are working on a worksheet, simply choose File ➤ Web Page Preview to see what it will look like when displayed in your Web browser.

Saving Your Web Pages to a Web Server

In the preceding steps, I saved my Web page to my local hard drive, but if you have access to a Web server (either via an intranet or through your Internet Service Provider), you can save Web pages to that server. To do so, you use a Web folder, which is really a shortcut to your Web server.

To create a Web folder, follow these steps:

1. Choose File ➤ Save As Web Page to open the Save As dialog box.
2. In the Places bar, click Web Folders.
3. Click the Create New Folder button to start the Add Web Folder Wizard, and follow the instructions on the screen.

After you create a Web folder, simply save your Web pages to it in the Save As dialog box. Your files are immediately placed on the Web server and are available to visitors.

NOTE NOTE NOTE NOTE NOTE NOTE NOTE NOTE NOTE NOTE NOTE NOTE NOTE NOTE NOTE

Before you can save a Web page created with Excel to a Web server, the server must have the Office Server Extensions installed. Normally, these extensions are installed, monitored, and maintained by your Web server administrator, and you don't need to worry about them. If you have any questions about this, see your server administrator.

Working with Hyperlinks

In terms of the Internet's World Wide Web, a *hyperlink* is a shortcut within a Web page that you click with your mouse to go from that resource to another. There are generally two types of hyperlinks:

Text Link text, which is underlined and in a different color than the surrounding text; you click the link text to activate the link.

Graphic An image that you click to jump to the target resource.

The target resource of a hyperlink can be a Web page, an Excel workbook, a sound file, a graphic image, a video file, or just about any other kind of file you can think of (although it's possible that your computer may not be able to handle the target file). That file might reside on your local drive, on your network, or on the Internet.

You can also specify an exact location within the target file, such as a cell address or range name within a workbook or a named anchor within a Web page.

You can create hyperlinks in an Excel worksheet that behave just like hyperlinks in Web pages:

- A text hyperlink is attached to a cell. All the text within the cell serves as the link text (you click the cell to activate the link, not any portion of the text that overhangs the width of the cell).
- A graphic image, such as a drawn object or a picture, in the worksheet can serve as a hyperlink.

You can create a hyperlink in Excel in three ways:

- By choosing Insert ➤ Hyperlink to open the Hyperlink dialog box
- By dragging and dropping a cell to create a link to that cell
- By inserting the HYPERLINK function

Whatever method you use, though, the results are the same—you click the hyperlink to open its target resource.

NOTE NOTE NOTE NOTE NOTE NOTE NOTE NOTE NOTE NOTE NOTE NOTE NOTE NOTE NOTE

Don't confuse a linking formula (as discussed in Skill 4) with a hyperlink. The formula returns a value from another workbook, and the hyperlink actually opens its target resource (which can be other file types besides a workbook).

Opening Different Types of Files

The result of clicking a hyperlink depends on the type of resource that will open. If it's an Excel workbook, it will be opened in Excel, just as when you choose File ➤ Open. Other file types open in the appropriate programs.

Files are associated with a program by being registered with Windows, according to their filename extensions. To view the current list of file associations, follow these steps:

continued ➧

1. In Windows Explorer, choose View ➤ Folder Options to open the Folder Options dialog box.

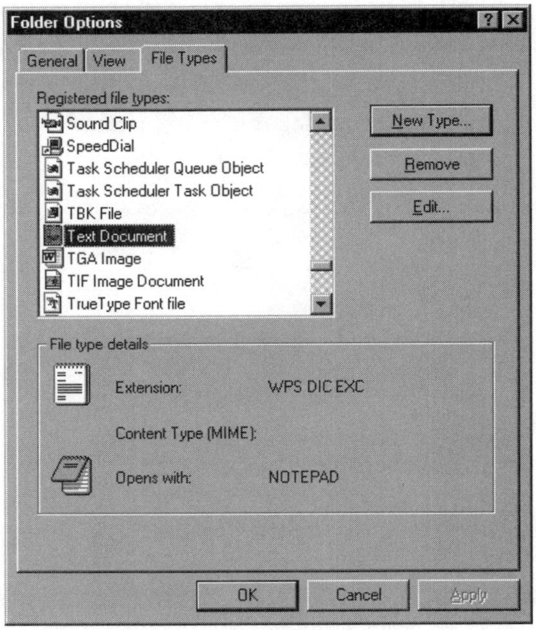

2. Click the File Types tab.
3. Scroll down the Registered File Type list, and click an item to see its associated program.

No magic is involved with associating a file type and the program that opens it. It's all based on the filename extension that is registered with Windows, and nothing more. When you double-click a file named ISLE.XYZ in Windows Explorer, for example, the program that opens that file (and all other XYZ files) will be the same program that will open that file when it is the target of an Excel hyperlink.

Using the Insert Hyperlink Dialog Box

You can insert hyperlinks in a worksheet while you are creating it or after the content and formatting are complete. To insert a hyperlink to another worksheet, follow these steps:

1. Select the cell in which you want the hyperlink.

2. Click the Insert Hyperlink button on the Standard toolbar, or choose Insert ➤ Hyperlink to open the Insert Hyperlink dialog box.

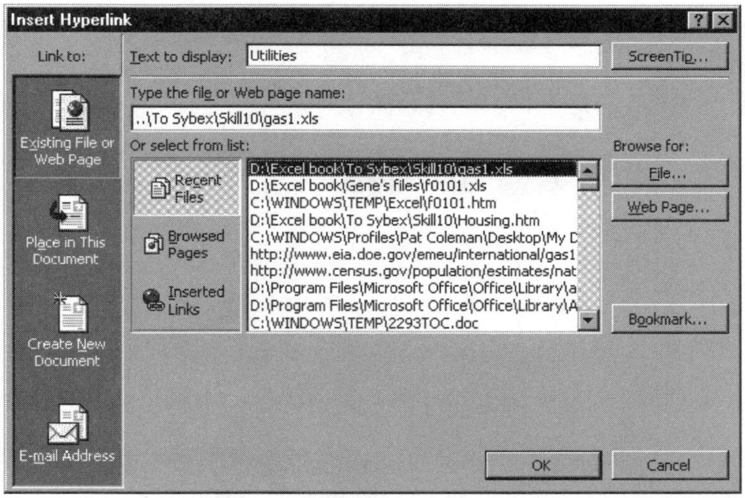

3. The Text to Display field shows the contents of the cell you selected. If you want to display other text, enter text.
4. In the Type the File or Web Page Name field, enter the name of the file to which you want to link. Or, click Recent Files, Browsed Pages, or Inserted Links, and select a file from the list. If you don't know the filename or see it in the list, click Browse for File or Browse for Web Page to locate it.
5. Click OK.

That's it. You've now inserted a hyperlink in your worksheet. To see if it works, simply click it as you would a hyperlink on any Web page.

To insert a hyperlink to another cell in the same worksheet, follow steps 1 through 4, click the Place in This Document shortcut, and then enter the cell reference in the Type the Cell Reference field.

To insert a hyperlink in a new worksheet, click the Create New Document shortcut, and enter the filename in the Name of New Document field.

TIP TIP TIP TIP TIP TIP TIP TIP TIP TIP TIP TIP TIP TIP TIP TIP TIP TIP TIP TIP TIP TIP TIP TIP TIP

To copy a hyperlink from one cell to another, right-click the hyperlink, and choose Copy from the shortcut menu. Click in the cell where you want to copy the hyperlink, and press Enter.

Adding a ScreenTip

A ScreenTip is text that appears in a little box when you place the cursor over a hyperlink. You can add a ScreenTip when you create a hyperlink or at a later time. To add a ScreenTip, follow these steps:

1. Select the cell in which you want to create a hyperlink, or select a cell that already contains a hyperlink.
2. Click the Insert Hyperlink button to open the Insert Hyperlink dialog box.
3. Click ScreenTip to open the Set Hyperlink ScreenTip dialog box:

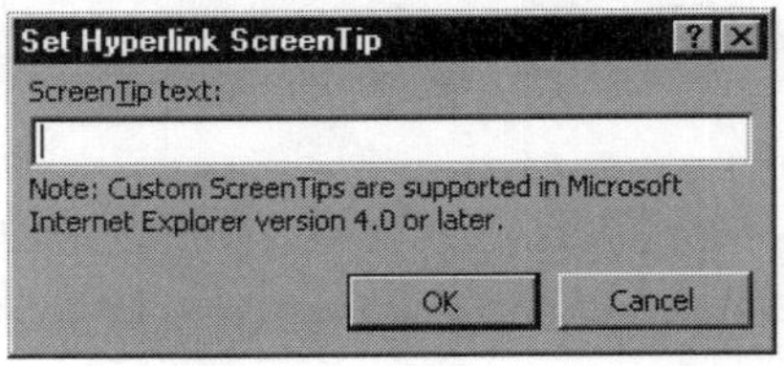

4. In the ScreenTip Text field, type the text you want to display.
5. Click OK twice.

Figure 10.4 shows a portion of a worksheet that includes a ScreenTip.

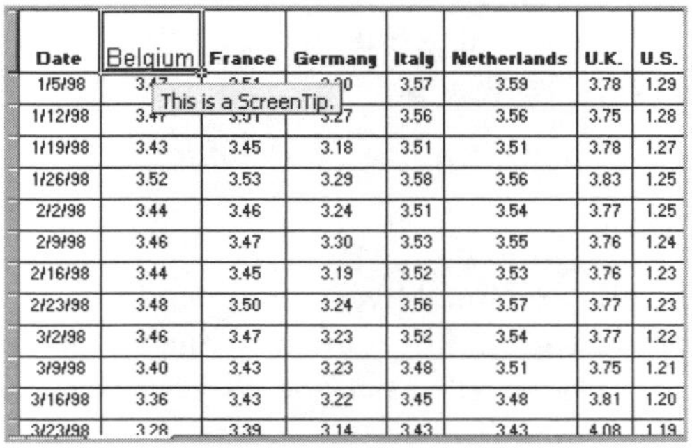

Date	Belgium	France	Germany	Italy	Netherlands	U.K.	U.S.
1/5/98	[illegible]	[illegible]	[illegible]	3.57	3.59	3.78	1.29
1/12/98	[illegible]	[illegible]	[illegible]	3.56	3.56	3.75	1.28
1/19/98	3.43	3.45	3.18	3.51	3.51	3.78	1.27
1/26/98	3.52	3.53	3.29	3.58	3.56	3.83	1.25
2/2/98	3.44	3.46	3.24	3.51	3.54	3.77	1.25
2/9/98	3.46	3.47	3.30	3.53	3.55	3.76	1.24
2/16/98	3.44	3.45	3.19	3.52	3.53	3.76	1.23
2/23/98	3.48	3.50	3.24	3.56	3.57	3.77	1.23
3/2/98	3.46	3.47	3.23	3.52	3.54	3.77	1.22
3/9/98	3.40	3.43	3.23	3.48	3.51	3.75	1.21
3/16/98	3.36	3.43	3.22	3.45	3.48	3.81	1.20
3/23/98	3.28	3.39	3.14	3.43	3.43	4.08	1.19

FIGURE 10.4: A hyperlink that includes a ScreenTip

Inserting a Hyperlink to an E-Mail Address

The easiest way to insert a hyperlink to an e-mail address is to simply type the address in a cell. As with other hyperlinks, however, you can specify text instead of the actual e-mail address, and you can add a ScreenTip. Follow these steps:

1. Select the cell where you want the e-mail address hyperlink.
2. Click the Insert Hyperlink button to open the Insert Hyperlink dialog box.
3. Click the E-mail Address shortcut:

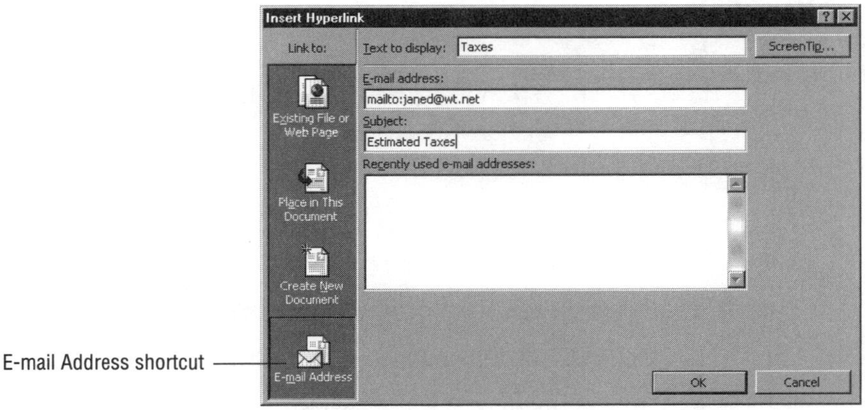

4. In the Text to Display field, accept the default text or enter something else.
5. In the E-mail Address field, type the address. Excel prefaces the address with "mailto."
6. If you want, add a subject line.
7. Click OK.

Clicking an e-mail hyperlink opens a message window in the user's e-mail program. The To: line is already filled in with the address of the hyperlink—and if you included a Subject line, that is also displayed.

Creating a Hyperlink with Drag and Drop

You can create a hyperlink to a cell in the same or another workbook by dragging the target cell to the cell in which you want to create the link. Follow these steps:

1. Select the cell or cells that you want as the target for the hyperlink.
2. Point to one of the cell's borders. When the mouse pointer becomes an arrow, hold down the *right* mouse button and drag the target cell to the cell where you want to create the hyperlink.
3. Release the mouse button, and choose Create Hyperlink Here from the shortcut menu.

Inserting a Hyperlink with the HYPERLINK Function

You can also create a text hyperlink in the worksheet by using the HYPERLINK function, which provides great variability in both the text that is displayed for the link and its target resource. (You learned about functions in Skill 5.) The syntax of the HYPERLINK function is:

```
HYPERLINK(link_location,friendly_name)
```

To use this function to create a hyperlink to a workbook, follow these steps:

1. Select the cell in which you want the hyperlink.
2. Click the Paste Function button to open the Paste Function dialog box.
3. In the Function Category list, select All.
4. In the Function Name list, select HYPERLINK (see Figure 10.5).

5. In the Link_location field, type the path and filename of the resource to which you want to link.
6. In the Friendly_name field, type the text to display in the cell.
7. Click OK.

Figure 10.6 shows the hyperlink and the friendly name created with the HYPERLINK function.

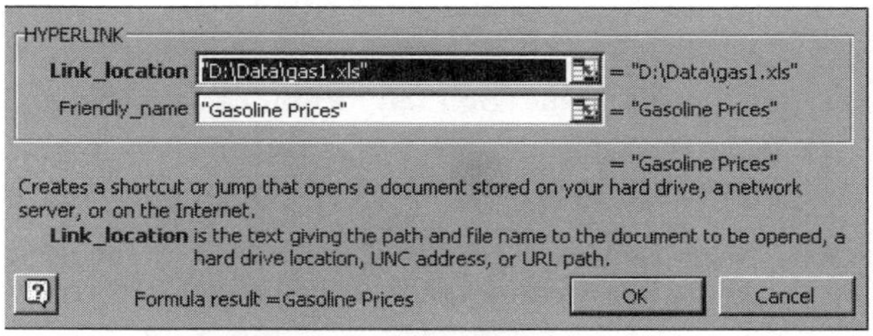

FIGURE 10.5: In this dialog box, enter the path and filename and the friendly name.

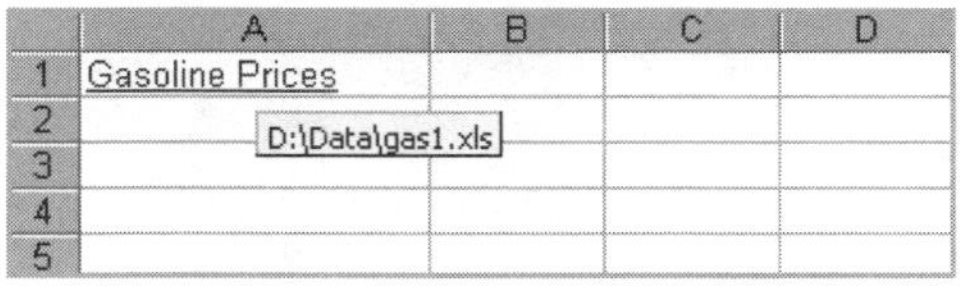

FIGURE 10.6: A hyperlink created with the HYPERLINK function

This type of hyperlink is essentially the same as one you create in the Insert Hyperlink dialog box. If you want to select a specific location in the target document, simply append it to the filename as you would in a linking formula. Here's how you would revise the first argument in the preceding formula so that cell B25 on Sheet 2 would be selected in the target workbook:

```
=HYPERLINK("[D:\Data\gas1.xls] Sheet2!B25",
```

As always, the link is more reliable if you specify a range name instead of a cell address.

The main advantage of creating a link with the HYPERLINK function is flexibility. Because the link is a formula, either argument (the friendly name or the link location) can automatically change as "outside" circumstances change. Those outside changes might be the current date or time, a value in another cell in the workbook, the name of the current workbook, the name of the person working on the link's workbook, and so on.

Formatting a Hyperlink

By default, hyperlinks are displayed in the default paragraph font, are underlined, and are in blue until they are clicked. Clicked hyperlinks are in "color 29," a light purple. This common format has become almost universally recognizable to those who browse the Web. Although you might want to think twice before reformatting your hyperlinks, you can do so. Follow these steps:

1. Choose Format ➤ Style to open the Style dialog box:

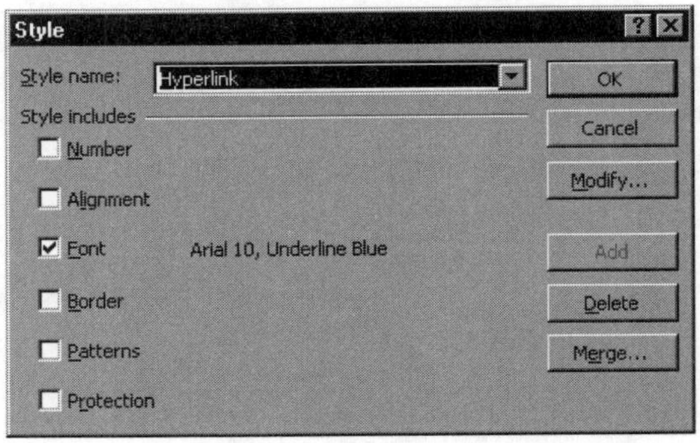

2. Click the down arrow in the Style Name box, and select Hyperlink.
3. Click Modify to open the Format Cells dialog box and make your changes.
4. Click OK to close the Format Cells dialog box.
5. Click OK to close the Style dialog box.

Editing a Hyperlink

Maintaining hyperlinks is an important task. Besides the annoyance factor associated with clicking a link that is unrelated to the task at hand, you can introduce error if you rely on a link that has not been updated.

Unless you create hyperlinks using the HYPERLINK function, hyperlinks don't update automatically when your cells or workbooks change. Follow these steps to edit a hyperlink:

1. Right-click the hyperlink you want to modify, choose Hyperlink from the shortcut menu, and then click Edit Hyperlink to open the Edit Hyperlink dialog box.

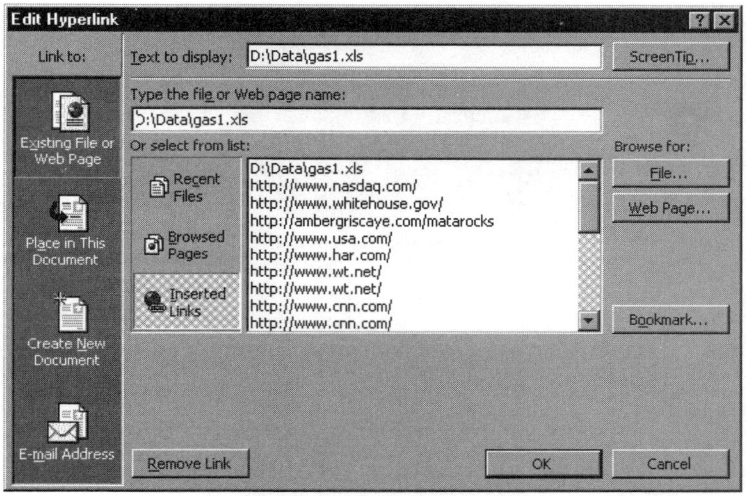

2. Follow the steps for inserting a hyperlink to change a filename, to rewrite a ScreenTip, to insert an e-mail address, and so on.

Deleting a Hyperlink

You'll soon find out, if you haven't already, that you can't delete a hyperlink by selecting it and pressing Delete. Selecting a hyperlink takes you to the target resource.

The easiest way to remove a hyperlink is to right-click the hyperlink, and choose Remove Hyperlink from the shortcut menu.

To delete a hyperlink you created with the HYPERLINK function, right-click it, and choose Clear Contents from the shortcut menu.

Navigating with the Web Toolbar

If you are working extensively with hyperlinked workbooks, the Web toolbar can help you navigate among them. You can display the Web toolbar in a couple of ways:

1. Right-click any toolbar, and click Web from the menu of toolbars.
2. Choose View ➤ Toolbars, and click Web.

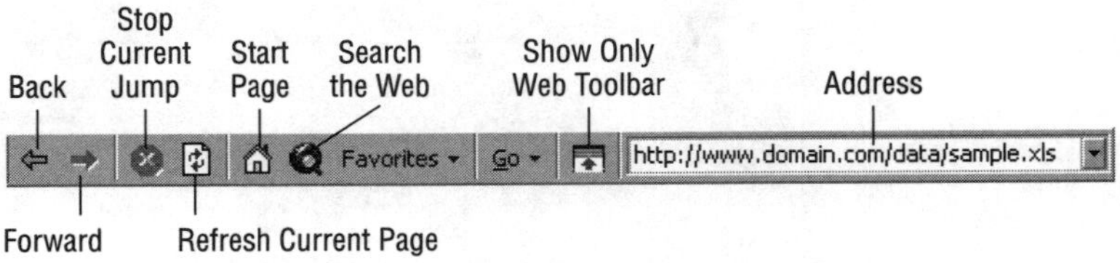

If you've used a Web browser before, you'll recognize most of the buttons on the Web toolbar:

- Back opens the previous resource (or page) you visited.
- Forward opens the succeeding resource from which you've returned.
- Stop Current Jump cancels the current opening of a target resource.
- Refresh Current Page reloads the current or active page.
- Start Page launches Internet Explorer and loads either your home page or the page you specified from the Set Start Page option on the Go menu (see the Go bullet, below).
- Search the Web launches Internet Explorer and opens to either the default search page or the page you specified from the Set Search Page option on the Go menu (see the Go bullet).
- Favorites displays a menu with a variety of folders and options, just like Internet Explorer.
- Go displays a menu with options on the Web toolbar, as well as Set Start Page and Set Search Page options.
- Show Only Web Toolbar closes all open toolbars except the Web toolbar. Click it again to restore all previously open toolbars.

- The Address text box allows you to enter a URL and press Enter to go to that resource or to select a URL that you've already visited from the drop-down list.

WARNING WARNING WARNING WARNING WARNING WARNING WARNING WARNING

Changing the destinations for the start and search pages will affect other programs on your computer, including the Internet Explorer browser and those in the Office suite.

Keep in mind that even though Excel can access addresses on the Internet, it is *not* a Web browser. As discussed earlier, when an Excel hyperlink opens almost any file other than a workbook, some other program will be called to open that file. For example, Excel can open a limited variety of HTML Web pages, but when an Excel hyperlink targets a Web page, that page will be opened by your Web browser, not by Excel (assuming your Windows installation is a typical one).

Once a hyperlink has caused a file to be opened in another program, perhaps a text file in Notepad, there is no automated way to navigate back to Excel. You return to it in the usual ways, such as by selecting its icon on the Windows taskbar or simply clicking the Excel window, if it's visible.

Therefore, the navigation arrow buttons on the toolbar only work for the Excel workbooks you have opened via hyperlinks.

Are You Experienced?

Now you can...

- ☑ Open files from the Internet
- ☑ Save Excel files as Web pages
- ☑ Save Web pages to a Web server
- ☑ Insert a hyperlink with the Insert Hyperlink dialog box
- ☑ Insert a hyperlink with drag and drop
- ☑ Use the HYPERLINK function to create a hyperlink
- ☑ Format, edit, and delete a hyperlink
- ☑ Navigate with the Web toolbar

SKILL 11

Turning Your Data into Charts

- Creating a simple chart
- Creating a chart with the Chart Wizard
- Using the Chart toolbar
- Manipulating an embedded chart
- Choosing a chart type
- Creating your own custom chart types
- Adding titles and legends
- Editing the components of a chart
- Printing a chart

In this skill, you'll learn about the basics of building and enhancing charts in Excel. You'll see how easy it is to create a dazzling chart of your data with just a few simple clicks of the mouse. Excel also provides tools and options that help you fine-tune the chart in a thousand ways.

In Skill 12, you'll learn how to add graphical enhancements—such as drawn objects, imported images, and free-form text—to your charts or worksheets.

Creating a Simple Chart

Before getting into the nuts and bolts of charting, I want to show you the easiest, fastest way to create a chart. You create a chart from the data in a worksheet. I'm going to use the data in the worksheet in Figure 11.1 to create a simple chart here, and then I'll use this same data later in this skill to illustrate how you can create other charts, modify them, and build custom charts.

	A	B	C	D	E	F	G	H
1		1980	1985	1990	1995	1996	1997	
2	Coal	15.4	17.5	19.1	20.1	21.0	22.6	
3	Gas	20.4	17.8	19.3	22.2	22.6	22.6	
4	Oil	34.2	30.9	33.6	34.7	35.9	36.3	
5	Total	70.0	66.2	72.0	76.9	79.4	81.5	
6								

FIGURE 11.1: The data I'll use to create charts

NOTE NOTE NOTE NOTE NOTE NOTE NOTE NOTE NOTE NOTE NOTE NOTE NOTE NOTE

The data in Figure 1.1 are in quadrillion Btu and are taken from *The World Almanac and Book of Facts 1999.* These are the most recent figures available.

Building the Worksheet

As you follow along in this skill, you can use the data in Figure 1.1, or you can, of course, create your own worksheet and use that or use an existing worksheet. Here are the steps to build the worksheet in Figure 1.1:

1. Open a new blank worksheet.
2. Enter the text and numbers shown in Figure 1.1, and enter SUM formulas in cells B5:G5 so that each totals the three cells above it.

3. Include the borders around the cells, apply the Number format with one decimal place, and shrink column widths to fit. None of these changes affect the chart, but they do make the worksheet easier to work with.
4. Save the worksheet.

Creating the Chart

To create the chart, follow these steps:

1. Select the data in your worksheet.
2. Press F11.

That's all there is to it. You'll see a chart similar to that in Figure 11.2.

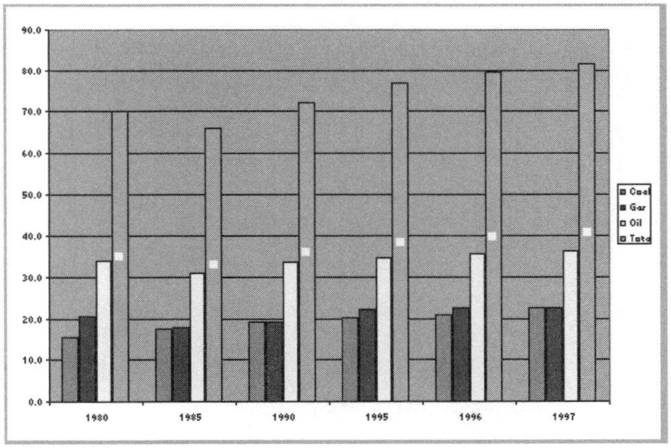

FIGURE 11.2: A simple chart created from the data in Figure 11.1

As you can see, whether you create a chart with the data in Figure 11.1 or with your own data, pressing F11 creates a simple column chart. Sometimes this may be all you need to get an instructive visual representation of your data. But most of the time, you'll want a chart that has a title, and depending on whether you'll print the chart or view it onscreen, you'll need to adjust the colors, the size, the labels, and so on. And certainly not all data are best charted in columns.

Now, let's look at the components, techniques, and terminology common to all charts.

Charting Overview

When you create a chart by pressing F11, the chart is displayed on a chart sheet, separate from the sheet that contains your data. You can, however, display the chart on the same page as your data, as Figure 11.3 shows.

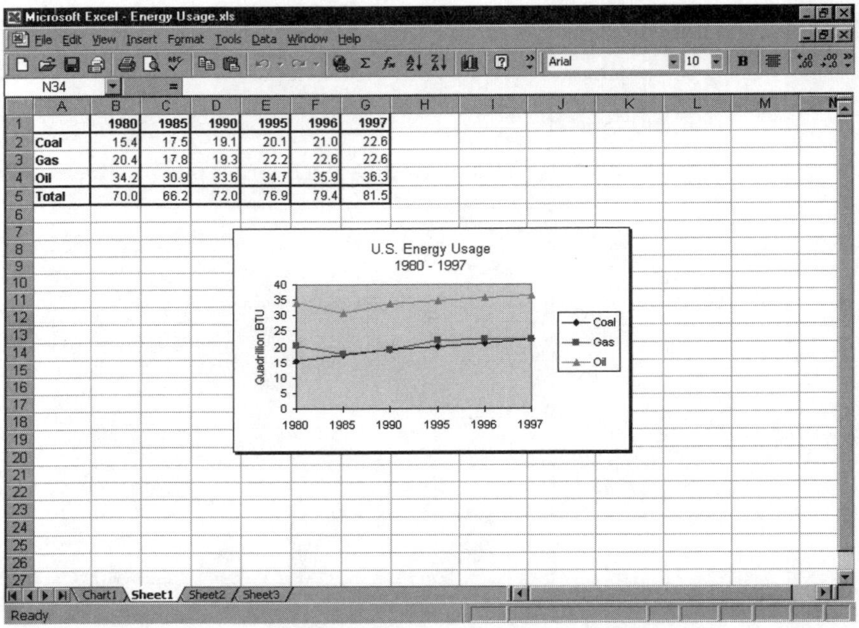

FIGURE 11.3: The chart in this worksheet illustrates the basic components of all charts.

Pointing to a component of a chart with the mouse displays a ScreenTip that includes the component's name, such as Chart Area or Plot Area, and the value of that component if the component is a data point. Yes, it's time to stop and define some terms.

Not all charts will have all the following components, but these are all the components that can be a part of any chart:

Type The chart in Figure 11.3 is a line chart. Excel has more than a dozen types of charts, such as bar, area, column, and pie, and each chart type has its own set of options and variations.

Location In Figure 11.3 the chart is *embedded* in the worksheet, where you can view it and, in this case, the data it plots (the range A1:G4). As I mentioned, the chart in Figure 1.2 is on its own *chart sheet* where, by default, it is sized to fit the current settings in the Page Setup dialog box for that sheet's printed page. Other than their location in the workbook, you'll find that most of the tools and options for working with charts apply both to chart sheets and to embedded charts.

Chart Area The rectangle that encloses all the other chart components is the Chart Area. You can change the style or color of its border, the pattern or color of its interior, and the font that is used for all text items within it.

Links No matter where you create a chart, it is linked to the data it plots in the same way that a formula is linked to data. If you change the value in a cell that is referenced by the chart, the corresponding point on the chart also changes.

X-Axis The *x-axis*, or *category axis*, is the horizontal line at the bottom of the chart along which the various categories, such as the six years in Figure 11.3, are laid out. A *major tick mark* identifies the position of each category on the axis; you can also display *minor tick marks* between each major one.

Y-Axis The *y-axis*, or *value axis*, is the vertical line on the left, to which the value of each data point is plotted. In Figure 11.3, the y-axis *scale* runs from 0 to 40, with each major tick mark being labeled accordingly. By default, Excel scales the axis so that its maximum is a little larger than the maximum value being plotted. But you can manually scale the y-axis if you want.

NOTE NOTE NOTE NOTE NOTE NOTE NOTE NOTE NOTE NOTE NOTE NOTE NOTE NOTE NOTE

Whether the x-axis and y-axis occupy the bottom and left sides of the plot area depends on the type of chart you choose and the type of data that you are plotting.

Plot Area In chart types that have an x-axis and a y-axis, those axes define two sides of the rectangular *plot area*. You can change the border of that area or the pattern or color of its interior. In a 3-D chart, the plot area is made up of the two *walls* and *floor* of the chart.

Data Series Three *data series* are represented in the chart in Figure 11.3 (Coal, Gas, and Oil), and each series has six *data points* (one for each year). Each point represents one cell in the range that is being graphed. In this line chart, a *data marker* shows each data point, and a line connects the markers for each series.

NOTE

You can have as many as 255 data series in a chart and as many as 32,000 data points in all the series in a chart. So get your magnifying glass out! In practice, however, your chart should tend toward the lean side, since its main purpose is to present a clear picture of the data that's behind it.

Titles *Titles* are at the top of the chart in Figure 11.3 and to the left of the y-axis. You can also place a title beneath the x-axis.

Legend To the right of the plot area is the *legend*, which identifies each of the data series.

Gridlines You can choose to display *gridlines* in the chart, which are lines that run from each tick mark on the x- and y-axes across the plot area. These lines can make it easier to identify the value of each data point within the chart. I turned off all gridlines in the chart in Figure 11.3 to avoid cluttering it.

Using the Chart Wizard to Create a Chart

Now you'll see how easy it is to create a chart using Excel's Chart Wizard, which is the best way to build a chart. In fact, you'll probably be letting the Chart Wizard guide your hand long after you've become the Van Gogh (or Salvador Dali?) of charting. Once you get the chart into the workbook, you can decide how you need (or want) to modify or enhance it.

Selecting the Data

In most cases, you start a chart by selecting the data you want to plot. the selected data in Figure 11.3 include the following chart components:

Data Series The three rows of data, B2:G2, B3:G3, and B4:G4.

Series Name The title in the cell to the left of each series.

Category Labels The titles in row 1 that will appear along the x-axis and identify each group of data points.

Legend Text In this case, the Series Names (A1:A3) will appear in the chart's legend, identifying each data series.

The data you select need not be in one contiguous block or even in the same sheet or workbook. However, if you select noncontiguous ranges, each range must be a rectangular selection. For example, I could add more data series to the chart in Figure 11.3 by selecting either a seven-cell row or column (to match the seven cells used for each data series and series name). You'll learn how to add series to a chart in the section "Editing a Series," later in this skill.

Choosing a Chart Type

After selecting the range, you can begin to create the chart. Follow these steps:

1. Click the Chart Wizard button on the Standard toolbar or choose Insert ‰ Chart to start the Chart Wizard.

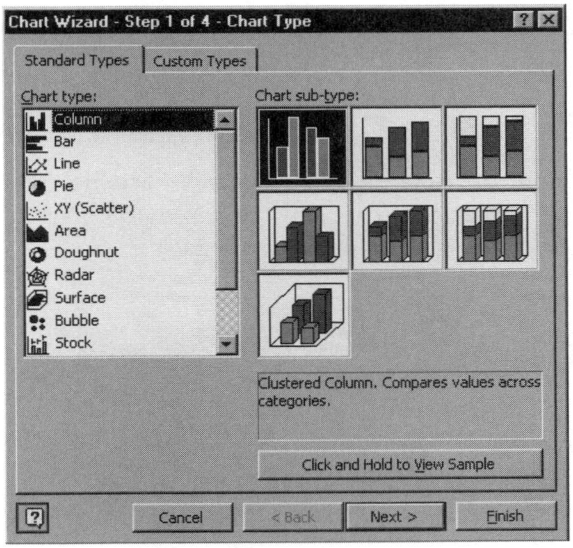

NOTE

If you select an existing chart in the worksheet or display a chart sheet, you can click the Chart Wizard button to modify that chart in the same way that you create a chart. On the other hand, you can make many enhancements to a chart that are *not* part of the Chart Wizard. You'll read about many of them later in this skill.

2. Select the type of chart you want to create in the Chart Type list.
3. In the Chart Sub-Type area, click the style you want. You'll see a description below the group of chart sub-types.

4. To get a preview of how your data will look with this type of chart, point to the Click and Hold to View Sample button and hold down the left mouse button.

5. Click Next to open Step 2 of the Chart Wizard.

TIP TIP TIP TIP TIP TIP TIP TIP TIP TIP TIP TIP TIP TIP TIP TIP TIP TIP TIP TIP TIP TIP TIP TIP TIP TIP

Like other Excel Wizards, you can back up a step in the Chart Wizard by clicking the Back button, or you can click Cancel to end the job without creating the chart. If you want to create the chart as it is currently defined and skip over any additional Chart Wizard options, click the Finish button in any of the Chart Wizard dialog boxes.

Specifying the Data Range and Series

Now you can make some decisions about how to plot the data you selected. Let's look at the choices in the Chart Wizard's Step 2 dialog box, which contains two tabs. Figure 11.4 shows the Data Range tab.

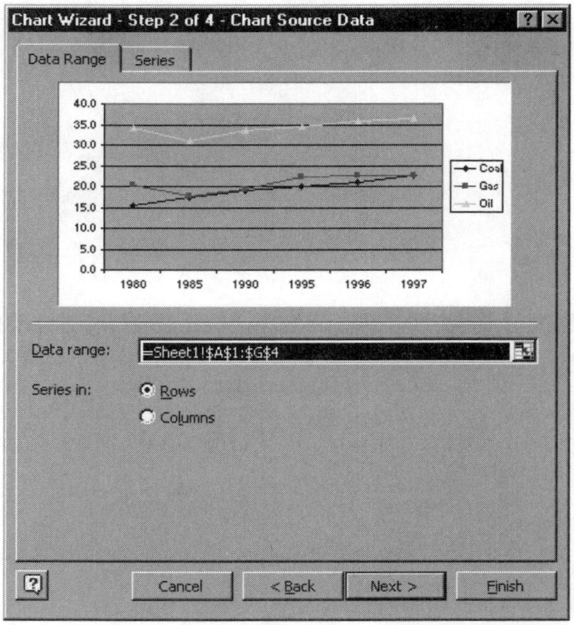

FIGURE 11.4: In Step 2 of the Chart Wizard, you specify how to plot the selected data.

NOTE

The Chart Wizard displays a sample of your chart as it looks at this point so that you can see the effects of any further changes you make.

The Data Range tab displays the range address that you selected for the chart (for our example, A1:G4 in Sheet1). You can verify that this is really what you want to plot or modify the address as needed.

You can also choose either Rows or Columns in the Series In section, which defines whether the chart series run across the rows or down the column. In Figure 11.3, each series occupies a row.

Now click the Series tab in the Step 2 dialog box. You'll see the same sample chart displayed, with a different set of options beneath it (as shown here).

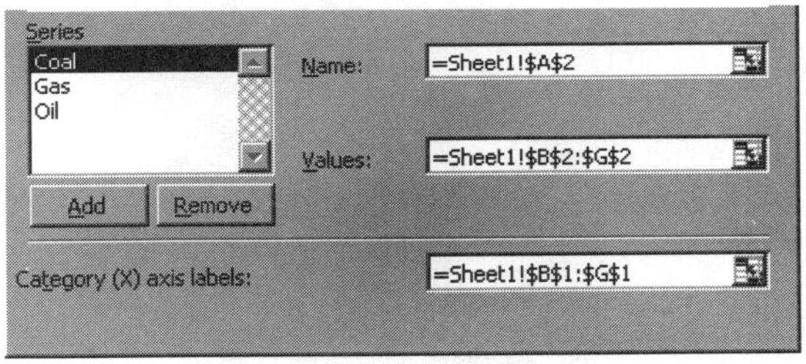

In the Series tab, you can change the cell references for each series with the following options.

Series Select one of the series in the chart; in our example, there are three—Coal, Gas, and Oil. The current range references for the one you select appear in the other fields in the dialog box. You can click Remove to eliminate the selected series from the chart (the data in the worksheet are not affected; that series is simply not included in the chart). You can add another series by clicking Add and filling in the range definitions for it.

Name Whatever is in this cell will serve as the name of the series. For example, cell A2 on Sheet1 contains the name for the Coal series. You can specify a different cell to serve as the name for this series, or when you return to the worksheet, you can enter a different name in the cell.

Values This is the range of cells that contains the values for the selected series. It is the range B2:G2 for the Coal series in our example worksheet.

Category (X) axis labels This range of cells contains the labels that will appear along the x-axis. In our example, that is the range B1:G1 (the years).

Click Next to open Step 3 of the Chart Wizard.

WARNING WARNING WARNING WARNING WARNING WARNING WARNING WARNING

If you adjust any of these references for a series, be sure that you also adjust the other series, if needed, or they may no longer be plotting related ranges.

Adding Titles and a Legend

The Step 3 dialog box of the Chart Wizard has six tabs in which you can specify a variety of options for the chart. The Titles tab is shown in Figure 11.5. At this point, I'll just use those that we need for this example; later in this skill, you'll learn about the others.

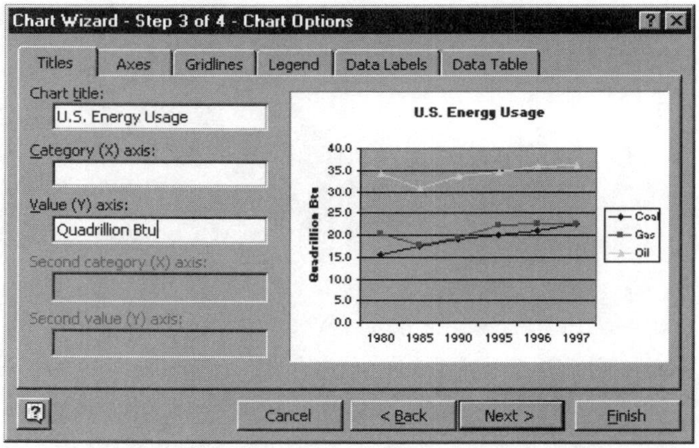

FIGURE 11.5: In Step 3 of the Chart Wizard, you create titles for the chart and define a variety of enhancements.

1. Click the Titles tab if it isn't already selected.
2. Type the title of the chart in the Chart Title field, **U.S. Energy Usage** for our example. We'll add the second line to this title later by editing the chart in the worksheet (see the "Entering or Revising a Title" section).
3. Select the Value (Y) Axis field, and notice how the chart title now appears in the sample chart in the dialog box. In this field, type **Quadrillion Btu**. We don't need a title for the x-axis because the category, years, is obvious in the chart.

4. Click the Gridlines tab, and clear its four options so that no gridlines appear in the chart. (In our example, we're turning them off so that they don't clutter this small chart.)

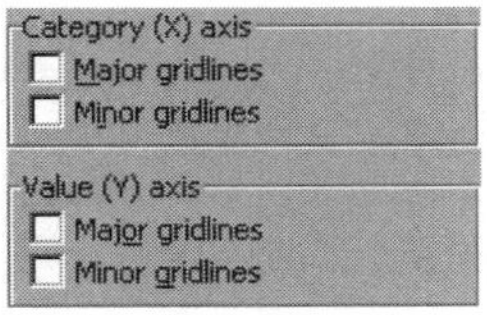

5. Click the Legend tab, click the Show Legend check box, and then select the option that you want. For our example, select the Right option so that the legend appears to the right of the plot area in the chart.

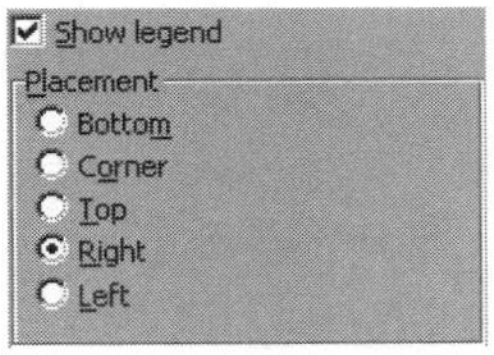

6. Click Next to open Step 4 of the Chart Wizard.

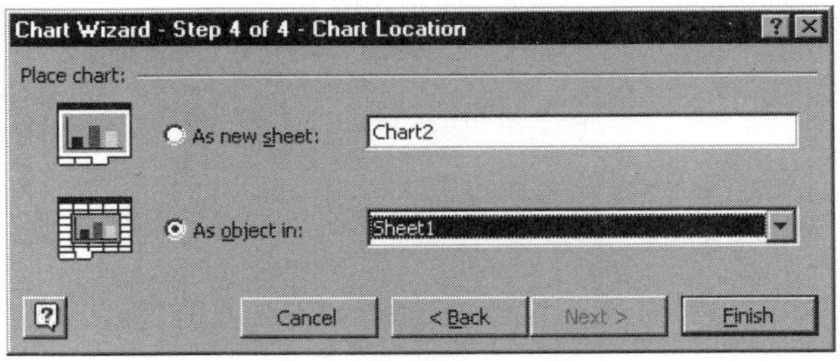

Deciding Where to Place the Chart

In the last Chart Wizard dialog box, Step 4, you specify where you want to create this chart (if you right-click an existing chart, you can choose Location from the shortcut menu to access this dialog box):

As New Sheet Creates the chart in its own chart sheet, out of the way of any data in other sheets. This gives you the largest viewing area for the chart and makes it easier to format and fine-tune it for printing on a separate page.

As Object In Embeds the chart within the worksheet you specify (Sheet1 in this case). Generally, you embed a chart so that you can view or print the chart along with any data in that worksheet, which is often the same data on which it is plotted. You can then watch the chart change as you make changes to the data that it plots.

After you select the location for the chart, click Finish. In our example, the chart is embedded in the worksheet that contains the data, as shown in Figure 11.6.

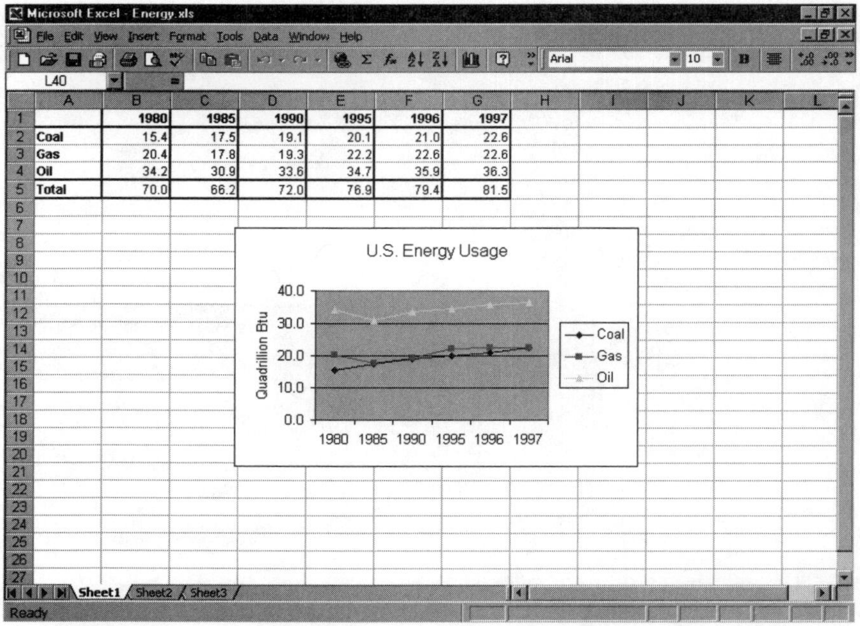

	1980	1985	1990	1995	1996	1997
Coal	15.4	17.5	19.1	20.1	21.0	22.6
Gas	20.4	17.8	19.3	22.2	22.6	22.6
Oil	34.2	30.9	33.6	34.7	35.9	36.3
Total	70.0	66.2	72.0	76.9	79.4	81.5

FIGURE 11.6: The "finished" chart in the worksheet, ready for lots of fine-tuning

You might want to add a few touches to your chart, but if you're reasonably happy with the results so far, go ahead and save the workbook.

SKILL 11

NOTE NOTE NOTE NOTE NOTE NOTE NOTE NOTE NOTE NOTE NOTE NOTE NOTE NOTE

It's easy to delete the embedded chart if you want to. Simply click the chart area, outside any of the chart components, and press Del. You can also modify, fine-tune, or enhance the chart or change any of its umpteen-dozen options, many of which you'll learn about in this skill.

Using the Chart Toolbar

Creating a chart displays the Chart toolbar above the Formula bar.

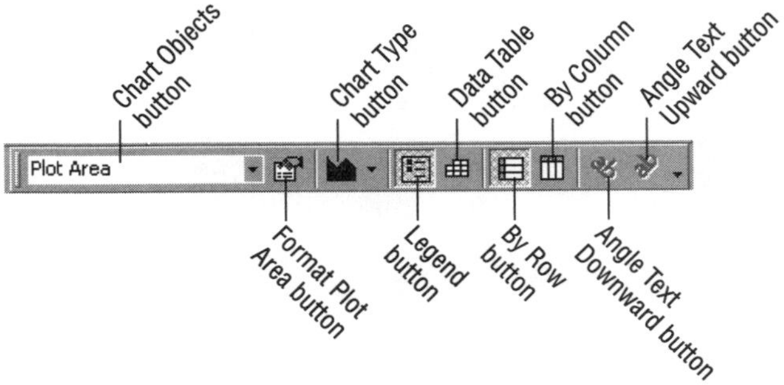

To display the Chart toolbar at any time, choose View ➤ Toolbars ➤ Chart. Especially useful is the Chart Objects drop-down list, which contains the name of every component in the chart. Simply select an object's name in the list to select that object in the chart.

Selecting, Moving, and Sizing an Embedded Chart

You can change the size and shape of an embedded chart or move it to a new location. You can do the same to the components within the chart; for example, you can move its main title to the left side of the chart or make its plot area smaller.

To select an entire embedded chart, click anywhere in its chart area (the mouse pointer appears as an arrow when it is over the chart), but outside any of the chart components, such as titles, legend, or plot area. You'll see selection handles appear at each corner of the chart area's perimeter and in the middle of each side.

After you select the chart, you can move or resize it in the usual Windows way. (You might move a chart into the lower-right corner of its worksheet to display as much of its source data as possible.)

To move a chart, point to the chart area (again, outside any of its components), and hold down the left mouse button; the mouse pointer appears as a four-headed arrow, indicating that you can move the chart. Now simply drag the chart to a new location.

When you select an embedded chart and then point to a selection handle, the pointer changes to a double-headed arrow, indicating that you can resize the chart. You can do so in three ways:

- To resize a chart in only one dimension, drag one of the selection handles that appears in the middle of a side. For example, you can widen a chart by dragging one of its sides. Make it just wide enough so that its x-axis labels have room to run horizontally instead of at an angle.
- To resize a chart in two dimensions, drag a corner selection handle.
- To resize a chart proportionally, so that its width and height retain the same relationship, hold down Shift while you drag one of the corner selection handles.

When you change the size of an embedded chart, Excel redraws the chart to fit the new dimensions. For example, if you give a chart lots of room, Excel will try to display the label for every major tick mark on the x-axis. As you shrink the chart, Excel will eliminate x-axis labels, as needed.

TIP

These methods for changing the size, shape, and position of an embedded chart apply to all objects that you place on a sheet, such as the drawn objects or imported graphic images discussed in the next skill.

To move a chart's titles, legend, or plot area, click the object to select it, and then drag it to a new position. You can also change the size of the plot area or legend by selecting it and dragging one of its selection handles.

Editing a Chart and Its Components

You can modify a chart (whether embedded or on a chart sheet) and its components in several ways, depending on what you want to change.

- Select the chart area or anything within it, and the menu bar displays a Chart menu. You use the items on the Chart menu to change the type of chart (the Step 1 dialog box for the Chart Wizard), its source data (Step 2), various chart options (Step 3), and the chart's location (Step 4).
- Right-click the chart area to display the shortcut menu, which contains the same commands that appear on the Chart menu as well as the Chart Window command, which displays the chart in a new window. This can make it easier to work on the chart, because you can resize, move, or hide that window without affecting the size or location of the embedded chart.
- Right-click a component within the chart, such as its legend, x-axis, a data series, or its title, and choose Format *Object* from the shortcut menu. For example, right-click the x-axis and choose Format Axis to open the Format Axis dialog box in which you can modify the way the axis looks and behaves. You can also double-click a chart component to display its Format dialog box.

You can also use the buttons and controls on the Chart toolbar to modify a chart.

After you finish editing the chart, click in the worksheet outside the chart area to return to the worksheet. You can also press Esc once or twice to deselect the chart.

Now we'll look at the many options you have when building a chart, starting with the chart's type.

Choosing a Chart Type

When you create a new chart and don't select a chart type, by default Excel selects the column chart. If you find that you often choose another chart type instead of the column chart, you can select another type to serve as the default (as described in the next section).

No matter what the default chart type is, though, when you're creating a new chart or revising an existing one, you can change chart types at any time. Excel redraws the chart using the same data series, titles, and so on—but in the new style.

Changing the Chart Type

To change the chart type of a chart you created, follow these steps:

1. Select the embedded chart or one of its components by clicking it, and then choose Chart ➤ Chart Type to open the Chart Type dialog box.

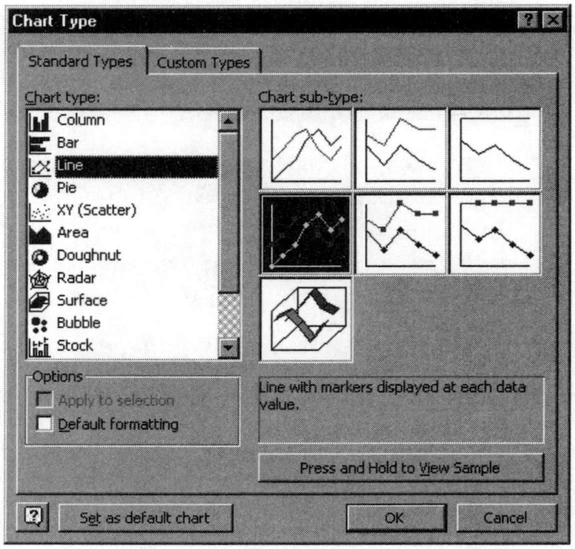

TIP TIP TIP TIP TIP TIP TIP TIP TIP TIP TIP TIP TIP TIP TIP TIP TIP TIP TIP TIP TIP TIP TIP TIP TIP

You can also right-click anywhere within the chart area but outside its other components and choose Chart Type from the shortcut menu.

2. Select one of the categories in the Chart Type list to choose a new chart type.
3. Choose a specific type from the Chart Sub-type group.
4. Click OK.

Among the sub-type are both 2-D and 3-D charts; most of the 3-D charts are essentially just 3-D versions of 2-D charts that add a nice "blocky" feel to the chart. Remember that you can press and hold down the button of that name to see a preview of the chart in the selected style. Three additional options are available in the Chart Type dialog box when you are revising an existing chart:

Apply to Selection This check box is selected when you select one or more series in the chart before displaying the Chart Type dialog box (if you haven't selected a series, this option is not available). If you leave this option selected, the chart type you choose applies only to the selected series. This allows you to mix different types of charts within a single chart so that, for example, some series are drawn as columns while another is drawn as a line (this is also discussed later in the "Editing a Series" section).

Default Formatting By default this check box is not selected so that any enhancements you've already applied to the chart will remain in effect even if you choose a new chart type. Select this option to remove all enhancements you've added and return the chart to its default look.

Set as Default Chart Click this button to make the currently selected chart type the default when you create a new chart.

You can click Cancel to leave your chart unchanged. You'll read about the Custom Types tab in the Chart Type dialog box a little later in the "Working with Custom Chart Types" section.

NOTE

You can also change the selected chart's type by clicking the Chart Type button on the Chart toolbar and making a selection from the drop-down palette, although there are many fewer chart types from which to choose. In general, stick with the Chart Type dialog box, which also displays a preview sample of your chart.

Line Charts

In a line chart, like those used in the examples so far in this skill, the x-axis consists of labels, and its tick marks are laid out evenly along that axis. Points for each series are plotted as small markers between the x- and y-axes, and a line connects the markers for each series.

Excel differentiates the series by the colors of their lines and markers, as well as by the shapes of the markers and styles of the lines.

A line chart is a good choice when you have many points to plot or when the up and down trend of the data is important.

NOTE

When both the x- and y-axes are numeric data, an XY, or scatter, chart may be the best choice. A section on XY charts follows shortly.

Column and Bar Charts

In a column chart, each data point in a series is represented by a column that rises from the x-axis. A bar chart is a column chart drawn sideways so that the x-axis is on the left.

Column and bar charts are useful when the height of any individual point is more important than the trend among points in a series. But avoid these chart types if you have many series or data points to plot, because the chart could look crowded and be difficult to interpret.

The x-axis, or *baseline*, in bar and column charts generally appears at the zero value on the y-axis, as shown in the column chart in Figure 11.7. If there are any negative values in the data, however, those points will extend *below* the baseline.

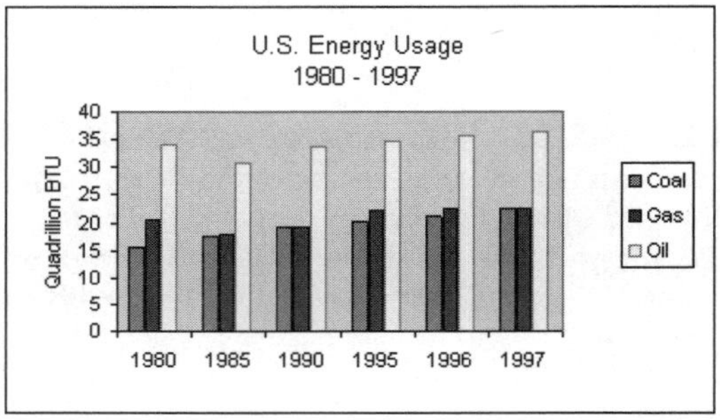

FIGURE 11.7: The energy data plotted in a column chart

See the discussion in "Stacked and Area Charts" for guidelines on creating a stacked chart, which is a subtype of the column and bar chart types.

XY (Scatter) Charts

Like a line chart, an XY chart plots each point with a marker and connects the points in each series with a line. But unlike a line chart, the x-axis consists of numbers, not text labels. This means that the x-axis tick marks are spaced according to their values and not just evenly spaced along the axis.

The XY chart is sometimes referred to as a scatter chart because it is often used without any lines connecting the data markers. You might use the scatter chart when your chart has many data points but no particular trend in their rising and falling. See the "Editing a Series" section, later in this skill, for more about changing the look of a series.

Figure 11.8 shows the difference between the two chart types. The data being plotted this time are for 1965, 1966, 1969, 1975, 1985, and 1990. Because these are not evenly spaced years, the line chart distorts their relationship, while the XY chart gives a more accurate picture.

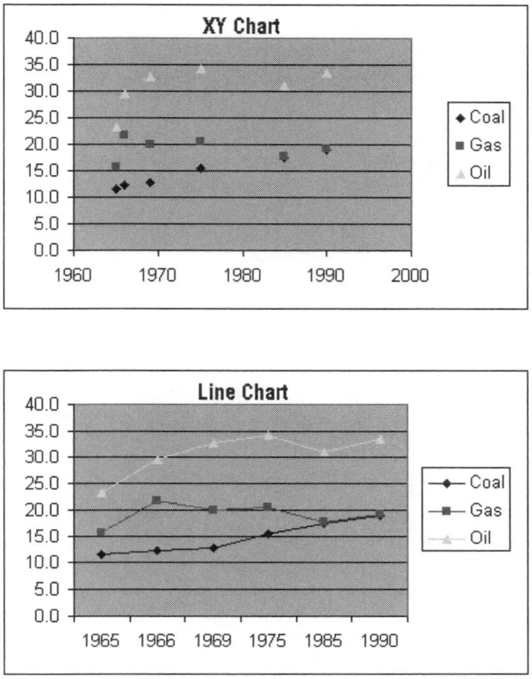

FIGURE 11.8: An XY chart plots one value against another, whereas a line chart plots values against evenly spaced text labels.

The XY chart at the top of Figure 11.8 treats the x-axis entries as numeric; so the data point markers for the three years in the 1960s all appear at that end of the axis.

In the line chart at the bottom of Figure 11.8, however, the tick marks are spaced evenly along the x-axis, with no regard for their actual numeric value. You can see how this treatment can distort the trend in the data.

Stacked Area, Column, and Bar Charts

The stacked-area chart is similar to a line chart, but plots the series one on top of another, thereby producing a total. The values along the y-axis increase accordingly. The data-point markers are not displayed, and the area between lines is filled with color.

Figure 11.9 shows the energy data in a stacked-area chart. Notice that the y-axis scale now runs to 80 and that the plotted areas bump into the left and right edges of the plot area. By default, Excel turns off the *Value (Y) axis crosses between categories* option for the x-axis for area charts (this is discussed in "Adjusting the Scale of a Category Axis" later in this skill).

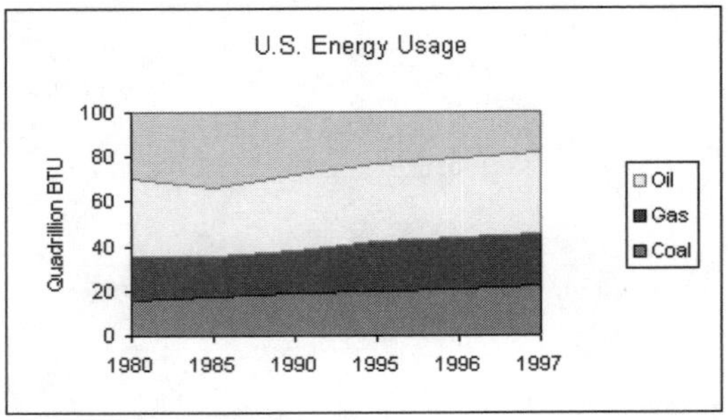

FIGURE 11.9: A stacked-area chart shows the total energy consumption as well as the contribution made by each energy source.

You can also create a stacked-column (or bar) chart to show accumulation. Each column represents the total of all the data points at that tick mark on the x-axis. Figure 11.10 shows the energy data in a stacked-column chart. In this case, the *Value (Y) axis crosses between categories* option for the x-axis is turned on (selected), so the bars at each end of the x-axis do not touch the left and right edges of the plot area.

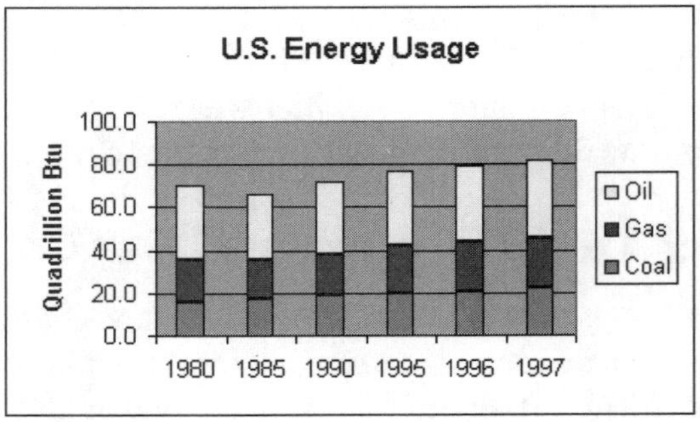

FIGURE 11.10: A stacked-column chart shows the total energy consumption, as well as the contribution made by each energy source.

Pie and Doughnut Charts

You use the pie and doughnut chart types to plot data for a single series. Both types are round, but the doughnut chart has a hole in its center (unless it's the jelly-filled doughnut chart). I'll use the pie chart for this discussion.

Each data point is represented by one "slice" of the circular pie chart. The size of each slice is proportional to the value it represents, so all the data points taken together make the complete circle.

You can choose to have Excel label each slice with any of the following:

- The underlying value of the data point
- Its percentage of the total
- Its underlying value in the worksheet, comparable to the x-axis labels in other chart types

Figure 11.11 shows a 3-D pie chart that plots the energy data used earlier for just a single year, 1997. Each slice is labeled with the text from column A of the worksheet, as well as that slice's percentage of the total pie.

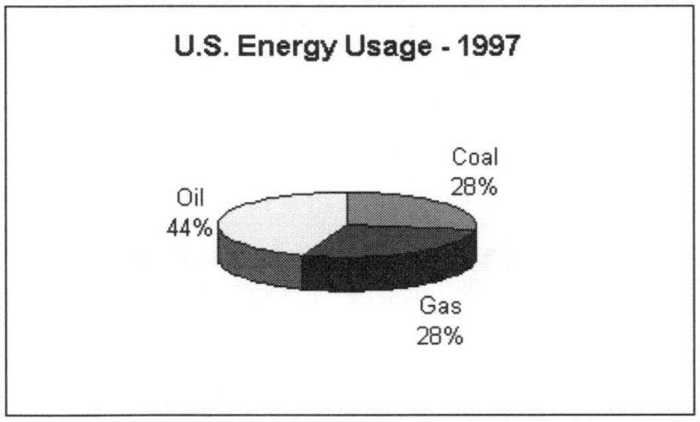

FIGURE 11.11: A pie chart plots a single series; each data point is represented by a slice of the pie.

TIP

To call attention to a slice, click once on the pie to select the pie, and then click a second time on the slice you want and drag it away in a big hunk. You can separate all the pie slices by clicking once on the pie and then dragging outward.

Radar Charts

The Radar chart takes a different view of your data by plotting it on concentric circles:

- The labels of the x-axis fall on the outer circle.
- The values on the y-axis begin in the center of the circle and grow as they head out to the x-axis circle.
- Each point in a series is plotted according to its position on the x-axis along the outer circle (its bearing in the language of radar and navigation) and how far out from the center it falls on the y-axis (its range).

Figure 11.12 shows a radar chart with the energy data we've been using.

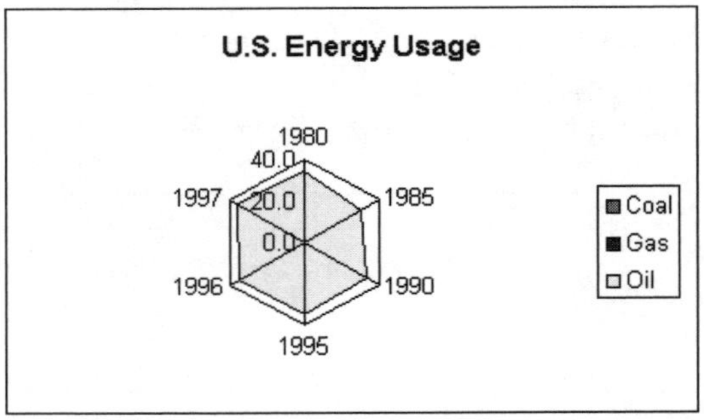

FIGURE 11.12: A radar chart plots the energy data.

TIP

A radar chart is particularly adept at showing cyclical data, such as the temperature at different times during the day.

3-D Surface Charts

The 3-D surface chart is a unique chart type that seems to drape a sheet over your data to create a three-dimensional view of it. A topographic map is a good example of one; it has many data points that fall along smoothly flowing curves in a chart (map).

If you were to leave your topographic map at home and try instead to refer to the numbers from which the map was drawn, you'd have a heck of time finding your way.

Figure 11.13 shows a 3-D surface chart that plots a function. The data cells for the chart are in a square range, B2:BJ62, that is 61 cells on a side and, therefore, contains 3,721 data points. Each point (cell) consists of a formula that was copied throughout the range. Here is the formula in the first plotted cell, B2:

```
=SIN(B$1^2+$A2^2)+SIN($A2)
```

Then I entered the number –3 in cell B1 and A2 and chose Edit ➤ Fill ➤ Series to fill each range B1:BJ1 and A2:A62, using a Step Value of 0.1 and a Stop Value of 3. When Excel recalculated all the formulas using these numbers, the chart could be plotted for the range B2:BJ62.

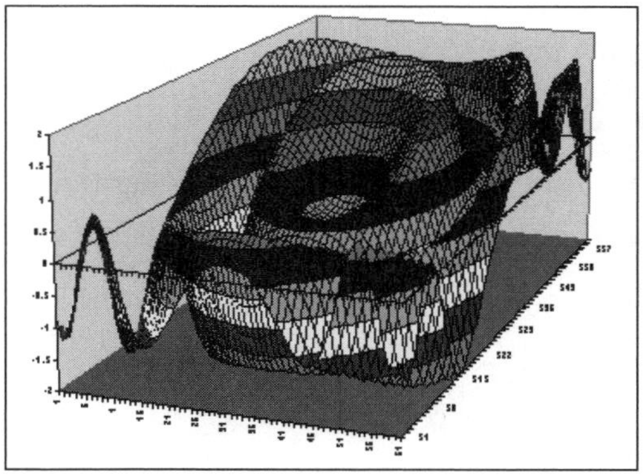

FIGURE 11.13: A 3-D surface chart plots a function.

NOTE NOTE NOTE NOTE NOTE NOTE NOTE NOTE NOTE NOTE NOTE NOTE NOTE NOTE NOTE

This is a very complex chart that may take Excel some time to draw on a slow computer (slow for the late 90s, that is). On a Pentium 133MHz computer with lots of RAM, Excel needed about six seconds.

Working with Custom Chart Types

You've already seen how to select a chart type from the Standard Types tab in the Chart Type dialog box. Now you'll learn how to take advantage of the charts offered in the Custom Types tab of that dialog box.

Excel's built-in custom chart types are similar to the standard chart types, but offer a bit more snap and sizzle in the formatting. You can select one of the built-in custom types just as you select one of the standard types.

The real advantage of custom charts, however, is that you can create user-defined charts. Once you define a chart type, it appears in the list of custom charts, and you can select it as you would any other chart type. Creating a variety of user-defined charts is the best way to build a "library" of your own chart types.

For example, with a custom chart type, all the departments in your company could produce standardized reports that all share exactly the same look—the plotted data and a title might be different in each department, but the charts would otherwise look the same. Every chart might display the same:

- Chart type, such as a 3-D column chart
- Background color and pattern for the chart area and plot area
- Colors and styles for each series in the chart
- Company logo above the chart title
- Titles on the x- and y-axes
- Fonts and font sizes

Choosing a Built-in Custom Chart Type

To choose a built-in custom chart, follow these steps:

1. Select the chart if it already exists in the workbook.
2. Choose Chart ➤ Chart Types to open the Chart Types dialog box, and click the Custom Types tab, as shown in Figure 11.14.
3. Click the Built- in option.
4. Click a chart type.
5. Click OK.

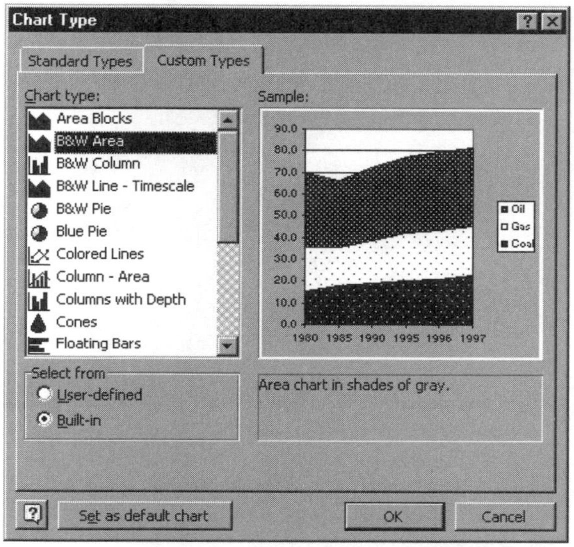

FIGURE 11.14: The Custom Types tab in the Chart Type dialog box

The built-in custom chart types are a bit more enhanced (or perhaps, eccentric) than the standard types we've looked at so far in this skill. In Figure 11.14, I selected the custom chart type called B&W Area, which is an area chart that is modified to display only shades of gray.

Other than getting a chart with a bit more pizzazz, selecting a custom chart type is no different from selecting one of the standard charts and later adding a few enhancements. The real payoff comes when you create your own custom charts.

Creating Your Own Custom Charts

Before you create a custom chart type, you need an existing chart that can serve as the model. Don't worry about getting it perfect the first time around, because you can change the definition of a user-defined chart type at any time.

Here's what to do after you create a chart that you want to use as the basis for a user-defined custom chart type:

1. Select the embedded chart or select the chart sheet.
2. Choose Chart ➤ Chart Type to open the Chart Type dialog box.

3. Click the Custom Types tab, and select the User-defined option.
4. Click Add to open the Add Custom Chart Type dialog box.

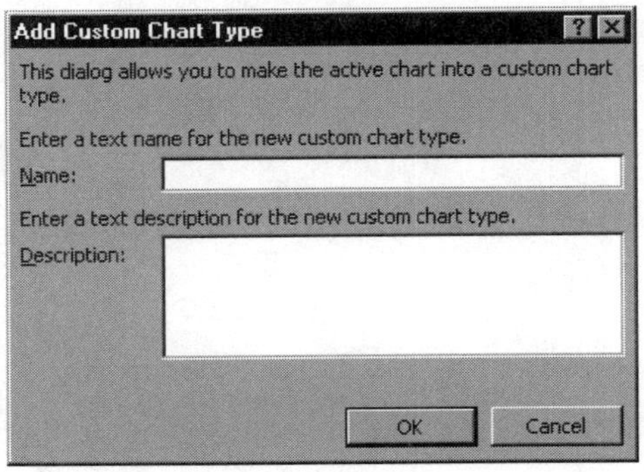

5. In the Name field, enter a name for the new chart type, which will appear in the list of user-defined custom formats. (The name can be a maximum of 31 characters.)
6. In the Description field, enter a description for the chart type, which will appear below the preview of the chart in the Chart Type dialog box.
7. Choose OK, and you should see your newly defined custom chart type appear in the list.
8. Choose OK to close the Chart Type dialog box.

The custom chart type you just defined is now available for you to apply to other charts you make—simply select it as you would any other custom or standard chart type. Just remember to select the User-defined option in the Custom Types tab in the Chart Type dialog box.

To remove a user-defined custom chart type, select it in the list in the Chart Type dialog box, and then click Delete.

TIP TIP TIP TIP TIP TIP TIP TIP TIP TIP TIP TIP TIP TIP TIP TIP TIP TIP TIP TIP TIP TIP TIP TIP TIP TIP TIP TIP

To distribute a user-defined custom chart to other Excel users, give them a workbook that contains the chart from which you created the custom chart type (or create a chart from that chart type). Then go through the steps described above to create a user-defined custom chart type for their copies of Excel.

Adding Titles to a Chart

By default, a chart has three built-in titles: a main title centered at the top of the chart area and titles for each axis. When you used the Chart Wizard earlier in this skill in "Adding Titles and a Legend," you entered a main chart title and a y-axis title (see Figure 11.6).

You're not limited to these three titles. You can create free-form text anywhere in a chart with the Text Box tool on the Drawing toolbar. You'll learn about this technique in the next skill. But remember that a chart is supposed to be a picture of the underlying data, so avoid creating long or overly descriptive titles.

Entering or Revising a Title

To add a title to an existing chart, follow these steps:

1. Select the chart or any of its components.
2. Choose Chart ➤ Chart Options to open the Chart Options dialog box.
3. Click the Titles tab.

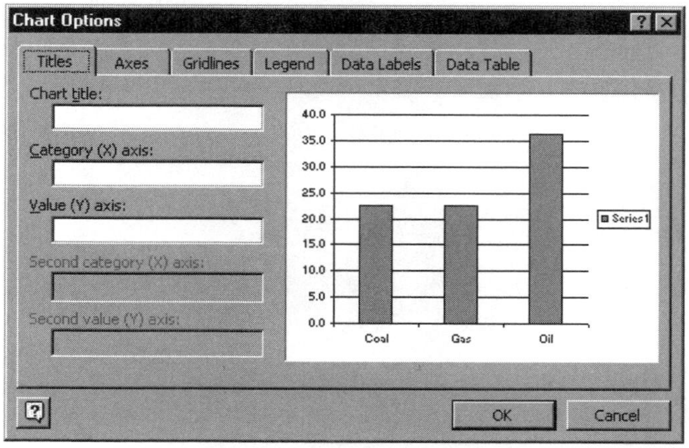

4. Enter a chart title and titles for the axes if you want, as you did earlier in the Step 3 dialog box of the Chart Wizard.
5. Click OK.

To revise an existing title within the chart, follow these steps:

1. Click the title within the chart to select it.
2. Click within the title to edit its text.
3. When you're finished, select another part of the chart or worksheet.

Formatting Titles

To change the font or alignment of a chart title or to enclose it in a box, follow these steps:

1. Right-click the title, and choose Format Chart Title from the shortcut menu to open the Format Chart Title dialog box.

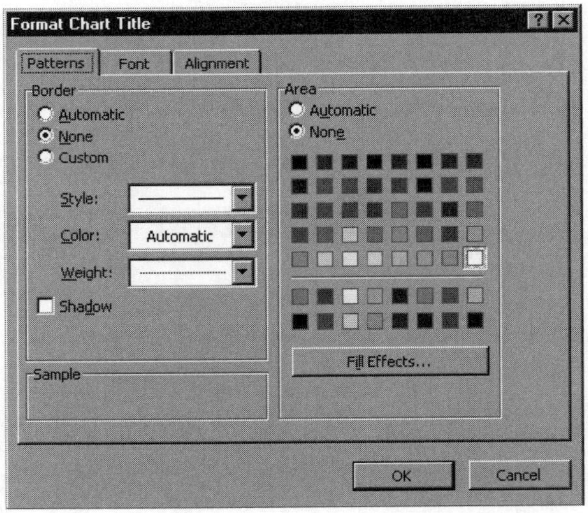

2. Choose formatting options much as you did in the Format Cells dialog box, earlier in this skill.
3. Click OK.

Linking a Title to a Cell

Instead of entering text for a title, you can create a link to a cell so that the title displays whatever is in that cell. The title must already exist in the chart, so, if necessary, create the title in the Titles tab of the Chart Options dialog box. Now follow these steps:

1. Click the title in the chart to select it.
2. Click in the Formula bar and enter a formula that references a worksheet cell. Be sure to include the sheet reference too, such as:

   ```
   =SHEET1!B15
   ```

3. Click the check mark to the left of the Formula bar or press Enter to enter that formula into the title.

The linked title will now display whatever is in the referenced cell.

When a workbook has many charts, linking the titles to worksheet cells can save you *lots* of time when you need to revise the chart titles. For example, suppose you've entered this year's data into last year's workbook so that it now charts current data. If the chart titles in all its charts are linked to cells, you can update them all to reflect the year simply by changing the dates in a few cells.

Adding a Legend to a Chart

A chart's legend describes each of the data series in the chart by displaying an example of the series, such as its line and marker style or color and its name. You may not need a legend in charts if the series are easy to distinguish and need no explanation.

You can create a legend while you're building a chart with the Chart Wizard, as you learned earlier in the "Adding Titles and a Legend" section. You can also create a legend or change the position of the legend by following these steps:

1. Select the chart.
2. Choose Chart ➤ Chart Options to open the Chart Options dialog box.
3. Click the Legend tab.
4. To change the position of the legend in the chart, select one of the legend placement options, such as Right, Bottom, or Top.
5. To remove the legend, clear the Show Legend option (you can also select the legend in the chart and press Del).
6. Click OK.

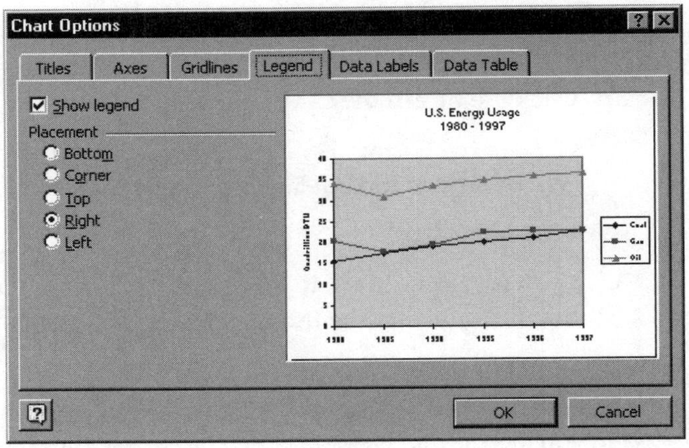

TIP

The Placement options make it easy to place the legend in a consistent manner, such as centered above or below the chart. You can also drag the legend anywhere you want in the chart.

To change the formatting of a legend, follow these steps:

1. Right-click the legend, and choose Format Legend from the shortcut menu to open the Format Legend dialog box.
2. Select options to format the text within the legend and the box that surrounds it.
3. Click OK.

You can select the text or markers within a legend and modify them, as well. For example, you can apply a different font to each of the series names in the legend. If you change the marker style in the legend, that change will also apply to the plotted series within the chart.

Editing a Chart to Make More Changes

Excel offers a tremendous variety of options for changing the look of the components in a chart. As you've seen, though, you can produce a nice chart with just a few clicks of the mouse, so you may not need these options often.

To modify just about any object in a chart, follow these steps:

1. Double-click the chart to select it.
2. Right-click, and choose Format *Object* from the shortcut menu to open the Format dialog box for that object. (*Object* is the name of the object.)

Here are a few editing tips:

- To select a component in a chart, click that object to display selection handles or a border around the object. You can also select its name from the Chart Objects list in the Chart toolbar, although not every chart component is listed there. For example, individual legend components are not listed.
- In a crowded chart, you may find it difficult to tell which object you've selected. Look in the Name box, to the left of the Formula bar, to see the name of the currently selected object.
- Choose Tools ➤ Spelling (F7) to check the spelling in the active (selected) chart.

Editing the Chart Area

To select the chart area, click the chart outside the plot area and not on any other chart objects. Selection handles surround the entire chart, and you'll see the name Chart Area appear in the Name box.

When you choose Format ➤ Selected Chart Area, the Format Chart Area dialog box appears. The tabs in it should look familiar by now:

Patterns Sets the style of the border that surrounds the chart and the color and pattern of its interior (the interior serves as the background for the other chart objects). If you click the Fill Effects button, you can choose from a variety of interior fills for the chart area, such as a picture that you import from a file.

TIP TIP TIP TIP TIP TIP TIP TIP TIP TIP TIP TIP TIP TIP TIP TIP TIP TIP TIP TIP TIP TIP TIP TIP TIP TIP TIP

If your chart overlaps your data and you want to display the cells beneath the chart, select None for the Area option.

Fonts Sets the font for all text elements in the chart; your choice overwrites any font changes you have already made to the titles, axes, and legend.

Properties Controls whether the chart can be modified or printed (see Skill 9). This tab appears when the chart area is part of an embedded chart. You can also specify how the chart moves when the cells that underlie it in the worksheet are moved, such as when you insert or delete columns. By default, the chart moves and changes size when the underlying cells change.

Including the Source Data as a Table

You can create a table of the chart's source data within the chart, which can sometimes be the only way to get the complete picture, such as when you print the chart separately from the worksheet data it references.

To add the underlying data to the chart, follow these steps:

1. Select the chart.
2. Choose Chart ➤ Chart Options to open the Chart Options dialog box.
3. Click the Data Table tab.

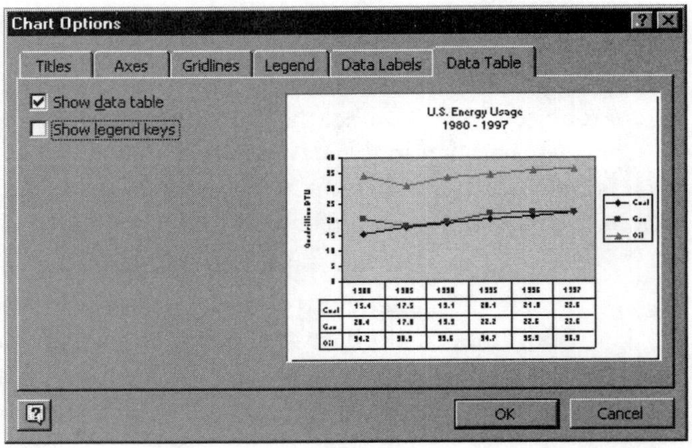

4. Click the Show Data Table option.
5. Click OK.

You'll see the table appear within the preview of the chart in the dialog box (some chart types won't offer the data table option, including pie and doughnut, XY, and surface charts).

The data table may be ineffectual if the chart is small and is embedded in a worksheet or if there are lots and lots of source data. The table will either stuff the chart to its limits, or Excel will skip some of its rows or columns so it will fit within the chart. Either result would not be very helpful. But the preview of your chart will tell you if inserting the data table is a good idea. To learn how to include all or only some of the data, see Skill 12.

Editing the Plot Area

To edit the plot area, follow these steps:

1. Select the plot area.
2. Choose Format ➤ Plot Area to open the Format Plot Area dialog box.
3. Use the options in this dialog box to change the border that surrounds the plot area and the color and pattern that fills it.
4. When you're done, click OK.

If you set the Area option to None, the color and pattern of the chart area show through the plot area. In many 3-D charts, you can also modify the two walls by choosing Format ➤ Walls, and you can modify the floor by choosing Format ➤ Floor.

Editing the Gridlines

In charts that have axes, you can display gridlines that run from either axis. Gridlines can make it easier to judge the value of any data marker, bar, or column in the chart.

To add gridlines to a chart or change their appearance, follow these steps:

1. Select the chart.
2. Choose Chart ➤ Chart Options to open the Chart Options dialog box.
3. Click the Gridlines tab.
4. Select the gridlines that you want to appear for either axis in the chart, or clear those that you want to hide. The major gridlines run from the major tick marks on the axis, and the minor gridlines run from the minor tick marks.
5. Click OK.

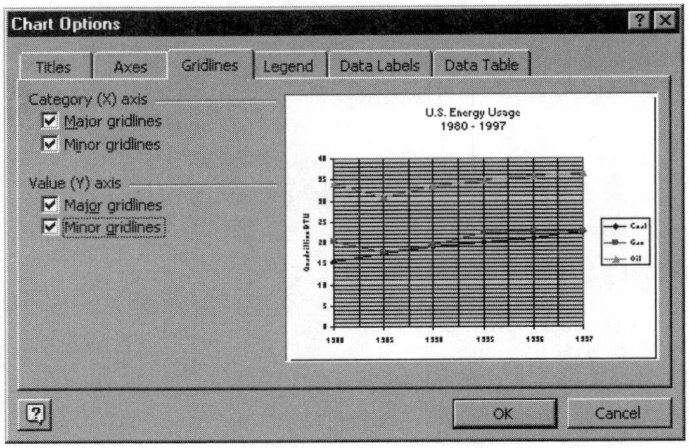

NOTE NOTE NOTE NOTE NOTE NOTE NOTE NOTE NOTE NOTE NOTE NOTE NOTE NOTE NOTE

You can display the major or minor gridlines even if you have hidden the axis tick marks.

You can also format the gridlines in a chart by right-clicking a gridline and choosing Format Gridline from the shortcut menu to open the Format Gridlines dialog box. You can format each of the four sets of gridlines independently. Watch the name box as you select gridlines to be sure which set you're getting.

The Format Gridlines dialog box has two tabs:

Patterns Changes the style and color of the selected gridlines.

Scale Adjusts the scale of the axis from which the gridlines run. The Scale choices are the same as the choices in the Scale tab for the axis and are discussed in the next section.

Editing an Axis and Its Scale

To change the format of an axis, use one of the usual methods for opening its Format dialog box, for example, by double-clicking it. You'll find that most of the choices in the Format Axis dialog box are the same whether you're working in a 2-D or 3-D chart or looking at the x-axis or y-axis. The Format Axis dialog box has these tabs:

Patterns Adjusts the look of the axis line and its major and minor tick marks (see the discussion in the next section).

Scale Adjusts the scale of the axis, such as specifying a maximum or minimum value for it (see the discussion below).

Font Chooses a font for the tick mark labels.

Number Sets the numeric format for the numbers on the tick marks along the axis.

Alignment Specifies whether the axis labels should run parallel, perpendicular, or at an angle to the axis.

Adjusting the Tick Marks

The axis tick marks calibrate the axis in the same way that the graduation lines on a thermometer or a tape measure do. You can adjust their look with the settings in the Patterns tab of the Format Axis dialog box, as shown in Figure 11.15.

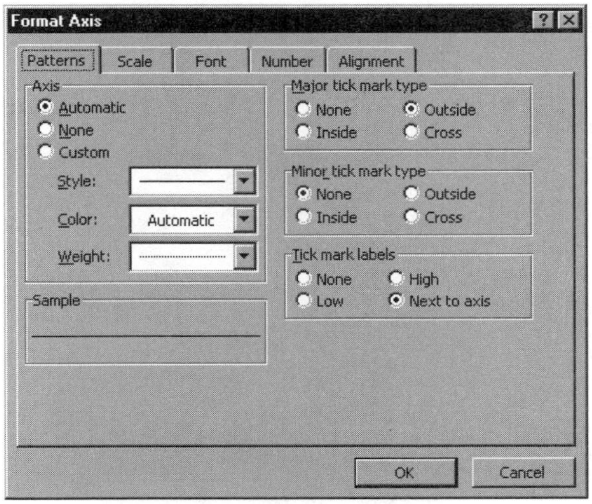

FIGURE 11.15: The Patterns tab in the Format Axis dialog box

There are duplicate groups of options for the major and minor tick marks, in which you choose how you want to display each type of tick mark on the axis. For example, choosing Inside draws the tick marks within the plot area side of the axis. Choosing None hides the tick marks altogether.

The Tick-Mark Labels option affects the number or text that appears next to each major tick mark on the axis. Choose None to hide the labels; the High option places the labels on the opposite side of the plot area.

Adjusting the Scale of a Numeric Axis

The choices in the Scale tab in the Format Axis dialog box vary according to the type of chart you're editing and whether the axis is numeric, such as the y-axis in Figure 11.3, earlier in this skill, or a category, such as the x-axis in that same figure.

NOTE

Although I used numbers to label the x-axis in Figure 11.3, I could have used text without affecting the look of the chart. In a line chart, the x-axis shows the categories but has no numeric significance (see the "XY (Scatter) Charts" section earlier in this skill).

Figure 11.16 shows the Format Axis dialog box and its Scale tab for the y-axis in Figure 11.3.

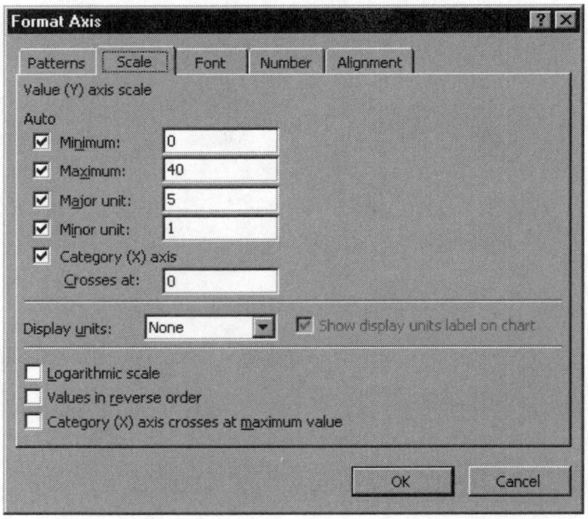

FIGURE 11.16: The Scale tab in the Format Axis dialog box for the y-axis in Figure 11.3

The choices in the Auto section are selected by default. This means that Excel automatically adjusts their settings based on the range of the numeric data being plotted along the axis.

You can clear the Auto check box for any of these options and enter your own numbers.

Minimum and Maximum By default, Excel automatically scales the axis so that the plotted data in the chart falls comfortably within the axis's minimum and maximum values. In Figure 11.16, the Minimum is set at 0 and the Maximum is set at 40. You can manually change these values to specify the lowest or highest number for the axis, regardless of the data.

TIP

At times, setting the Minimum or Maximum value is quite important. For example, when you are creating a series of line charts that will be compared with one another, you should give them all the same scale on the y-axis. Doing so makes it easy to compare them at a glance.

Major Unit and Minor Unit These options set the spacing of the major and minor tick marks (and those gridlines) along the axis. In Figure 11.16 these values are set to 5 and 1, so the major tick marks appear at 5-unit intervals and the minor tick marks at 1-unit intervals (although the minor tick marks are hidden in that chart).

Category (X) Axis Crosses At You can also set the point where the x- and y-axes meet (at zero in the chart in Figure 11.3), although in most cases Excel makes the best choice for this option.

To establish the unit of measure to display, make a selection from the Display Units drop-down list box.

The other three choices in the Scale tab for a numeric axis are optional and do not have automatic settings.

Logarithmic Scale Plots the log values of the data and scales the axis accordingly.

Values in Reverse Order Flips the axis upside down so that the lowest and highest ends of the axis swap places.

Category (X) Axis Crosses at Maximum Value Moves the x-axis to the highest point of this axis.

Adjusting the Scale of a Category Axis

In a line chart such as the one in Figure 11.3, the x-axis has no numeric value and therefore has no scale to adjust. The category labels are simply laid out evenly along the axis. When you open the Format Axis dialog box for a category axis, the Scale tab contains the options shown in Figure 11.17

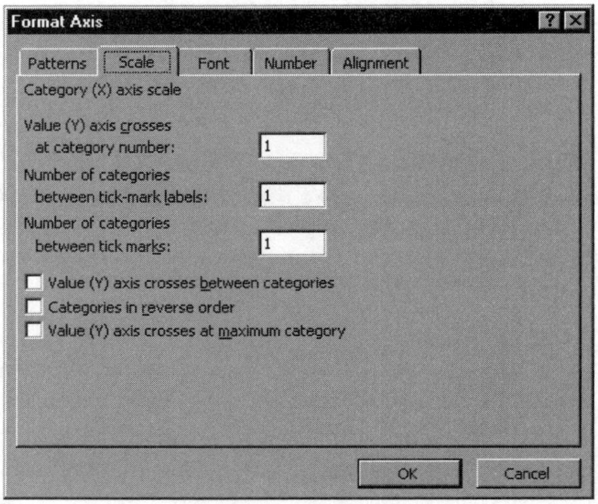

FIGURE 11.17: The Scale tab options for the x-axis in Figure 11.3

These are similar to the options discussed in the previous section for a numeric axis, but apply to the text-only axis:

Value (Y) Axis Crosses at Category Number This option specifies at which x-axis category the y-axis should meet the current axis.

Number of Categories between Tick-Mark Labels By default, this option is set to 1, so Excel tries to label every category along the axis, as it was able to do in Figure 11.3. To alleviate crowding, you can display every other category label by setting this to 2. Setting it to 3 displays every third category label, and so on. Of course, skipping labels might not be such a good idea if they are not in a regular series, as they were in Figure 11.3. Whether labels are printed or not, this setting affects only the look of the axis; all data points are displayed in any event.

TIP TIP TIP TIP TIP TIP TIP TIP TIP TIP TIP TIP TIP TIP TIP TIP TIP TIP TIP TIP TIP TIP TIP TIP TIP TIP TIP

When the number of categories between tick-mark labels is set to 1, Excel automatically adjusts the number of labeled tick marks as you shrink or expand the size of the chart or the fonts used on the axis.

Number of Categories between Tick Marks This is similar to the previous option, but affects only the display of the tick marks for the categories.

Value (Y) Axis Crosses between Categories When this option is selected, each data point is plotted *between* the two tick marks of a category. For example, this option was selected by default when I created the chart in Figure 11.6, and it is also selected for the column chart and stacked-column charts shown in Figures 11.8 and 11.11. It is cleared, however, for the finished line chart in Figure 11.3, so the data point markers fall directly over the tick marks on the x-axis. This option is also cleared for the stacked-area chart in Figure 11.10.

Editing a Series

Each series in a chart has its own formatting options, which vary somewhat depending on the type of chart. You can also manipulate a series in a chart, not just its appearance. For example, you can add or remove a series, change the cell addresses that a series references, and even move a data point in a series so that its source data changes.

To select a series in a chart you are editing, click any part of the series, such as one of its data points (marker, bar, and so on) or the line that connects them. A selection handle (small black box) appears over each data point in the series. You'll also see a border surround that series' source data in the worksheet, making it easy for you to spot their relationship.

Changing the Look of a Series

To change the cell references for each series in a chart, follow these steps:

1. Select the series.
2. Choose Chart ➤ Source Data to open the Source Data dialog box.
3. In the Data Range field, enter the new cell reference.
4. Click OK.

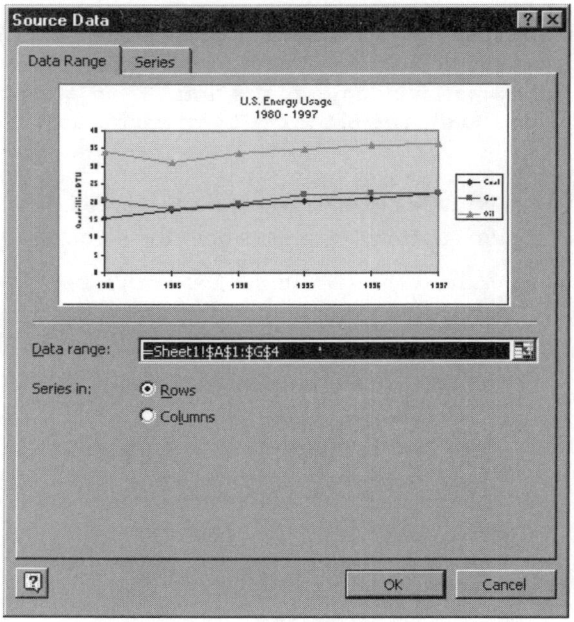

To change the appearance of a selected series in a chart, follow these steps:

1. Select the series.
2. Choose Format ➤ Selected Data Series to open the Format Data Series dialog box.

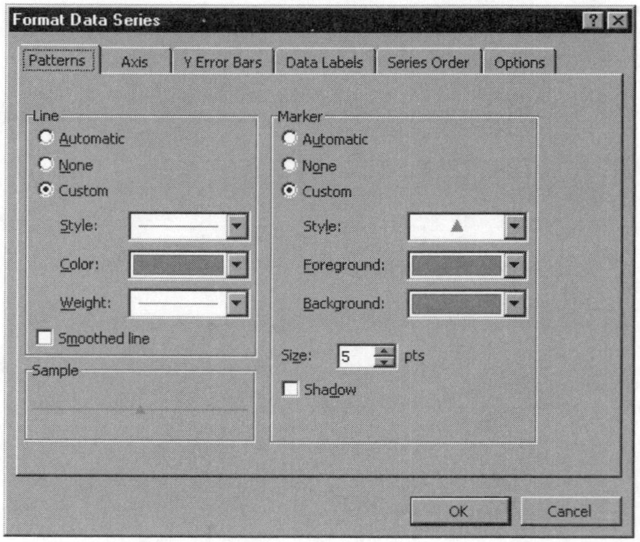

3. Select the formatting options you want, and click OK.

Although the options vary somewhat among the different chart types, most have the following tabs:

Patterns Use this tab to change the border or interior color and pattern of each data point in the series, such as each column in a column chart or the lines and markers in a line chart.

Axis On this tab, you can choose to plot the selected series against the primary or secondary axis. You may want two axes when plotting several series that vary widely in scale, such as the daily selling price of a stock and its daily sales volume. The secondary axis appears opposite the primary axis in the chart, and you can assign any series to either axis. You can format a secondary axis in the same way that you format the primary axis.

Y Error Bars An error bar is an extra plot line that appears at each data point in the series. The length of the error bar represents the amount of possible error, or uncertainty, for each point. You can specify how to determine the length of each error bar, such as by a fixed amount, a percentage, or the calculated standard deviation for the series. You can also format the error bars for a series by double-clicking one of them.

Data Labels A data label identifies a data point in the chart. You can choose to display the underlying number for each data point in a series or display its x-axis label.

Series Order By default, the series appear in the chart in the same order in which they appear in the worksheet; use this option to change their order in the chart. You might need to do this in a 3-D column chart if the first data series were the tallest and, by appearing in front of the other series, would therefore block them from view.

Options The choices in this tab vary among the chart types. For example, in a column chart you can specify the width of the gap between each group of columns in a category and whether the columns in a category should overlap.

Creating a Picture Chart

You can substitute a drawing or a picture for data markers in two-dimensional column and bar charts. Figure 11.18 shows a chart in which a drawing of a cellular phone represents each column in a column chart.

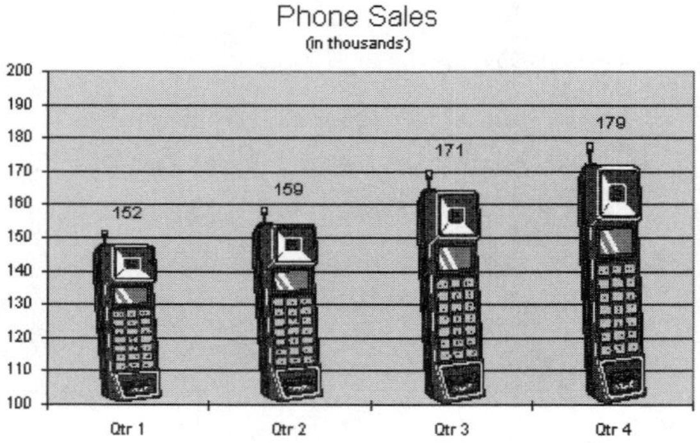

FIGURE 11.18: A drawing takes the place of each column in a column chart.

To insert a picture in a column or bar chart, follow these steps:

1. Right-click a column or bar, and choose Format Data Series from the shortcut menu to open the Format Data Series dialog box.
2. Click the Patterns tab, and click Fill Effects to open the Fill Effects dialog box.
3. Click the Picture tab.
4. Click Select Picture, and select a picture file.
5. Click OK in each dialog box to return to the chart.

NOTE NOTE NOTE NOTE NOTE NOTE NOTE NOTE NOTE NOTE NOTE NOTE NOTE NOTE NOTE

You can include a different picture for each series in a chart or even for each data point in a series. Realize, however, that a picture chart loses its punch rather quickly in a chart with more than a few data points.

To use a picture for a single data-point marker, select the series and then select the marker. When the selection handles surround that single marker, right-click it and follow the steps above.

You can also control the way the picture is displayed in a data marker with the options in the Fill Effects dialog box (step 2, above):

Stretch Stretches the image to fill the data marker. Figure 11.18 uses this option. Stretch may not be suitable for images that can't handle stretching, such as round ones that would turn into ovals, or when the data markers vary widely in size, which would make stretching more noticeable.

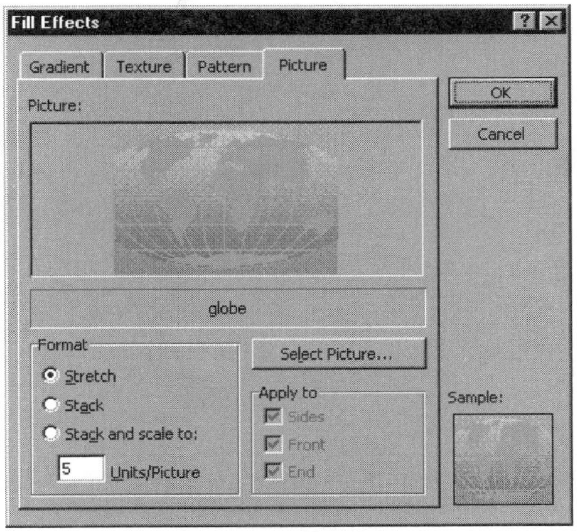

Stack Stacks multiple images within each data marker, and each image retains its original proportions.

Stack and Scale To Specifies how many units of the y-axis should be represented by each image and forms each data marker accordingly. For example, if you specify 25 as the Units/Picture in Figure 11.18, the first marker would be made from a little more than six images, since it spans 152 units of the y-axis.

Apply To Determines how the picture is displayed when it is filling the data point markers in a 3-D chart. You can choose to display or hide the picture for the sides, front, and ends of each marker.

NOTE NOTE NOTE NOTE NOTE NOTE NOTE NOTE NOTE NOTE NOTE NOTE NOTE NOTE NOTE

If you really want to dazzle them with your chart (or possibly annoy and confuse them), take a look at the other tabs in the Fill Effects dialog box.

Changing the Chart Type for a Series

If you select a series and then choose Chart ➤ Chart Type, you can select another chart type for only that series. For example, Figure 11.19 shows the energy data chart, which now includes a fourth series, the Total row from the data (A5:G5 in Figures 11.1 and 11.2).

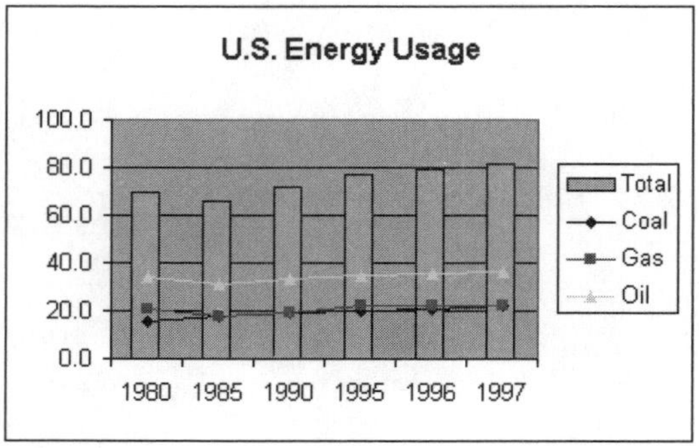

FIGURE 11.19: Plotting the Total series for the energy data as a column chart

The Total series has been plotted as a column chart, so that the effect is a tall column at each x-axis category, with three data-point markers falling within it for each of its three contributing values. Notice how the columns at each end of the axis butt into the left and right edges of the plot area. This is because the *Value (Y) axis crosses between categories* option for the x-axis is cleared, and each column is centered over its tick mark on the x-axis.

Adding Another Series

You can add a new series to a chart at any time. To remove a series, simply select it in the chart and press Del.

You can add a new series in several ways. Here are four of the easiest:

- When the chart is embedded in the worksheet, select the data in the worksheet for the new series, drag that selection onto the chart, and then release the button.
- To add a series either to an embedded chart or to a chart sheet, select the data and choose Edit ➤ Copy; select the chart, and choose Edit ➤ Paste. To specify how the new series should be plotted, choose Edit ➤ Copy and then choose Edit ➤ Paste Special to open the Paste Special dialog box. Specify precisely how to handle each row and column of the new series.
- Select the chart, choose Chart ➤ Add Data to open the Add Data dialog box, and enter the range of the data for the new series.

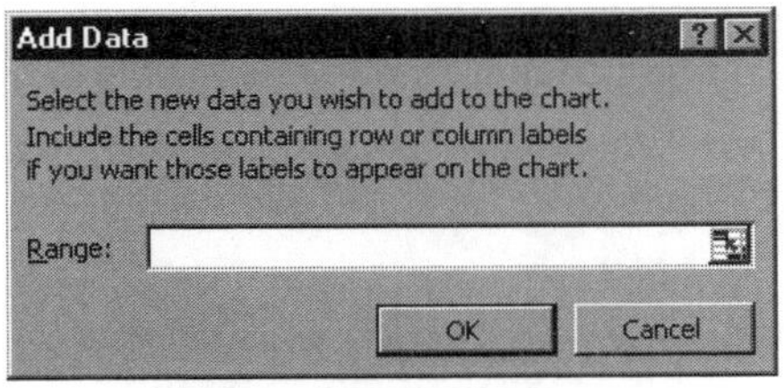

- Select the chart and choose Chart ➤ Source Data to open the Source Data dialog box (it's the same as the Chart Wizard's Step 2 dialog box). Click the Series tab, click Add, and then specify the new series (this was described earlier in the "Specifying the Data Range and Series" section).

Making the Source Data Fit the Chart

When you change the numbers in the source data for a chart, the chart is automatically redrawn to reflect the changes. Well, you can go the other way too and manipulate the data points on a chart to modify the source data.

The process is easy. All you have to do is drag a data-point marker up or down to increase or decrease that point's underlying value. Follow these steps:

1. Select the series (click it) that contains the data-point marker you want to adjust.
2. Click that data-point marker to select it, and the selection handles disappear from the other markers in the series. When you point to the marker (which is the top of a column or bar marker), the pointer changes to a double-headed arrow.

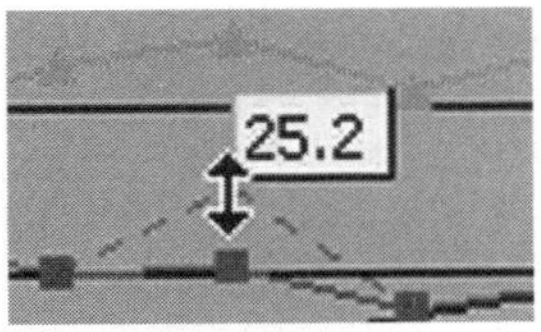

3. Drag the data marker up to increase its underlying number or down to decrease it. As you drag the marker, a ScreenTip displays the value; release the mouse button when you're finished.

If the cell for the data point contains a formula that references another cell, attempting to drag the marker displays the Goal Seek dialog box. You can then specify the value that you want for the formula's result and let Goal Seek do the rest (see Skill 4).

Printing a Chart

You can print a chart either as an embedded chart along with the worksheet or as a separate chart on its own chart sheet.

Printing an Embedded Chart

As you learned in Skill 8, when you print a worksheet that has embedded charts, the charts are printed along with the cells. You can eliminate embedded charts from printouts when you print the worksheet that contains them in two ways:

Don't Print Clear the Print Object option in the Properties tab of the Format Chart Area dialog box.

Hide All To eliminate all charts in all worksheets from the printout, choose Tools ➤ Options to open the Options dialog box, and click the View tab. Click Hide All in the Objects section (see Skill 9). Hiding graphic objects in the worksheet does not hide charts on their own chart sheets.

NOTE NOTE NOTE NOTE NOTE NOTE NOTE NOTE NOTE NOTE NOTE NOTE NOTE NOTE NOTE

When you are editing an embedded chart, you can choose File ➤ Page Setup and File ➤ Print to print it on a separate page, as though it were on its own chart sheet.

Printing a Chart Sheet

A chart sheet, like a worksheet, has its own print settings that you access by choosing File ➤ Page Setup. When you print from a chart sheet, you are printing just the chart it contains.

Most of the print settings discussed in Skill 8 also apply to chart sheets. The Page Setup dialog box for a chart sheet has the Page, Margins, and Header/Footer tabs, which have most of the options that you'll find on those tabs in the Page Setup dialog box for a worksheet.

The Chart tab replaces the Sheet tab in the Page Setup dialog box and includes the Printed Chart Size section, which determines how the chart will fit the printed page:

Use Full Page Sizes the chart so that it fills the printed page within the margins. The chart's proportions are, therefore, dependent on the margin settings. For example, if you specify large top and bottom margins, the chart could look somewhat "squashed" on the printout. This is the default option.

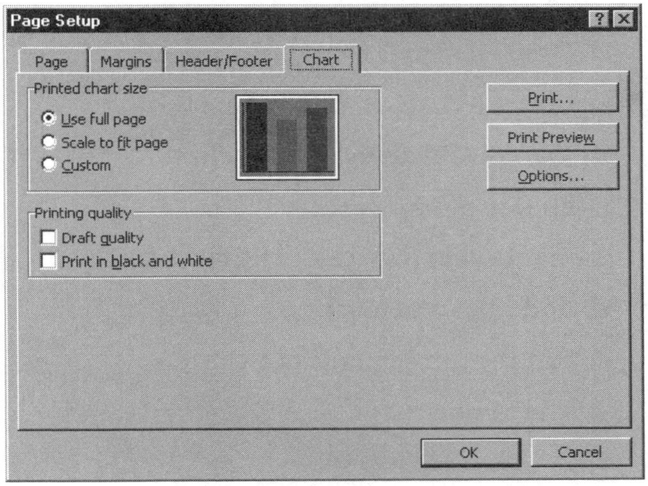

Scale to Fit Page Prints the chart as large as possible within the page margins while retaining the chart's proportions. If you specify large top and bottom margins, the chart's height shrinks to stay within those margins, but its width also shrinks to retain its proportions.

Custom Lets you size the chart within the chart sheet, which is how it will appear when printed.

NOTE NOTE NOTE NOTE NOTE NOTE NOTE NOTE NOTE NOTE NOTE NOTE NOTE NOTE NOTE

While a chart sheet is active, choose Tools ➤ Options to open the Options dialog box, and click the Chart tab. By default, the Chart Sizes with Window Frame option is not selected. If you select it, a chart will fill its sheet completely, no matter how you change that window's size.

The Print dialog box (choose File ➤ Print) offers the same choices as when you print a worksheet, minus the Selection option in the Print What section. By default, Excel prints charts in landscape orientation.

Are You Experienced?

Now you can...

- ☑ Create a simple chart
- ☑ Create a chart with the Chart Wizard
- ☑ Manipulate an embedded chart
- ☑ Choose a chart type
- ☑ Create your own custom chart types
- ☑ Add titles and legends
- ☑ Edit the components of a chart
- ☑ Print a chart

SKILL 12

Drawing in Worksheets and Charts

- Working with the Drawing toolbar
- Creating drawings with the Drawing tools
- Capturing pictures
- Inserting pictures
- Formatting a graphic object
- Moving and resizing objects
- Grouping and layering objects

In this skill you'll read about the Excel graphic tools that you can use to add drawings, arrows, pictures, text boxes, fancy text, and generally lots of sizzle to your workbooks. These tools won't make your numbers any more accurate, but they can emphasize the important data in a worksheet, help to explain data that might otherwise be a mystery, or just liven up the look of your worksheets and charts.

Working with the Drawing Toolbar

To create drawings or text boxes in a worksheet or a chart, you use the buttons on the Drawing toolbar. To display the Drawing toolbar, choose View ➤ Toolbars (or right-click one of the displayed toolbars) and then click Drawing. You can also click the Drawing button on the Standard toolbar (click it again to hide the Drawing toolbar).

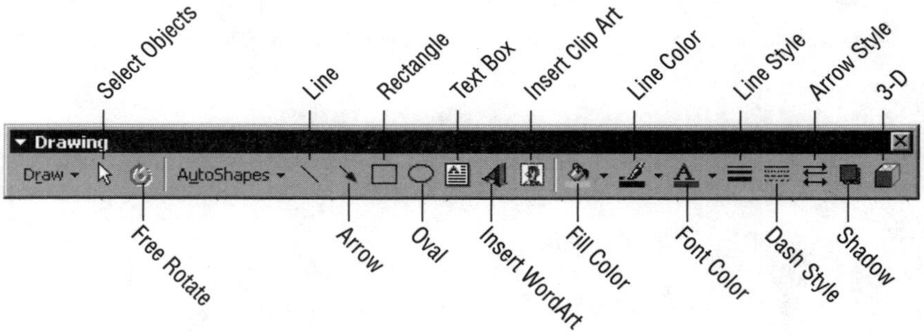

NOTE NOTE NOTE NOTE NOTE NOTE NOTE NOTE NOTE NOTE NOTE NOTE NOTE NOTE NOTE

You can also place a graphic image in a worksheet or a chart in the usual Windows way—via the Clipboard—by choosing Insert ➤ Picture, and by clicking the Insert Picture button on the Drawing toolbar. You'll learn how to use all these techniques in this skill.

You can create your works of art on a worksheet, on a chart sheet, or within an embedded chart. All drawn objects are independent of their locations; a drawing on a worksheet is not within any of the cells, and a drawing in a chart is not attached to any chart component.

Using a Drawing Button

You can do the following with the buttons on the Drawing toolbar:

- Draw lines and arrows.
- Draw rectangles, squares, ovals, and circles.
- Insert graphic images.
- Draw freehand lines and freeform shapes.
- Enter text in its own text box.
- Access a variety of ready-built shapes.
- Group objects as a single object.
- Change the color and style of an object's interior, border, and font.
- Rotate an object.
- Access commands on the Draw menu.

NOTE NOTE NOTE NOTE NOTE NOTE NOTE NOTE NOTE NOTE NOTE NOTE NOTE NOTE NOTE

The objects that serve as the basis for your drawings in Excel are called AutoShapes. Click AutoShapes on the Drawing toolbar to access them. You'll find that each shape has a similar set of properties and is quite "smart" when it comes to retaining its basic appearance when you change its size.

Follow this general procedure to work with any of the drawing tools:

1. Click the button on the Drawing toolbar; when you move the pointer over a workbook, the pointer changes to crosshairs.
2. Point to where you want the drawing to begin.
3. To create an object in a default size, click the mouse button once.
4. To create an object in the size you want, hold down the mouse button, drag to the ending point, and then release the mouse button.
5. The new object is selected, so you can change its size or position or choose Format ➤ AutoShape to change its look.
6. Start again with step 1 to draw another object.

To draw more than one of the same type of object, double-click its button on the Drawing toolbar. When you finish one object, you can immediately start the next one. When you're done, you can deselect that button by pressing Esc or by clicking the button again.

You can use the options in the Format AutoShape dialog box to change the look of the AutoShape, its size, its protection status, and how it behaves when the underlying worksheet or chart is changed. You can also use the buttons on the Drawing toolbar, such as Fill Color, Line Color, and Font Color. You'll learn how to do this in the "Formatting AutoShapes and Graphic Objects" section, later in this skill.

Using the Selection Pointer

Normally, the mouse pointer is a cross when it's over the worksheet, and it changes to an arrow when you move it over an object such as an AutoShape. The arrow indicates that the object, and not a cell, will be selected if you click the mouse button.

If you want the mouse pointer to remain an arrow, click the Select Objects button on the Drawing toolbar. This technique can be quite handy when you're working on multiple objects.

With the Select Objects button activated, you can select multiple objects with the mouse—simply drag to create a rectangle around the objects you want to select and then release the mouse button.

To return the pointer to its normal state, press Esc, double-click a cell, or click the Select Objects button again.

Drawing with AutoShapes

You create a drawing from AutoShapes in much the same way whether you're placing the drawing on a worksheet or in a chart. Once created, all drawn objects behave the same, so you can do the following:

- Select an object by clicking it; a rectangle of selection handles appears around the object.

- Select multiple objects by Shift+clicking each one or by using the Select Objects pointer, as described in the previous section.
- Move an object by dragging it or using the Edit ➤ Cut and Paste method.
- Copy an object by dragging it while holding down Ctrl or by using the Edit ➤ Copy and Paste method.
- Change the size of an object by dragging one of its selection handles.
- Change the look of an object, such as its border or interior color or pattern, via its Format AutoShape dialog box.
- Align an object with a worksheet gridline by holding down Alt while you draw, move, or resize the object.
- Move an object only horizontally or vertically by holding down Shift as you drag the object.
- Delete an object by selecting it and pressing Del.

Selecting an AutoShape

You can choose from literally dozens of simple and complex AutoShapes. You can select one by clicking the AutoShapes menu on the Drawing toolbar or by choosing Insert ➤ Picture ➤ AutoShapes. Pointing to an AutoShape button displays a ScreenTip with its name. An example is shown here.

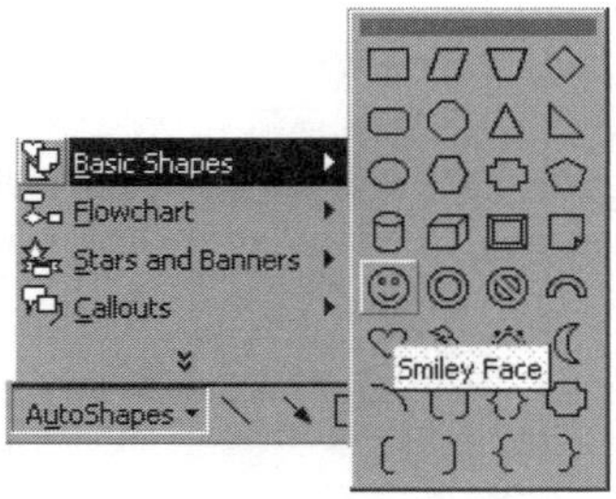

Each AutoShapes command offers a palette of shapes from which you can choose. Simply click a button in the palette, and create that shape in the worksheet or chart. You can also drag the bar at the top to "tear off" the palette and leave it displayed over the workbook so that its shapes are easy to access.

TIP TIP TIP TIP TIP TIP TIP TIP TIP TIP TIP TIP TIP TIP TIP TIP TIP TIP TIP TIP TIP TIP TIP TIP

To draw multiple objects that are all the same size and shape and have the same look, create one object and copy it as many times as you want.

Drawing Lines and Arrows

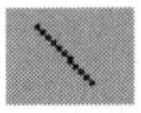

To draw a straight line, click the Line button and drag from the starting to the ending point, as described earlier in the "Using a Drawing Tool" section.

To draw an arrow, click the Arrow button and again drag from starting to ending point. The arrowhead appears at the end of the arrow's shaft, not at the beginning.

A line and an arrow both have the same attributes, so you can add an arrowhead to a line or remove the arrowhead from an arrow. To do so, use the options on the Colors and Lines tab in the Format AutoShape dialog box. You'll learn more about this in the "Formatting AutoShapes and Graphic Objects" section, later in this skill.

Drawing Rectangles, Squares, Ovals, and Circles

Drawing a rectangle or oval is essentially the same as drawing a line or an arrow. Click the Rectangle or Oval button, and drag out a rectangle the size you want. When you release the mouse button, the object is drawn to those dimensions.

TIP TIP TIP TIP TIP TIP TIP TIP TIP TIP TIP TIP TIP TIP TIP TIP TIP TIP TIP TIP TIP TIP TIP TIP

To draw a perfect square or circle, hold down Shift either when you drag to create the object or when you click once to create the object in its default size.

Don't worry about the object's exact size or shape. You can easily make adjustments once the object is drawn (see the "Moving, Resizing, and Rotating Objects" section later in this skill).

NOTE NOTE NOTE NOTE NOTE NOTE NOTE NOTE NOTE NOTE NOTE NOTE NOTE NOTE NOTE

To see even more AutoShapes, click the AutoShapes button and then click More AutoShapes.

Working with AutoShape Connectors

The AutoShapes Connectors palette includes a variety of line styles with which you can connect one AutoShape to another.

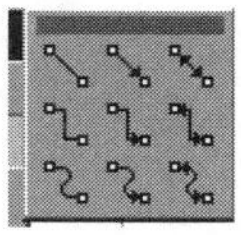

With the connectors, you can create diagrams such as flow charts (using the symbols on the Flow Charts palette) and organization charts. The AutoShape connectors may not seem all that exciting at first, but wait until you've tried them.

Connecting Two AutoShapes

To connect two AutoShapes with a connector, follow these steps:

1. Select the connector you want from the Connectors palette.
2. Move the mouse pointer (which is now crosshairs) close to the first object you want to join. You'll see small blue squares appear in the border of that object; each one is an attachment site to which you can join one end of the connector.
3. Click very close to one of the attachment sites, which will connect with the first end of the connector.

NOTE NOTE NOTE NOTE NOTE NOTE NOTE NOTE NOTE NOTE NOTE NOTE NOTE NOTE NOTE

When a connector is "locked" (joined) to an attachment site, you'll see a small red square at that site. If the connector end is "unlocked" (not joined to an AutoShape), you'll see a green square at that end of the connector.

4. Move the mouse pointer to the other AutoShape you want to join; you'll see the attachment sites appear on that object.
5. Point to, or very close to, an attachment site on that object and release the mouse button; the connector will attach to that site.

Figure 12.1 shows several examples of how you can join AutoShapes with connectors. You can see that the connectors are convenient ways to draw lines between AutoShapes, but they do a lot more than that.

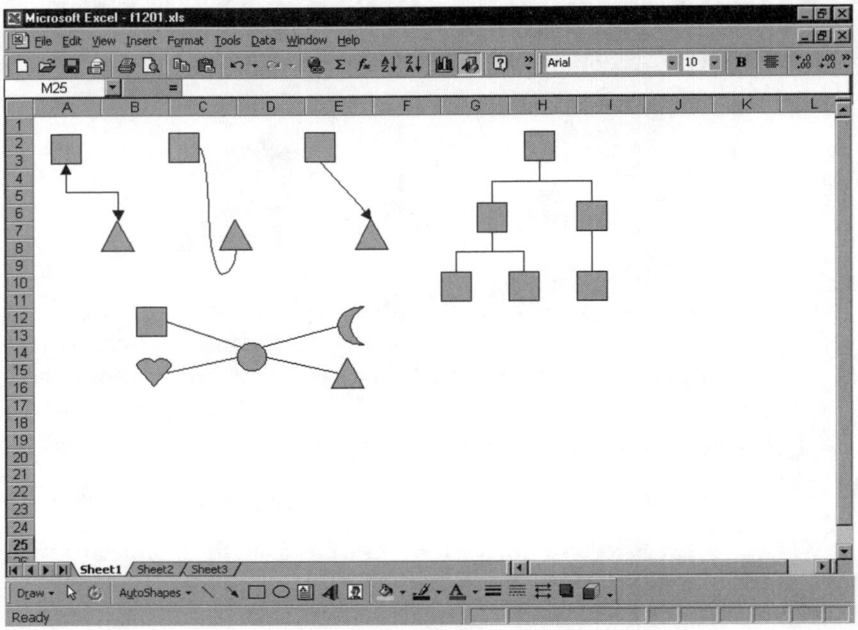

FIGURE 12.1: You can draw straight or curved lines between AutoShapes with the AutoShape connectors.

Moving Connected AutoShapes

The AutoShape connectors are cognizant of how to connect to AutoShapes of various sizes and shapes. They also display above-average intellect when you move or resize an AutoShape to which a connector is attached.

The best way to see how connectors behave is to connect two or more AutoShapes and start moving and resizing them. In the upper-left area of the worksheet in Figure 12.2 are the same two connected AutoShapes that appear in that area in Figure 12.1. I copied those first objects four times in Figure 12.2 and manipulated each of those four copies to show the effects on the connectors.

As you can see in Figure 12.2, a connector doesn't mind a bit when the AutoShape to which it is connected is moved or resized. The connector stays connected to the same attachment site and follows that site as needed.

A connector follows its AutoShape as needed, but it may end up following a strange route to do so. To make the route traveled by a connector more efficient,

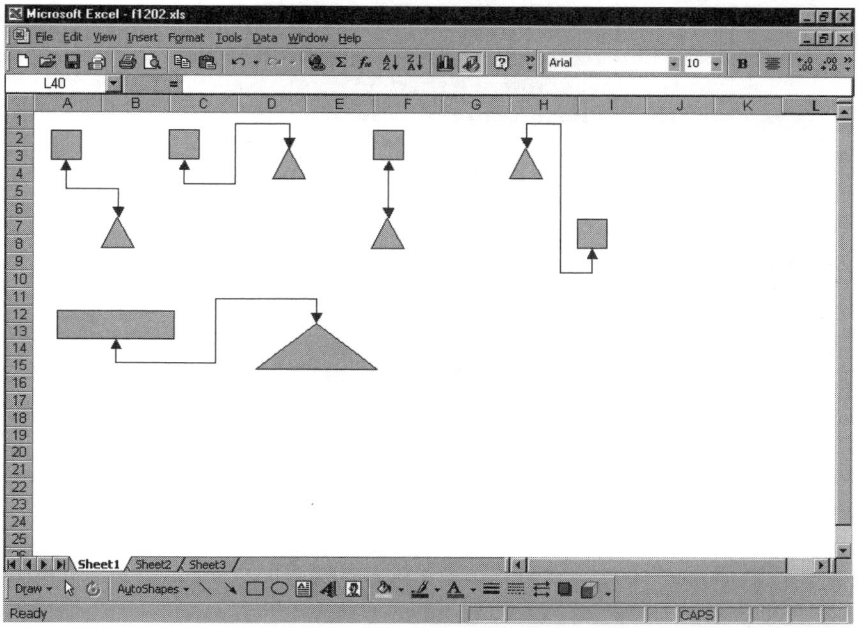

FIGURE 12.2: Connectors stay attached to an AutoShape and follow it when you move or resize the AutoShape.

select the connector or an AutoShape to which it is attached and choose Draw ➤ Reroute Connectors from the Drawing toolbar.

Shown below is a picture of a connector before (on the left) and after using the Reroute Connectors command. Before using the command the connector had four corners, while after it has only three.

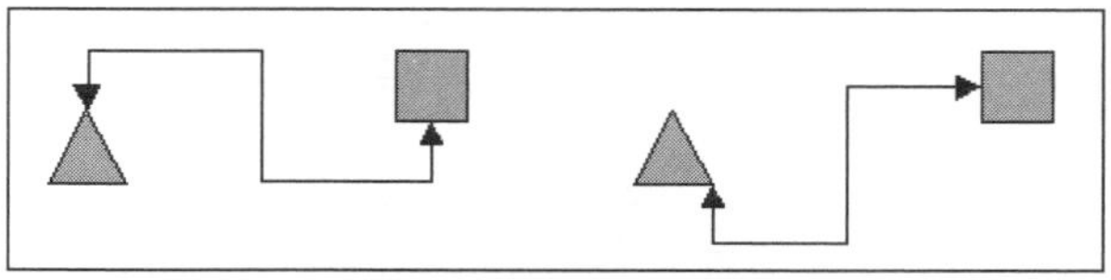

A connector isn't attached permanently to an AutoShape. You can drag either of its ends to another attachment site on the same or a different AutoShape. Be sure to drag the red square at the connector end; if you drag farther in on the connector, you'll move the entire connector and unlock it from the AutoShapes at both ends.

NOTE

Like the other AutoShapes, the connectors have their own set of properties, which you can modify by right-clicking the connector and choosing Format AutoShape from the shortcut menu. You can change the color and line style of the connector and the style of its end-point arrows, and you can make it a straight, elbow, or curved connector.

Adding Text

With the buttons on the Drawing toolbar, you can place text anywhere in a workbook. To place text within an AutoShape, just select the AutoShape and start typing (you cannot add text to lines and connectors). When you're finished, click outside the AutoShape.

You can also use the Text Box tool to add text. Follow these steps:

1. Click the Text Box button.
2. Drag out a rectangle to the approximate size you want and release the button.
3. Type the text that you want to appear within the box.
4. Click outside the box when you're finished.

Keep the following in mind when entering text in an AutoShape or a text box:

- The text automatically wraps within the width of the box; if you widen the box, you'll get longer lines of text.
- Press Enter to start a new paragraph.
- To edit the text later, click within the box.
- To replace all the text with new text, select the edge of the box or AutoShape and then start typing.
- To link the text box or AutoShape to a cell, select the box and create a formula in the Formula bar, such as =B4 or =Sheet2!A15, to refer to the contents of that cell (this is the same process that I discussed in Skill 11).

NOTE

If you want to create some really fancy text, choose Insert ➤ Picture ➤ WordArt, or click the WordArt button on the Drawing toolbar.

You can change the look of all or just some of the text within a text box or AutoShape. To change the font, follow these steps:

1. Select a text box.
2. Choose Format ➤ Text Box to open the Format Text Box dialog box.
3. Click the Font tab.
4. Select the options you want, and click OK.

If you select only some text within the box, you can change the font for just that text in the usual ways, such as with the controls on the Formatting toolbar.

The Format Text Box dialog box and the Format AutoShape dialog box also have an Alignment tab that is similar to that tab in the Format Cells dialog box (see Skill 6). Those dialog boxes also have a Margins tab in which you can adjust the margins between the text and the inside edges of the box or AutoShape that surrounds it.

Capturing a Picture

Another way to create a graphic object is by capturing a picture of a range of cells or a chart and then pasting that picture into a worksheet, a chart, or even another Windows application. The result is a graphic object that displays a picture of the captured area.

You can create either a static picture that won't change or a picture that is linked to its source and changes when the source changes.

Creating a Picture

To create an unlinked picture, follow these steps:

1. Select the part of the workbook that you want to capture in a picture, such as a range of cells, a range that includes embedded charts or other graphic objects, or the chart on a chart sheet.
2. Hold down Shift and choose Edit ➤ Copy Picture to open the Copy Picture dialog box.

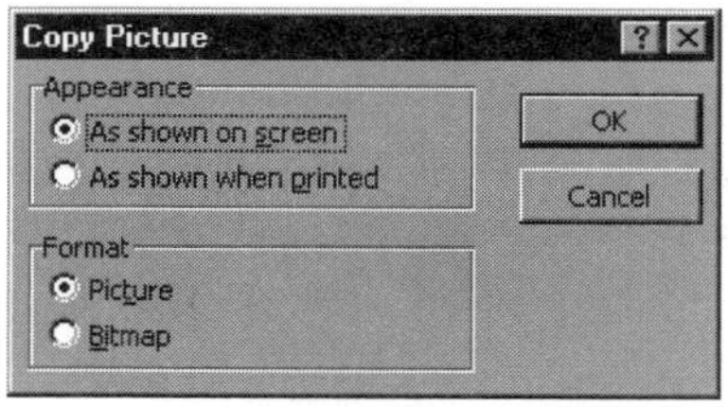

3. In the Appearance section, click the As Shown on Screen option to make a picture of the source as you see it on the screen. Or click the As Shown When Printed option to make a picture that will look like the source when it is printed (no gridlines, for example, if that print option is not selected).
4. In the Format section, click the Picture option if you selected As Shown On Screen. Choose Bitmap only if you are going to copy the picture to a program that can't handle graphic files in the Windows metafile format.
5. Click OK to close the Copy Picture dialog box.
6. Select the destination for the picture, such as a cell, a chart, or another Windows application.
7. Choose Edit ➤ Paste Picture if you're pasting the picture into an Excel worksheet. If you're in another application, choose Edit ➤ Paste, which may offer you options for how you paste the image into the document.

Linking a Picture to Its Source

When you create a picture of cells in the worksheet, you can link the picture to the cells so that when the cells change, the picture also changes. The process is similar to the one described above, with the following exceptions:

1. Select the source for the picture, and choose Edit ➤ Copy (do not hold down Shift).
2. Select the destination in Excel.
3. Hold down Shift and choose Edit ➤ Paste Picture Link.

The result looks the same as an unlinked picture. This time, however, if you change the data or the formatting of the picture's source, the picture reflects the change.

NOTE NOTE NOTE NOTE NOTE NOTE NOTE NOTE NOTE NOTE NOTE NOTE NOTE NOTE NOTE

If you select a linked object and look on the Formula bar, you'll see a formula referencing its source cells, such as =Sheet1!$A$1:$G$5. If you want, you can change that reference, and the linked picture will update accordingly.

The process for pasting a linked picture of the worksheet into a chart is slightly different. In Skill 11, you learned how to include a chart's source data within the chart. When there are too many rows or columns in that data, however, it's almost a detriment to the chart to do so.

Here's how to include all or only some of a chart's source data as a linked picture within a chart:

1. Select the range of data cells, hold down Shift, and choose Edit ➤ Copy Picture.
2. Select the As Shown on Screen option, select the Picture option, and click OK.
3. Open the chart sheet or select the embedded chart.
4. Choose Edit ➤ Paste to create an *unlinked* picture.
5. Select the new picture, and enter the linking formula in the Formula bar, such as =Sheet1!A1:G5.
6. Press Enter to complete the formula.

That last step creates the link to the worksheet. Figure 12.3 shows a chart with its underlying data displayed as a linked picture. When the data change, both the chart and its picture of the data are updated.

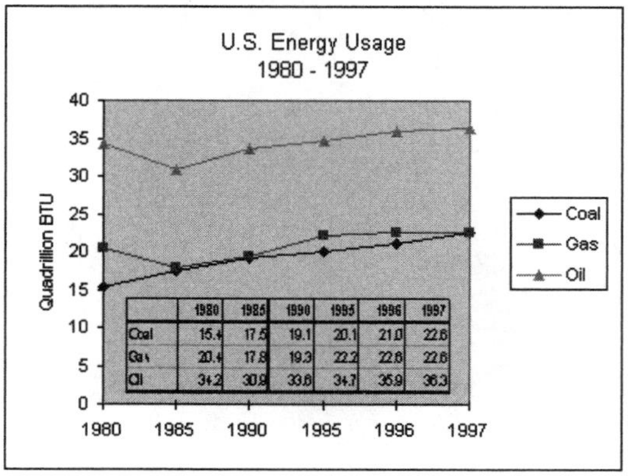

FIGURE 12.3: A chart containing a linked picture of its source data

Inserting Graphic Images

You can insert graphic images into a worksheet or a chart in three ways:

- By clicking the Insert Picture button on the Drawing toolbar

- By choosing Insert ➤ Picture and selecting a command from the shortcut menu
- By copying an image from another Windows program

NEW

To insert a graphic image using the Insert ClipArt dialog box, follow these steps:

1. Open the worksheet or chart into which you want to insert the image.
2. Click the Insert Picture button or choose Insert ➤ Picture to open the Insert ClipArt dialog box.

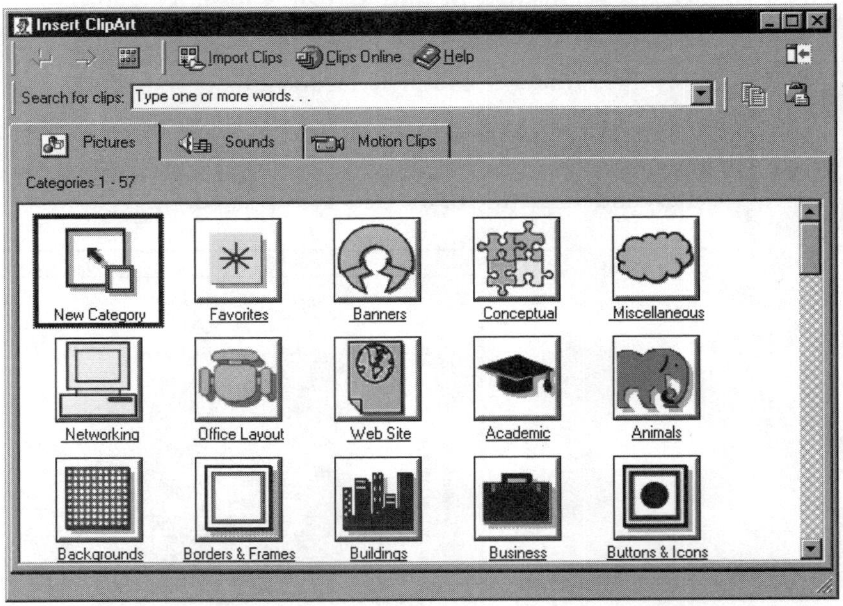

3. Select a category and then select an image within the category.
4. Click Insert Clip to insert the image.

To insert a graphic image other than a picture, choose Insert ➤ Picture and then select an item from the menu:

Clip Art Lets you select an image from the clip art gallery that comes with Excel and Microsoft Office. If you have access to the Internet, you should really try the Clips Online button in the Insert ClipArt dialog box. It loads your Web browser and opens the Web site called Microsoft Clip

Gallery Live, from which you can browse through and download hundreds of clip art, photograph, video clip, and sound files.

From File Lets you choose a graphic file from disk; Excel can handle a variety of file types, including BMP, EPS, GIF, JPEG, PCX, and TIF.

AutoShapes Displays the AutoShapes toolbar, from which you can choose one of the AutoShapes palettes, such as Lines or Connectors.

Organization Chart Starts the program Microsoft Organization Chart, which gives you handy tools for creating organization charts. The result is a picture in Excel of the chart you create.

WordArt Displays the WordArt Gallery from which you can select a design on which to base your WordArt picture (try it; it's fun).

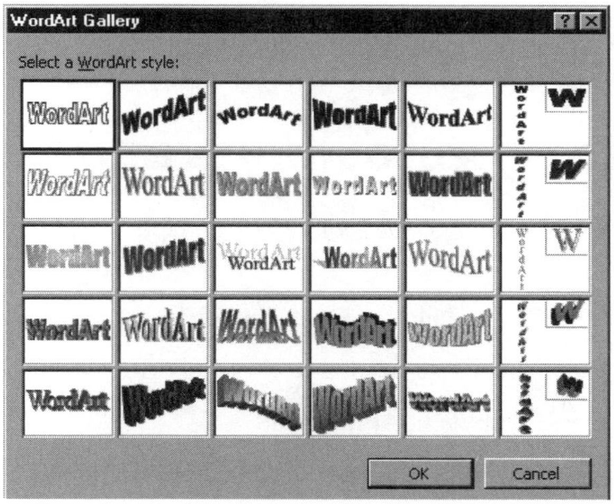

NEW

From Scanner or Camera Inserts an image from your scanner or digital camera into Excel.

NOTE NOTE NOTE NOTE NOTE NOTE NOTE NOTE NOTE NOTE NOTE NOTE NOTE NOTE NOTE

All these commands, except From File, depend on those features being installed with Excel or Office. In the case of the From Scanner or Camera command, you must also have a scanner or a digital camera installed on your computer system.

You can also copy an image from another program. Follow these steps:

1. Select the object/image in the source program.
2. Choose Edit ➤ Copy.
3. In Excel, choose Edit ➤ Paste to import the image.

No matter which method you choose, you'll end up with a graphic object in Excel that you can move, size, and copy, and whose attributes you can modify via its Format dialog box.

As I mentioned in Skill 9, if your computer seems to run a bit slow when you have pictures in a worksheet, you can hide the pictures or just show boxes in their place. Choose Tools ➤ Options to open the Options dialog box, click the View tab, and choose either Hide All or Show Placeholders in the Objects section.

Formatting AutoShapes and Graphic Objects

You can change the look of AutoShapes and graphic objects in Excel in the usual way:

- Right-click the object, and choose Format *Object* from the shortcut menu.
- Select the object, and choose Format ➤ *Object*.
- Double-click the object.
- Select the object, and click a button on a toolbar.

TIP TIP TIP TIP TIP TIP TIP TIP TIP TIP TIP TIP TIP TIP TIP TIP TIP TIP TIP TIP TIP TIP TIP TIP TIP

You can apply a name to an object, much as you can to a cell—select the object, enter the name in the Name box (to the left of the Formula bar), and press Enter. That name appears in the Name box whenever you select the object.

Figure 12.4 shows the Format AutoShape dialog box that opened when I selected a group of connected objects in Figure 12.2.

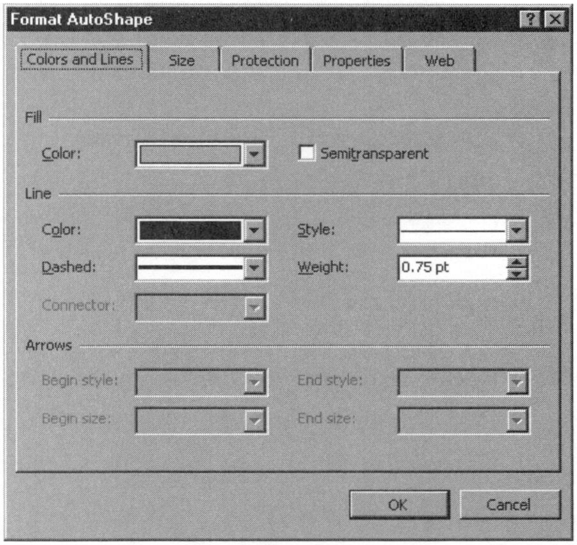

FIGURE 12.4: The Format AutoShape dialog box has some of the tabs that are commonly found in the Format *Object* dialog box.

Here are the tabs you can find in the Format *Object* dialog box (only some of these will appear for some types of objects):

Colors and Lines Includes the Line, Arrows, and Fill options, which affect the look of the border that surrounds the object, its end points (if it's a line), and its interior color and pattern.

Size Lets you specify the exact dimensions of the object, rotate the object, and change its scale (width to height ratio). If you select the Lock Aspect Ratio option when changing its scale, the object will scale proportionally.

Picture Crops the picture within its borders, changes its brightness and contrast, and changes its colors to shades of gray or black and white.

Alignment Changes the alignment of any text within the object.

Margins Sets the margins that surround any text within the object.

Protection Protects the object or only the text within it; the Locked option is selected by default. An object that also contains text will have a Locked Text option, which protects the text within the box from being changed. To enable protection, you must first turn on sheetwide protection, as you learned in Skill 9.

Properties Includes options that affect how the object reacts when the underlying cells in the worksheet are moved, such as when you insert or delete rows or columns (see Skill 11).

NEW

Web Lets you supply alternative text to display if the object is in a Web page. The text displays while the graphic loads, if the visitor has graphics turned off, or if the visitor is using a text-only browser.

When an object is within a chart and not a worksheet, its Properties tab has the following two choices:

Size with Chart Resizes the object along with the chart.

Do Not Size with Chart Fixes an object at its size, no matter how the chart changes size.

TIP TIP TIP TIP TIP TIP TIP TIP TIP TIP TIP TIP TIP TIP TIP TIP TIP TIP TIP TIP TIP TIP TIP TIP

You can use the Format Painter button to transfer an object's formatting to another object, just as you can with cells. Select the source object, and click the Format Painter button. Then select the target object, and its formatting will match that of the source.

You can have a lot of fun changing the look of a selected AutoShape when you click the 3-D button on the Drawing toolbar. You choose one of the 3-D perspectives from the menu, which adds a third dimension to the selected object or objects. To display the 3-D Settings toolbar, click the 3-D Settings button on the menu for the 3-D button.

You'll be able to waste at least a half-hour playing with the controls on this toolbar, as you change the degree of rotation of the AutoShape, the direction of the apparent lighting on it, its depth, the look of its surface, and more.

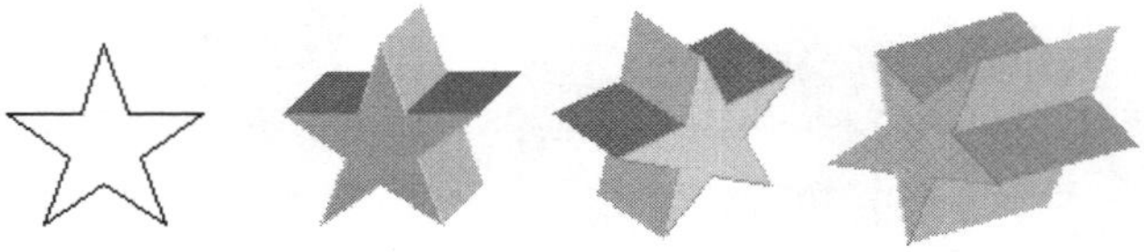

Clicking the Shadow button on the Drawing toolbar applies a shadow effect to a 2-D AutoShape; it's almost as much fun as the 3-D button. It also has a toolbar you can display, which lets you adjust the color and position of the shadow.

If you find that you frequently format AutoShapes in the same style, you can save the formatting of an existing AutoShape as the new default for all AutoShapes that you create. Follow these steps:

1. Right-click an existing AutoShape.
2. From the shortcut menu, choose Set AutoShape Defaults.

The new AutoShapes that you create will have the new look.

Moving, Resizing, and Rotating Objects

You can move or resize an AutoShape or other graphic object at any time with a few strokes of your mouse, and you can rotate AutoShapes, as well. You can also adjust the layering of multiple objects so that the one you choose overlaps the others.

Before you can do any of this, though, you must select the object or objects you want to work on:

- Click an object to select it.
- Shift+click to select several objects.
- Click the Select Objects button on the Drawing toolbar, and drag a rectangle over the objects you want to select.

NOTE NOTE NOTE NOTE NOTE NOTE NOTE NOTE NOTE NOTE NOTE NOTE NOTE NOTE NOTE

You can select an object that is filled by clicking anywhere within it. If it is not filled, however, you must click one of its edges.

Selection handles appear around a selected object, which you use to resize the object. Remember, if you have selected multiple objects, any action you take on one of them will be performed on all of them.

To move an object:

- Drag it to its new location.
- Use the Edit ➤ Cut and Paste method.

- To align an object with the nearest worksheet gridline, hold down Alt while you move the object. You can also enable the Draw ➤ Snap ➤ To Grid command on the Drawing toolbar, so that objects you create or move will snap to the gridlines by default (you don't need to hold down Alt).
- To move the selected object or objects a tiny bit in one direction (a difficult task with a mouse), use the commands on the Draw ➤ Nudge menu on the Drawing toolbar.

To copy an object:

- Hold down Ctrl, drag the object, and release the mouse button to create the duplicate.
- Use the Edit ➤ Copy and Paste method.

To resize an object:

- In one dimension only, drag the selection handle on the side you want to adjust.
- In two dimensions, drag a corner selection handle.

To resize an object so that it maintains its proportions, hold down Shift while you drag a corner selection handle.

You can rotate an AutoShape in two ways:

- To specify an exact amount of rotation (in degrees), open the Format AutoShape dialog box, click the Size tab, and in the Rotation field enter the number of degrees you want to rotate the object. Zero degrees is the default, and the rotation is clockwise.
- To rotate the object by hand, click the Free Rotate button on the Drawing toolbar; green circles appear as rotation points in place of some of the sizing handles on the selected AutoShape. Drag one of the rotation points to rotate the object, and release the mouse button when you're finished.

TIP

To rotate the AutoShape more smoothly and in smaller increments, move the mouse pointer away from the object. Greater distance reduces the effect of the mouse's movement on the object's rotation.

Changing the Order and Alignment of Objects

When objects overlap, you can adjust their order in the layering with the commands on the Order menu, which you'll find on an object's shortcut menu as well as on the Draw menu on the Drawing toolbar.

If you select an object that overlaps a second object, the Send to Back command places the selected object beneath the second. You can also select an object that is partially hidden by one or more other objects and use the Bring to Front command to place it on top.

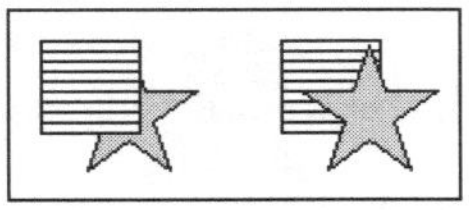

In the previous section, you learned how to align an object with the worksheet gridlines when you move or create the object. You can also align objects with one another, independent of the gridlines, with the commands on the Draw ➤Align or Distribute menu on the Drawing toolbar.

For example, if you want to line up four objects with one another horizontally, select the four objects, and choose Draw ➤ Align or Distribute ➤ Align Top. The top edge of all four objects are now aligned. It doesn't matter what shape each object may be; the top edge of an object will be aligned with that point on the other three objects.

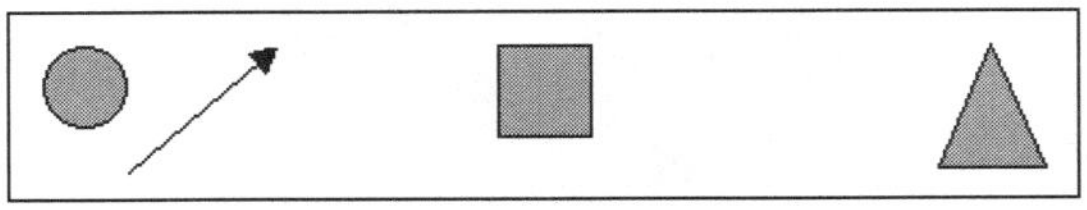

You can also space objects evenly, either horizontally or vertically. In the above example, after you align the top edges of the objects, you can choose Draw ➤ Align or Distribute ➤ Distribute Horizontally to adjust the four objects so that they are evenly spaced. The outside objects remain fixed, while the inner objects are spaced appropriately.

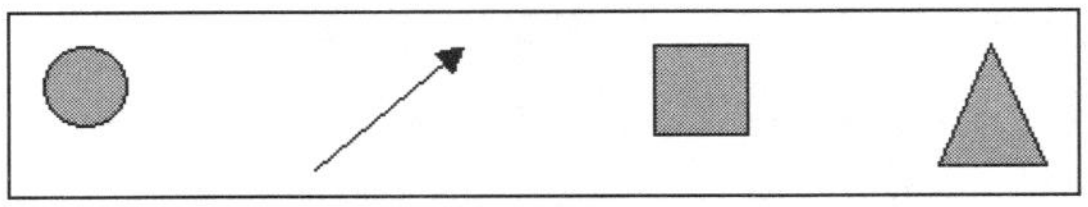

Grouping Objects

When you create a drawing from multiple objects, you can *group* them so that they behave as a single object. Simply select all the objects that you want in the group, and choose the Group command either from the Draw menu on the Drawing toolbar or from the Grouping menu on a selected object's shortcut menu.

Lots of advantages are associated with creating a group from multiple objects:

- You can select the group with a single click on any one of its objects, instead of having to select each object in the group.
- You never accidentally lose a piece of the drawing by forgetting to select it along with the rest of the objects in the drawing.
- When you change the formatting of any object in the group, the change applies to all the objects in the group for which that change is relevant (changing the margins has no effect on an object that cannot contain text).
- The objects within the group maintain their relationship when you make the grouped object larger or smaller.

The left side of Figure 12.5 shows a drawing made up of three rectangles and two lines that form one image. If you group these objects and then shrink them, the result is shown in the center of the figure. The image retains its proportions in its new size.

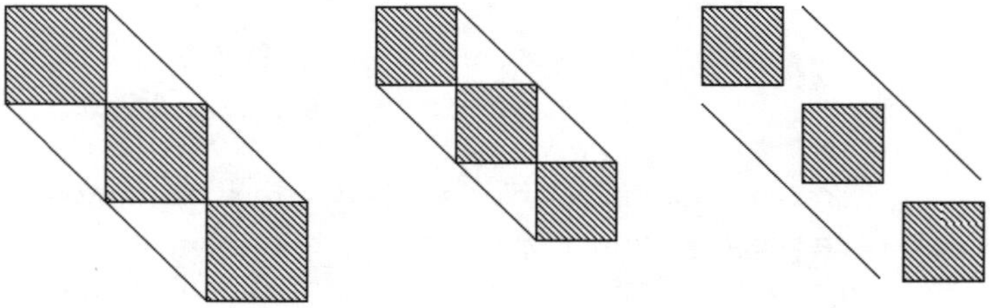

FIGURE 12.5: The effect of changing an object's size when it is grouped and ungrouped

On the right of Figure 12.4, you see the result of shrinking the first image when it is *not* grouped. The upper-left corner of each object remains in its original position, and the spaces between the objects increase.

You can ungroup a grouped object at any time by selecting it and choosing the Ungroup command, either from the Draw menu on the Drawing toolbar or from the Grouping menu on the object's shortcut menu.

Are You Experienced?

Now you can...

- ☑ **Work with the Drawing toolbar**
- ☑ **Draw with AutoShapes**
- ☑ **Connect AutoShapes**
- ☑ **Add text boxes and text**
- ☑ **Capture a picture of a worksheet**
- ☑ **Insert a graphic image**
- ☑ **Format AutoShapes and graphic images**
- ☑ **Move, resize, and rotate objects**
- ☑ **Change the order and alignment of objects**
- ☑ **Group objects**

SKILL 13

Working with Databases (Lists) in Excel

- Understanding lists in Excel
- Sorting the rows or columns in a range
- Working on a list through a form
- Validating cell entries
- Filtering the data in a list
- Performing an advanced list query
- Creating subtotals in a list
- Structuring a list as an outline
- Summarizing a list with a PivotTable

Excel is great at crunching numbers, and it's also well-qualified for crunching data. In this skill, you'll learn about some of the data-handling tools that appear on Excel's Data menu.

When Data Becomes a List

Have you ever written a phone number on a slip of paper and tucked it away for future reference? Tucked it away, no doubt, with all the other scraps of paper that you use for making quick notes!

Well, that's not the type of data we're talking about in this skill. We're going to take all those scraps and organize them into an Excel *list,* which is actually a range of cells whose data are structured so that you can use Excel's list-handling tools on them.

NOTE NOTE NOTE NOTE NOTE NOTE NOTE NOTE NOTE NOTE NOTE NOTE NOTE NOTE

When a list is referred to as a *database,* generally the list is being used for traditional database purposes, such as sorting, querying, and summarizing. In the language of databases, a row is called a *record,* and a column is called a *field.*

Figure 13.1 shows a small example of a name and address list in a worksheet. It looks straightforward, and yet it contains all the elements you need to work with lists in Excel.

	A	B	C	D	E	F	G	H
1	Last	First	Address	City	State	Zip	Age	
2	Kork	Elwood	7 Broadway	Tumbleweed	NV	87201	43	
3	Smithen	Carol	46 Over St	Cypress	CA	96802	32	
4	Pilz	Patricia	12-A West St	Seaside	CA	94025	22	
5	Smythe	Gerald	123 4thSt	Cypress	CA	96803	59	
6	Pilz	Amanda	2021 4th Ave	Hard Rock	NV	87203	32	
7	Shumway	Gordon	123 I St	Seaside	CA	94022	27	
8	Sebetta	Frank	656 Miguel Wy	Cypress	CA	96803	36	
9	Kenwood	Julie	PO Box 455	Red Pine	WA	82027	19	
10	Schnapp	Iris	23 9th Ave	Olive Hill	WA	82033	36	
11								

FIGURE 13.1: A worksheet list contains the same type of data in each column, and the data in each row are all related.

NOTE NOTE NOTE NOTE NOTE NOTE NOTE NOTE NOTE NOTE NOTE NOTE NOTE NOTE NOTE

The list in Figure 13.1 illustrates various list-handling features in Excel. I'll use this same list throughout this skill. You can either create this list in a worksheet or create a similar one using information from your own address book.

The names and addresses in Figure 13.1 are structured as an Excel list:

- The cells in each column (field) contain similar information, such as first name, last name, or age.
- Each column has a unique title directly above the data.
- All the cells in each row relate to only one individual (a record) and never occupy more than one row.
- There are no completely blank rows within the data. If you create a record, it should contain at least some data.
- All entries within a column are of the same type and scale. For example, all the states are abbreviated consistently, and all the ages are numbers and are expressed as years.

So what can you do with this type of data in Excel? Here are some ideas:

- Sort the list, for example, by last name or age.
- Add to or modify the data via a form.
- Filter the list so that it shows only the rows that match the criteria you specify, such as only rows whose state is CA.
- Create subtotals automatically that display the average age of the people in each state.
- Create an outline of the list.
- Create a PivotTable that instantly summarizes the data in a list.

NOTE NOTE NOTE NOTE NOTE NOTE NOTE NOTE NOTE NOTE NOTE NOTE NOTE NOTE NOTE

If you plan on running your business's inventory in a 10,000-row Excel list, think twice. Excel has some wonderful tools for handling data, but it's a wimp compared with a database program such as Microsoft Access or Borland's Paradox. Even when your data is in a database program, you can still access it in Excel, although those techniques are beyond the scope of this book.

Sorting a List

You can sort the data in any columns or rows in Excel, but you'll generally be sorting data within an organized list, such as the one in Figure 13.1.

Selecting the Range to Sort

You can select the sort range yourself, but you can also let Excel select it for you. To do so, follow these steps:

1. Select any cell within the range you want to sort and within the column that you want to serve as the *primary sort key.*
2. Choose Data ➤ Sort to open the Sort dialog box. (We'll look at this dialog box in the next section.)

NOTE NOTE NOTE NOTE NOTE NOTE NOTE NOTE NOTE NOTE NOTE NOTE NOTE NOTE NOTE

The primary sort key is the field by which you want to arrange the data. For example, if you want to arrange the list in Figure 13.1 by last name, the Last column is the primary sort key.

Excel selects all the occupied cells around the selected one but, by default, excludes the very first row, which it assumes contains column titles (see the Header Row option discussed in the next section).

Since specifying the wrong rows or columns can produce disastrous results, exercise caution when letting these big decisions happen "automatically." If you want to be absolutely sure of the range that will be sorted, select the range you want in the usual way. So in Figure 13.1, you could select the range A1:G10 and then choose Data ➤ Sort (again, read about the Header Row option in the next section).

WARNING WARNING WARNING WARNING WARNING WARNING WARNING WARNING

The most important part of sorting is ensuring that the range you sort includes all the required columns and rows and excludes any that you do not want sorted.

Here's an example of one of the hazards of sorting. In Figure 13.1, you definitely do *not* want to sort the titles in row 1 along with the other data rows in the list. Column titles that have been alphabetized within the data won't really serve their purpose.

Also, never leave out any columns from the sort range, such as column G in Figure 13.1. If you omit a column from the sort range, the data in that column will remain unsorted while the data in the rows to its left are placed in a new order. Not nice at all.

Before you sort a range for the first time, save your workbook. If you then accidentally exclude a few columns from the sort range, you can always close the current workbook and load it again from disk. Choosing Edit ➤ Undo undoes a sort but, as always, only if you have not yet performed 16 other actions in the workbook.

TIP TIP TIP TIP TIP TIP TIP TIP TIP TIP TIP TIP TIP TIP TIP TIP TIP TIP TIP TIP TIP TIP TIP TIP TIP

If you have several ranges that you sort from time to time, give each a name. When you want to sort one, select the range by selecting its name from either the Name box or the Go To dialog box (choose Edit ➤ Go To), and then choose Data ➤ Sort.

Performing the Sort

To sort the name and address list in Figure 13.1 so that it is alphabetized first by last name and then by first name, follow these steps:

1. Select any cell in column A of the data range, rows 1 through 10.
2. Choose Data ➤ Sort to open the Sort dialog box.

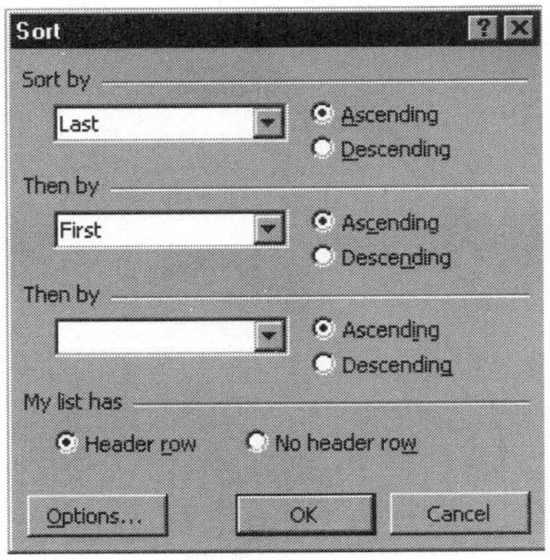

Excel selects the range A2:G10. The Header Row option in the Sort dialog box is selected by default. Excel assumes that there are titles in the top row of the sort range and that you would not want to include that row in the sort. If there are other occupied rows above the range you selected, Excel does not make this assumption.

If there is no titles row, you can select the No Header Row option to have Excel include the very first row in the sort. Try selecting either option and watch how Excel either includes or excludes the titles row.

Since you started by selecting a cell in the last name column, the Sort By drop-down list displays Last as the column used for sorting the list. This list conveniently displays all the column titles in the heading row. If there were no column titles, the list would offer the usual column labels instead.

3. Click Ascending for the Sort By option to sort from A to Z.

   We need to sort by a secondary column, too, in order to break any ties when two rows have the same last name.

4. Choose First from the Then By drop-down list and again click Ascending.
5. Click OK to sort the list; the sort may be too fast to notice.

Figure 13.2 shows the resulting worksheet. Because you defined a secondary column for determining the sort, the two rows with identical last names are also sorted by their first names.

	A	B	C	D	E	F	G	H
1	Last	First	Address	City	State	Zip	Age	
2	Kenwood	Julie	PO Box 455	Red Pine	WA	82027	19	
3	Kork	Elwood	7 Broadway	Tumbleweed	NV	87201	43	
4	Pilz	Amanda	2021 4th Ave	Hard Rock	NV	87203	32	
5	Pilz	Patricia	12-A West St	Seaside	CA	94025	22	
6	Schnapp	Iris	23 9th Ave	Olive Hill	WA	82033	36	
7	Sebetta	Frank	656 Miguel Wy	Cypress	CA	96803	36	
8	Shumway	Gordon	123 I St	Seaside	CA	94022	27	
9	Smithen	Carol	46 Over St	Cypress	CA	96802	32	
10	Smythe	Gerald	123 4thSt	Cypress	CA	96803	59	
11								

FIGURE 13.2: The results of sorting the range A2:G10 by the Last and First columns

Sorting from the Toolbar

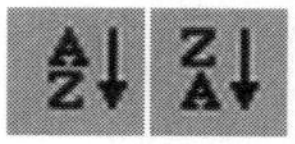

You can sort a range of cells by clicking the Sort Ascending or Sort Descending button on the Standard toolbar, but I highly recommended that you use caution when doing so. Sorting from the toolbar works so quickly that if you sort the wrong range, you might not even realize it.

If the sort range has adjoining occupied columns, for example, Excel automatically includes them in the sort. That could spell disaster after the sort, so don't rely on Excel to select the range for you until you're well practiced with sorting. When in doubt, it's safer to choose Data ➤ Sort, as described in the previous section.

But when you want to sort via the toolbar buttons, here's how to do it:

1. Select a cell within the range you want to sort in the column that you want to use to determine the sort order. You cannot select a secondary or tertiary sort column.
2. Click the Sort Ascending button to sort the range in A to Z order, or click the Sort Descending button to sort in Z to A order.

NOTE

After you perform a sort, check to see that the correct range was sorted, and don't forget that you can always choose Edit ➤ Undo.

The sort buttons are a real convenience when you want to sort a range in several ways, such as by age, state, or last name. Simply select a cell in a different column and click the appropriate sort button.

WARNING

You can't use the toolbar buttons to sort if your range contains any merged cells.

Looking at Your Sorting Options

As you have seen you can sort a list alphabetically, but you can also sort in other ways. To do so, click the Options button in the Sort dialog box to open the Sort Options dialog box.

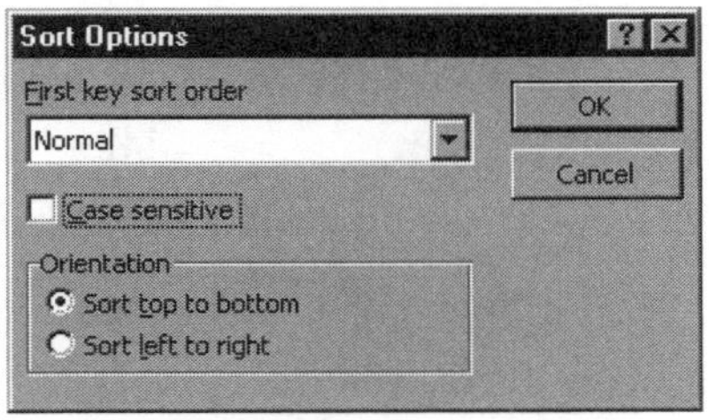

The three options in the Sort Options dialog box affect the outcome of the sort:

First Key Sort Order Is a drop-down list that includes all the custom lists defined in this workbook (as described in Skill 2). Normal is the default, which sorts according to the usual alphabetic and numeric rules. If you choose one of the lists, such as the months of the year or the days of the week, the sort is based on the items in that list. Without this feature, you could only sort a column of month names or days of the week alphabetically.

Case Sensitive Is not selected, by default, which means that the case of a letter has no effect on the sort order. Select this option if you want an uppercase letter to follow its lowercase counterpart when you sort in ascending order, such as aAbBcC.

Orientation Determines the direction in which the data is sorted. By default, the option Sort Top to Bottom is selected, which rearranges the rows of the sort range during the sort. Select Sort Left to Right to rearrange the columns of the sort range.

Entering and Viewing Data via a Form

When you're going to work with the data in a list, you may find it frustrating if there are so many columns that you can only see some of them without scrolling the screen. This means you can't see all the information that belongs to each row.

NOTE NOTE NOTE NOTE NOTE NOTE NOTE NOTE NOTE NOTE NOTE NOTE NOTE NOTE NOTE

Since the discussion that follows is more data related than spreadsheet related, I use the database terms *records* and *fields* instead of the spreadsheet-related terms *rows* and *columns*.

The solution is to select any cell within the list and choose Data ➤ Form to display a data-entry form. Figure 13.3 show the data-entry form for my name and address list used in the previous examples.

The data-entry form displays all the fields in the list, each identified on its left by its column title. The buttons on the right are for navigating the list.

When you first open the form, it displays the data for the first record in the list (the row beneath the column titles), the current record number, and the total number of records in the list (1 of 9 in Figure 13.3).

The buttons perform the following functions:

New Creates a new blank record that is added after the last record in the list. Enter data into its fields, and when you're finished, either press Enter or click one of the navigation buttons to go to another record.

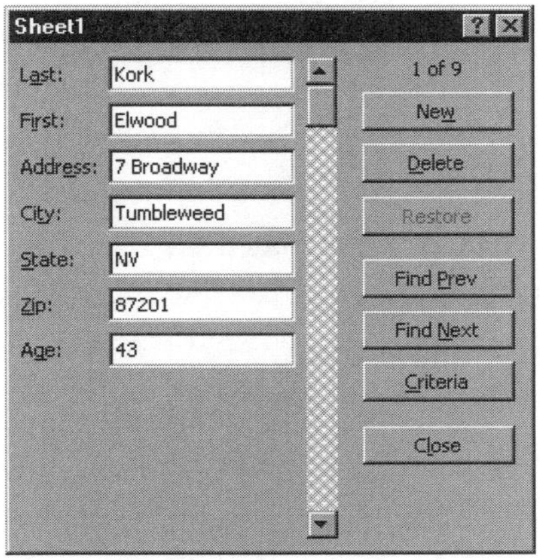

FIGURE 13.3: Use the data-entry form to view, modify, or search through the rows of a list.

Delete Removes the current record from the list.

Restore Acts as an Undo command for any changes you may have made to the current record (other than actually deleting it), as long as you use it *before* you move to another record.

Find Prev Displays the previous record in the list. You can also press the up arrow on the keyboard or use the vertical scroll bar to scroll through the records.

Find Next Displays the next record. You can also press the down arrow on the keyboard.

Criteria Lets you specify criteria in any of the fields so that you can find all matching records, essentially filtering the list so only records that match your criteria are displayed in the form.

Close Returns you to the worksheet.

To move through the fields in the form, press Tab or Shift+Tab. To move to the very first record, press PgUp or Ctrl+up arrow. Press PgDn or Ctrl+down arrow to move to the last record. (Actually, you'll end up in a new blank record, but the last occupied record is just above the new record.) When you get to the last field on a form, you can press Enter to move to the next record.

You can edit any of the fields in a record; the changes you make aren't entered into the list until you select another record in the form or close the form.

To find records, select the Criteria button. The fields of the form are emptied and ready for your search criteria. After you enter the criteria, select Find Prev or Find Next to display the next record that matches your criteria. Using my example name and address list, here are some ways that you can search on criteria that you specify:

- Enter **CA** in the State field. As you move through the data with the Find buttons, only records that have CA in their State field are displayed.
- Enter **>30** in the Age field to find all records whose entries in the Age field are greater than 30.
- Enter both those criteria to find all records that have CA in their State field and whose entries in the Age field are greater than 30.
- Enter **Sm** in the Last field to find all records whose last name begins with Sm, such as Smithen and Smythe.
- Enter **<>CA** in the State field to find all records whose state is *not* CA.

NOTE NOTE NOTE NOTE NOTE NOTE NOTE NOTE NOTE NOTE NOTE NOTE NOTE NOTE NOTE

To create a new set of criteria, click Clear to delete anything that you entered previously in the criteria fields. Otherwise, the previous criteria will be considered in the search.

Validating Cell Entries

Entering data in a cell seems like a simple and harmless exercise, especially when compared with writing a complex formula. But plenty of problems can arise from a cell entry that isn't quite right, and those problems often fall into the categories of data range, type, and consistency.

Suppose a worksheet for an upcoming project has a cell with the title *Days Worked Last Month* next to it. You can imagine what type of entry should be made in that cell. Here are some entries that are even *more* imaginative:

- –23
- 93,562,724

- Twenty-three
- 23.8

The first two items are out of an acceptable range; the last two are of the wrong type (text and a number with a decimal fraction). Of course, I'm only assuming that all these numbers would be invalid when, in fact, from the information I have, there's really no way to be completely sure.

Another problem, consistency, often crops up when data is part of a list (a database). In a column whose title is *State*, for example, you might expect the standard, two-letter designations, such as WA, but not Washington, Wash., or WG. When data is entered inconsistently, it is virtually impossible to perform standard database actions on the data. In this example, there could be a variety of spellings for any one state, so sorting the data by the State column would give a meaningless result.

To the rescue comes Excel's Data ➤ Validation command. It can prevent all three types of data-entry problems, while also making your worksheets easier to use. This is especially important when you are designing worksheets that will be used by others.

You apply data validation to a selected cell or range much as you would apply cell formatting, and if you copy or move the cell, its validation criteria end up on the target cell. To set validation, follow these steps:

1. Select the cell to which you want to apply validation.
2. Choose Data ➤ Validation to open the Data Validation dialog box, which is shown in Figure 13.4.
3. Using the tabs in this dialog box, specify validation criteria.
4. Click OK when you are done.

You use the tabs in the Data Validation dialog box to do the following:

Settings Specify the type of data that will be allowed in the cell and the range of numeric data. You can also specify that the entry come from a list of acceptable entries.

Input Message Create a message that will be displayed when a user selects the cell; this message can prompt the user to make an appropriate entry.

Error Alert Define the message that will appear when a user attempts to enter unacceptable data and specify whether that data will be allowed or rejected.

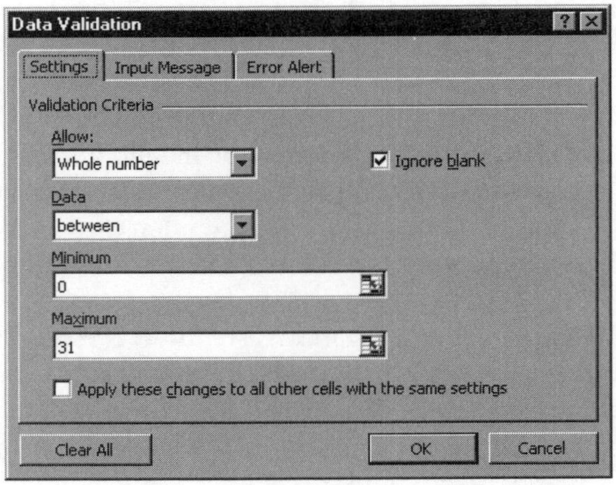

FIGURE 13.4: You specify the allowable data for a cell in the Data Validation dialog box.

Specifying the Allowable Data

To illustrate data validation, I'll use the cell labeled *Days Worked Last Month* that I mentioned in the previous section.

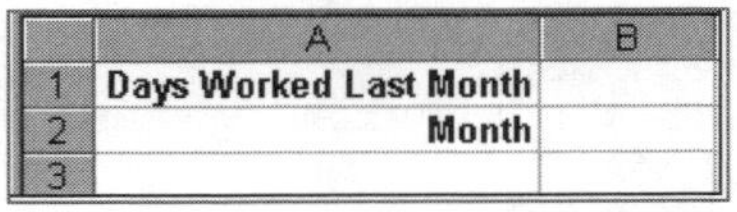

In Cell B1, I'll require that the entry be a whole number in the range 0 through 31, the maximum number of days in a month. (Later you might try making this maximum month-specific.) Later, in the section named "Specifying Other Validations," I'll set up validation for entering a month name from a list into another cell labeled *Month*. Here are the steps:

1. Select the cell where the number of days will be entered.
2. Choose Data ➤ Validation to open the Data Validation dialog box, and then click the Settings tab as shown in Figure 13.4.
3. In the Allow drop-down list, choose Whole Number.

4. In the Data drop-down list, choose Between. The other choices in this list are logical operators, such as *less than*, *greater than*, and *equal to*, each of which offers one or two fields in which you specify the comparison values.
5. Set the Minimum data-entry field to 0 and the Maximum to 31.
6. The Ignore Blank check box is selected, by default, which means that the user does not have to make an entry in this cell. The importance of the cell would determine whether an entry is required.
7. Click OK to return to the worksheet.

Even though you have not yet completed the process, validation is enabled in this cell. To prove it, enter the number **1** in the cell and press Enter. Now enter **10** and press Enter, then try **31** and press Enter. All numeric entries from 0 to 31 should be accepted, with no indication that validation has been applied to the cell.

Now enter a number outside the acceptable range, and you should see Excel's generic error dialog box, "The value you entered is not valid." You can click Retry and enter another number, or click Cancel. An invalid entry will not be allowed.

TIP

Data validation is removed from a cell when you erase the cell by choosing Edit ➤ Clear ➤ All. You can also turn off validation by clearing the *Show error alert after invalid data is entered* option on the Error Alert tab in the Data Validation dialog box.

In order to make data validation complete, I'll define an input message and a more specific error message.

Defining the Input Message

If you're going to restrict a cell to only certain entries, you can make it easier for the user by creating a message that will be displayed when the validation cell is selected (much as a cell comment is displayed when you point to a cell).

The message could say something like "Watch out! If you make any mistake here, we'll catch you!" You could also try something more helpful, such as "The number of workdays you enter can range from 0 to 31."

To define an input message, follow these steps:

1. Select the cell to which you applied data validation.

2. Choose Data ➤ Validation to open the Data Validation dialog box, and click the Input Message tab.

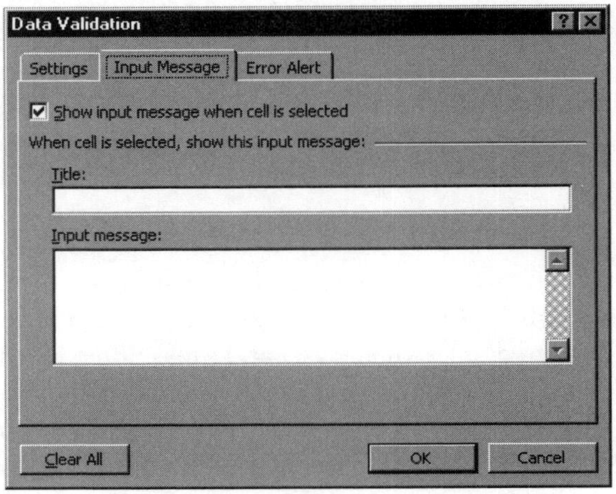

3. Verify that the *Show input message when cell is selected* check box is checked. If you clear this check box, no input message is displayed.
4. In the Title field, enter the title of the input message, such as **Days Worked Last Month** in my example.
5. In the Input Message field, enter the text of the message, such as **The number of workdays you enter here can range from 0 to 31.** If you're not sure at this time, you can leave this blank.
6. Click OK to go back to the worksheet.

NOTE NOTE NOTE NOTE NOTE NOTE NOTE NOTE NOTE NOTE NOTE NOTE NOTE NOTE NOTE

If the Office Assistant is active, that is where you will see the input message displayed. Otherwise, the message will appear next to the cell as a ScreenTip.

You should see your input message, looking something like the one shown below. The message will remain on the screen until you select another cell. You can also press Esc to hide the message, or you can move the message by dragging it to another location. Once you move it, all input messages for other validation cells in this worksheet will be displayed there, as well.

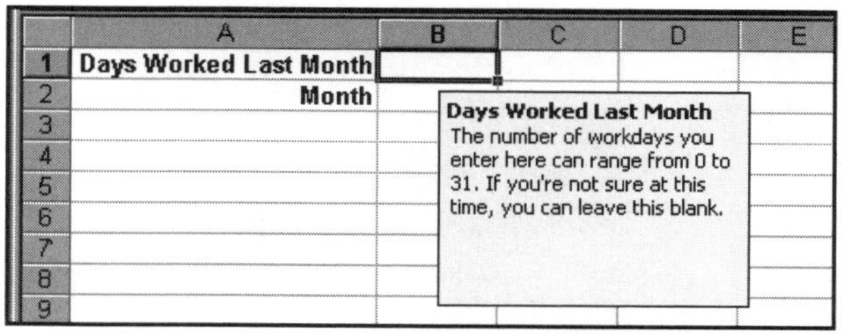

Defining the Error Message

Let's complete the data validation for this cell by defining the invalid-data message. Follow these steps:

1. Select the validation cell, choose Data ➤ Validation to open the Data Validation dialog box, and then click the Error Alert tab.

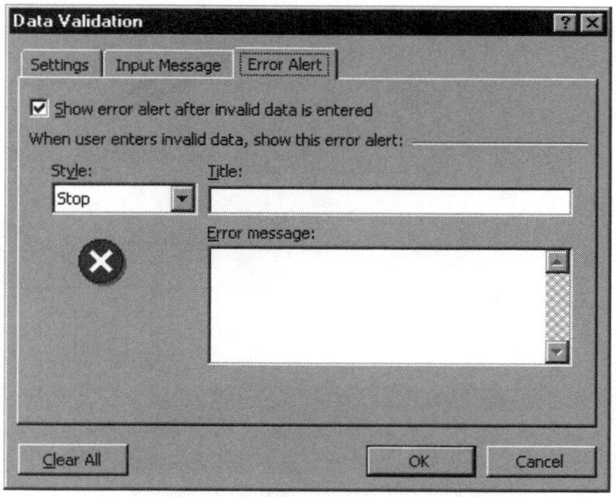

2. The *Show error alert after invalid data is entered* check box is selected by default. If this option is not selected, not only will no message be displayed for an invalid entry, but data validation will not be enforced—all cell entries will be allowed.

3. Now you must decide whether an invalid entry will be accepted or rejected. In my example, it seems reasonable to require that the entry be within the validation limits, 0 to 31, so I chose Stop from the Style drop-down list.

The dialog box that is displayed for the Stop alert has Retry and Cancel buttons. The user will have no option to place the invalid entry in the cell. The other two alerts are:

Warning Displays the message you create along with the prompt *Continue?* and has Yes, No, and Cancel buttons. This allows the user to enter the invalid data (Yes), revise the entry (No), or cancel the entry altogether.

Information Displays only the message you enter along with the OK and Cancel buttons; choosing OK completes the cell entry.

4. Enter the message and title that you want to appear when an invalid entry is attempted. In my example, I entered the title **Invalid Number**, and the message **The number of workdays must be from 0 to 31**.
5. Click OK.

Now try making an invalid entry in this cell, such as a number outside the range 0 to 31 or a text entry. You'll see the dialog box appear displaying your error-alert message. At this point you can click the Retry button to revise the entry or click Cancel.

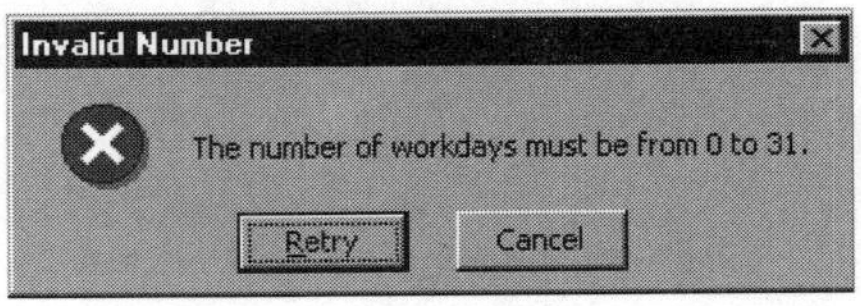

NOTE NOTE NOTE NOTE NOTE NOTE NOTE NOTE NOTE NOTE NOTE NOTE NOTE NOTE NOTE

You cannot enter a formula in this cell if its result falls outside the acceptable validation parameters (0 to 31 in this case). However, once a formula is in the cell, if its result becomes invalid, it will still not trigger the error message.

Specifying Other Validations

In this example, I defined a valid cell entry as a whole number in the range 0 through 31. But there are many more validations on the Allow list of the Settings tab in the Data Validation dialog box:

Any Value Allows any cell entry and essentially turns off validation; but the input message will still be displayed.

Decimal Allows only real numbers, which include whole numbers and fractions.

List Requires that the entry be from a list of acceptable entries (see an example below).

DateTime Allows only a valid date entry.

Time Allows only a valid time entry.

Text Length Allows only a text entry, and you can specify its length.

Custom Allows any cell entry, but only if the result of the logical formula you enter for this option is True. For example, the formula =MONTH (NOW())=1 allows an entry only when the current month is January.

You can also enter a formula in any of the comparison fields for each type of validation. For example, here's how you could require entry of a date that is no earlier than today's date, but no later than 90 days from that date.

1. Choose the Date option from the Allow list and the *between* comparison operator from the Data list.
2. For the Start Date comparison value, enter the formula =TODAY(); for the End Date enter =TODAY()+90.

Filtering a List with Your Criteria

You can *filter* a list so that only the rows you want to see are displayed. In my example, you could hide all rows except those whose entry in the State column is CA or whose entry in the Age column is greater than 30 but less than 40. You do so by choosing Data ➤ Filter and then selecting an item on the submenu.

Turning on the AutoFilter

In this first example, I'll filter the name and address list from Figure 13.1 so that all rows are hidden except those that contain CA in the State column. Here are the steps:

1. Select a cell anywhere within the list.

NOTE NOTE NOTE NOTE NOTE NOTE NOTE NOTE NOTE NOTE NOTE NOTE NOTE NOTE NOTE

AutoFilter assumes that the first row of the range contains column titles and does not consider the first row part of the data rows. You can also filter only one list on a worksheet at a time.

2. Choose Data ➤ Filter ➤ AutoFilter to turn on AutoFilter for this list. Excel places a list arrow next to the title in each column.
3. Click the arrow next to State in cell E1 to display a list of every unique entry in that column. This list is similar to the pick-list feature that was discussed in Skill 2.

   Figure 13.5 shows the worksheet at this point. The trick now is to select an item from the list, that AutoFilter will use to filter the list.

	A	B	C	D	E	F	G	H
1	Last	First	Address	City	Sta	Zip	A(	
2	Kork	Elwood	7 Broadway	Tumblev		87201	43	
3	Smithen	Carol	46 Over St	Cypress		96802	32	
4	Pilz	Patricia	12-A West St	Seaside		94025	22	
5	Smythe	Gerald	123 4thSt	Cypress		96803	59	
6	Pilz	Amanda	2021 4th Ave	Hard Ro		87203	32	
7	Shumway	Gordon	123 I St	Seaside	CA	94022	27	
8	Sebetta	Frank	656 Miguel Wy	Cypress	CA	96803	36	
9	Kenwood	Julie	PO Box 455	Red Pine	WA	82027	19	
10	Schnapp	Iris	23 9th Ave	Olive Hill	WA	82033	36	
11								
12								

FIGURE 13.5: The AutoFilter feature offers a drop-down list of the unique entries in each column.

4. Select CA from the AutoFilter list for the State column, and in an instant the list is filtered, as shown in Figure 13.6.

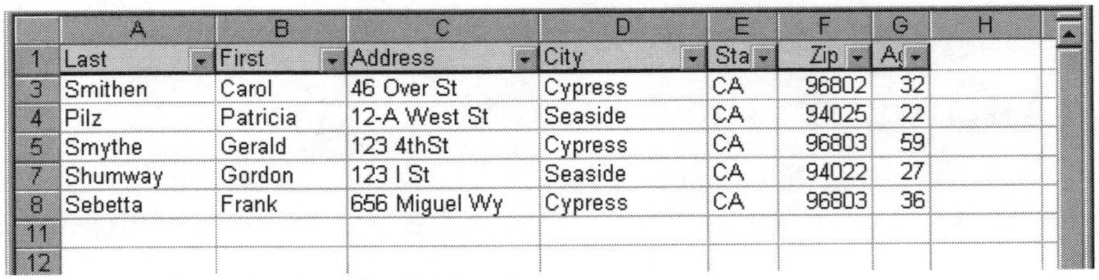

	A	B	C	D	E	F	G	H
1	Last	First	Address	City	Sta	Zip	A(	
3	Smithen	Carol	46 Over St	Cypress	CA	96802	32	
4	Pilz	Patricia	12-A West St	Seaside	CA	94025	22	
5	Smythe	Gerald	123 4thSt	Cypress	CA	96803	59	
7	Shumway	Gordon	123 I St	Seaside	CA	94022	27	
8	Sebetta	Frank	656 Miguel Wy	Cypress	CA	96803	36	
11								
12								

FIGURE 13.6: The list after selecting CA from the AutoFilter list for the State column

All rows that do not contain the criteria you specified are hidden, as though you had chosen Format ➤ Row ➤ Hide. Now it's easy to work on only the rows you want to see, whether you edit their data, copy them elsewhere, or print them.

NOTE NOTE NOTE NOTE NOTE NOTE NOTE NOTE NOTE NOTE NOTE NOTE NOTE NOTE NOTE

When the list is filtered, the row numbers of the list are shown in blue to remind you that there may be hidden rows. The AutoFilter down arrow is also shown in blue in any column where you selected a filter, such as column E in Figure 13.6.

You can turn off filtering in these ways:

- Click the All selection in the AutoFilter drop-down list.
- Choose Data ➤ Filter ➤ AutoFilter.

TIP TIP TIP TIP TIP TIP TIP TIP TIP TIP TIP TIP TIP TIP TIP TIP TIP TIP TIP TIP TIP TIP TIP TIP TIP

Because the SUBTOTAL function ignores all hidden rows, you can use it to perform a calculation on a column in a filtered list. You'll learn about it later in the "Creating Subtotals in a List" section.

Creating a Custom Filter

You can create a more flexible filter by choosing Custom from an AutoFilter drop-down list. In this next example, I'll filter the list through the Age column and hide all rows except those that contain an age greater than 30 and less than 40.

As you'll see here, you can filter the same list through multiple columns to refine the scope of the search. The list will get smaller and smaller each time as your comparison criteria allow fewer and fewer rows to "make it through" the filter.

To add a second filter to the one in the previous example, follow these steps:

1. Click the arrow next to Age in cell G1.
2. Select Custom from the drop-down list to open the Custom AutoFilter dialog box, shown here.

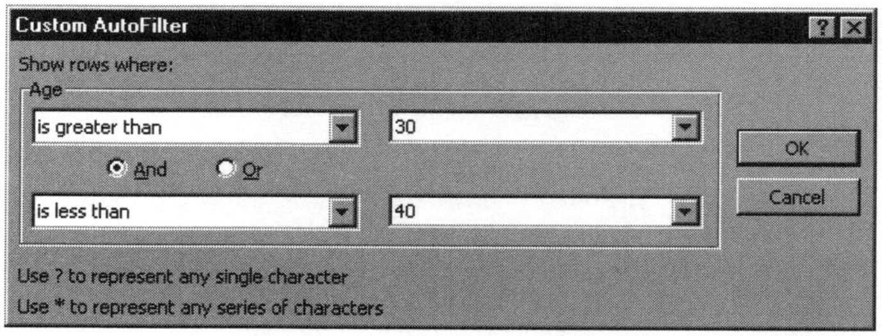

The Custom AutoFilter dialog box has two fields for creating comparison criteria that define the filter. Each consists of a drop-down list of logical operators and a field where you enter the comparison item.

3. Select *is greater than* in the first drop-down list.
4. Enter 30 in the field to its right. This entry filters out all rows except those whose entry in the Age column is greater than 30. If there is already an entry in the column that would serve as the comparison criteria, you can select it from the drop-down list.
5. Click the And button so that the second filter will be used in conjunction with the first.
6. Choose *is less than* in the second drop-down list.
7. Enter 40 in the field to its right.
8. Click OK to close the dialog box.

Now the list is filtered even more and looks like the worksheet in Figure 13.7. If you compare this worksheet with the worksheet in Figure 13.5, you can see that seven rows are hidden. The remaining rows have CA in the State column and a number greater than 30 and less than 40 in the Age column.

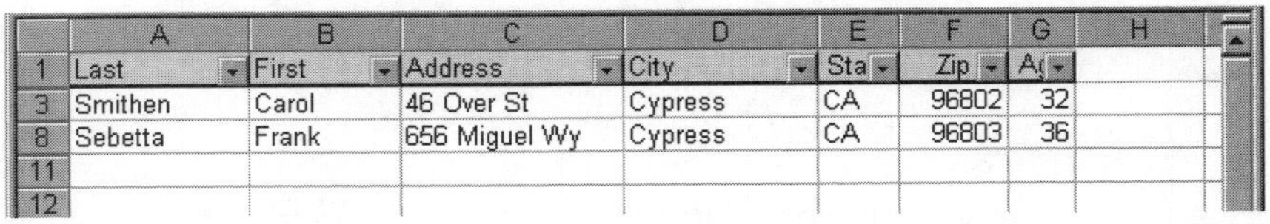

	A	B	C	D	E	F	G	H
1	Last	First	Address	City	Sta	Zip	A(	
3	Smithen	Carol	46 Over St	Cypress	CA	96802	32	
8	Sebetta	Frank	656 Miguel Wy	Cypress	CA	96803	36	
11								
12								

FIGURE 13.7: The list after filtering it for all rows that have CA as the state and have ages greater than 30 and less than 40

You can choose one of the less-specific logical operators, such as *begins with* or *ends with*, and enter just those characters you're looking for. You can also include the asterisk to represent all characters or the question mark to represent any single character. For example, entering

```
equals Jo?n
```

would find John and Joan.

If you select the Or option in the Custom AutoFilter dialog box instead of And, Excel applies both filters independently. For example, if you apply these two filters in the State field

```
equals CA
equals WA
```

and connect them with the Or option, Excel displays all rows that contain either CA or WA.

NOTE NOTE NOTE NOTE NOTE NOTE NOTE NOTE NOTE NOTE NOTE NOTE NOTE NOTE NOTE

When you filter multiple columns, you are, in effect, creating an "and" relationship between the filtered columns. Excel displays only rows that meet this criteria *and* that criteria *and* the other criteria.

Using the Top Ten AutoFilter

Another way to filter a list is by selecting Top 10 from an AutoFilter drop-down list for a numeric column (it won't work for text columns). This choice displays the Top 10 AutoFilter dialog box, shown in Figure 13.8.

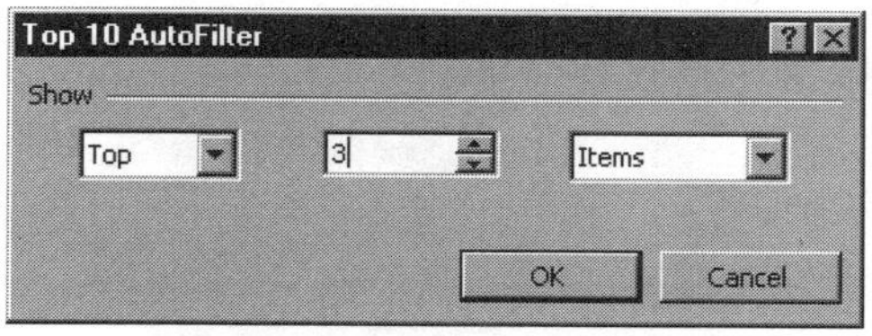

FIGURE 13.8: The Top 10 AutoFilter dialog box

This feature works by defining a range of values for the filter—any rows whose entries in this column fall within the range are displayed, and the rest are hidden.

Suppose I want to see only those rows that contain the oldest ages in the Age column in my example. Here are the steps to create a filter that shows only the top three items among the ages.

1. Turn off all filtering by choosing Data ➤ Filter ➤ Show All to display all rows.
2. Select the Top 10 choice from the AutoFilter list in the Age column.
3. Set its three options to Top, 3, and Items so that the list displays only the rows that contain the top three ages.

NOTE NOTE NOTE NOTE NOTE NOTE NOTE NOTE NOTE NOTE NOTE NOTE NOTE NOTE NOTE

You can set the first option to Bottom to display the lowest values in the column. Set the last option to Percent to display rows that fall within, for example, the top 3 percent for that column.

4. Choose OK, and the worksheet now looks like the one in Figure 13.9. Four rows, not three, are displayed in the list because the third oldest age is found in two rows.

	A	B	C	D	E	F	G	H
1	Last ▼	First ▼	Address ▼	City ▼	Sta ▼	Zip ▼	A(▼	
2	Kork	Elwood	7 Broadway	Tumbleweed	NV	87201	43	
5	Smythe	Gerald	123 4thSt	Cypress	CA	96803	59	
8	Sebetta	Frank	656 Miguel Wy	Cypress	CA	96803	36	
10	Schnapp	Iris	23 9th Ave	Olive Hill	WA	82033	36	
11								
12								

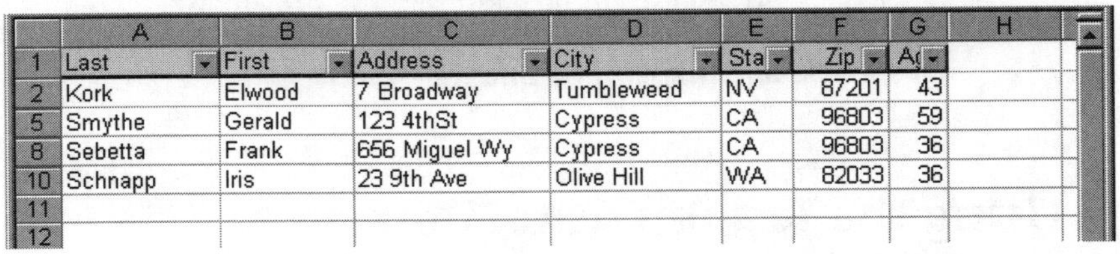

FIGURE 13.9: The name and address list after using the Top 10 AutoFilter to display only the top three items in the Age column

Creating an Advanced Filter

You can carry the filtering concept a lot further with the Data ➤ Filter ➤ Advanced Filter command. Although the Advanced Filter can be rather confusing at first, it offers several advantages over the filtering we've discussed so far:

- You create the comparison criteria within a range in the worksheet, which can be more convenient than going to multiple AutoFilter lists.

- You can filter for multiple items in one column, whereas a Custom AutoFilter allows only two.

- You can create multiple "or" comparison criteria between the columns, which you can't do with the AutoFilter techniques discussed so far.

- You can include formulas in the comparison criteria so that, for example, only rows with ages greater than a value in some other cell are selected.

- Instead of hiding the rows that don't meet the criteria, you can choose to copy the rows that do meet the criteria elsewhere as a new list.

- You can choose to show only unique results and hide any duplicates (although each row must have exactly the same data in every column to be considered a duplicate).

Unfortunately, the Advanced Filter tends to be just that—advanced—and falls outside the scope of this book. But one example should help you decide if you need to pursue the topic.

Figure 13.10 shows the name and address list from the previous examples, with these modifications:

- I chose Data ➤ Filter ➤ AutoFilter to turn off the AutoFilter feature.
- I inserted four rows above the table to leave room for the comparison criteria (it can go anywhere you want, but this is a convenient spot, right next to the list).
- I entered the comparison criteria in the range B1:B3.

	A	B	C	D	E	F	G
1		State					
2		CA					
3		WA					
4							
5	Last	First	Address	City	State	Zip	Age
6	Kork	Elwood	7 Broadway	Tumbleweed	NV	87201	43
7	Smithen	Carol	46 Over St	Cypress	CA	96802	32
8	Pilz	Patricia	12-A West St	Seaside	CA	94025	22
9	Smythe	Gerald	123 4thSt	Cypress	CA	96803	59
10	Pilz	Amanda	2021 4th Ave	Hard Rock	NV	87203	32
11	Shumway	Gordon	123 I St	Seaside	CA	94022	27
12	Sebetta	Frank	656 Miguel Wy	Cypress	CA	96803	36
13	Kenwood	Julie	PO Box 455	Red Pine	WA	82027	19
14	Schnapp	Iris	23 9th Ave	Olive Hill	WA	82033	36
15							

FIGURE 13.10: The name and address list with a comparison criteria range, ready for the Advanced Filter command

The criteria can consist of multiple columns; each must have a column title from the list in its first cell. In Figure 13.10, the criteria select any row that contains CA *or* WA in its State column.

TIP

The column titles you use in the criteria must match those in the table exactly. The quickest and safest way to ensure this is by copying the titles you need from the table to the criteria.

Here's how to put the Advanced Filter to work:

1. Select a cell anywhere inside the list.
2. Choose Data ➤ Filter ➤ Advanced Filter to open the Advanced Filter dialog box.

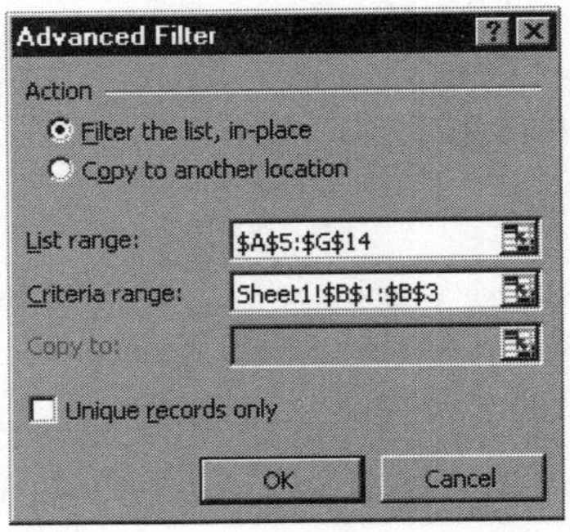

3. Edit the List Range field if it doesn't already show the address of the list. (Note that this range must include the list's column titles.)
4. Enter the criteria address in the Criteria Range Field.
5. Leave the Action field set to Filter the List In-Place. If you choose Copy to Another Location, specify the address in the Copy To field.
6. Leave the Unique option cleared.
7. Click OK to apply the advanced filter.

Creating Subtotals in a List

A function that references a range of cells continues to refer to the same cells even though their rows or columns are hidden. Thus, most functions are unsuitable for performing calculations on a list that you have filtered—their results won't change after filtering.

The SUBTOTAL function is an exception, because it ignores any cells whose rows or columns are hidden. It is also smart enough to ignore any cells that contain another SUBTOTAL function, which allows you to create subtotals within a list without affecting the grand total for the entire list.

You can use the SUBTOTAL function in two ways:

- Alone like any other function
- By choosing Data ➤ Subtotal

Using the SUBTOTAL Function

The syntax of the SUBTOTAL function is:

```
=SUBTOTAL(number,range)
```

The *number* argument is a number between 1 and 11, which indicates the type of calculation you want to perform. For example, 1 is Average, 2 is Count, 4 is Max, 5 is Min, and 9 is Sum. The *range* argument is the range of cells on which you want to perform the calculation.

You learned how to filter the name and address list in the AutoFilter examples earlier in this skill; now I'll use the SUBTOTAL function to calculate both the number of rows displayed and the average of their ages.

Figure 13.11 shows the name and address list from Figure 13.6 after filtering the State column for CA.

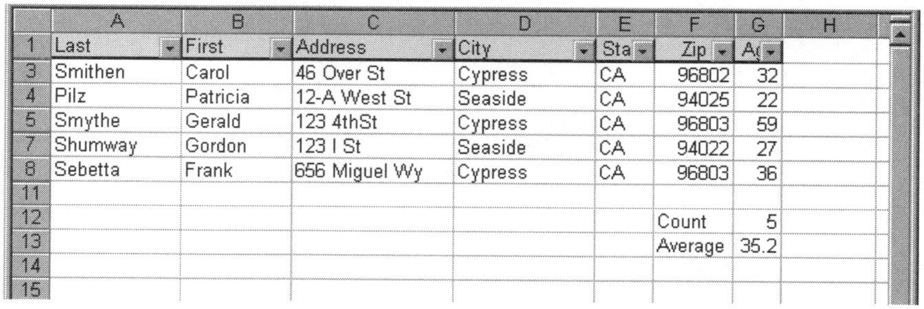

	A	B	C	D	E	F	G	H
1	Last	First	Address	City	Sta	Zip	A(	
3	Smithen	Carol	46 Over St	Cypress	CA	96802	32	
4	Pilz	Patricia	12-A West St	Seaside	CA	94025	22	
5	Smythe	Gerald	123 4thSt	Cypress	CA	96803	59	
7	Shumway	Gordon	123 I St	Seaside	CA	94022	27	
8	Sebetta	Frank	656 Miguel Wy	Cypress	CA	96803	36	
11								
12						Count	5	
13						Average	35.2	
14								
15								

FIGURE 13.11: With the SUBTOTAL function, you can perform calculations on a filtered list.

Here are the steps to create the functions:

1. Enter the **Count** label in cell F12, and enter the **Average** label in cell F13.
2. Enter the function **=SUBTOTAL(2,G2:G10)** in cell G12 to count the displayed rows in the range G2:G10.
3. Enter **=SUBTOTAL(1,G2:G10)** in G13 to average the ages in the displayed rows.

NOTE NOTE NOTE NOTE NOTE NOTE NOTE NOTE NOTE NOTE NOTE NOTE NOTE NOTE NOTE

Always leave at least one blank row below a list you intend to filter; otherwise, AutoFilter includes any adjacent data. Of course, any data in the same rows as the list could end up being hidden when you filter out those rows from the list.

Now when you change the filtering in the list, the formulas update their results and perform their calculations only on the displayed rows. For example, change the filter in the State column to select only those rows that contain WA. The two formulas will update their results to reflect the rows that are displayed.

Using the Data ➤ Subtotals Command

When you work with a list, such as the name and address list you've seen throughout this skill, choosing Data ➤ Subtotals can quickly create subtotals for each category you specify. It's an amazingly helpful tool that saves you many, many steps.

NOTE NOTE NOTE NOTE NOTE NOTE NOTE NOTE NOTE NOTE NOTE NOTE NOTE NOTE NOTE

Before you can choose Data ➤ Subtotals, you must sort your list on the column that you want to perform the subtotal on. For example, you could sort the list by State and then average all the ages for each state in a subtotal.

Choosing Data ➤ Subtotals performs two rather complex tasks.

- It inserts a row and creates a SUBTOTAL function at each change in the data in the column you specify; the function automatically references the correct number of cells above it.
- It creates an outline of the list so that you can show more or less detail at the click of a button.

Here's how easy it is to create subtotals for the name and address list used earlier. The process will summarize the list by state and average the ages in each state.

NOTE NOTE NOTE NOTE NOTE NOTE NOTE NOTE NOTE NOTE NOTE NOTE NOTE NOTE NOTE

If you're using the list from the previous example, erase the contents from F12:G13, and choose Data ➤ Filter ➤ AutoFilter to turn off the AutoFilter.

1. Sort the list by state. Select a cell in that column in the list (column E in the earlier figures) and click the Sort Ascending button on the Standard toolbar.
2. With a cell anywhere in the list selected, choose Data ➤ Subtotals to open the Subtotal dialog box.

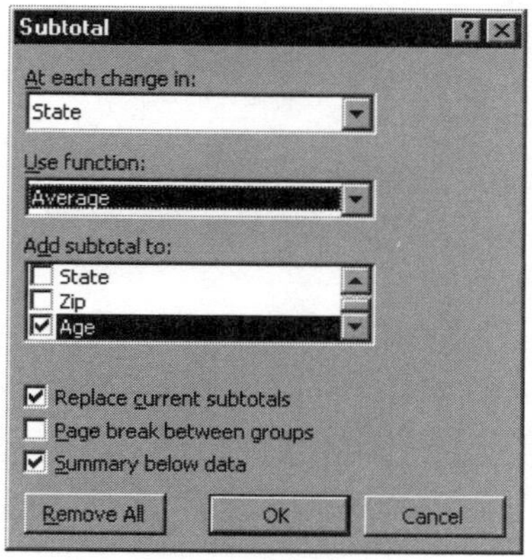

3. Select State from the At Each Change In drop-down list. This step puts a SUBTOTAL function at each change in the data in the State column, such as when CA ends and NV begins (that's why you needed to sort by the State field).
4. Select Average from the Use Function drop-down list because you want to average the ages for each group of states.
5. Select Age from the Add Subtotal To list so that the formula will average the ages in that column. The last three options are less important, and you can set them to their defaults:
6. Select Replace Current Subtotals.
7. Do not select Page Break between Groups.
8. Select Summary below Data.
9. Click OK to create the subtotals.

In no time at all, the subtotals will be entered as you specified. Figure 13.12 shows the result.

	A	B	C	D	E	F	G	H
1	Last	First	Address	City	State	Zip	Age	
2	Smithen	Carol	46 Over St	Cypress	CA	96802	32	
3	Pilz	Patricia	12-A West St	Seaside	CA	94025	22	
4	Smythe	Gerald	123 4thSt	Cypress	CA	96803	59	
5	Shumway	Gordon	123 I St	Seaside	CA	94022	27	
6	Sebetta	Frank	656 Miguel Wy	Cypress	CA	96803	36	
7					**CA Average**		35.2	
8	Kork	Elwood	7 Broadway	Tumbleweed	NV	87201	43	
9	Pilz	Amanda	2021 4th Ave	Hard Rock	NV	87203	32	
10					**NV Average**		37.5	
11	Kenwood	Julie	PO Box 455	Red Pine	WA	82027	19	
12	Schnapp	Iris	23 9th Ave	Olive Hill	WA	82033	36	
13					**WA Average**		27.5	
14					**Grand Average**		34.0	
15								

FIGURE 13.12: The list after subtotaling by the groups in the State column and averaging their ages

NOTE NOTE NOTE NOTE NOTE NOTE NOTE NOTE NOTE NOTE NOTE NOTE NOTE NOTE NOTE

To remove all the subtotals from a list, select a cell in the list, choose Data ➤ Subtotals to open the Subtotal dialog box, and click Remove All.

Notice the outlining symbols on the left side of Figure 13.12. The Subtotals command automatically creates an outline of the list in which each outline level includes one of the groups you subtotaled.

Grouping and Outlining Your Data

Excel's outlining feature lends itself perfectly to the way we work in the columns and rows of Excel and organize data by groups. Instead of looking at hundreds of rows of data, you can collapse any level of the outline to hide the detail and leave only the summary rows.

As you saw in the previous section and in Figure 13.12, when you choose Data ➤ Subtotals to apply subtotals by group, Excel automatically applies an outline structure to the data. Figure 13.12 shows Excel's outlining controls and symbols on the left side of the worksheet.

NOTE NOTE NOTE NOTE NOTE NOTE NOTE NOTE NOTE NOTE NOTE NOTE NOTE NOTE

A worksheet outline can organize data by rows, as in Figure 13.12. It can also organize data by columns, as you saw in Skill 9 when we created a Scenario Summary sheet. The discussion that follows uses the row-centric view.

Outline Terminology

An outline in Excel is structured around *groups* of data, such as the grouping by state in the name and address list. Without groups, there would be no structure on which to base the outline.

An outline can have multiple *levels.* Each level is subordinate to the level above it and may have other levels subordinate to it.

The lowest level of the outline, subordinate to all others, contains the *detail* rows that hold the actual data you want to subtotal or otherwise organize into an outline.

Between each group of detail rows is a *summary* row, which is often a subtotaling function, such as the subtotal rows in Figure 13.12.

Navigating through an Outline

Figure 13.13 shows the same worksheet from Figure 13.12, but this time with only the summary rows displayed—the detail rows are hidden.

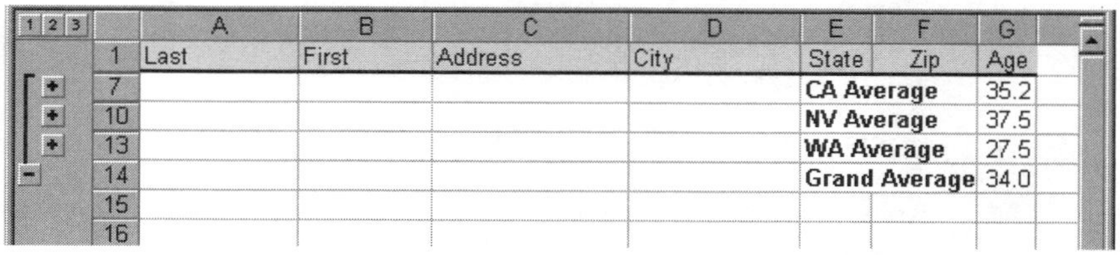

1 2 3
A B C D E F G
1 Last First Address City State Zip Age
7 CA Average 35.2
10 NV Average 37.5
13 WA Average 27.5
14 Grand Average 34.0
15
16

FIGURE 13.13: You can collapse an outline to hide its details.

The outline controls at the left of the worksheet serve both to indicate outline levels and to let you collapse or expand the levels. You can also use the commands on the Data ➤ Group and Outline submenu.

You can turn on or off the display of the outline controls without affecting the structure of the outline. Follow these steps:

1. Choose Tools ➤ Options to open the Options dialog box.
2. Click the View menu.
3. Click the Outline Symbols option.
4. Click OK.

Even with the controls hidden, you can manipulate the outline with the commands on the Data ➤ Group and Outline submenu.

Expanding or Collapsing a Level

To expand (show detail) or collapse (hide detail) one group in the outline, click the + or – button for that group. Or click anywhere on the bar that extends from the – button along its group. To select all the cells in a group, hold down Shift and click that group's + or – button.

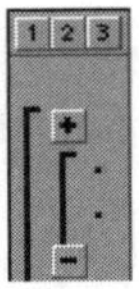

You can also select any cell in the outline and choose either Hide Detail or Show Detail from the Data ➤ Group and Outline submenu. Of course, Show Detail will only work if there is a subordinate level to show.

By using these buttons, you can expand or collapse individual groups within the outline, but you can also expand or collapse all groups within a level.

Expanding or Collapsing All Levels

To expand or collapse all groups at and below a specific level, click the appropriate number button above the outline symbols.

Figure 13.13 shows three number buttons, one for each level in the outline:

Level 3 The lowest, most subordinate level consists of the detail rows in each group. The rows within that group have the same entry in the State column.

Level 2 The subtotals level, which summarizes each group of detail rows.

Level 1 The grand total level, which summarizes all the groups.

In Figure 13.13, you can see the effects of clicking the level 2 button. The grand total and subtotals rows are displayed, but the detail rows (level 3) are hidden. Clicking the level 1 button hides the level 2 summary rows as well, leaving only the grand total (average) row displayed.

Creating an Outline

You can create an outline in several ways. The best and the easiest is to choose Data ➤ Subtotals, as described earlier in this skill, which inserts subtotals for the groups you specify and builds the outline automatically.

NOTE NOTE NOTE NOTE NOTE NOTE NOTE NOTE NOTE NOTE NOTE NOTE NOTE NOTE NOTE

To remove an outline from the worksheet, select any cell within the outline and choose Data ➤ Group and Outline ➤ Clear Outline. The outline will be removed, but the data will not be affected.

If your data already has formula (summary) rows whose formulas reference the cells directly above or below them, you can let Excel create an outline for you. For example, you might have SUM formulas that total the values in the rows above them. Simply select all the relevant rows, and choose Data ➤ Group and Outline ➤ Auto Outline.

If your data is not structured for an automatic outline, you can create an outline completely "by hand." Simply select the rows (or columns) you want within a group of the outline, and choose Data ➤ Group and Outline ➤ Group. There should be at least one row (or column) between each group, which will serve as the summary row for the group above or below it (or to the left or right for columns).

Enhancing an Outline

You can change the formatting of any cells in an outline, but keep in mind that all the groups in each level of an outline represent the same type of data and should therefore have a consistent look. Instead of trying to apply this consistent look yourself, you can let Excel do it automatically via styles (specifically for outlines) or the AutoFormat feature (both were discussed in Skill 6).

Applying Styles to an Outline Automatically

To apply a style to each summary row, follow these steps:

1. Select all the rows in the outline.
2. Choose Data ➤ Group and Outline ➤ Settings to open the Settings dialog box.

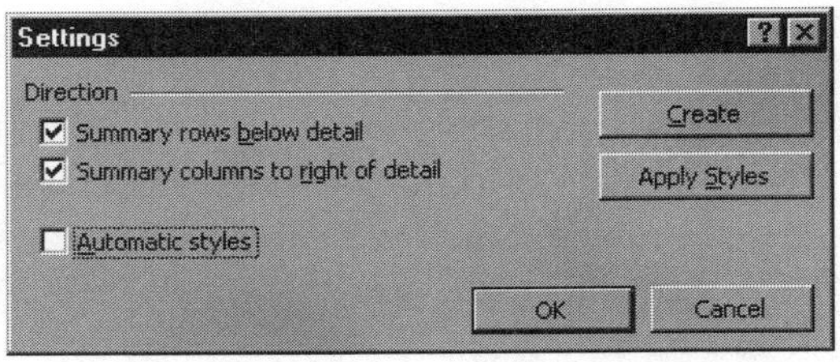

3. Click Apply Styles to apply a special outline style to each summary row in the outline. For example, the first level gets the style named RowLevel_1, and the second level style is named RowLevel_2.

4. Click OK.

To apply these styles automatically when you next create an outline on the current worksheet, click the Automatic Styles check box.

Once applied, these styles behave like any other styles. You can remove them from a row or apply a different style. You can also modify the definitions to apply a new look to each summary row that uses that style.

Using AutoFormat on an Outline

The AutoFormat feature is a great way to enhance an entire range, and you can also use it for outlines. (AutoFormat was discussed in Skill 6.) To use AutoFormat, follow these steps:

1. Select all the cells of the outline.
2. Choose Format ➤ AutoFormat to open the AutoFormat dialog box.
3. Select one of the formats from the Table Format list.
4. Click OK.

The outline is formatted so that the summary rows for each level look the same.

Figure 13.14 shows the outlined name and address list after enhancing it with AutoFormat. As you can see, AutoFormat figured out the outline structure and formatted it accordingly.

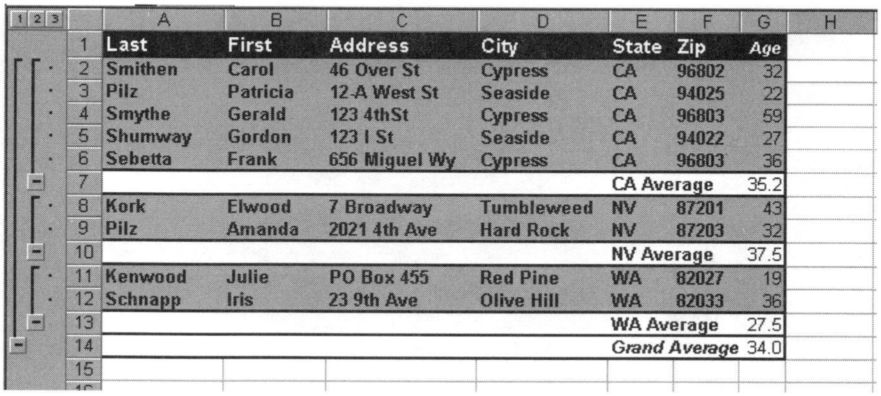

	A	B	C	D	E	F	G	H
1	Last	First	Address	City	State	Zip	Age	
2	Smithen	Carol	46 Over St	Cypress	CA	96802	32	
3	Pilz	Patricia	12-A West St	Seaside	CA	94025	22	
4	Smythe	Gerald	123 4thSt	Cypress	CA	96803	59	
5	Shumway	Gordon	123 I St	Seaside	CA	94022	27	
6	Sebetta	Frank	656 Miguel Wy	Cypress	CA	96803	36	
7					CA Average		35.2	
8	Kork	Elwood	7 Broadway	Tumbleweed	NV	87201	43	
9	Pilz	Amanda	2021 4th Ave	Hard Rock	NV	87203	32	
10					NV Average		37.5	
11	Kenwood	Julie	PO Box 455	Red Pine	WA	82027	19	
12	Schnapp	Iris	23 9th Ave	Olive Hill	WA	82033	36	
13					WA Average		27.5	
14					*Grand Average*		34.0	
15								

FIGURE 13.14: You can use AutoFormat to enhance the detail and summary rows of an outline.

Creating Instant Reports with PivotTables

So far in this skill you've tried a variety of tools for organizing and summarizing your data using:

- Sorting to arrange rows or columns in alphabetic or numeric order.
- AutoFilter to display only the rows that match the criteria you specify.
- Subtotals to quickly create subtotaling functions for each group.
- Outlining to assign the groups in a range to levels in the outline and to collapse or expand the outline to hide or show more detail.

Now we'll look at Excel's PivotTable, yet one more tool for organizing and summarizing data. It actually combines a number of the features found in these other tools. A PivotTable is an interactive table that summarizes your data so that you can organize and analyze it many ways.

Figure 13.15 shows a PivotTable that was created from the data I've been using throughout this skill (worksheet gridlines were turned off so the PivotTable's border would stand out). I'll build this PivotTable in the sections that follow.

	A	B	C	D	E	F
1			Age			
2	State	City	Count	Average	Youngest	Oldest
3	CA	Cypress	3	42.3	32	59
4		Seaside	2	24.5	22	27
5	CA Total		5	35.2	22	59
6	NV	Hard Rock	1	32.0	32	32
7		Tumbleweed	1	43.0	43	43
8	NV Total		2	37.5	32	43
9	WA	Olive Hill	1	36.0	36	36
10		Red Pine	1	19.0	19	19
11	WA Total		2	27.5	19	36
12	Grand Total		9	34.0	19	59

FIGURE 13.15: The finished PivotTable summarizes the data in the name and address list.

NOTE NOTE NOTE NOTE NOTE NOTE NOTE NOTE NOTE NOTE NOTE NOTE NOTE NOTE NOTE

Granted, this is some wimpy data for putting the PivotTable to the test. Nonetheless, the data is easy for you to create, so you can follow along if you want, and it's easy to verify how the PivotTable arrived at its results.

Building a PivotTable

I'll build the PivotTable from the name and address list in Figure 13.1. If you want to follow along and have been using this example, choose Data ➤ Subtotals to open the Subtotal dialog box, and then click Remove All to eliminate any subtotals or outlining in the list.

Specifying the Source Data

The first step in building a PivotTable is to determine what data you want to use. The source data requirements for a PivotTable are similar to those for the other list-related tools that I have covered in this skill, as discussed in the "When Data Become a List" section. Here are the steps:

1. Select a cell anywhere within the source range (the list) for the PivotTable.
2. Choose Data ➤ PivotTable and PivotChart Report to start the PivotTable and PivotChart Wizard.

3. Choose the type of data you want for the PivotTable in the Step 1 dialog box. For the example, choose Microsoft Excel List or Database, click the PivotTable option, and then click Next.

4. In the Step 2 dialog box, verify that the range the Wizard selected is correct—A1:G10 for our sample data. Then click Layout.

Remember, in a Wizard you can click the Back button to go back one step.

Placing the Rows, Columns, and Data

The PivotTable and PivotChart Wizard - Layout dialog box is shown in Figure 13.16. This is where you design the PivotTable.

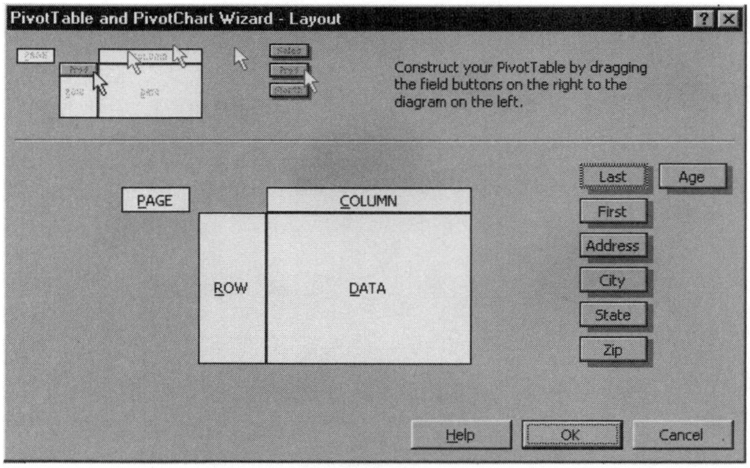

FIGURE 13.16: The PivotTable and PivotChart Wizard - Layout dialog box, where you design the PivotTable by dragging field buttons into the PivotTable model

A labeled button represents each column (field) title in the list. You simply drag a button onto the PivotTable model in the dialog box to add that column to the PivotTable. The model has four areas:

Row The chosen field name appears as a row label in the finished PivotTable.

Column The chosen field name appears as a column label in the PivotTable.

Data The data within the chosen field is summarized in one column of the PivotTable. Like the Subtotals feature, you can choose the type of calculation that is performed.

Page The chosen field is assigned to a separate drop-down list above the finished PivotTable. When you choose one of the data items from that list, the PivotTable updates its values using the data associated with that item.

To add columns to the PivotTable, follow these steps:

1. Drag the State button to the Row area on the left side of the model.
2. Drag the Age button to the Data area.

By default, Excel sums the values in the data field, as evidenced by the *Sum of Age* text on the button. In many cases, summing the data will be relevant, but not for the ages in this case.

Modifying a PivotTable Field

Instead of summing the ages, we want to count them. Follow these steps:

1. Double-click the Age button that you just placed within the model to open the PivotTable Field dialog box.

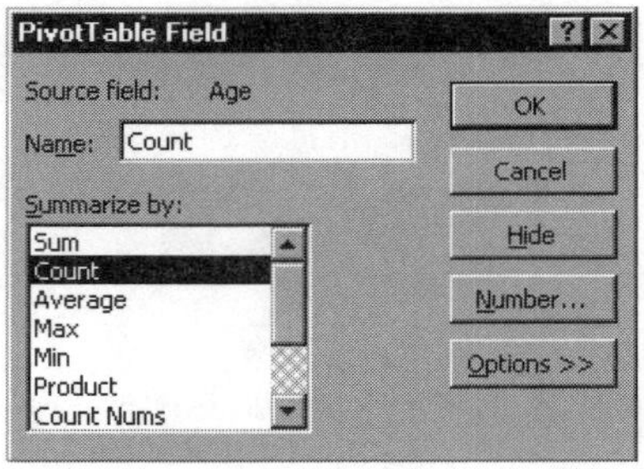

2. Select Count in the Summarize By list to count all the ages in each state.
3. Shorten the title that appears in the Name field to **Count** and then click OK. Now this button is simply called Count, which is how it will appear within the finished PivotTable.

Adding More Data

I also want to average the ages and find the smallest (youngest) and largest (oldest) ages in each state. Here are the steps:

1. Drag the Age button into the Data area of the model three more times (so that there are four buttons in the Data area).
2. Double-click the first button below the Count button.
3. In the PivotTable Field dialog box, choose Max, enter **Oldest** in the Name field, and then click OK.
4. Double-click the button beneath the Oldest button.
5. In the PivotTable Field dialog box, choose Min, enter **Youngest** in the Name field, and click OK.
6. Double-click the last button in the PivotTable model.
7. In the PivotTable Field dialog box, choose Average, and shorten the entry in the Name field to **Average**.

Don't click OK yet; we're not quite done with this one (if you did click OK, just double-click the Average button again).

Applying a Numeric Format

Because the averages won't be whole numbers, we specify a numeric format for this field that has a fixed number of decimal places. Here are the steps:

1. Click the Number button in the PivotTable Field dialog box.
2. Select the Number format, and set its Decimal Places option to 1.
3. Click OK.

The PivotTable model in the PivotTable and PivotChart Wizard - Layout dialog box should now look like the one shown in Figure 13.17.

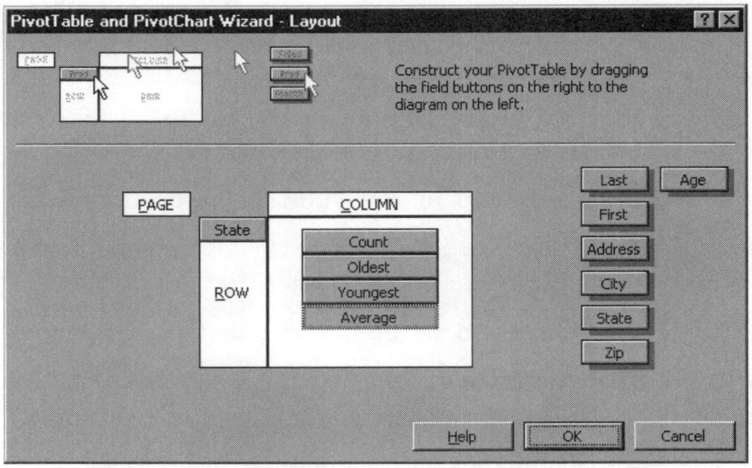

FIGURE 13.17: The PivotTable model after adding four fields to the Data area

Finishing the PivotTable

We've finished designing the PivotTable—although like most things we do on the computer, we can easily modify the finished PivotTable later. Let's wrap up.

1. Click OK to return to the Step 3 PivotTable and PivotChart Wizard dialog box, shown in Figure 13.18, in which you specify where the PivotTable should be created.

FIGURE 13.18: The Step 3 PivotTable and PivotChart Wizard dialog box

2. Choose the Existing Worksheet option and enter **Sheet2!A1** as the address at which to create the PivotTable. (If you choose New Worksheet, the PivotTable is placed on a new inserted worksheet.) You can also choose the Options button and select from a variety of PivotTable options. You might experiment with them after finishing this example.

3. We're through, so choose Finish, and then save the workbook as PivotTable.

Excel creates the PivotTable on Sheet2, as shown in Figure 13.19. Also shown in that figure is the PivotTable toolbar, which you'll find to be a great convenience when you're manipulating a PivotTable.

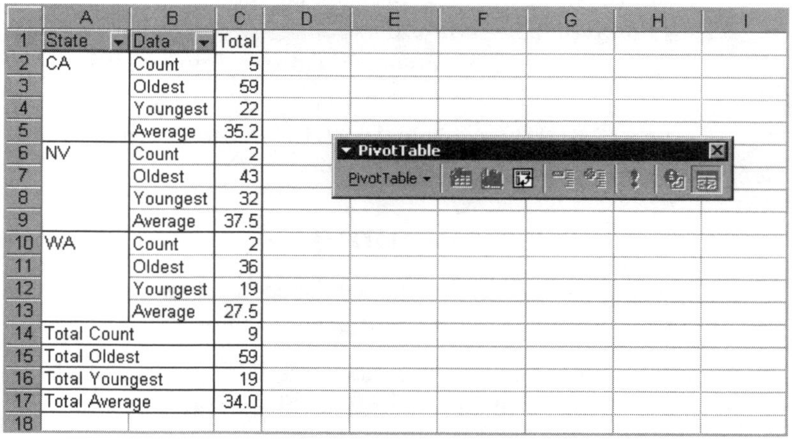

	A	B	C
1	State	Data	Total
2	CA	Count	5
3		Oldest	59
4		Youngest	22
5		Average	35.2
6	NV	Count	2
7		Oldest	43
8		Youngest	32
9		Average	37.5
10	WA	Count	2
11		Oldest	36
12		Youngest	19
13		Average	27.5
14	Total Count		9
15	Total Oldest		59
16	Total Youngest		19
17	Total Average		34.0
18			

FIGURE 13.19: The finished PivotTable was created on its own worksheet.

Here's what the PivotTable summarizes:

- Each unique entry in the source data's State column appears as a row in the column labeled State in the PivotTable. The entries in that column are sorted alphabetically.

WARNING WARNING WARNING WARNING WARNING WARNING WARNING WARNING

If there are far more entries than you expected in your PivotTable, such as in the State column, very likely those entries were inconsistent in the source data. For example, since Excel reads CA, Calif, and Cal as three unique entries, it would place all three items in the PivotTable.

- In the Data column, the names of the four calculations we specified are listed for each state.
- In the Total column, the calculations are performed on the data in the Age column in the source data.
- By default, totals have been added to summarize each of the four calculations (one of the options in the Step 3 dialog box).
- By default, the PivotTable has been formatted with the AutoFormat feature so that there are borders around the appropriate cells.

Imagine how useful this PivotTable would be if the source data had contained hundreds or thousands of rows. Now let's see how easy it is to manipulate a finished PivotTable so it will look like the one in Figure 13.15.

You can redefine a PivotTable at any time by selecting a cell within it and choosing Data ➤ PivotTable Report, which opens the PivotTable and PivotChartWizard's Step 3 dialog box. You can also click the PivotTable Wizard button on the PivotTable toolbar.

Pivoting Rows or Columns

Let's revise the PivotTable so that each calculation appears as a separate column next to the states, as shown earlier in Figure 13.19.

1. Point to cell B1, the shaded cell that looks like a button. It's labeled Data and is the PivotTable control for the second column.
2. Drag the control to the right over the Total column. An icon near the pointer indicates the orientation this field will take if you release the mouse button. The icon switches from a multiple-row orientation to a multiple-column orientation.
3. Release the mouse button, and the task is done.

The Total column title is replaced by the four calculated columns, as shown in Figure 13.20.

TIP TIP TIP TIP TIP TIP TIP TIP TIP TIP TIP TIP TIP TIP TIP TIP TIP TIP TIP TIP TIP TIP TIP TIP TIP

The Figure 13.20 example shows how the PivotTable got its name—you can pivot a row or column button to change the orientation of the PivotTable, and all calculations are refreshed accordingly.

	A	B	C	D	E	F	G	H	I	J
1		Data								
2	State	Count	Oldest	Youngest	Average					
3	CA	5	59	22	35.2					
4	NV	2	43	32	37.5					
5	WA	2	36	19	27.5					
6	Grand Total	9	59	19	34.0					
7										
8										

FIGURE 13.20: The PivotTable after pivoting a group of rows to columns

You can change a field in the PivotTable with the PivotTable Field dialog box, which was discussed earlier in the "Building a PivotTable" section. To open the PivotTable Field dialog box, select a cell within the field and choose Field Settings from the menu on the PivotTable toolbar. You can also click the Field Settings button on the PivotTable toolbar or right-click a cell and choose Field Settings from the shortcut menu.

Adding a New Element

You can add or remove a field at any time. Let's add the City column from the source data in our example so that it appears next to the State column in the PivotTable. Here are the steps:

1. Select a cell anywhere in the PivotTable and either choose Data ➤ PivotTable Report and PivotChart Report, or click the PivotTable Wizard button on the PivotTable toolbar to open the Step 3 dialog box.
2. Click Layout to open the PivotTable and PivotChart Wizard – Layout dialog box.
3. Drag the City button to the Row area on the left side of the PivotTable, and place it beneath the State button that's already there.
4. Click OK.
5. Click the Finish button.

Excel adds the City column to the PivotTable, as shown in Figure 13.21. It looks very much like the model in Figure 13.15.

	A	B	C	D	E	F
1			Data			
2	State	City	Count	Oldest	Youngest	Average
3	CA	Cypress	3	59	32	42.3
4		Seaside	2	27	22	24.5
5	CA Total		5	59	22	35.2
6	NV	Hard Rock	1	32	32	32.0
7		Tumbleweed	1	43	43	43.0
8	NV Total		2	43	32	37.5
9	WA	Olive Hill	1	36	36	36.0
10		Red Pine	1	19	19	19.0
11	WA Total		2	36	19	27.5
12	Grand Total		9	59	19	34.0
13						

Sheet1 Sheet2 Sheet3

FIGURE 13.21: The PivotTable after adding the City field from the source data

TIP TIP TIP TIP TIP TIP TIP TIP TIP TIP TIP TIP TIP TIP TIP TIP TIP TIP TIP TIP TIP TIP TIP TIP TIP

You can expand and collapse the data elements in a PivotTable in much the same way that you can expand and collapse an outline. For example, think of the State entries as being one level of the outline and of the City entries as a second level. Double-click a state entry, such as CA, to hide its city entries. Double-click again to display the detail. You can also use the Hide Detail and Show Detail commands on the Data ➤ Group and Outline submenu or the buttons on the PivotTable toolbar.

Changing the Column Order

The four calculation columns in Figure 13.21 aren't in the same order as those shown in Figure 13.15. Here's how to change them:

1. Right-click a cell within the PivotTable and choose Wizard from the shortcut menu to open the Step 3 dialog box.
2. Click Layout to open the PivotTable and PivotChart Wizard - Layout dialog box.
3. Rearrange the four buttons displayed in the Column area. Drag the Average field button from the bottom of the four up to second from the top.

4. Drag the Youngest button so it is above Oldest. The PivotTable model in the dialog box now looks like the one shown here.

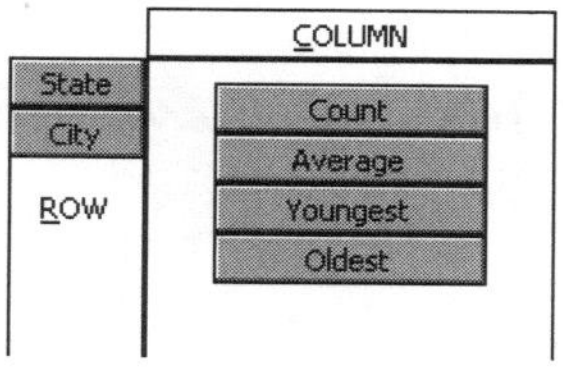

5. Drag the City button to the Row area, below the State button.
6. Click OK, and then choose Finish to complete the changes and return to the worksheet. The four calculation columns are now rearranged in the PivotTable.

Formatting a PivotTable

You can enhance a PivotTable much as you would any range in the worksheet. Instead of changing the format of individual cells, however, it's easier to let AutoFormat do the job for you.

TIP TIP TIP TIP TIP TIP TIP TIP TIP TIP TIP TIP TIP TIP TIP TIP TIP TIP TIP TIP TIP TIP TIP TIP TIP TIP

By default, Excel applies an AutoFormat to the PivotTable when you create it. But you can change the formatting afterward to any style that suits you.

Simply select a cell within the PivotTable and choose Format ➤ AutoFormat to open the AutoFormat dialog box. Choose one of the format names, and proceed as described in Skill 6.

AutoFormat knows the structure of a PivotTable, just as it understands outlines and subtotals. AutoFormat applies the chosen format to emphasize the groups and subtotals within the PivotTable.

You can change the title in a PivotTable control by selecting the control and typing the new label for it (or edit its label in the Formula bar).

NOTE NOTE NOTE NOTE NOTE NOTE NOTE NOTE NOTE NOTE NOTE NOTE NOTE NOTE NOTE

This is as far as we go with the topic of PivotTables. It's a powerful tool for summarizing and analyzing large amounts of data, and its complexity quickly surpasses the scope of this book. If you have data to analyze, though, you should spend more time experimenting with PivotTables.

Are You Experienced?

Now you can...

- ☑ Sort a list
- ☑ Sort the rows or columns in a range
- ☑ Work on a list through a form
- ☑ Validate cell entries
- ☑ Filter the data in a list
- ☑ Perform an advanced list query
- ☑ Create subtotals in a list
- ☑ Structure a list as an outline
- ☑ Build a PivotTable
- ☑ Modify a PivotTable

SKILL 14

Changing the Look of Excel

- Setting defaults for Excel
- Creating new windows
- Arranging windows
- Hiding windows
- Splitting the window into panes
- Freezing panes
- Changing the screen magnification
- Saving custom views of the workbook
- Customizing toolbars
- Creating new toolbars

This skill covers some of the issues that affect the look and feel of Excel. You'll learn how to modify the program and its behavior so that Excel suits your own work habits.

Setting Defaults

In the Options dialog box (choose Tools ➤ Options) are a variety of settings that control the way Excel looks and works. You learned about many of them in the earlier skills in this book. In general, if you want to adjust an aspect of Excel, open the Options dialog box, shown here.

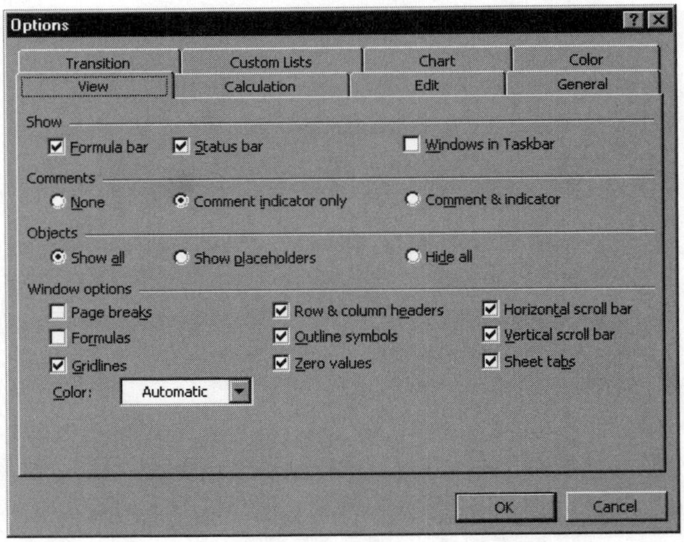

As a reminder, here's a list of what you can do with each tab:

View Change the look of Excel. Choose to display or hide the Formula bar, status bar, gridlines, scroll bars, sheet tabs, formulas, and graphic objects.

Calculation Specify how Excel calculates formulas.

Edit Set the options for the way you work in cells. Choose to enable or disable in-cell editing and drag-and-drop cell operations, and specify whether the cell selector moves when you press Enter.

Transition Set the default file save format and set defaults for operations that may be confusing to users of Lotus 1-2-3. Choose to have the forward slash key (/) activate Excel's menu bar and specify how to handle formulas with range names. This tab is important to users of other spreadsheet programs and those working in an environment of mixed versions of Excel.

General Alter several program options; choose the defaults for the font and font size, file folder, and user name.

Custom Lists View, create, or modify custom lists.

Chart Specify how empty cells are plotted in the active chart and whether ScreenTips are displayed for chart components.

Color Change the color palette that Excel uses, for example, when you change the fill color for a cell or the markers in a chart.

Remember that the changes you make to most of these settings apply only to the active workbook. The next time you open that workbook, the changes you made in the Options dialog box will still be in effect.

TIP TIP TIP TIP TIP TIP TIP TIP TIP TIP TIP TIP TIP TIP TIP TIP TIP TIP TIP TIP TIP TIP TIP TIP TIP

If you want to make changes that will affect all new workbooks, create a workbook template, as described in Skill 7.

Arranging Windows on the Screen

Excel has all the windowing features that you expect of a well-written Windows application. It also has some features that are specific to its worksheet-and-cell personality.

Here's a quick refresher on working with windows in Excel (and most other Windows programs):

- To switch between windows, click within another window, choose a window name from Excel's Window menu, or press Ctrl+F6.
- To make a window full size, click the Maximize button, choose Maximize from the Control menu, or double-click the window's title bar.
- To return a window to its previous size and location on the screen, click the Restore button, choose Restore from the Control menu, or double-click the window's title bar.

- To move a window, drag it by its title bar or choose Move from the Control menu.
- To resize a window, drag any of its borders or corners with the mouse. To cancel resizing, press Esc. You can also choose Size from a window's Control menu.

Creating a New Window

When you choose File ➤ New to create a new workbook, by default a single window opens to display the worksheet. But you can open multiple windows on the same workbook by choosing Window ➤ New Window.

NOTE

In a worksheet that contains 65,536 rows and 256 columns, a typical window displays only about nine-millionths of that one worksheet. That's about the same as viewing the Queen Elizabeth ocean liner through one of her portholes!

Each window can have a different view of the workbook, as well. For example, if you have two windows open for one workbook, you can turn off the display of gridlines and change the screen magnification in one window but not in the other.

You can move or size any of the windows to suit your needs, and you can change the workbook in any window. For example, when you want to move or copy a range or graphic object to another part of the workbook, you can first display the source in one window and the destination in another. Then it's easy to perform the operation between the two locations.

When you open a new window for a workbook, Excel gives it the same name as the original window, with the addition of a numeric suffix after a colon. If the workbook is named Housing, for example, the first new window you open for it is named Housing:2, and the original window is named Housing:1.

You can close a window at any time by clicking the Close button in its title bar or by choosing Close from the window's Control menu. Closing a window does not affect any other windows that may be open on the workbook. However, if the window you close is the only one open on the workbook, you will be closing the file, as though you were choosing File ➤ Close.

Arranging Windows

When you have multiple windows open in Excel, you'll quickly run out of screen real estate for displaying them. But you can change the size or move individual windows as needed, and you can also rearrange all open windows at one time by choosing Window ➤ Arrange to open the Arrange Windows dialog box.

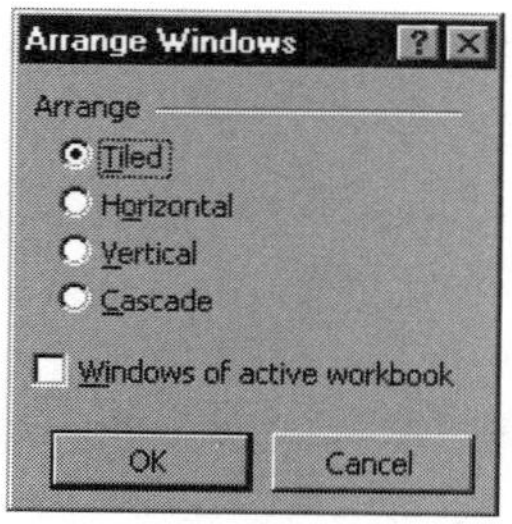

Figure 14.1 illustrates the window layouts you can choose from the Arrange Windows dialog box.

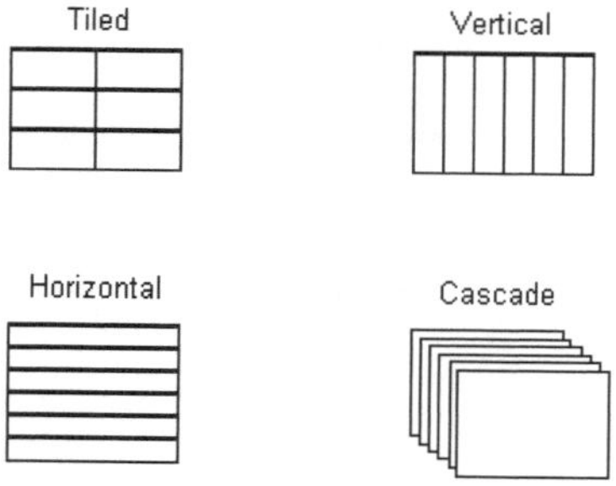

FIGURE 14.1: You can arrange the open windows in Excel in four ways with the choices in the Arrange Windows dialog box.

Hiding Windows

You can hide a window without actually closing it by choosing Window ➤ Hide, as you learned in Skill 9. Doing so can free up some acreage on your screen, while still allowing you to access the hidden window with formulas or commands.

NOTE

To display a hidden window, choose Window ➤ Unhide, select the hidden window from the list of all hidden windows, and then choose OK. Hiding portions of a workbook was discussed in Skill 6.

Splitting the Window into Panes

Another way to view different parts of a workbook is to split one window into two or four panes. You can do so with your mouse or by choosing Window ➤ Split.

Splitting the Window with Your Mouse

To split the window into two panes with your mouse, drag one of the two split boxes into the worksheet.

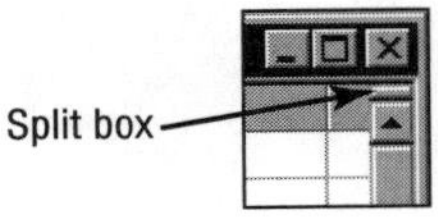

To split the window horizontally, follow these steps:

1. Point to the split box above the vertical scroll bar; the mouse pointer changes to a double-headed vertical arrow.

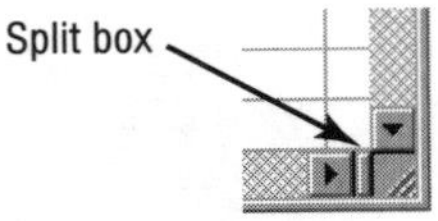

2. Drag the split box down and into the worksheet.
3. Release the mouse button when it is positioned where you want it.

To split the window vertically, drag the split box at the right of the horizontal scroll bar to the left and into the worksheet; then release the mouse button.

NOTE NOTE NOTE NOTE NOTE NOTE NOTE NOTE NOTE NOTE NOTE NOTE NOTE NOTE NOTE

Don't confuse the vertical pane splitter with the tab split box, which is to the left of the horizontal scroll bar.

Moving between Panes

Once you've split the window into panes, you can move between the panes simply by clicking in a pane with your mouse. You can also press F6 to select a cell in the next pane (Shift+F6 goes in the opposite direction).

When you scroll through the worksheet in one pane, the worksheet in the opposite pane scrolls along with it. For example, the worksheet in Figure 14.2 has been split horizontally, and the two panes always display the same columns.

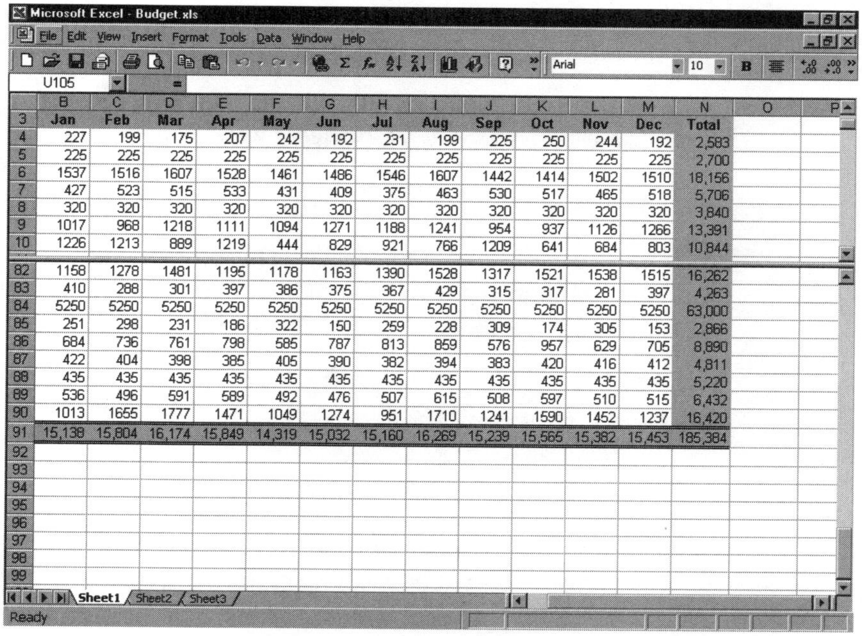

Microsoft Excel - Budget.xls
File Edit View Insert Format Tools Data Window Help
Arial
10
U105
B C D E F G H I J K L M N O P
3 Jan Feb Mar Apr May Jun Jul Aug Sep Oct Nov Dec Total
4 227 199 175 207 242 192 231 199 225 250 244 192 2,583
5 225 225 225 225 225 225 225 225 225 225 225 225 2,700
6 1537 1516 1607 1528 1461 1486 1546 1607 1442 1414 1502 1510 18,156
7 427 523 515 533 431 409 375 463 530 517 465 518 5,706
8 320 320 320 320 320 320 320 320 320 320 320 320 3,840
9 1017 968 1218 1111 1094 1271 1188 1241 954 937 1126 1266 13,391
10 1226 1213 889 1219 444 829 921 766 1209 641 684 803 10,844
82 1158 1278 1481 1195 1178 1163 1390 1528 1317 1521 1538 1515 16,262
83 410 288 301 397 386 375 367 429 315 317 281 397 4,263
84 5250 5250 5250 5250 5250 5250 5250 5250 5250 5250 5250 5250 63,000
85 251 298 231 186 322 150 259 228 309 174 305 153 2,866
86 684 736 761 798 585 787 813 859 576 957 629 705 8,890
87 422 404 398 385 405 390 382 394 383 420 416 412 4,811
88 435 435 435 435 435 435 435 435 435 435 435 435 5,220
89 536 496 591 589 492 476 507 615 508 597 510 515 6,432
90 1013 1655 1777 1471 1049 1274 951 1710 1241 1590 1452 1237 16,420
91 15,138 15,804 16,174 15,849 14,319 15,032 15,160 16,269 15,239 15,565 15,382 15,453 185,384
92
93
94
95
96
97
98
99
Sheet1 Sheet2 Sheet3
Ready

FIGURE 14.2: When you split the window into horizontal panes, both panes always display the same columns.

Scrolling up or down in one horizontal pane does not affect the other, however, so you can work in two distant places in the same column. In fact, you can see in Figure 14.2 that each pane has its own vertical scroll bar. When you split the window vertically, each pane always displays the same rows.

Adjusting and Removing Panes

You can adjust the position of a pane by dragging the split with your mouse. Again, watch for the mouse pointer to change to a double-headed arrow when you point to a split.

The portion of the split that you drag determines whether the split will align with a worksheet gridline. For example, to reposition a horizontal split:

- Drag a split at a point that is over the worksheet cells to align the split with the nearest row.
- Drag at a point that is over the scroll bar or the row headings to drag the split to any position.

You can double-click a split to remove it and the panes it creates. You can also remove all splits from the worksheet by choosing Window ➤ Remove Split.

Splitting the Window with the Split Command

You may often want to split the worksheet into panes at a specific row or column. You could do so with your mouse, but it may be easier to use the Split command. Follow these steps:

1. Select a cell that is in the row below or the column to the right of where you want the split.
2. Choose Window ➤ Split.

If there is both a row above and a column to the left of the selected cell, you will create a four-pane split. Otherwise, selecting a cell at the edge of the worksheet creates a two-pane split. For example, selecting cell A6 and choosing Window ➤ Split creates a two-pane horizontal split between rows 5 and 6.

Freezing Panes

You can split the window into two or four panes in a different way by *freezing* the top or left-side pane. Freezing allows you to view column titles, for example, while working many rows below them.

To create frozen panes, follow these steps:

1. Select a cell that is in the row below or the column to the right of where you want the split.
2. Choose Window ➤ Freeze.

For example, Figure 14.3 shows a worksheet that has both column titles (row 3) and row titles (column A) as well as many rows and columns of data. To freeze both the row and column titles, select cell B4 and choose Window ➤ Freeze Panes. You can scroll anywhere in the worksheet, and the column and row titles in the frozen panes will still be displayed.

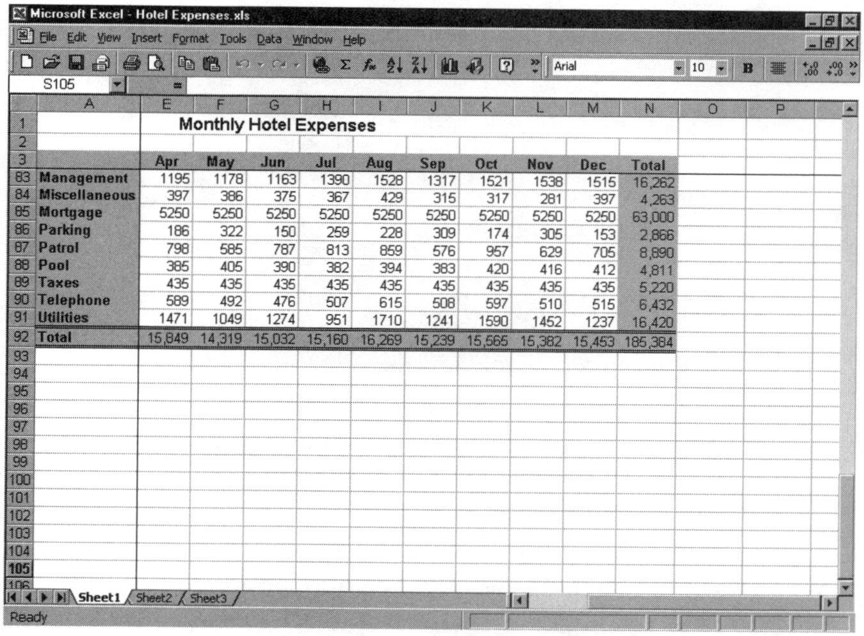

FIGURE 14.3: Freezing the panes at cell B4 in this worksheet allows you to view the column and row titles while you work in the rows below or the columns to the right.

Changing the Screen Magnification

You can easily change the magnification of the current sheet. For example, when you are working with small fonts, you can zoom in on the screen to make it more readable, but also show fewer cells.

More likely, you will want to zoom out on the screen to show more rows and columns, so you can see the rolling landscape and wide vistas of your work (even if you have to squint to see what's in the cells!). To see more of the worksheet without changing the magnification, choose View ➤ Full Screen.

To change the screen magnification for the active sheet, choose View ➤ Zoom to open the Zoom dialog box:

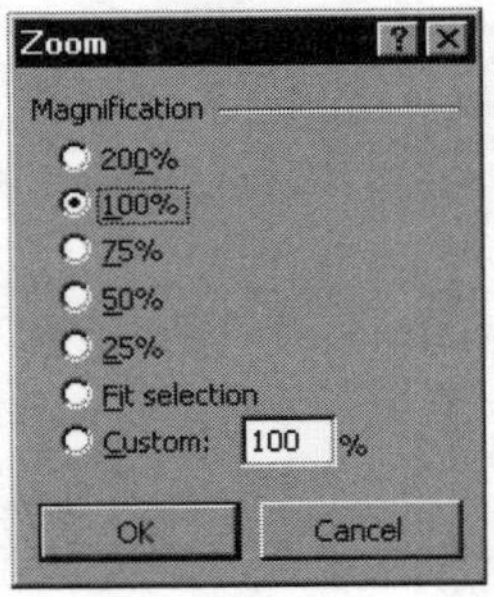

You can set the magnification in three ways:

Percent Select one of the percentages, either to increase magnification (200%) so that fonts look bigger or to decrease magnification (25%, 50%, or 75%) so that more cells are displayed. The 100% option, the default, shows your work at its actual size.

Fit Selection The magnification factor is set automatically so that the selected range of cells or the current chart sheet fits the window size.

Custom Specify a percentage for screen magnification, from 10 to 400 percent.

You can also use the Zoom control on the toolbar to set the magnification for the current sheet. From its drop-down list, select a percentage, such as 75% or 200%, or choose Selection to adjust the magnification to the selected range or chart. You can also simply type a percentage in the Zoom control.

Using a Mouse with a Wheel to Zoom

If you are using a mouse with a wheel, such as Microsoft's IntelliMouse, you can change the zoom factor simply by holding down Ctrl and rolling the wheel—backward to decrease magnification, and forward to increase it.

If you want the wheel to change the screen magnification by default (without your holding down Ctrl), follow these steps:

1. Choose Tools ➤ Options to open the Options dialog box.
2. Click the General tab.
3. Click the Zoom on Roll with IntelliMouse check box.
4. Click OK.

NOTE

Shrinking a worksheet's magnification to 10 or 20 percent is a great way to find out what's in that worksheet. You'll see about 100 columns and 140 rows of pinhead-sized cells. But you should be able to pick out cells that are occupied and any cells that have borders or are shaded.

Don't worry about the sheet's magnification when you want to print it. In this case, what you see on the screen has no effect on the printout. If you want to increase or decrease the magnification of the printout, do so with the Scale options, which you'll find on the Page tab in the Page Setup dialog box, as you learned in Skill 8.

Working with Custom Views

It's great to be able to change the look of your workbook in so many ways. It's even greater that you can save the current look as a *custom view*, which is simply a way to save many of the current workbook settings under a name. You can save multiple views of the same workbook and return to any one of those views at any time.

Here are some of the settings that are saved when you create a custom view:

- Screen magnification
- Page break preview

- Most of the options on the View tab in the Options dialog box, such as the display of gridlines, scrollbars, and the Formula bar
- Hidden rows, columns, and worksheets
- The current print settings, making custom views a great way to handle multiple print jobs in the same workbook
- AutoFilter settings

Keep in mind that saving a custom view is like taking a snapshot of these settings for the entire workbook, not just of the active worksheet. For example, the screen magnification of every worksheet is saved when you create a new custom view. When you later show that view, each worksheet displays in the magnification that was in effect when you created the view.

To create a custom view, follow these steps:

1. Create the workbook look you want.
2. Choose View ➤ Custom Views to open the Custom Views dialog box.

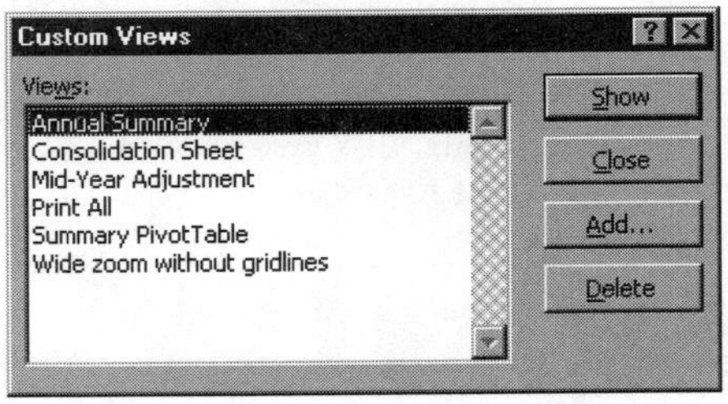

3. Click Add to open the Add View dialog box.

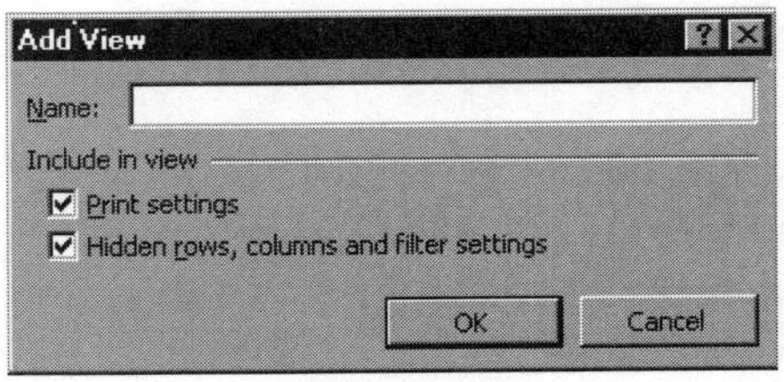

4. In the Name field, enter a name for your view.
5. Clear the Print Settings check box if you don't want to save those features.

6. Clear the *Hidden rows, columns and filter settings* check box if you don't want to save those features.

7. Click OK.

In the Custom Views dialog box, click Show to display the current workbook with the settings saved under the selected custom view. To remove a custom view, select it in the list, and click Delete.

NOTE NOTE NOTE NOTE NOTE NOTE NOTE NOTE NOTE NOTE NOTE NOTE NOTE NOTE NOTE

You can never damage your work by adding or deleting a custom view. However, you could be in for a surprise when you select a view in the Custom Views dialog box and choose Show. Every worksheet will return to the way it looked when you created that view, including the print settings and the state of all filtered lists. You won't lose any data, but your workbook may look quite different under the new view. To return to Normal view, choose View ➤ Normal.

Custom views are much like scenarios (which you learned about in Skill 9), in that they save certain aspects of the current state of the workbook. As you learn how to take advantage of both these features, you'll be able to combine them to take control of the workbook's data and appearance.

For example, you can recall a named scenario to return to the data in that scenario's changing cells. You can also recall a named custom view to set the look of the worksheet for that scenario, perhaps making it ready to print.

Customizing Toolbars

Throughout this book, I've mentioned the various toolbars in Excel. Their buttons and controls often serve as shortcuts for commands on Excel's menus. In other cases, such as with the Drawing toolbar, the buttons are the only means for accessing some features.

In Skill 1, you learned how to hide or display Excel's toolbars and how to add and remove buttons from the Standard and Formatting toolbars. But you're not limited to using only those toolbars; you can create your own, and you can adjust the controls on any toolbar.

Adjusting the Controls on a Toolbar

You can change the appearance of the buttons (and other controls) on a toolbar in several ways. Before you can do so, though, you *must* do the following:

1. Display the toolbar you want to work with.
2. Choose Tools ➤ Customize to open the Customize dialog box.

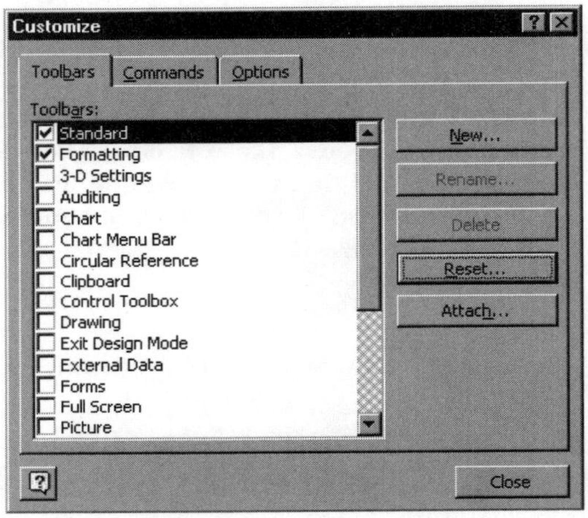

Now you can make the following changes:

- Place a button anywhere you want on a toolbar by dragging it to a new position.
- Adjust the width of a drop-down list by selecting it and dragging one of its edges to the right or to the left.
- Insert a vertical line between groups of buttons by right-clicking a button to the right of where you want the line and choosing Begin a Group from the shortcut menu.
- Copy a button by holding down Ctrl and dragging the button. You can drag it to another toolbar or another worksheet.

Another way you can change a toolbar button is by changing its look—you can modify the picture or text that appears on its face. Follow these steps:

1. Display the toolbar.
2. Choose Tools ➤ Customize to open the Customize dialog box.

3. Right-click the button in the toolbar that you want to change to display the shortcut menu.

- To change the text for a button, enter it in the Name field.
- Click Copy Button Image to copy the picture on the face of the button to the Windows Clipboard.
- Click Paste Button Image to paste whatever picture is in the Clipboard into the button.
- Click Edit Button Image to open the Button Editor and dabble in iconoclastic iconography to your heart's content.

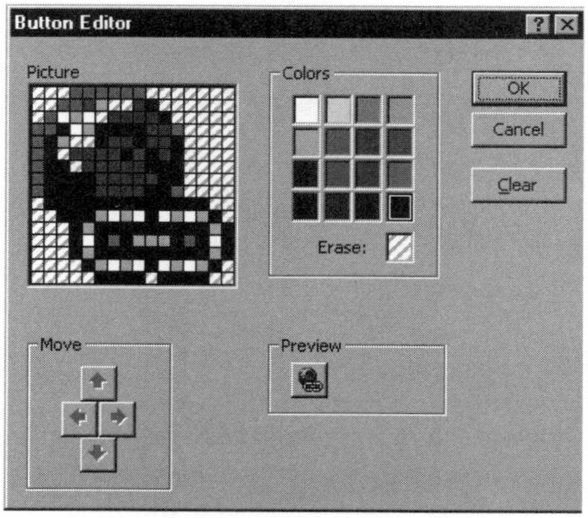

- Click Change Button Image to select a new icon from a palette of icons.

NOTE

Experiment with the other items on the shortcut menu. The secret to becoming a daring, confident button artist, however, is one other choice that appears on the shortcut menu for a button whose face you have changed. Click Reset Button Image to change the button back to its original look.

Creating a New Toolbar

It's also easy to create your own toolbars that contain the buttons and controls you want. Follow these steps:

1. Choose Tools ➤ Customize to open the Customize dialog box.
2. Click New to open the New Toolbar dialog box, shown here.

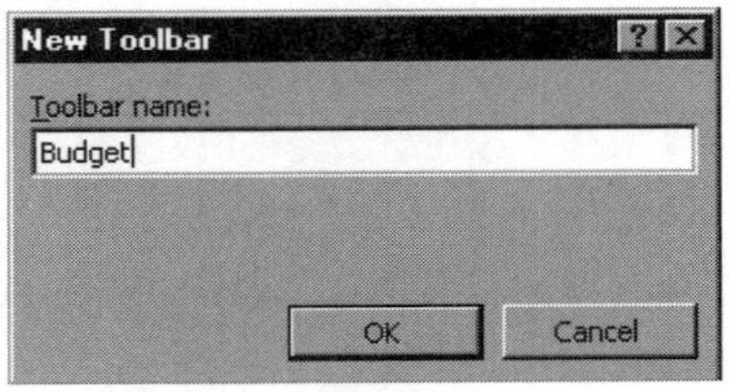

3. In the Toolbar Name field, enter a name for your new toolbar, and then click OK. A new, empty toolbar is displayed over the worksheet.
4. Simply drag the buttons you want onto it. It expands as you add buttons.
5. When you are finished, click Close in the Customize dialog box.

The new toolbar is now available for use, just like any other toolbar. You are free to move it, change its size, or dock it at the top or bottom of the Excel window. You can delete a custom toolbar at any time. Select its name in the Toolbars tab of the Customize dialog box, and then click Delete.

Making Custom Toolbars Available

By default, Excel stores your custom toolbars with its own default settings so that they are available to any workbook. However, they won't be available when you open one of your workbooks on another computer, under someone else's copy of the Excel program.

But you can *attach* one or more custom toolbars to a workbook so that the toolbar stays with the workbook. Follow these steps to attach a toolbar to the active workbook:

1. Choose Tools ➤ Customize to open the Customize dialog box.
2. Click the Toolbars tab, and then click Attach to open the Attach Toolbars dialog box.

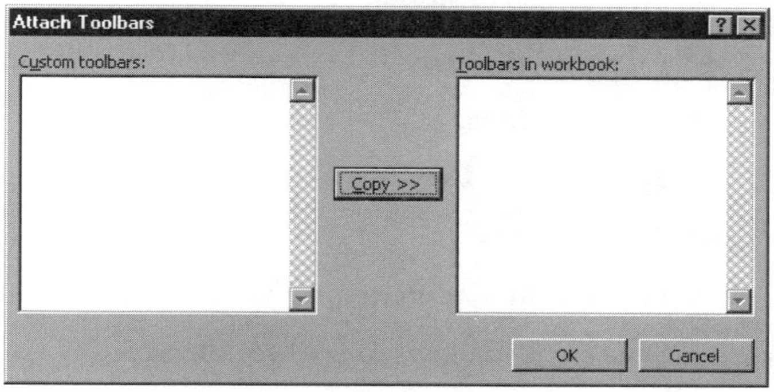

3. Select a toolbar name in the Custom Toolbars list on the left side of the dialog box.
4. Click the Copy button in the center of the dialog box to copy the selected toolbar name to the Toolbars in Workbook list on the right side of the dialog box.
5. Continue to select custom toolbars and copy their names to the Toolbars in Workbook list.

NOTE NOTE NOTE NOTE NOTE NOTE NOTE NOTE NOTE NOTE NOTE NOTE NOTE NOTE NOTE

If you select a toolbar name in the Toolbars in Workbook list, the Copy button changes to Delete. Click the button to remove that name from the list.

6. Click OK when you are finished.

You won't notice any difference, but the custom toolbars you selected are now attached to the workbook and will be available for that file no matter where you take it. For example, if you send the workbook file to a friend, that person will be able to use your attached custom toolbars by selecting them in the usual ways.

Are You Experienced?

Now you can...

☑ Use the Options dialog box to set defaults for Excel

☑ Create new windows

☑ Arrange windows

☑ Hide windows

☑ Split the window into panes

☑ Freeze panes

☑ Change the screen magnification

☑ Save custom views of the workbook

☑ Customize toolbars

☑ Create new toolbars

☑ Edit a button image

GLOSSARY

#

The pound sign is used in Excel as a preface in formula error messages, such as #DIV/0!, and in custom numeric formats where it serves as a placeholder for any number. You will also see pound signs displayed for a cell when its column is too narrow to display the number in that cell.

2-D

A range whose cells all occupy the same worksheet, such as B10:J55; a chart that is drawn with two dimensions.

3-D

A range of cells that consists of the same 2-D range on multiple, consecutive pages, such as Sheet1:Sheet3!B10:J55; a chart that is drawn to show depth in the third dimension.

a

absolute

A formula reference to a cell or range that will remain unchanged when the formula is copied, such as =$A$1. A *relative* reference, such as =A1, will adjust when the formula is copied.

active

The currently selected object and the object that will receive the data you enter or the results of the command you invoke, such as the active workbook, worksheet, cell, chart, chart object, drawn object, or picture.

add-in

An optional, accessory program that you enable or disable by choosing Tools ➤ Add-Ins. You can install several add-ins when you install Excel, and you can find other add-ins that are published by third parties, as well.

address

The location of a cell, identified by its column and row, such as A1; a range address includes its upper-left and lower-right cells, such as A1:B10. You can also include the worksheet in the address, such as Sheet2!A1, as well as the workbook's filename and path or URL, such as `'C:\DATA\[MyFile.xls]Sheet1'!A1`.

argument

An item that you enter within the parentheses of an Excel worksheet function that defines the scope of the function. A few functions take no arguments; some functions take several arguments, some of which may be required while others are optional. You separate arguments with a comma.

audit

To trace the chain of references for worksheet formulas, using the commands on the Tools ➤ Auditing menu or the buttons on the Auditing toolbar.

autotemplate

A worksheet or workbook template file that you create and save in Excel's XLStart folder. The autotemplate is loaded automatically by Excel, such as when you create a new worksheet.

c

cell

The junction of a row and column in the worksheet, in which you enter data or formulas.

chart sheet

A sheet in a workbook that contains a single chart (see also *embedded chart*).

circular reference

A formula that references its own cell, either directly or indirectly.

Clip Art gallery

A collection of graphic designs, images, backgrounds, textures, photos, sounds, and video that you can add to your worksheet or chart.

comment

A note you attach to a cell by choosing Insert ➤ Comment; when you point to the cell with your mouse, the comment is displayed.

concatenate

To combine two or more text items within a formula; the ampersand (&) is the concatenation operator.

constant

An unchanging datum, such as a number you include in a formula (see also *variable*).

contents

What is contained within a cell, as opposed to what is displayed on the screen for that cell (see also *display*).

d

dependent

When a cell contains a formula that references another cell, that formula is dependent on the other cell, changing the cell's contents affects the result of the formula in the dependent cell (see also *precedent*).

display

What you see on the screen, as opposed to what might actually reside within the cells of a worksheet. For example, if cell B2 displays the number 3, it might contain that number, but it could also contain the formula =INT(PI()) or =10–7.

e

embedded chart

A chart within a worksheet. You can view the chart and the worksheet data at the same time and make changes to the data and see the effects on the chart (see also *chart sheet*).

external reference

A formula that refers to a cell or range outside its own workbook (see also *link* and *reference*).

f

filter

A set of criteria that you create to limit the type of data that is displayed or selected (as with the Data ➤ Filter command).

format

The attributes that taken together determine the way an object appears. A cell's format consists of a number style, font, alignment, color, and border.

function

A named mathematical shortcut that produces a result; Excel has hundreds of functions, such as SUM, DATE, PI, and NOW. Each function is followed by a pair of parentheses, which may require one or more *arguments*.

g

group (worksheets, objects, outlines)

Two or more objects that are combined so that they behave as a single object. You can group multiple worksheets by selecting them; changing one of the worksheets in the group changes them all. You can group graphic objects by selecting them and choosing Draw ➤ Group from the Drawing toolbar. You can group rows or columns of similar data by creating an outline of the data with the commands on the Data ➤ Group and Outline submenu.

h

HTML

An abbreviation for HyperText Markup Language, the language used to create Web pages.

hyperlink

Text or a graphic image that when clicked opens another document or selects another cell in the current workbook. You create a hyperlink by choosing Insert ➤ Hyperlink or by using the HYPERLINK function.

l

link

A formula that refers to cells outside its own worksheet or workbook is called a linking formula. The series in a chart are usually linked to data in a worksheet; when the data change, the chart updates automatically. You can also link data between Excel and another program.

list

A range in the worksheet that serves as a database, especially when used with the Sort, Filter, Form, Subtotals, Group and Outline, and PivotTable commands on the Data menu.

m

macro

An automated routine (actually, a computer program) that completes a task in Excel in one step; you can record a macro or write your own with the Visual Basic for Applications language.

n

name

You can use a name instead of the actual address of a cell or range in any formula or command. You create a range name by choosing Insert ➤ Name.

natural language formula

A formula that references cells by referring to text titles above or to the left of the cells in the worksheet.

nest

To include one formula or function within another.

noncontiguous

A range of cells that do not adjoin one another, or two or more selected worksheets that do not adjoin one another. You select noncontiguous cells or worksheets by holding down Ctrl as you click them.

normal

The default style for all cells in a workbook. If you change the definition for the style called Normal (choose Format ➤ Style), all cells in the workbook (except those to which you've applied another style) will take on the new look.

o

object

A generic name for any component that you can manipulate, including a cell, row, column, worksheet, workbook, chart, component in a chart, or graphic object.

OLE

Object linking and embedding is the Windows process that allows you to exchange data, such as text, cells, charts, or pictures, between Excel and other OLE-compliant Windows programs. When you embed data via OLE, you can later edit the embedded data within the program in which it was created.

p

path

The location of a file, which can include the file's disk drive and folder, such as `C:\Data\Summary\MyFile.xls`.

Personal toolbar

The Standard and Formatting toolbars displayed on one line. The buttons it contains depend on those you most often use.

PivotChart

A chart that uses the summarized data of a PivotTable.

PivotTable

An interactive table that summarizes your data so that you can organize and analyze it many ways.

point

To select a cell or range with your mouse when you are prompted to specify a range for a formula you are writing or a command.

precedence, order of

Formulas are generally evaluated from left to right, but rules govern which mathematical operations are performed first. The formula =5+3*2 equals 11, not 16, because multiplication has precedence over addition.

precedent

A cell to which a formula refers, usually in the sense of tracing the path of the reference from the formula with the commands on the Tools ➤ Auditing menu or Auditing toolbar (see also *dependent*).

protection

Preventing changes by locking a cell, worksheet, workbook, chart, chart component, or graphic object and applying protection via the Tools menu.

r

random number

A number selected at random; Excel's RAND function returns a random number between 0 and 1 and returns a new result every time the worksheet recalculates.

range

Any group of cells in one or more worksheets, but usually a rectangular group of cells in one worksheet (see also *2-D*, *3-D*, and *address*).

range name

See *name*.

reference

A cell or range that is included in a formula. If the data in the cell or range changes, the result of the formula changes, as well (see also *external reference*).

relative

See *absolute*.

s

status bar

The horizontal bar at the bottom of Excel's window that displays various information and indicators.

style

A named collection of formats, such as font, color, or numeric format. You can define a style or apply one to a cell or range with the Format ➤ Style command.

t

template

A model for creating new items that are all based on the same features. In Excel, when you create a new worksheet or workbook from a template, the result looks just like the template.

u

URL

A *uniform resource locator* identifies a document on the World Wide Web, in the same way that a file's *path* identifies it on your computer.

v

variable

A cell that is referenced by a formula; you can enter a new value in the cell to affect the formula's result, which is often much preferred to placing the value within the formula (see *constant*).

w

Web folder

A shortcut to your Web server. Placing a file in your Web folder publishes it to your Web server if you have access to a Web server.

workbook

The basic document in Excel, which consists of one or more worksheets.

worksheet

A single page of a workbook, consisting of rows, columns, and cells, which can also include graphic objects such as charts or drawings.

workspace

The current layout of all open documents, their window sizes, and their positions. You can save the workspace by choosing File ➤ Save Workspace (it uses the file extension XLW). You can later open a workspace by choosing File ➤ Open, which will open all the files associated with that workspace.

x

XLStart

Each time you start Excel, it looks in the folder named XLStart and loads any workbooks or workspaces it finds there. You can also store *autotemplates* in XLStart, which will be used to create new, default worksheets or workbooks.

Index

Note to the Reader: Page numbers in **bold** indicate the principal discussion of a topic or the definition of a term. Page numbers in *italic* indicate illustrations.

Numbers

Symbols

A

D

E

G

H

I

N

O

P

R

S

T

U

V

W